THE TRUE God

INTELLIGENT,

Isaac Newton

Into His PRESENCE

Volume 2

Encountering the God of the Prophets

To Elizabeth:

It is my prayer that as you read about the encounters of the God of history with Haggai & Zechariah you will realize how much He invested in you—His temple—and that He was to come & live in His Temple. As this realization warms your heart may you find yourself drawn ever more deeply into His Presence.

Napoleon Burt

Your friend & colleague,

ISBN 978-1-64515-982-7 (paperback)
ISBN 978-1-64515-983-4 (digital)

Christian Faith Publishing, Inc.
832 Park Avenue
Meadville, PA 16335
www.christianfaithpublishing.com

Printed in the United States of America

Dedication

To my son, Justin Burt, my daughter, Sarah Burt, and my many students over the years. As our heavenly Father loved us and gave of Himself in order that we could reach our full potential, so I offer this work, as I have given of my life to help each of you reach your full potential in God. I pray that each of you will spend a lifetime getting to know and love the God of history. May this work become a seed planted in your hearts that brings forth rich fruit in each of your lives.

I have invested much of my life to teaching others. I see the heart for teaching as one of the gifts God has planted in my life. Much of my effectiveness as a teacher, I owe to you. Being your teacher has moved me closer to reaching my God-given potential. You have helped me become a better person.

Contents

Foreword

We have waited too long for what we longed for. We now have it in this marvelous work. It speaks about the God of creation and it lets that God speak about himself.

God's worshipping servant and my brother, lifts accurate and needed information from the pages of the Bible, then we experience God lowering Himself and bending toward us, and lifting us up into His presence.

In order for us to intimately know this God, he must invade our world and consciousness, because we surely cannot invade His. Men and women of the OT met him and found it impossible to ever be the same.

This distinct and studious book will separate the reader from the abysmal mental pit of persons who seem to delight in seeking to reduce the sovereign glorious power of Almighty God.

Professors, bishops, pastors, teachers, or choir members will find insight and motivation in the revelatory truths which flow from every chapter. The OT God is magnified as the NT God who is crystalized.

The author is used by God to do what our electronic gadgets and the internet can not. Namely - to place awe and worship on automatic.

Rick "Soup" Campbell
Soup For The Soul International Ministries

Acknowledgements

I would like to thank my father, James E. Burt, Sr. and my mother, Nellie M. Burt. They taught me discipline, work ethic, and persistence in pursuing goals despite the presence of challenges. They have sacrificed for me, and my seven brothers, throughout our lives. They prayed for me and fought for me during my childhood when my very survival seemed uncertain. They taught me to pray and believe that God cared about me as a person and that He would intervene in my life. He did! They planted seeds in my life and cultivated my gifts until my life began to yield fruit from the seeds they had planted. Good parents are a gift from God.

I owe a great debt of gratitude to three other men--Bishop Francis L. Smith, Brother Jeff Robinson, and Elder Soup Campbell. Bishop Francis L. Smith pastored First Apostolic Faith Church in Akron, Ohio. He was the man of God who laid the foundation upon which my faith has been built. He instilled in me a fervent love for the word of God. Bishop Smith's life convinced me that biblical faith was not incompatible with personal intellectual advancement. He emphasized to me that "Christianity is the thinking man's religion."

Often men walk through life without male contemporaries who will support them when needed, challenge them when they need correction, and provide them healthy, godly friendship that establishes their path in righteousness. A man who finds one such male comrade is truly blessed. From my youth, I have been blessed to have two such honorable men grace my life, Brother Jeff Robinson and Elder Soup Campbell. They have my gratitude for their investments in this project and in my life, investments too numerable to attempt to recite.

Acknowledgments

Introduction

In the year that I graduated high school and went off to Kent State University, Buckminster Fuller created the "Knowledge Doubling Curve." Within the last decade, it was estimated that the fund of available knowledge was doubling every year and the rate of change of the slope of this curve was increasing each year. The number of different knowledge disciplines has proliferated since Fuller introduced the concept of the "Knowledge Doubling Curve." The cumulative amount of information in any one field of study now is so vast that one person cannot possibly know everything about everything. One of the characteristics consistently attributed to the God of the Bible, however, is omniscience. This means that He knows all things about all things—past, present, and future. The idea that any individual can master the entire body of all present-day knowledge is unfathomable. The God of history is the one person who possesses all past, present, and future knowledge. There is simply no way to verify that a person possesses this fund of knowledge. God's demonstrations of His knowledge of future events provides a line of evidence to support the claim that He is omniscient.

The writer of Hebrews informs us that, in time past, the omniscient God spoke to the fathers of Israel by the prophets (Heb. 1:1). Throughout documented history, at His discretion, the God of the Bible offered glimpses of His omniscience by giving detailed and precise revelations of future events to His prophets. While it is not the only measure of whether a statement concerning the future is from God, prophetic accuracy is one measure; because God knows all things, when He gives a revelation concerning future events, His statements are always accurate (Deut. 18:21-22).

In order to validate the historical veracity of biblical prophecies two pieces of evidence must be provided. First, it must be established that the prophetic utterance predated the event prophesied. The fulfillment of the prophesied event at a later date, must then be established. Proclaiming His unique ability to know the future, Jehovah declared to one of His prophets, "Behold, the former things are come to pass, and new things do I declare: before they spring forth I tell you of them" (Isaiah 42:9). He also proclaimed, "Remember the former things of old: for I am God, and there is none else; I am God and there is none like Me, Declaring the end from the beginning, and from ancient time the things that are not yet done, saying, My counsel shall stand, and I will do all My pleasure" (Isaiah 46:9-10).

Examples of Jehovah's repeated demonstrations of omniscience throughout history abound. Before the nation of Israel was even formed and centuries before they were enslaved in Egypt, Jehovah told Abraham which generation of his descendants would leave Egypt in a great exodus (Gen. 15:13-16 and Exodus 6:16-18). Shortly before the death of Moses, Jehovah used him to foretell the fall of Israel to their Assyrian and Babylonian captors. This was around 1406 BC, hundreds of years before these Neo-Assyrian and Neo-Babylonian empires even existed (Leviticus 26, Deuteronomy 28, 2 Kings 17:6-23 and 2 Kings 24-25). The circumstances surrounding the death of the sons of the man who would eventually rebuild Jericho after Joshua's conquest of this walled city were revealed to Joshua more than five hundred years beforehand (Joshua 6:26 and 1 Kings 16:34). The birth and actions of King Josiah were predicted over three hundred years beforehand and proclaimed to King Jeroboam by an unnamed prophet (1 Kings 13:1-3 and 2 Kings 23:14-17). And there are literally hundreds of messianic prophecies spoken by Old Testament prophets giving phenomenally accurate and precise details concerning events in the life of the coming messiah, Jesus Christ.

God spoke prophetically in the days of Adam, Abraham, Job, Moses, David and many others. But the prophetic ministry became firmly entrenched in Israel and Judah during the days of Elijah, Elisha, and Joel. The foundation of prophetic ministry was laid by the efforts of these men in response to the imminent threat to Jehovah-worship that arose from the calculated efforts of Ahab and Jezebel. Elijah and Elisha established the school of the prophets in Israel and Joel was their counterpart in Judah as a father of prophetic ministry. From the efforts of these fathers of prophetic ministry arose multiple generations of prophets. Isaiah and his four contemporaries—Jonah, Hosea, Amos, and Micah—formed the next generation of prophets. They prophesied during the time just before, during, and shortly after the fall of Israel to Assyria. The third generation of prophets included Nahum, Habakkuk, and Zephaniah. These three men prophesied during the seventh century BC. The fourth generation of prophets were the mouthpieces of Jehovah during the time immediately before, during and after the fall of Judah to Babylon. The fifth, and final group of prophets and writers of the Old Testament included Ezra, Nehemiah, Esther, Zechariah, Haggai, and Malachi. They lived during the post-captivity era. In each of these generations of prophets, Jehovah demonstrated His omniscience by making proclamations about future events which were later shown to be accurate descriptions of events that took place after Jehovah described them to His prophets.

As you read through Volume 2 of Into His Presence, I encourage you to contemplate several tough questions, examine the evidence that is presented regarding the questions raised, and embrace the conclusion that the preponderance of evidence supports. One difficult question that this book addresses is, "Are the people and events recorded in the Bible congruent with current knowledge in the disciplines of history and observational science?" The evidence laid out in this manuscript will argue convincingly that a significant body of evidence from the scientific discipline of archaeology supports the fact that the events and persons recorded within the pages of the Bible were historical and not fictional. By establishing a historical timetable for the life and times of the prophets in the Bible, it can and will be demonstrated that these events and persons were historically contemporary with non-biblical events and characters, whose historicity is not considered up for debate. In addition, dating the persons and events written about in the Bible enables us to see how God demonstrated His accurate and precise knowledge of the future by showing the many times when He gave details about events years before the events transpired.

In addition to establishing the historicity of the prophets, this volume advances the argument that the selected biblical personalities all had encounters with the same divine person they each knew as God, the Lord, or Jehovah. The nature of their interactions with this divine person indicates that He was not a mere concept or figment of their imaginations, but— just as they were persons on the stage of history—He was a person interacting with them on the stage of history. The consistency of the perceived attributes and character of this divine person, as observed through His interactions with His prophets over the expanse of history, argues as well that He is not conceptual, but instead, one and the same timeless person Who interacted with each of them as documented in the Bible.

This manuscript, like Volume 1 of Into His Presence, relies heavily upon the concept of "divine pronouns" to bring clarity to the understanding of the person of God. By way of review, a divine pronoun can be defined as a word that can function as a noun and that refers to the person(s) that the men and women of the scripture encountered as the God of the Bible (e.g. I, Me, Mine He, Him, His).

Consistent with the previous volume, grammatical principles that govern our understanding of the link between nouns and pronouns are faithfully applied to provide clarity to our understanding of the personhood of God. It is critical to reemphasize that to gain this clarity on the personhood of God, one must pay attention to the following two factors:

1. The student must follow the use of divine pronouns by God, the other persons of history that interacted with Him, and the people that recorded these interactions within the pages of the Bible.
2. The student must understand the singularity or the plurality of the personhood of God as it was discerned by the people of history with whom God interacted.

I hope that your perspective when reading the Bible will be changed forever after reading this book. After reading this book, you will read the Bible for what it is—a book that captures a portion of human history. While reading this book, you will become keenly aware that there is a body of scientific evidence in the established field of archaeology that confirms the veracity of the Bible's historical narrative. You will see the prophets and the events in their lives in the context of non-biblical events that were contemporary with them. You will understand that the God of the Bible—though He resides outside the realm of time because He is eternal—interacted with the prophets over the course of generations and over a span of many centuries. In addition to intervening in their personal lives, He spoke to them about future events, demonstrating His omniscience.

He was perceived as a person by His prophets and others with whom He interacted. You will read the writings of the prophets as a series of encounters between them and the divine person with Whom they interacted. After reading this book, you will never again be able to read the Bible account without noticing the presence of the divine pronouns that reference the person of the God of history.

Encountering the God of Israel's Great Non-Writing Prophets

Elijah and Elisha remain towering figures in Israel's history. Though they are quite contrasting characters, each man stood as Jehovah's mouthpiece, the arm of His strength, and the symbol of His presence during their period of ministry to an apostate nation. The apostate state of the northern kingdom, commonly called Israel, began as a consequence of Solomon's sins. Solomon made the grave mistake of disregarding the commandment Jehovah had given at Sinai in 1446 BC not to marry the women of the nations of the land that He would give to His people (Exodus 34:14–17). Because of Solomon's sin, the kingdom had been divided into two after his death in 931 BC (1 Kings 11:11–13, 12:31–39). Jeroboam became the first king of the northern kingdom. The throne of the southern kingdom passed to Solomon's son, Rehoboam.

After he became the first king of the northern kingdom, Jeroboam established a false religion, worshipping idols he had erected at Dan and Bethel (1 Kings 12:26–33). Jeroboam's error was based on earthly wisdom and the fear that the people would depose him and return to Jerusalem, the center of worship the united kingdom had known under David and Solomon. This act became Jeroboam's evil legacy, being referenced throughout Israel's history for hundreds of years as "the sin of Jeroboam which he sinned and made Israel to sin." The actions of Solomon and Jeroboam set the kingdom of Israel (the northern kingdom) on a downward spiral away from the pursuit of intimate relationship with Jehovah and embracing the worship of other gods.

Less than a century after Solomon began to have his heart turned away from the worship of Jehovah as the only true God (after 959 BC) and about six decades after Jeroboam first instituted idol worship on a national level (around 931 BC), Ahab took the throne of the northern kingdom. He married Jezebel around 874 BC. Together, they plotted to uproot the worship of Jehovah throughout the nation of Israel. The prophetic ministries of Elijah and Elisha were the primary sources preserving the worship of the God of Abraham, Isaac, and Jacob throughout the reign of Ahab and his descendants in the northern kingdom.

The godly influence of the ministries of Elijah and Elisha also countered the detrimental effects of the descendants of Ahab who infiltrated the royal line of David in the southern kingdom (Jehoram, Ahaziah, and Athaliah). Without the ministries of these prophets, the work of Ahab, Jezebel, and their descendants in the southern kingdom might have destroyed the foundation of Jehovah worship throughout the entire nation, including Judah. The ministries of Elijah and Elisha helped preserve Jehovah worship in Judah from the twilight of the life of David's fourth generation son, Asa, through the entire reign of David's fifth generation son, Jehoshaphat.

These two prominent prophets did not leave any personally written records of their ministry or their encounters with Jehovah and are therefore categorized as Israel's great non-writing prophets. This chapter will explore the lives and ministries of Israel's two great non-writing prophets. The attributes of each prophet are discussed. The historical and chronological framework within which each man's ministry unfolded will be established. Some extra-biblical archaeologic evidences for the existence of key historical contemporaries of Elijah and Elisha will help provide the historical and chronological context of their ministries. The divine person each prophet knew as the Lord will become clear in the context of their historically framed encounters with Jehovah. These encounters are enumerated and explored in this chapter.

CHAPTER ONE

Elijah—My God is Jehovah

Elijah was an enormously influential historical figure. While notable prophets like Gad and Nathan preceded Elijah, it was the prophetic ministry of Elijah that marked the beginning of prophetic ministry's role as a highlight in Jewish history. From the beginning of Israel's kingdom age, kings and priests were considered highly significant, but prophetic ministry was catapulted into its own sphere of significance with the beginning of Elijah's ministry. From his time forward, prophetic ministry never relinquished this lofty platform.

With great personal fortitude, Elijah challenged Israel's wicked political leaders and the existing religious system that was dismissive of the person Israel had known as God since its birth as a nation. He instituted a school of the prophets that would perpetuate the impact of prophetic ministry beyond his lifetime. Elijah was mentioned by Jesus and the apostles more times than any other old testament prophet. He was the prototypical prophet as demonstrated by the fact that, along with Moses, it was Elijah that appeared with Jesus on the mount of transfiguration (Matt. 17, Mark 9).

This rugged and impactful man who withstood the forces that would have otherwise cast an entire nation into utter spiritual darkness must have had his commitment to his mission sustained by an immeasurably deep intimate relationship with the divine person he knew as the Lord. During his decade or so of prophetic ministry, he had twenty-one documented divine encounters which gave insight into his relationship with Jehovah. These encounters are discussed sequentially and designated EJ1–EJ21 in this chapter.

Before exploring the divine encounters of Elijah with the person he knew as God, one final necessary prerequisite is to give a brief description of the historical setting and the other historical figures of importance during Elijah's lifetime. Ahab became the king of Israel while Asa, David's fourth generation heir, was still king in Judah in about 874 BC (1 Kings 16:29). In contrast to the mistaken view that Ahab may have been a fictional character created to represent the forces that opposed Israel's "fictional God," non-Jewish archaeological findings confirm the existence of this evil king and his evil wife, Jezebel.

Ahab was the son of Omri who established Samaria as the capital city of the northern kingdom of Israel. The Moabite Stone, or Mesha Stele, confirms the historicity of Ahab's father, Omri. The Khurk Stele, an Assyrian record, confirms Ahab's presence in history. Ethbaal was the founder of a Phoenician royal dynasty (878–847 BC) and worshipper of the Phoenician god named Baal according to a noted Greek historian named Menander.

The marriage of Ethbaal's daughter, Jezebel, to the heir of Omri's dynasty in Samaria was a brilliant move to expand his political influence and spread the worship of his god into Israel (1 Kings 16:30–33). The close cultural ties of Israel and Sidon, the capital of Ethbaal's kingdom, are apparent throughout the biblical record of Elijah's ministry. The plan of Ethbaal and his daughter, Jezebel, might well have succeeded if not for the strong oppositional prophetic ministry of Elijah.

Meanwhile, Jehoshaphat, David's fifth generation royal descendant, sat on the throne of Judah and led his nation in the continued worship of the God of his fathers (Abraham, Isaac, Jacob, Moses, David, and Asa). In fact, in the third year of his reign (about 867 BC), Jehoshaphat implemented a systematic educational program to embed the teachings of his fathers throughout Judah during his time (2 Chronicles 17:7–9). For his efforts, unlike Ahab, Jehoshaphat was held in high regard by Elijah and his contemporaries in prophetic ministry in Israel.

One of the consistent personal attributes of the God of Israel is His omniscience and His ability to foretell the future with amazing accuracy. A significant display of Jehovah's prophetic accuracy was revealed during the reign of Ahab. The walls of Jericho were rebuilt during this time, and a prophecy concerning this event was fulfilled and documented. In 1406 BC, after Israel's conquest of Jericho, Joshua prophesied (by the inspiration of Jehovah) that the man who rebuilt the walls of Jericho would do so at the cost of the life of two of his sons (Joshua 6:26). During Ahab's reign (874–853 BC), Hiel coordinated the rebuilding of the walls of Jericho with Abiram, his firstborn, dying at the beginning of the project, and his youngest son, Segub, dying as the project was being completed (1 Kings 16:34).

With amazing accuracy, Joshua's God, the God of Elijah and the God Whom Ahab rejected predicted this unfortunate occurrence over 500 years in advance. But this is only a small example of the strength and consistent character of the person Moses and Joshua knew as God and with Whom Elijah, the first prophet to be evaluated in this chapter, had an intimate relationship.

Elijah's Encounters with Jehovah

EJ1—Elijah prophesies a drought (1 Kings 17:1).
EJ2—Elijah sustained by food from ravens (1 Kings 17:2–7).
EJ3—Elijah is sustained by food from a widow at Zarephath (1 Kings 17:9–16).
EJ4—Elijah resurrects the son of the widow of Zarephath (1 Kings 17:17–24).
EJ5—Elijah prophesies the end of the drought (1 Kings 18:1–2).
EJ6—Elijah prays and Jehovah answers by fire (1 Kings 18:36–39).

From the beginning of Ahab's reign, he and Jezebel did a great deal to undermine the foundation of Israel's worship of Jehovah and replace it with Baal worship. In so doing, they enslaved the minds of the people of the nation to this foreign, false, and frail deity. After a little more than a decade of this, Elijah's ministry erupted into the spotlight, highlighting Jehovah's strength, and giving Israel an opportunity to turn their hearts back to the worship of the true and living God. Six documented divine encounters between Elijah and Jehovah over a period of three years marked the historical record of the start of Elijah's ministry.

One of Baal's purported divine powers was his ability to control the weather; he was the storm god or the god of weather. Much like Jehovah had done when He discredited the false gods of Egypt by bringing ten plagues on the land in 1446 BC, the proclaiming of a drought in Israel in 861 BC was a direct challenge to the power of Baal. It would provide evidence to the children of Israel and their new oppressors—Ahab, Jezebel, and the prophets of the false religion of Baal—that Jehovah alone was God. No doubt, Elijah reminded Ahab that the God Whom he had forsaken was the same person Who had brought Israel out of Egypt and planted them in Palestine almost 600 years previously.

Elijah identified the fact that he answered to a different deity than Ahab when he said to Ahab, "As the Lord God of Israel liveth, before Whom I stand, there shall not be dew nor rain these years, but according to my word" (1 Kings 17:1). The use of the pronoun *Whom* established the fact that Elijah saw his God as a divine person. The Lord followed up Elijah's proclamation with specific directions on how He would provide for Elijah during the drought. Elijah's water would come from the brook Cherith, while ravens would bring his daily nutrition. God used a first person singular divine pronoun in identifying Himself to Elijah on this occasion (1 Kings 17:2–7).

When the brook dried up—likely several months later—the Lord directed Elijah to leave Israel and go to Zarephath, a city in Phoenicia, the home country of Baal and his high priest, Ethbaal. God told Elijah, "I have commanded a widow woman there to sustain thee" (1 Kings 17:9). Elijah's conversation with this Phoenician woman revealed that she and Elijah did not worship the same deity. She called Jehovah "the Lord thy God" when speaking to Elijah. When Elijah prophesied Jehovah's provision for himself and for the household of the widow in response to her obedience to his request, he referenced "the Lord God of Israel" as opposed to Baal. Jehovah's supreme power of provision and His mercy and grace to His followers was demonstrated through this miraculous provision which sustained Elijah through the remainder of the drought—likely a period of more than two years.

During his time living in Zarephath, Elijah was also credited with the prayer that led to the first documented case of a person being resurrected from the dead. When the widow's child died, Elijah questioned God for allowing this to occur. Elijah's God no doubt used this miracle, in conjunction with His continued miraculous provision of sustenance for Elijah and the widow, to strengthen Elijah's faith and to convert some of Baal's followers into believers in the power of Israel's God. Elijah prayed three times for the child, and the child's life was restored. The record does not indicate that this was a resuscitation, but rather a resurrection. The credibility of both Elijah and his God were established in the eyes of the widow and any who heard of this miracle.

In late 858 BC, the third year of the drought, Elijah's God directed him saying, "Go, show thyself unto Ahab, and I will send rain upon the earth" (1 Kings 18:1). With the use of the first person singular divine pronoun *I*, the Lord—as a divine person—took credit for the directive to Elijah and the return of the rain that would soon follow. In order to openly and publicly demonstrate His superiority over the pagan god, Baal, and to give the people of Israel a clear reason to abandon the false religion and return to Him, Jehovah sent His agent, Elijah, to issue a public challenge to Baal and his prophets.

The event described in 1 Kings 18:17–40 amounted to an utter humiliation of Baal and those who had dared believe that his power could compare with that of the God of Abraham, Isaac, and Israel. Elijah's challenge was, "Call ye on the name of your gods, and I will call on the name of the Lord: and the God that answereth by fire, let Him be God!" (1 Kings 18:24).

Baal's followers were granted a generous time allotment to seek his response. He did not answer their petitions. After taking additional measures to emphatically contrast his God's power with the impotence of Baal, Elijah successfully invoked the intervention of Jehovah Who sent fire to consume the offering Elijah had prepared. The answer of God by fire, consuming the sacrifice offered by Elijah, was reminiscent of the response of God that occurred when Aaron and Moses dedicated the tabernacle and the priests to the service of the Lord in 1445 BC (Leviticus 9:24). As God had stamped His approval on the religious process implemented by Moses and the Aaronic priesthood in 1445 BC, so He stamped His approval on the religious process offered by Elijah in contrast to that offered by Ahab, Jezebel, and the priests of Baal in 858 BC. It was clear to all in attendance that "the Lord, He is God" (1 Kings 18:39) and that He was calling His people back to fellowship with Him as the only deity worthy of their worship.

Jehovah sanctified Himself from the Phoenician gods and simultaneously demonstrated their inability to answer the petition of their worshippers. The Lord completed His discrediting of Baal, the storm god, by demonstrating that He alone controlled the medium of rain. He accomplished this by allowing the rain to fall at Elijah's prophetic utterance after the prophets of Baal had been slaughtered (1 Kings 18:40–45). In addition to proving His superiority over Baal and the Phoenician gods, Jehovah demonstrated the consistency of His character through this public display of His power.

Elijah's God was the same person that had covenanted with Abraham (approximately 2091 BC), Isaac (around 1977 BC) and Jacob (about 1928 BC). To the Israelite who knew anything about their history (particularly Elijah and Ahab), the God Who had answered by fire on Mount Carmel was the same divine person Who had distinguished Himself from the Egyptian pantheon of gods in 1446 BC. After delivering His people from the oppression of the Egyptians, Jehovah had answered Moses and Aaron by fire in the wilderness nearly six centuries before answering Elijah by fire on Mount Carmel. Jehovah confirmed His omnipotence, His mercy, and His covenant-keeping, relationship-oriented personal nature by each of these public acts though they had been separated by a lengthy stretch of history. Additionally, He showed that He was a God Who had expectations of His people and that when these expectations were unmet, at some point, consequences ensued. It is notable that the divine person Elijah knew as God used the first person singular divine pronoun *I* in three separate conversations with Elijah during this three year window of time (1 Kings 17:3–4, 17:9, 18:1).

EJ7—Elijah fed by an angel (1 Kings 19:4–6).
EJ8—Elijah fed by an angel (1 Kings 19:7–8).
EJ9—Elijah counseled in a cave at Horeb after a 40 day fast (1 Kings 19:9–18).

While the power of Jehovah was magnificently displayed and He sanctified Himself from the false gods of Ahab, Jezebel, and the Phoenicians, this whole process was exhausting work for His prophet, Elijah. The biblical account indicates that a feeling of isolation and a physical, emotional, and intellectual strain gripped Elijah. This literally left him exhausted because man is a physically limited being, unlike the inexhaustible, limitless living God. After the public humiliation of Jezebel and her deity by Jehovah's prophet, Jezebel issued a personal threat on the life of Elijah. In his state of physical and emotional fatigue and knowing that this woman was fully capable of carrying out her threat, Elijah was unable to mount his typical stoic, rugged, undaunted response when he faced this new challenge.

Elijah's response to this new challenge was a request for the ultimate escape—his death. This event in Elijah's life has a historical parallel to the ministry of Moses. In 1445 BC, immediately after Moses had received the law, ordained and implemented the worship process and the priests, organized and mobilized the nation, and set out with them to go to the land of promise, the people murmured because they had no meat. It was more than Moses could endure as a human vessel of ministry and a tool for the work of Jehovah on earth. In his exasperated, emotionally and physically depleted state, Moses asked the Lord to take his life, rather than make him endure the challenge of leading the people any longer (Numbers 11:9–15).

Like Elijah, Moses had reached his human limits. The compassionate, intimate person Moses knew as the Lord miraculously provided meat for the people and also met the need of His human agent by providing other human counterparts to assist him with his ministerial tasks. At least four first person singular divine pronouns were used by the Lord in this exchange with Moses (Numbers 11:16–17, 23). Moses used one additional first person singular divine pronoun in reference to the divine person with Whom he had this conversation at this time (Numbers 11:21).The personhood of Moses's God was clear. The compassion, mercy, grace, and the ability of Moses's God to provide for the needs of each of His servants was abundantly evident.

Elijah's plight in 858–857 BC was similar. He had been used by God to deliver the people from the bondage of serving an impotent idol god in a fruitless, lifeless, religious institution. He had seen Jehovah perform miracles before his eyes and before the eyes of the believers and the unbelievers on Mount Carmel. Surely, this should have settled the matter once and for all. Instead, the dogged determination of Jezebel to destroy Jehovah and His servants had intensified, and Elijah's very life was threatened, this time directly. He ran for his life and cried out to God, "It is enough; now, O Lord, take away my life; for I am not better than my fathers" (1 Kings 19:4).

He may well have had the experience of Moses with the Israelites in the wilderness in his mind at this point. Regardless, the response of the Lord to Elijah's emotional and physical state in 858–857 BC was quite similar to that of Moses's God in 1445 BC. He provided sustenance to Elijah in a miraculous way (1 Kings 19:4–8) and then proceeded to give Elijah a human counterpart to assist him with his ministerial tasks.

Elijah was sustained on the strength of the miraculous provision of Jehovah for forty days. He saw the glory of God manifested before him in a manner reminiscent of the way Moses's God had allowed Moses to see His glory in Exodus 33:18–23. He heard the Lord use at least two first person singular divine pronouns in identifying Himself and reaffirming His sovereignty and control of the situation. The Lord instructed Elijah to anoint a political successor to the leader of Syria and a political successor to the wicked leader of Israel. Elijah also received a successor and assistant for his work in the prophetic ministry. As well, Jehovah reassured Elijah—thus reviving his spirit—that thousands of Israelites had remained faithful to their covenant relationship with Jehovah (1 Kings 19:9–18).

Elijah did not know that nearly a decade would pass before Elisha would succeed him and that almost two decades would pass before the political leaders that he anointed would actually come to power. The mere promise of a change was enough to revive Elijah's spirit and give him the renewed stamina he needed to continue on in the ministerial post to which his God had assigned him. Elijah's God was concerned about His servant and gave him what he needed to sustain him physically, emotionally, and spiritually in his time of need. Jehovah is a relationship-oriented, compassionate, divine person.

Unnamed prophet prophesies military victory over Syria at Samaria (1 Kings 20:13–14).
Unnamed prophet prophesies Syria's return to fight against Israel (1 Kings 20:22).
Unnamed prophet prophesies military victory over Syria at Aphek (1 Kings 20:28).

The next three prophetic utterances documented during the span of Elijah's ministry were attributed to unnamed prophets. These prophecies may have occurred during the time Elijah was completing the directive to anoint his ministerial successor and the political successors of Israel and Syria. He had received this directive from the Lord at Mt. Horeb when he was spent emotionally, physically, and spiritually, and otherwise simply needed a reprieve from the prophetic ministry. Jehovah may have used these other human vessels of prophetic ministry to continue the work of the ministry while Elijah was allowed a season of recovery.

Each of the prophetic utterances that occurred during this time concerned military conflicts between Israel and Benhadad II, king of Syria. The first occurred in 857 BC and predicted that Israel's small military force would defeat Benhadad II and the thirty-two kings that helped him in a battle in the hills around Samaria (1 Kings 20:13–14).

The second occurred after Israel's victory and warned of the return of Benhadad II for another battle early the following year (1 Kings 10:22). The third occurred in 856 BC (1 King 20:28) when the Syrian led forces regrouped and came against Israel in the valleys near Aphek, instead of the hills near Samaria. Israel defeated the Syrians and their allies a second time.

On each occasion, the divine person Who instructed the prophets was the Lord. The Lord used a total of four first person singular divine pronouns to associate Himself with these prophets while accurately predicting future events. In the second battle, Ahab spared the life of Benhadad II and—three years later—this decision cost him his own life as prophesied by one unnamed prophet (1 Kings 20:35–43, 22:1).

Because of the dramatic presentation of the prophet's message in 1 Kings 20, some scholars have speculated that this unnamed prophet may have, in fact, been the Micaiah who prophesied Ahab's death in 1 Kings 22.

EJ10—Ahab judged for wrongful death of Naboth (1 Kings 21:17–24).
EJ11—Ahab's humility leads to delayed judgment (1 Kings 21:29).

Ahab's failure to negotiate a deal to acquire possession of the land of Naboth and Jezebel's plot to have Naboth killed so that Ahab could assume possession of this land occurred during a three year window between Ahab's final two wars with Syria (856–853 BC). The unjust murder of Naboth was an evil act in the sight of God. Consistent with His character over hundreds of years, the God of Israel showed that He had standards for acceptable conduct in Israel and that He would judge anyone who failed to live by these standards. He also showed that while judgment may be delayed, it is imminent and that He was merciful even in issuing forth judgment. The words of the Lord in issuing judgment on the matter of Naboth are recorded in 1 Kings 21:17–24, 1 Kings 21:29, and 2 Kings 9:25–37. A total of eight first person singular divine pronouns were credited to the Lord in addressing the moral and spiritual failures of Ahab by the murder of Naboth.

Ahab's death prophesied by unknown prophet in 857/856 BC (1 Kings 20:42).
Ahab's death prophesied by Micaiah in 853 BC (1 Kings 22:14–26).

Ahab's death is an important event during the ministry of Elijah. Ahab began to reign in 874 BC and married Jezebel before

Elijah began his ministry. Ahab died in 853 BC in a battle that can be verified and dated by non-biblical archaeological evidence. The Bible dates Ahab's final battle as having occurred three years after the battle of Aphek (1 Kings 22:1) between Syria (led by Benhadad II) and Israel (led by Ahab). Earlier that same year, Benhadad II and Ahab had combined forces to defeat Shalmaneser III, an event documented on the Kurhk Monolith which dates this battle at 853 BC. The biblical accounts of Ahab's death and the prophesies of his death contain six singular divine pronouns. These accounts remind us historically that the Lord is just, that He has expectations regarding behavior for those who are affiliated with Him, and that there is ultimately a cost for transgressions against Him and against His standards, though that judgment may be delayed.

Ahab was a notable figure in Israel's history for several reasons. He was arguably Israel's most wicked king. Jeroboam was the first king of the northern kingdom of Israel. Jeroboam's legacy was evil. He introduced idol worship, setting up idols in Bethel and Dan to keep his constituents from returning to Jerusalem to worship and risk instability in his new kingdom.

Ahab took idolatry to a much greater level, however. He introduced the worship of a set of pagan idols and, largely through a coordinated effort led by his wife Jezebel, engaged in an active war against the worship of Jehovah, the God of his fathers. Ahab made himself an enemy of Jehovah and had malicious intent to destroy the worship of Jehovah altogether. The evil of Ahab and Jezebel was a cancer that impacted both the northern kingdom and the southern kingdom beyond their lifetimes.

The next two kings of the northern kingdom, Ahaziah and Jehoram, were the sons of Ahab. The biblical epitaph of Ahaziah states, "He did evil in the sight of the Lord, and walked in the way of his father, and in the way of his mother, and in the way of Jeroboam, the son of Nebat, who made Israel to sin, for he served Baal, and worshipped him, and provoked to anger the Lord God of Israel, according to all that his father had done" (1 Kings 22:52–53).

Jehoram's epitaph is less scathing but still records that he did evil in the sight of the Lord (2 Kings 3:1–3). The rise of Jehu gave the northern kingdom a fresh start; he purged the land of the descendants of Ahab.

Ahab's evil was far-reaching, impacting the southern kingdom for several generations as well. One significant strike against the good reign of Jehoshaphat, David's fifth generation royal descendant and king of Judah, was his penchant to form political alliances with ungodly rulers. He formed alliances with Ahab (1 Kings 22:1–4), Ahaziah (2 Chronicles 20:35–37), and Jehoram (2 Kings 3:6–9) during each of their evil reigns. Furthermore, Jehoshaphat opened the door for the expansion of Baal worship into the southern kingdom by consenting to have his son, also named Jehoram, marry the daughter of Ahab.

The biblical epitaph of Jehoram, the son of Jehoshaphat, states, "He walked in the way of the kings of Israel, like as did the house of Ahab: for he had the daughter of Ahab to wife: and he wrought that which was evil in the eyes of the Lord" (2 Chronicles 21:5–6). When Jehoram, king of Judah, died, his youngest son, Ahaziah, became king. The mother of Ahaziah and wife of Jehoram was Athaliah, the daughter of Ahab (2 Chronicles 21:6 and 22:2–3). Ahaziah was only king in Judah for one year. Athaliah, the daughter of Ahab, ruled over Judah after the death of Ahaziah.

A divinely inspired act by Jehoshabeath, the daughter of King Jehoram and the wife of Jehoiada, the priest, saved the southern kingdom from being completely overtaken by the house of Ahab. She hid Ahaziah's son, Joash, from Athaliah when Athaliah attempted to murder all of the children of Jehoram after the death of Ahaziah. Had Athaliah's plot succeeded, the Davidic line would have been extinguished, and the Davidic Covenant would not have been fulfilled.

Six years later, Jehoiada proclaimed Joash as king of Judah and had Athaliah killed. This removed the threat of the takeover of the Davidic throne by the house of Ahab. This historical sequence of events demonstrated a critical lesson: evil should not be tolerated nor its significance underestimated; because left unchecked, it will increase and eventually seek to rule where it once was only tolerated. The historical case of the evil perpetuated by Ahab, Jezebel, and Baal worship in Israel and Judah emphatically illustrates this truth.

> *EJ12—Elijah prophesies the death of Ahaziah (Ahab's son and King of Israel)(2 Kings 1:3–4).*
> *EJ13—By Elijah's prayer, fire consumes a regimen of 50 and their captain (2 Kings 1:9–10).*
> *EJ14—By Elijah's prayer, fire consumes a second military regimen of 50 (2 Kings 1:11–12).*
> *EJ15—Elijah is commanded to go with the third military regimen of 50 (2 Kings 1:15–16).*

After the death of Ahab, his son, Ahaziah, became king of Israel and ruled for just over a year before dying. The Bible credits him with ruling for two years. Bible scholars have determined that when credited in years, the reign of kings in Israel were always rounded up. Thus, a reign lasting anywhere between thirteen to twenty-four months might be rounded to two years. During his brief evil reign from 853–852 BC, Ahaziah neither worshipped nor pursued any relationship with the God of Israel. When he grew terminally ill, he sought the counsel of other gods instead of seeking Jehovah. Because Ahaziah alienated himself from Jehovah, Elijah was given a directive from the Lord to confront him. The omniscient God of Israel, through the prophet Elijah, foretold the imminent death of Ahaziah.

When this offensive and threatening message reached Ahaziah, he sent several small military regiments to bring Jehovah's messenger to the king's court for reckoning. Two of these regiments and the captains over them were consumed by fire from heaven at the request of Jehovah's messenger, Elijah. Subsequently, the captain of the third regiment of fifty men humbled himself before Elijah and pleaded for mercy instead of coming against him in the same threatening manner of the first two captains. Jehovah directed Elijah to go with this captain and his regiment and personally confirm the prophetic message of Jehovah to Ahaziah.

When Elijah confronted Ahaziah and delivered the message of Jehovah concerning Ahaziah's imminent death, Elijah used the third person singular divine pronoun *His* to reference the divine person Who had commissioned him to deliver the message (2 Kings 1:16). Elijah's God showed Himself to be omniscient (knowing all things, including the future). He demonstrated His omnipotence by sending fire from heaven. He also displayed His omnipresence by knowing the actions of the king when the king sent to inquire of a false god. Jehovah informed His servant, Elijah, of the king's actions and sent him to challenge the wicked king. Jehovah showed His mercy to the captain of the third fifty instead of destroying him like He had done the previous two captains. Finally, Jehovah's relationship to Elijah and His protection of Elijah, His servant, are clearly displayed in this series of encounters.

EJ16–Elijah's letter rebukes Jehoram, the son of Jehoshaphat (2 Chronicles 21:12–15)

In what might have been his last official act before visiting three schools of the prophets and concluding his earthly ministry, Elijah penned a message of rebuke to Jehoram, the king who had succeeded Jehoshaphat on the throne of Judah. Jehoram had married Athaliah, the daughter of Ahab, and he and his leadership team were implementing an aggressive agenda to institute Baal worship in Jerusalem and throughout Judah (2 Chronicles 21:5–11). Elijah claimed that he was writing this letter at the prompting of the person he called "the Lord God of David." During David's lifetime (1040–970 BC), he had an intimate walk with the person he knew as the Lord. David's relationship with Jehovah is evidenced through the eleven documented divine encounters and the twenty-three additional significant life events recorded about his life, along with the use of about 600 singular divine pronouns referencing David's God in the Psalms and in historical records of David's life. Thus, the designation of the Lord as "the Lord God of David" by Elijah is very appropriate.

Elijah contrasted the evil ways of Jehoram—his choosing to turn away from covenant relationship with Jehovah to worship Baal—with the right ways of Asa and Jehoshaphat, his predecessors. Both Asa and Jehoshaphat had implemented programs to bring the nation into closer fellowship with the God of Israel (2 Chronicles 14:2–5, 17:3–9). Asa (910–870 BC) had two documented divine encounters. Jehoshaphat (870–850 BC) had five documented divine encounters. Both had a personal relationship with the Lord God of David, to some extent. Each had experienced the Lord's protection, provision, and His personal intervention on their behalf, and they taught the nation to seek after a covenant relationship with this God.

Asa was Jehoram's grandfather. Jehoshaphat was Jehoram's father. Despite this rich history of having his royal predecessors come to know the person of the God of Israel, His provision, and His positive character, Jehoram defiantly turned away from the pursuit of the Lord and thus threatened the perpetuation of the Davidic Covenant.

At this point (probably 850 BC), Elijah had spent over a decade in prophetic ministry as the advocate of the Lord in a battle against the spiritual cancer of Baal worship in northern Israel. He certainly would not sit by quietly and not make some effort to influence the wayward young king of Judah. Neither would the Lord, the divine person using the prophet Elijah. The message of the Lord to Jehoram, and the written rebuke through the pen of Elijah, prophesied adverse consequences for Jehoram personally and for the nation as a whole because of their rejection of a covenant relationship with the Lord. The details of the fulfillment of these prophecies are recorded in 2 Chronicles 21:16–20 and include a graphic description of a horrible physical ailment that resulted in the death of this king who did not turn from his evil agenda even after being reprimanded by Elijah. The recorded prophesies came years before their fulfillment.

EJ17—Elijah is sent to Bethel (2 Kings 2:2).
EJ18—Elijah is sent to Jericho (2 Kings 2:4).
EJ19—Elijah is sent to Jordan (2 Kings 2:6).
EJ20—Elijah parts the Jordan River (2 Kings 2:8).
EJ21—Elijah's ascension (2 Kings 2:11–13).

Once Elijah had completed this final earthly ministerial assignment, cautioning Judah's current political leader, he sensed the closure of his sojourn on earth. Around 858 BC, he had commissioned his successor, Elisha (1 Kings 19:16), and planted seeds in the minds of political figures who would help eradicate the evil influences of Ahab (Jehu and Hazael). He had trained his successor for nearly a decade, along with training a whole generation of prophets who would continue the work of the ministry through the school of the prophets.

The second chapter of 2 Kings records the efforts of a man who had invested himself in passing on his passion for pushing people to pursue covenant relationship with the person he knew as the Lord. Elijah, again sensing the end of his earthly ministry, left the city of Gilgal and went to do a final check on the young prophetic ministry students at Bethel, Jericho, and Jordan. Elijah's God prompted him each step of the way during his final visitations.

The Bible does not record how Jehovah prompted Elijah. Each prompting may have been a mere conviction in Elijah's spirit as this is a means by which God has encountered His people throughout history as well. We only know that each prompting was an encounter of Elijah with the Lord because Elijah testified on each occasion that the Lord had sent him to the next destination (2 Kings 2:2,4,6). In his conversations with the students, Elijah must have communicated something of a parting blessing, because each time, the students warned Elisha, "Knowest thou that the Lord will take away thy master from thy head today?"

Elijah had also been preparing Elisha for this transition; Elisha's response to the students at each of the stops was, "Yes, I know it." Having grown very close to his mentor and sensing that something extraordinary was going to occur and that his mentor's departure was at hand, Elisha refused to be separated from Elijah.

Elisha witnessed God's power on the life of his mentor as Elijah performed his final miracle and parted the Jordan river with his mantle, allowing him and his student to cross over on dry ground (2 Kings 2:8). The suspending of the natural laws governing water had occurred in the life of Moses in 1446 BC at the crossing of the Red Sea (Exodus 14:14–22) and in the life of Joshua in 1406 BC at the crossing of the Jordan (Joshua 3–4). Each time, it had signaled a significant transition for the leader and his followers. With Moses and his followers, it signaled the end of their oppression in Egypt. It marked the end of their daily encounters of the many gods of Egypt and their freedom to move toward a close encounter with the God of their fathers. It was a historical marker of their transition to a complete dependence upon Jehovah and His words as they headed toward the land this God had long ago promised to give them.

With Joshua, it had signaled the end of a time of wandering in the wilderness in the vicinity of the land of promise and a transition into actually occupying the land of promise. With the crossing of the Jordan River, the nation was now depending completely on their God as they took on the people that were currently living in the land He had promised to them.

So when Elijah miraculously parted the Jordan with his mantle, it signaled a significant transition. It signaled the end of the earthly ministry of Elijah and the beginning of the independent prophetic ministry of Elisha. Despite the greatness of the ministry of Elijah, the overall accomplishments of the prophetic ministry of Elisha would be even greater. Elijah had set in motion the processes that would bring to an end the formidable challenge to the worship of Jehovah that had been posed by Ahab, Jezebel, and Baal worship. It was time to surrender the reins of ministry to one who would do greater works.

As Elijah spoke with Elisha, a supernatural event occurred that separated the two of them, leaving no evidence of Elijah's continued physical existence except that his mantle fell to the earth. Elisha took possession of the mantle of Elijah and received a double portion of the spirit of his teacher. The supernatural event is variously described as a whirlwind and as a horse-drawn chariot of fire. Nothing of its kind was ever described before or after it in the annals of history.

Elisha—God is Savior

Elisha's ministry stands on its own and is unique and powerful in its own essence. Nonetheless, because he was the student of Elijah, and because his period of ministry was launched by and immediately followed that of Elijah, and because the character of his ministry was quite different from that of his immediate predecessor, Elisha's ministry is often contrasted to that of Elijah.

While Elijah was a rugged outsider who seemed to relish in condemning the leaders of the establishment and ushering in judgment and destruction upon those who stood in opposition to his God, Elisha seemed to be a people oriented ambassador of his God. As Jehovah's minister, Elisha was always working to meet the needs of people of all walks of life and bringing them to an experiential knowledge of the grace, mercy, and power to provide, which was characteristic of his God. While Elijah's ministry was best characterized as a ministry of judgment, Elisha's ministry is best characterized as a ministry of mercy and salvation.

The two ministries and the two prophets are complimentary components of the whole ministry of one God. The divine person Who authored and empowered both ministries is truly one and the same. Only when viewed together and in the light of a historical perspective can these two ministries give the most accurate and comprehensive insight to the character of the divine person these two prophets knew as Jehovah.

Elisha was a historical contemporary of Elijah. He was called to learn under and eventually succeed Elijah only three to four years after the historically documented beginning of Elijah's ministry (around 858 BC). After Elijah's ministry came to a miraculous, dramatic, and abrupt conclusion, Elisha succeeded him in the office of prophetic ministry for almost half a century. A review of the historical contemporaries of Elijah will, therefore, familiarize the student of history with the figures who dominated the historical setting in which Elisha was a student of the ministry.

Two of the contemporaries of Elijah and Elisha were named Jehoram. If Elijah's ascension did not take place until about 850 BC, then he had as much as a two-year overlap with Jehoram, the son of Ahab, in the northern kingdom. History does not record an encounter between these two men. King Jehoshaphat's son and successor was also named Jehoram. History does record a letter of staunch rebuke from Elijah to this monarch of the southern kingdom (2

Chronicles 21:12–15) at the end of Elijah's term of prophetic ministry (~851–850 BC). However, since Elisha's ministry continued for almost fifty more years, some additional historical contemporaries should be mentioned briefly.

Three additional kings of the northern kingdom, three additional monarchs of the southern kingdom of Israel (Judah), and two additional kings of Syria should be considered among the contemporaries of Elisha. The Moabite Inscription, or the Mesha Stone, archaeologically confirms the account of the battle of Israel, Judah, and Edom against Moab in 850 BC. Therefore, it confirms the existence of Jehoshaphat (King of Judah) and Jehoram (King of Israel).

The Black Obelisk of Shalmaneser III archaeologically confirms the reign of Jehu over the northern kingdom (841–813 BC). Jehu's son, Jehoahaz, ruled from 813–796 BC. Jehoash, the grandson of Jehu, was the king who witnessed the death of the great prophet Elisha around 796 BC.

The Tell al Rimah Inscription of Adad-Nirari III (king of Assyria) provides extra-biblical archaeological evidence for the existence of Jehoash.

Additionally, the Victory Stele of Hazael, who was anointed king of Syria by Elijah in 858 BC (1 Kings 19:15) and had his divine appointment reconfirmed by Elisha in 841 BC (2 Kings 8:8–15) gives extra-biblical archaeological evidence of the historicity of Hazael. This Victory Stele also confirms that Jehoram (king of Israel from 852–841 BC) and Ahaziah (king of Judah from 842–841 BC) were actual historial characters along with Hazael (king of Syria from 841–800 BC). As a corollary, these archaeological finds allow the student of history to accept the existence of Jehoram (850–842 BC), Athaliah (841–835 BC), and Joash (835–795 BC), who were the father, mother, and brother, respectively, of Ahaziah, the aforementioned king of Judah.

The ministry of Elisha, it has been noted, contained more miracles than that of any other historical character of the Old Testament, with the exception of Moses, the deliverer and the lawgiver. The bulk of Elisha's divine encounters were evidenced by these miracles and occurred during the decade of 851–841 BC. Additional historically based divine encounters of Elisha associated with miracles occurred on his death bed and after his death in 796 BC.

Because it is extremely difficult to irrefutably confirm the historicity of miraculous occurrences, especially without the ability to interview eyewitnesses, the divine encounters of Elisha are more difficult to confirm than those of the majority of the prophets. Nonetheless, having confirmed his place in history and the historicity of some key persons contemporary with Elisha, we will proceed to at least briefly describe what we know of the attributes of the person Elisha knew as the Lord from the divine encounters Elisha had with Him.

ES1—Elisha parts the Jordan River (2 Kings 2:14).
ES2—Spring of waters cured at Jericho (2 Kings 2:18–22).
ES3—Detractors at Bethel judged and cursed (2 Kings 2:23–24).
ES4—Prophetic deliverance of three kings from Moab (2 Kings 3:1, 10–26).

Elisha witnessed the closure of the prophetic ministry of his friend and mentor, Elijah, in a miraculous event of unprecedented proportions and had the power of Elijah's ministry transferred to him at that time. From its inception, Elisha's ministry was filled with miraculous deeds. Using Elijah's mantle, which he retrieved as it fell to the earth from the whirlwind that carried him away, Elisha performed the same miracle he had that very day seen Elijah perform. With the parting of the Jordan by Elisha in 850 BC came the confirmation that the Lord God of Elijah would be the source of the strength of Elisha's own ministry in the absence of Elijah. With the confirmation that he had indeed received a double portion of the spirit of Elijah as he had requested, Elisha never showed any doubt in his calling or his capacity for ministry.

The miraculous was present at each of Elisha's stops as he went back to visit each of the schools of the prophets established by Elijah. In Jericho, Elisha's God confirmed Elisha's ministry and confirmed His presence with Elisha when He healed the spring of waters on which the people were dependent for their livelihood. When it was discovered that the waters were toxic, Jehovah said to Elisha, "I have healed these waters; there shall not be from hence any more death or barren land" (2 Kings 2:21).

Elijah's God had shown His command of water just before Elisha became Elijah's student by withholding rain for over three years and again at the close of Elijah's ministry by parting the Jordan River hours before Elisha's first recorded miracle. The God of Moses had performed a miracle much like He did for Elisha when He healed the waters of Marah during Israel's trek from Egypt to Sinai in 1446 BC (Exodus 15:22–25).

Interestingly, Jehovah made a covenant with Israel at Marah, promising to heal them or protect them from the plagues and diseases they had witnessed in Egypt if they would serve Him. He is Jehovah-Ropheka in Exodus 15:26. The healing of the waters at Jericho may well have reminded Elisha of this covenant between Jehovah and His people and the fact that Jehovah is the person Who heals, protects, and miraculously provides for His covenant people.

From Jericho, Elisha journeyed to the school of the prophets at Bethel. Another notable miracle occurred in Jericho where, in 931 BC, Jeroboam had set up a golden calf for Israel to worship in the stead of worshipping Jehovah (1 Kings 12:26–33). This idol worship was well-entrenched in Bethel and continued nearly eighty years later, in 850 BC, when Elisha was visiting the school of the prophets there.

The children who mocked Elisha during his visit were likely challenging his presence because he was a Jehovah worshipper, and they were the products of a city given to idol worship. Elisha's cursing of these youngsters, and thus, Jehovah's judgment on them in allowing their death at the hands of bears was a swift and miraculous judgment through the hands of nature on a people who had given themselves to transgress their covenant relationship with Jehovah. They had removed themselves from covenant relationship with Jehovah Ropheka and no longer enjoyed the benefit of His protection. Elisha merely spoke the judgment of Jehovah over them. After all, throughout His history with mankind, Jehovah had been a God Who had expectations of His people, and consequences followed those who chose to live outside of these standards.

Finally, within the same year, the first year of Elisha's ministry, he encountered Jehoram (king of Israel), Jehoshaphat (king of Judah), and the king of Edom in the wilderness of Edom as they were journeying to Moab to crush Moab's rebellion against Israel. These three kings and their armies found themselves in dire straits, and the faithless evil king of the northern kingdom blamed their grave situation on Jehovah Whom he did not worship.

Jehoshaphat, on the other hand, a Jehovah worshipper, sought the assistance of Jehovah to rescue them. Jehoshaphat was well familiar with Jehovah's favor and power. Jehovah had spared him from certain death in a battle in 853 BC (2 Chronicles 18:30–32) and had given Judah a miraculous victory over Ammon, Moab, and Edom soon after that during a battle in which the army did not even have to fight against the opposing forces (2 Chronicles 20:16–17). Jehoshaphat requested the counsel of a prophet of Jehovah when Jehoram blamed Jehovah (2 Kings 3:11).

Elisha, out of respect for Jehoshaphat, interceded to seek Jehovah for the desperate kings and their men. Elisha's God miraculously provided water for the people and gave them another military victory in which they did not even have to fight against their enemies to win (2 Kings 3:16–25). Jehovah demonstrated His ability to control the weather (omnipotence), His propensity to intervene on behalf of those in covenant relationship with Him, and His knowledge of future outcomes (omniscience) with this miracle.

Elisha's perception of the personhood of the Lord is seen in his reference to "the Lord of hosts…before Whom I stand" (2 Kings 3:14); and his statement, "And this is but a light thing in the sight of the Lord: He will deliver the Moabites also into your hand" (2 Kings 3:18). This was Elisha's first ministerial assignment on the international stage, and the historicity of the battle involved in this ministry is confirmed archaeologically by the Moabite Inscription dated around 850 BC.

ES5—Oil of the widow of Shunem multiplied (2 Kings 4:1–7).

ES6—Prophesies the conception of the great woman of Shunem (2 Kings 4:16–17).

ES7—Resurrection of the dead child of the great woman of Shunem (2 Kings 4:18–37).
ES8—Axe head floats (2 Kings 6:1–7).

Elisha's ministry extended over a period of more than five decades, but the vast majority of the miracles, for which we have documentation, appear to have occurred during his first full decade of ministry, 850–841 BC. The chronological order of these miracles and associated events is controversial, difficult to establish, and—for the purpose of establishing the personhood of Elisha's God—unimportant. What is important is what each of these miracles or events revealed about the nature of Elisha's God Who, because miracles are supernatural, must have been the authority responsible for the occurrence of these miracles.

The multiplying of the oil for the widow of the city of Shunem demonstrated the consistency of the Lord's character as the provider for His people and His limitless power. Over 1,100 years previously, God had revealed Himself as Jehovah-Jireh to Abraham on Mount Moriah (Genesis 22:1–18). On that occasion, Jehovah's personhood was made clear when He used at least seven first person singular divine pronouns in His series of exchanges with Abraham. This attribute—the Lord as provider for His people—was also manifested to Moses and the Israelites in the wilderness between 1446–1406 BC. No less than five first person singular divine pronouns were used in the Lord's discussions with Moses in the event documented in Exodus 16:1–17, during which the Lord first fed the nation with manna and miraculously provided meat for them to eat.

There are no divine pronouns used in the record of His exchanges with Elisha during the miracle of providing an endless supply of oil for the widow of Shunem. Nonetheless, the divine person Who interacted with Elisha at this time was the Lord (or Jehovah) and is the same divine person Who encountered Abraham and Moses.

The same personal attribute of caring for and providing for His people is clearly manifested again. While the woman of Shunem, previously mentioned, was of low socioeconomic status, the next miracle involved a Shunammite woman of a high socioeconomic status. The great woman of Shunem, as she is called by Elisha, took care to use her resources to meet a need of the prophet. Elisha sought to serve her in return. She had no ulterior motive for her service to him and rejected his offers of reciprocation. The prophet discovered that, like Sarah, Rebecca, and Hannah in years past, the great woman of Shunem was childless and sought God's intervention on this matter. Like Sarah, the widow of Shunem did not think this thing possible. As He had made conception possible for Sarah around 2066 BC (Genesis 21:1), Rebecca around 2006 BC (Genesis 25:23–26), and Hannah around 1105 BC (1 Samuel 1:20), Jehovah allowed the great woman of Shunem to conceive a child around 850–845 BC.

The impossible was not impossible to the omnipotent God of Elisha. A few short years after his conception, the child of the great woman of Shunem was playing in the fields, had a sudden onset of a severe headache, and suddenly died. The great woman of Shunem sought the intervention of Elisha and his miracle-working God in the face of this great loss. The resurrection of the widow's child from the dead after his untimely death was the second such miracle recorded in the records of the scripture.

Elisha's mentor had performed the first during the drought of 861–858 BC (1 Kings 17:17–24). The miraculous recovery of the axe head from the water was another miracle demonstrated by Elisha's God. It was the only miracle of its kind recorded in the scripture. Both of these events demonstrated the omnipotence of the God of Elisha as He was working in Elisha's ministry.

ES9—Famine foretold (2 Kings 8:1–2).
ES10—Toxic pottage cured at Gilgal (2 Kings 4:38–41).
ES11—Loaves of barley multiplied at Gilgal (2 Kings 4:42–44).
ES12—Naaman healed of leprosy (2 Kings 5:1–19).
ES13—Gehazi stricken with leprosy and removed from prophetic service (2 Kings 5:20–27).

Elisha was credited with foretelling a seven-year famine. He stated that the Lord had called for a famine (1 Kings 8:1). Thus, again, Elisha's God was omnipotent and omniscient, both dictating that a famine was going to occur and knowing how long the famine would continue. Armed with this information, Elisha was able to give counsel to the great woman of Shunem to help her best position her family to survive the coming famine conditions. The famine appears to have occurred during the decade of Elisha's most prominent ministerial activity.

The curing of the toxic pottage and the miraculous multiplication of the barley loaves at Gilgal may have also occurred during this famine. Regardless, both miracles demonstrated Jehovah's ability to provide for His people during difficult times. These miracles remind the student of history once again of the Lord's provision for His people in the wilderness during the great Exodus of 1446–1406 BC.

The famine must have occurred before 841 BC because Gehazi was still the servant of Elisha, and Benhadad II was still king of Syria. Gehazi was removed from his office as assistant to Elisha after the healing of Naaman the leper (2 Kings 5:21–27) but still held this office at the end of the famine. It was Gehazi who was conveying a report of Elisha's miracles to Jehoram, king of the northern kingdom when the famine ended, and the great woman of Shunem and her family returned to Israel. This occurred before the death of Benhadad II (2 Kings 8:3–6).

Benhadad II was succeeded on the throne of Syria by Hazael in 841 BC (2 Kings 8:7–15). Naaman, like Hazael, was a great general of Syria under Benhadad II (2 Kings 5:1). He would have probably been perceived as a threat by Hazael, thus was likely not a military presence after 841 BC when Hazael became king of Syria.

Elisha's perception of the personhood of the Lord was revealed when he refused the gifts offered in exchange for the miraculous healing Naaman received. Elisha responded to Naaman's offer by saying, "As the Lord liveth, before Whom I stand, I will receive none" (2 Kings 5:16). Elisha indicated, thereby, that he saw Jehovah as the divine person to Whom he was accountable and Who, in fact, had performed this miracle. It was Jehovah Who deserved a response from Naaman.

Naaman then gave the response that Elisha and Elisha's God really sought after; Naaman expressed a new understanding that there was no God, beside Jehovah, worthy of praise and a commitment to live a life guided by this new understanding. Gehazi's plot to receive gifts from Naaman threatened to undermine the impact of the work of the ministry in Naaman's life and received a just response from Elisha and Jehovah.

Jehovah's judgment of Gehazi reiterated that He was a God of compassion and a God of judgment, a character trait that the first man, Adam, could verify (Genesis 3). When God judged Adam's sin, He also uttered the first messianic prophecy during the same series of verbal exchanges (Genesis 3:15–24). Elisha had also used the expression, "As the Lord liveth, before Whom I stand," when he responded to the kings of Israel, Judah, and Edom in the wilderness as they were on their way to war against Moab in about 850 BC (2 Kings 3:14). He seemed to be ever aware of the fact that there was an eternal person to Whom he must answer and Who was the source of the supernatural insights and events associated with his ministry.

ES14—The strategic plans of the Syrian king (Benhadad II) revealed (2 Kings 6:8–13).
ES15—The strategic plans of the Syrian king (Benhadad II) revealed (2 Kings 6:8–13).
ES16—The strategic plans of the Syrian king (Benhadad II) revealed (2 Kings 6:8–13).
ES17—The armies of Jehovah revealed to Elisha's young servant (2 Kings 6:17).
ES18—The armies of Syria blinded by Elisha's request (2 Kings 6:18).
ES19—The armies of Syria healed by Elisha's request (2 Kings 6:20).
ES20—Elisha prophesies Jehovah's provision during the Syrian siege (2 Kings 6:24–7:20).

The Syrian nation was a perpetual menace to the whole land of Palestine during the reign of Benhadad II. Again and again, they raided the countries of Palestine and lived on the spoils that they took. Israel's plight as one of these countries was well-documented in 2 Kings 5–8. One of Syria's raids had netted the capture of the maid from Israel who mentioned the prophet Elisha to Naaman's wife. This resulted in Benhadad II sending a message to Jehoram, king of Israel, that he was sending Naaman to Israel to be recovered of his leprosy. Jehoram had interpreted this in the light of Syria's frequent unprovoked raids as a ploy by the Syrian king to justify yet another raid of the land.

In chapter 6, there were at least three raids planned by the Syrians. Israel's God thwarted these three raids by revealing the plans of the Syrians to Elisha before the raids could be executed. This repeated thwarting of his newest plans to raid Israel caused Benhadad II to become very uneasy. He blamed this development on the presence of a traitor within the ranks of the Syrians.

In reality, this was a demonstration of the omniscience of Jehovah and His close relationship with His servant Elisha to whom He revealed inside information on the plans of the Syrians. On no less than three occasions, Jehovah encountered Elisha and revealed the thoughts and plans of Benhadad II.

When the Syrians determined that Elisha was the informant of Benhadad's plans for raiding Israel, Benhadad II dispatched a military contingent to capture Elisha. Elisha's God miraculously disabled the contingent with blindness and then miraculously restored their sight when their ability to accomplish their mission was neutralized. Jehovah used this situation to reveal His omnipotence to Elisha's new ministry student, Jehoram (king of Israel), and Benhadad II and the Syrians. Elisha was already quite aware of the omnipotence, omnipresence, and omniscience of the person He knew as the Lord. It was at Elisha's request that *He*, the Lord, smote the Syrians with blindness and later restored their sight (2 Kings 6:18,20).

After these raids, the Syrians again raided the land and besieged Samaria. Jehoram had agreed to Elisha's counsel when the Syrian army was at his mercy and had not destroyed them, leaving them at full strength at the time of this subsequent siege. So Jehoram blamed Elisha for Syria's successful raid and the siege that resulted. The condition in the city was so desperate during this siege that the people resorted to cannibalism to survive.

During this crisis, when a divine move would be absolutely unmistakable, Jehovah revealed His remedy for the crisis to Elisha who spoke a prophetic utterance that could scarcely be believed. The prophecy was fulfilled when the Syrians inexplicably abandoned the siege. Not only were the omnipotence and omniscience of Jehovah displayed, but His care, compassion, and provision for His people were also shown. This was done, despite the fact that the king, Jehoram, and the nation as a whole remained outside of the protection of a covenant relationship with Jehovah (2 Kings 3:1–3, 3:13).

Thus, while the vulnerability of the nation to repeated raids by Syria may well have been the consequence of their broken covenant relationship, the provision of Jehovah for them was a demonstration of His mercy toward His people.

ES21—Prophesies the death of Benhadad II and the reign of Hazael of Syria (2 Kings 8:7–15).
ES22—Prophesies the death of Jehoram and the rise of Jehu's dynasty (2 Kings 9:1–13).

By around 841 BC, the busiest phase of the public prophetic ministry of Elisha seemed to be winding down. After he prophesied the end of Jehoram's reign and the death of Benhadad II with their replacement by Jehu and Hazael, respectively, there are no more records of Elisha's prophetic ministry until he is on his deathbed. During this period, the evil political influence of Ahab and Jezebel continued to be widespread. Elijah had contended with their evil throughout his time in prophetic ministry. Elisha had taken up the mantle and continued the struggle throughout the reign of Jehoram. Elijah had initially anointed Jehu in 858 BC. Elisha effectively sent Jehu, the appointed successor of Jehoram, to accomplish his appointed task some sixteen to seventeen years after Elijah had anointed him.

At the same time that Jehu had been anointed by Elijah, Hazael had also been anointed. When Elisha sent Jehu to go and fulfill his appointment, he also sent Hazael to go and fulfill his commission. Elisha's God had known nearly two decades before the death of Benhadad II that Hazael would be his successor. By His omniscience, He had also foretold the end of the dynasty of Ahab in the northern kingdom which became a historical eventuality in 841 BC.

When Jehovah sent Elisha to activate Jehu to step into his appointment, He used first person singular divine pronouns according to the historic record (2 Kings 9:3, 6–10). The divine pronoun *I* was used at least once. The statements of both Elisha and Jehu only record the use of this divine pronoun once. The student whom Elisha sent, however, attributed the use of the divine pronoun *I* to the Lord four times and the use of the divine pronoun *My* once in his actual message to Jehu. In any case, the divine personhood of Elisha's God and master was evidenced as Elisha's decade of ministerial prominence was closing. Elisha witnessed the beginnings of the political regime changes that his mentor, Elijah, had seen long before this time.

ES23—Elisha prophesies three victories of Israel over Benhadad III and Syria (2 Kings 13:17–19). Elisha's bones credited with the resurrection of a dead man (2 Kings 13:20–21).

Nothing is recorded of the ministry of Elisha during the reigns of Jehu and Hazael. Elisha lived through the reigns and deaths of Jehoram, Jezebel, and Jehoahaz in the northern kingdom. He saw the rise and fall of Jehoram, Ahaziah, and Athaliah in the southern kingdom. Joash—the young king who took the throne of David when he was only seven years old—was the king of Judah when Elisha died.

Jehoash, the grandson of Jehu, was on the throne of Israel when Elisha was on his deathbed. It was this king, Jehoash, to whom the prophet spoke the words of his last prophecy. Elisha's God had revealed to him that Jehoash would determine his own military success by the fervor of his response to Elisha's direct commands to him during an encounter between the two men while Elisha was on his deathbed (2 Kings 13:17–19). The king's response predicted three victories over Syria and the son of Hazael (Benhadad III). The final prophecy of Elisha was fulfilled according to 2 Kings 13:24–25.

The final miracle associated with the prophet Elisha occurred after his death and was quite possibly the most dramatic and the least believable. The biblical record states that a dead body was cast into the grave of Elisha and that the body was restored to life upon contacting the body of Elisha.

Elisha's God had already proven that He could restore a dead body to life when He caused the resurrection of the son of the great woman of Shunem sometime between 850–841 BC. It would have been no great feat for this same divine person, Who had created the universe from nothing and created life on earth by the power of His spoken word and had restored a body to life forty to fifty years earlier, to do this miraculous deed at the site of Elisha's grave. It was not the power of Elisha's holiness, but the presence of the power of Elisha's God that caused this miracle of unprecedented proportions to occur. A miracle of this magnitude rivals that of the earthly departure of Elijah the prophet, which marked the end of Elijah's earthly ministry and the beginning of the independent prophetic ministry of Elisha.

Summary and Conclusions

The prophetic ministries of Elijah and his ministerial successor, Elisha, are intricately interwoven. During the majority of the recorded history of Elijah's ministry, Elisha accompanied him as his student and servant. Thus, Elisha got to know the God of Elijah while training under him for nearly a decade. Moreover, Elisha's experiences with the Lord confirm that his God had the same attributes and was the same divine person as the God of his mentor, Elijah.

Between 861–851 BC, Elijah made at least eight major prophesies, was associated with nine major miracles, had ten clearly identified conversations with the Lord, and three additional interactions in which a divine conversation is inferred. Each of these is listed below (Table 1.2, 1.3, and 1.4). Through His prophetic accuracy, Elijah's God demonstrated His perfect knowledge of the future (omniscience). Five of these prophecies were judgments upon the nation and/or its rulers for their spiritual infidelity. Jehovah had described Himself to Moses as a jealous God in 1446 BC (Exodus 20:5, 34:14). As He had distinguished Himself from the false gods of Egypt then, so He distinguished Himself from the false gods of Ahab and Jezebel and showed His consistent tendency to ultimately judge His people when they turned their loyalties to other gods.

Four of the miracles associated with Elijah's ministry were demonstrations of Jehovah as the Jehovah-Jireh, known to Abraham between between 2166–1991 BC (God Who provides for His people). A fifth miracle was done without any active role by the prophet; he was the recipient of the miracle during his ascension via a chariot or a whirlwind. Five additional miracles involved the active participation of the prophet.

Elijah had no less than thirteen interactions with Jehovah in which a direct conversation with the Lord was at least inferred. In his final visitations to the schools of the prophets at Jericho, Bethel, and Jordan, the divine communication was inferred by Elijah's comment that the Lord had sent him to each location. Both of the divine communications in reference to the judgment of King Ahaziah of the northern kingdom were clearly direct verbal exchanges between Elijah and Jehovah.

The divine personhood of the Lord, the God of Israel, is referenced by the use of the third person singular divine pronoun *His,* spoken by Elijah in 2 Kings 1:16. And in Elijah's letter to King Jehoram of Judah at the end of Elijah's ministry, the communication from Jehovah was again a direct exchange. Though no divine pronouns are used by Elijah or Jehovah in this historically documented communication, the God of Elijah is here identified as the same person Who was God to David, Jehoshaphat, and Asa.

Elijah began his ministry with a confrontation with Ahab after a directive from the Lord God of Israel, the person before Whom Elijah said he stood. The divine pronoun used here was *Whom,* identifying the personhood of Jehovah. In each of the remaining six direct communications from Jehovah to Elijah, the Lord actually used first person singular divine pronouns when referring to Himself while speaking to Elijah. In total, during these six communications, the Lord used eleven first person singular divine pronouns (*I* and *Me*).

The person Elijah knew as the Lord was an omniscient, omnipotent, omnipresent person Who performed miracles, defying the limitations of mere humanity. He provided protection and sustenance for His people. He controlled the elements, had no divine equal, and repeatedly held His people to a standard of conduct. If Jehovah's people transgressed His standards and breached their covenant relationship with Him, He was apt to bring judgment upon them, although the judgment was accompanied by a measure of mercy.

Micaiah and the unnamed prophets who were contemporary with Elijah also heard the Lord use divine pronouns which established His personhood in His interactions with them. The Lord used the first person singular divine pronoun *I* five times in these exchanges. Micaiah used at least five third person singular divine pronouns as he referenced the divine person to Whom he was subject. They were recorded when Micaiah confronted Ahab and Jehoshaphat before their joint military engagement with Benhadad II that ended in the death of Ahab (1 Kings 22).

After the miraculous conclusion of Elijah's ministry and the passing of Elijah's mantle to Elisha, the same divine person Who had directed and kept Elijah for over a decade directed and kept Elisha as he continued the work of Elijah, and of Jehovah, for over a half-century. During the first year of Elisha's ministry, His God performed three miracles and gave one prophecy. In one of these miracles, Elisha stated that the Lord said, "I have healed these waters," thereby establishing the personhood of Elisha's God.

In delivering the prophecy which God gave him to speak that same year, Elisha referenced "the Lord of hosts before Whom I stand." Thus, in his first year, Elisha unquestionably established the personhood of his God. During his most active decade of ministry, extending from 850–841 BC, Elisha saw this God perform eleven additional miracles. Elisha received nine additional words of prophecy from Jehovah over this period of time. God is repeatedly referred to as the Lord (Jehovah) during this decade, but there is a scarcity of divine pronouns documented by the historical accounts.

In the account of Naaman's healing, Elisha used the divine pronoun *Whom* to reference his God. First person singular divine pronouns were used by Elisha's God when Elisha commissioned Jehu to proceed with the uprooting of Ahab's dynasty. At least one and as many as five first person singular divine pronouns were spoken by God in association with this event (including the use of the pronouns *I* and *My*).

At least four of the miracles performed during Elisha's ministry were clearly associated with a direct communication from the Lord. The historical record clearly reflects a direct communication between Jehovah and Elisha in five of the prophecies attributed to Elisha while this communication is safely, albeit only, inferred in the other five prophetic words spoken by Elisha. The miracles attributed to Elisha's God and associated with Elisha's ministry bore record of the Lord's omnipotence, omniscience, omnipresence, mercy, power to provide and protect and His intricate involvement with the lives of His people. The resurrection of a dead body that touched Elisha's bones may be one of the most dramatic illustrations of Jehovah's omnipotence associated with the ministry of Elisha. The personal attributes demonstrated by Jehovah as He performed these miracles had consistently characterized Him throughout the ministry of Elijah and the other men of history that had even preceded Elisha. Elisha's God was the same divine person the men who had preceded him in ministry had known.

The prophecies associated with the ministry of Elisha further confirmed the personhood and divine attributes of Elisha's God. In all, through Elisha's ministry, less than ten first person singular divine pronouns and the divine pronoun Whom (which appears twice) are associated with His God. However, His personhood is solidly established by the context of the historical accounts recording the interaction of Elisha with his God.

The God of Elijah and Elisha was the same covenant-keeping, relationship-oriented, omnipotent, omniscient, omnipresent, sovereign God of the fathers of Israel. He was the God Who had given promises to Abraham, Isaac, and Jacob, the fathers of Israel. He had given the law to Moses, Israel's lawgiver and deliverer. He had given the promised land to Joshua, the agent of Jehovah's salvation to a people who had wandered in the wilderness for decades. He had given the kingdom to David, Israel's great psalmist and king. This same divine person commissioned and empowered Elijah and Elisha for the work they did, laying the foundation for the prophetic ministry. The work of Jehovah through His relationship with Elijah and Elisha laid the foundation that would undergird the prophetic ministry for hundreds of years.

Table 1.1 Elijah's encounters with Jehovah

	Description	Reference	FPSP	3PSP
	The early years of Elijah's ministry			
EJ1	Elijah prophesies a drought	1 Kings 17:1		
EJ2	Elijah sustained by food from ravens	1 Kings 17:2-7	1	
EJ3	Elijah is sustained by food from a widow at Zarephath	1 Kings 17:9-16	1	1
EJ4	Elijah resurrects the son of the widow of Zarephath	1 Kings 17:17-24		
EJ5	Elijah prophesies the end of the drought	1 Kings 18:1-2	1	
EJ6	Elijah prays and Jehovah answers by fire	1 Kings 18:36-39		2
	Jehovah gives Elijah a season of rest			
EJ7	Elijah fed by an angel	1 Kings 19:4-6		
EJ8	Elijah fed by an angel	1 Kings 19:7-8		
EJ9	Elijah counseled in a cave at Horeb after a forty day fast	1 Kings 19:9-18	2	1
	Jehovah judges Ahab's social/ moral misconduct			
EJ10	Ahab judged for wrongful death of Naboth	1 Kings 21:17-24	2	
EJ11	Ahab's humility leads to delayed judgment	1 Kings 21:29 2 Kings 9:25-37	4 2	
	Jehovah and Elijah and the end of Ahab's dynasty			
EJ12	Elijah prophesies the death of Ahaziah (Ahab's son and King of Israel)	2 Kings 1:3-4		
EJ13	By Elijah's prayer, fire consumes a regimen of fifty and their captain	2 Kings 1:9-10		

EJ14	By Elijah's prayer, fire consumes a second military regimen of fifty	2 Kings 1:11-12		
EJ15	Elijah is commanded to go with the third military regimen of fifty	2 Kings 1:15-16		1
EJ16	Elijah's letter rebukes Jehoram, the son of Jehoshaphat	2 Chron. 21:12-15		
	The final days of Elijah's ministry			
EJ17	Elijah is sent to Bethel	2 Kings 2:2		
EJ18	Elijah is sent to Jericho	2 Kings 2:4		
EJ19	Elijah is sent to Jordan	2 Kings 2:6		
EJ20	Elijah parts the Jordan River	2 Kings 2:8		
EJ21	Elijah's ascension	2 Kings 2:11-13		

FPSP First person singular divine pronouns
3PSP Third person singular divine pronouns

Table 1.2 Communication between Jehovah and Elijah documented

Date BC	Event	Reference
861 BC	Beginning of drought of rain	1 Kings 17:1
861 BC	Provision by ravens	1 Kings 17:4
861 BC	Provision by widow of Zarephath	1 Kings 17:14-16
858 BC	End of drought of rain	1 Kings 18:1
858 BC	Encouragement at Mt. Horeb	1 Kings 19:9-18
856-3 BC	Confronting Ahab in field of Naboth	1 Kings 21:17-24
856-3 BC	Ahab humbled, judgment delayed	1 Kings 21:29
853-2 BC	Confronting the messengers of Ahaziah	2 Kings 1:3-4
853-2 BC	Conceding to third captain; message to Ahaziah	2 Kings 1:15
851 BC	Letter to chastise Jehoram of Judah	2 Chronicles 21:12-15
850 BC	Sent to Bethel	2 Kings 2:2
850 BC	Sent to Jericho	2 Kings 2:4
850 BC	Sent to Jordan	2 Kings 2:6

Table 1.3 Major prophecies of Elijah

Date BC	Prophecy	Reference
861 BC	Drought of rain	1 Kings 17:1
861 BC	Endless supply of oil and meal	1 Kings 17:14-16
858 BC	End of drought of rain	1 Kings 18:41
858 BC	Political rise of Hazael (Syria) and Jehu (Israel)	1 Kings 19:15-16
856-3 BC	Death of Ahab and Jezebel	1 Kings 21:21-24
856-3 BC	Judgment of Ahab's house	1 Kings 21:29
853-2 BC	Death of Ahaziah	2 Kings 1:3-4, 16
851 BC	Judgment of Jehoram of Judah	2 Chronicles 21:12-15

Table 1.4 Major miracles associated with Elijah (to Elijah or through Elijah)

Date BC	Miracle	Reference
861 BC	Provision by ravens	1 Kings 17:6
861 BC	Provision by endless supply of oil/meal	1 Kings 17:14-16
861 BC	Provision (twice) by an angel	1 Kings 19:5-8
860-58 BC	Resurrection of widow's son	1 Kings 17:20-22
858 BC	Calls for fire to consume offering at Mt. Carmel	1 Kings 18:30-39
853-2 BC	Calls for fire to consume captain and his fifty men	2 Kings 1:10
853-2 BC	Calls for fire to consume second captain and his fifty men	2 Kings 1:12
850 BC	Parts Jordan with his mantle	2 Kings 2:8
850 BC	Ascension via whirlwind/chariot of fire	2 Kings 2:11

Table 1.5 Elisha's encounters with Jehovah

	Description	Reference	FPSP	3PSP
	The establishing of Elisha's ministry			
ES1	Elisha parts the Jordan River	2 Kings 2:14		
ES2	Spring of waters cured at Jericho	2 Kings 2:18-22	1	
ES3	Detractors at Bethel judged and cursed	2 Kings 2:23-24		
ES4	Prophetic deliverance of three kings from Moab	2 Kings 3:1, 10-26		1
	The most prominent years of Elisha's ministry			
ES5	Oil of the widow of Shunem multiplied	2 Kings 4:1-7		
ES6	Prophesies the conception of the great woman of Shunem	2 Kings 4:16-17		
ES7	Resurrection of the dead child of the great woman of Shunem	2 Kings 4:18-37		
ES8	Axe head floats	2 Kings 6:1-7		
ES9	Famine foretold	2 Kings 8:1-2		
ES10	Toxic pottage cured at Gilgal	2 Kings 4:38-41		
ES11	Loaves of barley multiplied at Gilgal	2 Kings 4:42-44		
ES12	Naaman healed of leprosy	2 Kings 5:1-19		
ES13	Gehazi stricken with leprosy and removed from prophetic service	2 Kings 5:20-27		
ES14	The strategic plans of the Syrian king (Benhadad II) revealed	2 Kings 6:8-13		
ES15	The strategic plans of the Syrian king (Benhadad II) revealed	2 Kings 6:8-13		
ES16	The strategic plans of the Syrian king (Benhadad II) revealed	2 Kings 6:8-13		

ES17	The armies of Jehovah revealed to Elisha's young servant	2 Kings 6:17		
ES18	The armies of Syria blinded by Elisha's request	2 Kings 6:18		1
ES19	The armies of Syria healed by Elisha's request	2 Kings 6:20		
ES20	Elisha prophesies Jehovah's provision during the Syrian siege	2 Kings 6:24-7:20		
ES21	Prophesies the death of Benhadad II and the reign of Hazael of Syria	2 Kings 8:7-15		
ES22	Prophesies the death of Jehoram and the rise of Jehu's dynasty	2 Kings 9:1-13	7	
	The end of Elisha's ministry			
ES23	Elisha prophesies three victories of Israel over Benhadad III and Syria	2 Kings 13:17-19		

FPSP First person singular divine pronouns
3PSP Third person singular divine pronouns

Table 1.6 Communication between Jehovah and Elisha documented

Date BC	Event	Reference
850 BC	Waters healed at Jericho	2 Kings 2:18-22
850 BC	Water and military victory for armies of Israel/Judah/Edom	2 Kings 3:1, 10-26
850-41 BC	Oil multiplied for the widow of Shunem	2 Kings 4:1-7
850-41 BC	Great woman of Shunem would conceive a child	2 Kings 4:16-17
850-41 BC	Jehovah called for a famine	2 Kings 8:1-2
850-41 BC	Loaves multiplied	2 Kings 4:42-44
850-41 BC	Healing of Naaman of Syria	2 Kings 5:1-19
850-41 BC	Military strategy of Benhadad II revealed (three times)	2 Kings 6:8-13
850-41 BC	Heavenly military host revealed	2 Kings 6:17

850-41 BC	Syrian army blinded	2 Kings 6:18
850-41 BC	Syrian army's sight restored	2 Kings 6:20
850-41 BC	Provision during Syrian siege of Samaria	2 Kings 6:24-7:20
841 BC	Death of Benhadad II/rise of Hazael of Syria	2 Kings 8:7-15
841 BC	Death of Jehoram/rise of Jehu of Northern Kingdom	2 Kings 9:1-13
796 BC	Three military victories of Israel over Syria	2 Kings 13:17-19

Table 1.7 Major prophecies of Elisha

Date BC	Prophecy	Reference
850 BC	Water and military victory for armies of Israel/Judah/Edom	2 Kings 3:1, 10-26
850-41 BC	Oil multiplied for widow of Shunem	2 Kings 4:1-7
850-41 BC	Great woman of Shunem would conceive a child	2 Kings 4:16-17
850-41 BC	Jehovah called for a famine	2 Kings 8:1-2
850-41 BC	Military strategy of Benhadad II revealed (three times)	2 Kings 6:8-13
850-41 BC	Provision during Syrian siege of Samaria	2 Kings 6:24-7:20
841 BC	Death of Benhadad II/rise of Hazael of Syria	2 Kings 8:7-15
841 BC	Death of Jehoram/rise of Jehu of Northern Kingdom	2 Kings 9:1-13
796 BC	Three military victories of Israel over Syria	2 Kings 13:17-19

Table 1.8 Major miracles associated with Elisha

Date BC	Miracle	Reference
850 BC	Parts Jordan River with Elijah's mantle	2 Kings 2:11-15
850 BC	Waters healed at Jericho	2 Kings 2:18-22
850 BC	Bears maul idol worshippers at Jericho	2 Kings 2:23-24
850-41 BC	Resurrection of child of Great woman of Shunem	2 Kings 4:18-37
850-41 BC	Axe head floats	2 Kings 6:1-7
850-41 BC	Toxic pottage healed	2 Kings 4:38-41

850-41 BC	Loaves multiplied	2 Kings 4:42-44
850-41 BC	Healing of Naaman of Syria	2 Kings 5:1-19
850-41 BC	Gehazi becomes leprous	2 Kings 5:20-27
850-41 BC	Heavenly military host revealed	2 Kings 6:17
850-41 BC	Syrian army blinded	2 Kings 6:18
850-41 BC	Syrian army's sight restored	2 Kings 6:20
796 BC	Dead man resurrected by touching bones of Elisha	2 Kings 13:20-21

References

The Holy Bible. 2010. *Authorized King James Version.* Nashville, Tennessee: Holman Bible Publishers.

Wiersbe, Warren W. 2007. *The Wiersbe Bible Commentary: Old Testament.* Colorado Springs, Colorado: David C. Cook.

https://teldan.wordpress.com/house–of–david–inscription/

http://www.jewishencyclopedia.com/articles//2871–ben–hadad

Mark, Joshua J. "Jezebel: Princess of Sidon, Queen of Israel." *Ancient History Encyclopedia.* http://www.ancient.eu/article/92/

Encountering the God of Joel: The God of Judah's Prophet of Pentecost

Joel was a prophet in the southern kingdom of Israel (Judah) during the same century that Elijah and Elisha were prophets in the northern kingdom of Israel (Israel). He was the earliest of the writing prophets, predating Isaiah, Hosea, Amos, Jonah, and Micah by fifty to one hundred years. He probably delivered his prophecy around 860–830 BC. Historically then, the rulers of Judah during Joel's lifetime might have been Jehoshaphat, Jehoram, Ahaziah, Athaliah, and/or Joash. International rulers that were probably contemporary with Joel included Ahab, Ahaziah, Jehoram, and Jehu of the northern kingdom (Israel), Benhadad II and Hazael of Syria, and Shalmaneser III of Assyria.

The Kurkh Monolith and the Black Obelisk of Shalmaneser III are Assyrian artifacts that confirm the historicity of some of the people who were contemporary with Joel. Admittedly, none of these people are mentioned by name in Joel's writing. Joel does, however, mention the Grecians (Joel 3:6). The Great Amphictyonic League—a cultural and political allegiance of Greek states—was in place during the time of Joel's ministry. Joel's reference to the Grecians may have been the first direct confirmation of ancient Greece and its interactions with or historical link to Palestine in the Old Testament. Pinpointing the precise historical window of Joel's writing to a timespan narrower than 860–830 BC is a significant challenge. Establishing a historical setting within which the prophet lived and the historical figures contemporary with him is sufficient evidence of Joel's historicity.

Joel begins his writing by describing a plague of locusts that had recently caused devastation within his country. This plague of locusts could have been contemporary with the famine which the Lord called for during the ministry of Elisha to the Northern Kingdom (2 Kings 8:1–2) and thus, it may have occurred during the decade of Elisha's greatest ministerial prominence (851–841 BC). Some evidence suggests that it occurred during Judah's dark days under the reign of Jehoram, Ahaziah and Queen Athaliah, extending from 853–835 BC (2 Chronicles 21:16–23:21). Because of his evil choices, Jehoram, king of Judah, incurred judgment by Jehovah (2 Chronicles 21). A revolt by the Edomites (2 Chronicles 21:5–10) and an invasion by an international coalition including the Philistines, Arabians, and others (2 Chronicles 21:16–17) were the consequence of Jehovah's judgment upon Judah during Jehoram's eight-year reign.

King Ahaziah and his mother, Queen Athaliah, who succeeded him on the throne, were also evil rulers of Judah. The locust infestation mentioned by Joel may well have been sent as a judgment during these dark days. Neither of these three rulers may have been considered worthy of mention by Joel, the prophet of Jehovah. Hence, the fact that no ruler of Judah is named in his writings. When Jehovah speaks of judgment and retribution for evil committed against Judah (Joel 3), it may be for the losses Judah sustained at the hands of other nations during the reigns of these three evil rulers.

Joel's writing probably occurs during the end of the dark days of Judah under Jehoram, Ahaziah, and Athaliah (853–835 BC) or the beginning of the reign of Joash (835–795 BC). Despite the fact that Joash was very young when he became king, he left the legacy of being one of the few good kings of Judah. The document that records Joel's work and his relationship with Jehovah is readily divided into three parts. A historical description of Jehovah's recent judgment upon the land is found in Joel 1. A warning or prophecy of coming judgments is recorded in Joel 2:1–11. Joel finishes his writings with a call to repentance and a promise of Jehovah's future judgment upon Judah's enemies and Jehovah's mercies upon His people (Joel 2:12–3:21).

Joel's record contains a single series of exchanges between him and his God. Jehovah speaks in Joel 2:12–14, is credited with the words recorded in Joel 2:19–20, and speaks continuously from Joel 2:24 through the remainder of this short book. Joel 2:12–14 contains Jehovah's plea to His people to return to faithfulness to the covenant relationship He has sought with them for centuries. In Joel 2:19–20, the prophet speaks but conveys the words of a promise spoken by Jehovah. Jehovah's promise is for restoration of His people in a short timeframe if they return to covenant relationship with Him.

In Joel 2:24–32, Jehovah's promise of restoration is extended to include a prophecy beyond the immediate historical time frame and into the more distant future. At this point, the promise also extends beyond the Hebrew nation to include all of God's chosen people in the future, a group that includes all believers. The extended reach of this prophecy spoken by Jehovah to Joel is confirmed by Peter on the day of the birth of the New Testament church (Acts 2:1–21).

The remainder of Jehovah's prophecy in Joel likely references the nation's coming restoration to prominence that ultimately occurred during the reign of King Uzziah, the grandson of Joash, who sat on Judah's throne from 790–740 BC.

Joel knows Jehovah as Judah's sovereign judge and the One Who can provide or withhold provision at His sovereign discretion. Joel's God is divinely responsible for the judgment of the people, brought by the plague of locusts described in Joel 1. Joel calls Jehovah the Almighty in Joel 1:15. He references the Day of the Lord (a reference to a day of judgment by Jehovah) five times in his short book (1:15, 2:1, 2:11, 2:31, 3:14).

Joel also knows Jehovah as the God Who seeks to restore His people to covenant relationship with Him (Joel 2:12–14,24–32). Jehovah says of Himself, "He is gracious and merciful, slow to anger, and of great kindness" (Joel 2:13). Joel's God offers hope in the midst of judgment upon His people and promises to protect His people in the face of their enemies (Joel 2:24–3:21). Upon their return to Him, Jehovah promises to "restore the years that the locust hath eaten" (Joel

2:25). He calls Himself "the Hope of His people" and "the strength of the children of Israel" (Joel 3:16).

There are thirty-four first person singular divine pronouns attributed to Joel's God in his written record. There are sixteen third person singular divine pronouns in this prophetic book. The person Joel knows as Jehovah is not unlike the person Joel's contemporaries in Israel, Elijah and Elisha, described. He is the omnipotent, omniscient, and sovereign judge of all the earth.

Table 2.1 Outline of Joel's Encounter with Jehovah

Subject	Reference	Divine titles	FPSP	3PSP
Reflecting on the past				
Joel laments plague of locust	1:1–20	Almighty		
Prophecy of future events				
Joel warns of further judgments	2:1–11			5
Call for repentance, Jehovah's promises to His people				
Jehovah calls Judah to repentance	2:12–14		1	4
Joel encourages a response to Jehovah's call for repentance	2:15–23		3	5
Jehovah promises restoration	2:24–32		11	
Jehovah describes judgment of Judah's enemies	3:1–21	Hope of His people, Strength of the children of Israel	19	2

FPSP First person singular divine pronouns
3PSP Third person singular divine pronouns

References

The Holy Bible. 2010. *Authorized King James Version.* Nashville, Tennessee: Holman Bible Publishers.

Wiersbe, Warren W. 2007. *The Wiersbe Bible Commentary: Old Testament.* Colorado Springs, Colorado: David C. Cook.

Leston, Stephen. 2011. *The Bible in World History.* Urichsville, OH: Barbour Publishing Inc.

Encountering Isaiah's God: The God of Judah's Eagle-Eyed Prophet

The prophet Isaiah occupies a prominent position in Jewish history. He began his ministry around 740 BC, approximately fifty years after the death of the great prophet Elisha who died around 796 BC. You will recall that Elisha was the student of Elijah who had established the school of the prophets around 858 BC. Elisha, whose name means "God is salvation," perpetuated the school of the prophets after Elijah's departure. Elijah and Elisha were, therefore, effectively the fathers of prophetic ministry in Israel, particularly in the northern kingdom.

After the death of these fathers of prophetic ministry who left no personal writings of their own prophetic ministry, the next generation of great prophets included the writing prophets Jonah (around 760 BC), Amos (around 760 BC), Hosea (around 750–720 BC), Micah (around 735 BC), and Isaiah. Of this generation of prophets—appropriately considered the successor generation to Elijah and Elisha—Isaiah, whose name means "salvation of Jehovah," had the most far-reaching impact.

Isaiah has been commonly referred to as "the eagle-eyed prophet." This moniker is justified, because Isaiah's ministry was filled with numerous prophecies concerning short-ranged, mid-ranged, and even long-ranged future events. A great many of these prophecies have been proven, by their fulfillment, to have been accurately forecast by the prophet. In this chapter, we will discuss the God of the prophet Isaiah, while in subsequent chapters, we will evaluate the God of Isaiah's prophetic contemporaries.

Elijah and Elisha were the human vessels used by Jehovah to challenge the evil political and spiritual influences of Israel's political leaders over a century before Isaiah's day. In a similar fashion, Isaiah was the human vessel used by Jehovah to influence the political leaders of Judah throughout his life. Isaiah's ministry style resembled that of Elisha more than that of Elijah. He was a political insider, sought out by and well-received by those in political power, and he used his high social status for the work of the ministry of his God.

Isaiah's ministry began during the latter portion of the reign of Uzziah (790–740 BC) and continued through the reigns of Jotham (740–722 BC), Ahaz (730–716 BC), and Hezekiah (716–686 BC). The scriptures reveal that Isaiah was married, his wife was a prophetess, and he had two sons (Isaiah 7–8). It can be deduced, in fact, that his family was a part of his ministerial work. The ministry of Isaiah extended over a period of approximately fifty to seventy-five years, beginning sometime before 740 BC and concluding with his death around 686 BC.

A comprehension of the historical setting of Isaiah's life is essential to understanding his ministry and his perception of the person of Jehovah, his God. The spiritual state of both the northern and the southern kingdoms influenced Isaiah's ministry. The political climate within Judah, international political alliances within the land of Palestine and the influence of existing and emerging world powers of Isaiah's day, should also be taken into consideration when examining Isaiah's writings.

The idolatrous practices instituted by Jeroboam in 930 BC and expanded by Ahab and Jezebel around 870 BC had plagued Israel for a long time by the time Isaiah began his prophetic ministry. These idolatrous practices had brought the nation to a state of spiritual crisis with imminent impending judgment. Though periods of spiritual revival were interspersed in Israel's history since the times of Jeroboam and Ahab, the overall spiritual trajectory was away from the worship of Israel's God, Jehovah.

The northern and southern kingdoms were separate political entities and were often hostile toward each other. The other countries in the land of Palestine were often hostile to each of the kingdoms of the divided nation of Israel, Syria being a chief example from the times of Elijah and Elisha. Egypt remained a world power to be reckoned with by the countries of the land of Palestine.

Assyria, however, had become a world power around 900 BC and was among the greatest threats to all of the countries in the land of Palestine during Isaiah's day, including Israel and Judah. The Babylonian empire did not formally exist until after the close of Isaiah's ministry but could be considered an emerging world power during his lifetime. As the countries of Palestine struggled for supremacy or even survival in this political climate, many lines of political allegiance or political alliances were formed with surrounding nations and with the nations that were considered to be world powers.

When any nation experienced a military conquest of another nation, they attributed their successes to the favor of the gods of their land and considered it a testimony of the strength of their gods in comparison to the gods of the conquered people. Much of this is reflected in the writings of the prophet Isaiah. An understanding of these dynamics is evident as Isaiah dialogues with his God, interacts with political leaders, and ministers to the people of Judah and to us through his prophetic ministry.

The major extra-biblical source of confirmation of the historicity of the persons and events discussed in the Bible that were contemporary with the prophet Isaiah come from Assyrian archaeology. The leaders of the Assyrian empire during the ministry of Isaiah included Tiglath-Pileser III (also known as Pul), Shalmaneser V, Sargon II, and Sennacherib.

Tiglath-Pileser III ruled Assyria from 745–727 BC. It was under his reign that Assyria began to really oppress the countries of the land of Palestine, including Israel. His successor, Shalmaneser V, began a siege of Samaria around 725 BC but died before the northern kingdom was actually conquered.

While under Uzziah's reign, Judah was a strong and independent nation; under Ahaz, the nation formed an allegiance with

Assyria because of perceived threats to its national sovereignty posed by the allegiance formed between Israel and Syria. The Nimrud Tablet provides archaeological confirmation of the military activities of Assyria in the land of Palestine during this era—under Pekahiah, Pekah, and Hoshea, kings of the northern kingdom (2 Kings 16–18; 2 Chronicles 28).

One of the sons of Tiglath-Pileser III, Shalmaneser V (727–722 BC) or Sargon II (722–705 BC), actually captured Samaria in 722 BC. Other countries of Palestine formed alliances to ward off the Assyrian empire. For example, Judah formed an alliance with Philistia and considered an alliance with Egypt for this purpose. Sargon II crushed these revolts and alliances and ultimately posed a significant threat to Judah's sovereignty.

Archaeological evidence of the activity of Assyria in the land of Palestine during the days of Isaiah abound. The Prism of Sargon II provides extra-biblical archaeological support for the Bible's account of Assyria's activity in Palestine after the fall of Samaria and during the reign of Ahaz (Isaiah 7–12; 2 Chronicles 28). However, the greatest biblically recorded challenge of Assyria to Judah's sovereignty came during the reign of Assyria's next king, Sennacherib (705–681 BC). This was during the rule of Hezekiah, king of Judah.

The Sennacherib Relief directly records Assyria's assault on the land of Judah in 701 BC. It is important to note its omission of any comment proclaiming the conquest of Jerusalem, which is consistent with the Bible's account in Isaiah's writings (2 Kings 19–20; 2 Chronicles 29–32; Isaiah 36–39). Finally, the Azekah Inscription also provides a record of Sennacherib's campaign against Hezekiah.

Significant secular historical developments were also occurring outside of the land of Palestine during Isaiah's time. The Greek city-states were just beginning to form around 700 BC. According to history, the first ancient Olympic Games were held in Athens in 776 BC, just before Isaiah began his prophetic ministry. Homer, it is believed, may have written his epic, *The Iliad*, as late as 750 BC. It is postulated that work on the Great Wall of China may have begun during this era as well. These developments, while contemporary with Isaiah's ministry, shed no light on the historicity of Isaiah, his people, and his God.

No other Old Testament historical personality comes close to Moses, Israel's lawgiver, in terms of number of historically documented encounters with the person they each knew as Jehovah. Among the list of Old Testament historical personalities, Isaiah comes closer than the vast majority. Ezekiel and Jeremiah, as we will see later, arguably rival Isaiah for this distinction. Certainly, none of Isaiah's contemporaries in the prophetic ministry rival him in the number of historically documented divine encounters they experienced.

As to the scholarly controversy of whether Isaiah is, in fact, the author of the complete volume which bears his name, this is a modern dilemma not shared by the men of history more proximate to its writing. The Jewish historian, Josephus, understood that a single person had written the book of Isaiah. The prophets of the Old Testament who quoted Isaiah (Zephaniah, Nahum, Jeremiah) did not question the authorship of this book. Jesus himself, and the writers of the New Testament who referenced Isaiah (Matthew, Mark, Luke, John, James, Peter, and Paul) had no doubt concerning the singleness of the authorship of Isaiah's writing. In his work, *Explore the Book*, J. Sidlow Baxter does a masterful job of summarizing the argument for the single person authorship of the book of Isaiah.

Having authenticated Isaiah's historicity, established his prominent role in prophetic ministry, and addressed the singleness of the authorship of his writings, we should turn our attention to understanding Isaiah's perception of the personhood of God. The personhood of Isaiah's God is a prominent theme throughout his writings. As Isaiah's view of Jehovah becomes clear, a comparison of the God of Isaiah with the God of Isaiah's predecessors in history will further establish the immutability of the personal attributes of Israel's God over time. An examination of Isaiah's encounters with Jehovah will confirm that Isaiah's God is the same omnipotent, omniscient, omnipresent, sovereign, covenant-keeping, relationship-oriented person that Adam, Noah, Abraham, Isaac, Jacob, Moses, David, Elijah, and Elisha had each known.

Job had established the personhood of God (Job 13:8) and used the title "The Holy One" in reference to this divine person (Job 6:10) over 1,500 years before Isaiah. At least three times, psalmists used the divine title "The Holy One of Israel" when referring to this divine person (Psalms 71:22, 78:41, 89:18). The idea of the person of Jehovah as "The Holy One" and "The Holy One of Israel" is, however, central to Isaiah's ministry. Isaiah refers to Jehovah as "The Holy One of Israel" over two dozen times, "The Holy One of Jacob" once, and simply "The Holy One" on four other occasions in the written record of his ministry.

As He had done when He was searing the newly minted law into the culture of the Israelites in 1446–1445 BC (see the book of Leviticus), Jehovah repeatedly used the phrases "I the Lord" and "I am the Lord" throughout his encounters with the prophet Isaiah. In Leviticus, Jehovah used the phrase "I the Lord" seven times. He used the phrase "I am the Lord" forty-five times during this period in the wilderness before the nation of Israel left Sinai for their first encounter with the inhabitants of the land Jehovah had promised to give them. The statement "I the Lord" appears fourteen times in Isaiah's writing, while "I am the Lord" occurs nearly a dozen times (eleven, to be precise).

In his prophetic ministry, Isaiah tackles the heretofore sparingly addressed Messianic role of Jehovah, like no previous writer of the Old Testament. Jehovah had foretold the coming of a Messiah 2,000 to 3,000 years previously as He meted out judgment in the Garden of Eden (Genesis 3:15). He had alluded to this coming Messiah when He called Abram about 1,400 years ago (Genesis 12:1–5). Moses made mention of this Messiah in 1406 BC before his death (Deuteronomy 18:15–20). The Davidic Covenant, established around 1000 BC, made the coming of the Messiah more palpable than ever as his royal lineage was revealed by Jehovah (2 Samuel 7:4–16; 1 Chronicles 17:4–14). This was a revelation that, though he did not fully comprehend, David revelled in (Psalm 2, 16, 110).

This human manifestation of the Jehovah that the men of Israel's history had known is prophesied with unprecedented clarity and accuracy throughout the ministry of the prophet Isaiah, over 700 years before Jehovah would make His appearance as the Messiah. Messianic terms documented in Isaiah include rod, stem, branch, righteous servant, branch of the Lord, arm of the Lord, man of sorrows, Light of the Gentiles, glory of the Lord, Zion's salvation, angel of His presence, Immanuel, Prince of Peace, Wonderful, Counsellor, The mighty God, The Everlasting Father, the son, and the sure mercies of David.

These titles, while clarifying the work of Jehovah as the coming Messiah, still refer to a single eternal person. That the eternal person known as Jehovah would make Himself manifest as a human person is evinced by the fact that Isaiah records over a thousand singular divine pronouns to reference the God with Whom he had over forty documented encounters over the course of approximately five to six decades of prophetic ministry.

Encounter one: Jehovah Presents His Case Against Judah (Isaiah 1–5)

The historical time setting of Isaiah 1–5 is not definitively established by the biblical text. Some of the ambiguity is due to difficulties with the dating of the reigns of the various kings of Judah. The scripture is clear that Uzziah reigned fifty-two years (2 Kings 15:1–7; 2 Chronicles 26), Jotham reigned sixteen years (2 Kings 15:32–38; 2 Chronicles 27), Ahaz reigned sixteen years (2 Kings 16:1–20; 2 Chronicles 28), and Hezekiah reigned twenty-nine years (2 Kings 18–20; 2 Chronicles 29–32).

However, scholars debate how much of the reign of each of these kings overlapped with the reign of their successor (i.e. length of co-regencies). It is certain that Uzziah and Jotham had a lengthy co-regency as a result of Uzziah's leprosy—a consequence of his personal transgression during an otherwise good and godly reign. How many of Jotham's sixteen years of reign were shared with his leprous father before Uzziah died is unclear.

Establishing dates is important, because Isaiah 1–6 is a record of the final years of Uzziah's life and his death, while Isaiah 7–12 occurs during the reign of Ahaz. It may be that the vast majority of Jotham's reign was a co-regency, hidden in the reigns of Uzziah and Ahaz; hence, there is no distinct mention of Jotham's reign in the book of Isaiah. The latter days of the reign of Uzziah (and Jotham) provide the historical time setting for the first five chapters of Isaiah; this is probably around the 740s BC.

In the first five chapters of his book, Isaiah presents a summary of the state of Jehovah's relationship with Judah over the course of his prophetic ministry. Jehovah's accusations against the nation of Judah are summarized first. Jehovah's counsel to Judah, in light of His accusations and their guilt, is given next. The consequences or payment which would be exacted because of the transgressions of Judah and the measure of mercy which Jehovah would extend to them along with this judgment are also presented in the first five chapters of Isaiah.

Repeatedly, throughout this section, Isaiah communicates statements which he received from the mouth of Jehovah. He follows these statements with his personal elaboration on these divine proclamations and their implications. Direct statements from Jehovah are found in Isaiah 1:2–3, 1:11–20, 1:24–26, 3:1–4, 3:15–16, 5:3–6, and 5:9–10.

The first chapter of this section of Isaiah is written like a court scene in which Jehovah presents His case and Isaiah is His authorized spokesperson. Chapters 2–4 outline some of the judgments. Chapter 5 reiterates Jehovah's case against Judah, presented by His authorized spokesperson, Isaiah, in the form of a song or a parable involving a well-cared for but unfruitful vineyard.

Much can be deduced of the character of Isaiah's God from this portion of scriptural history, the first of Isaiah's documented encounters or series of encounters with Jehovah. Isaiah uses the divine title "The Holy One of Israel" for the first time during his record of this first encounter (Is. 1:4, 5:19, 5:24). Nine times in this section of Isaiah, he also uses the titles "The Lord of hosts" (1:9, 24, 2:12, 3:1, 5:7, 9, 16, 24) and "The Lord God of hosts" (3:15), These titles were used over sixty times by the prophet Isaiah through the course of his prophetic ministry. In Isaiah 1:24, he also refers to Jehovah as "The Mighty One of Israel."

In these opening chapters, Isaiah attributed forty first person singular divine pronouns to having been spoken by Jehovah in communicating His thoughts. Additionally, twenty-five third person singular divine pronouns are used in reference to Jehovah by His authorized spokesperson in this encounter. This opening encounter masterfully presents Isaiah's God as a person Who establishes a standard of conduct for His people and ultimately judges those who choose to transgress His covenant but remains a God of mercy even when He issues forth His judgments.

The omnipotence, omniscience, sovereignty, and relationship orientation of Isaiah's God is also clearly seen. The parable of the vineyard is a beautiful poetic summary of the state of Jehovah's relationship with Judah and gives a poetic illustration of many of the personality traits of Jehovah that have been consistent throughout history.

Encounter two:
In the Throne Room of Jehovah (Is. 6)

The year of the death of King Uzziah was the year of greatest transition in the ministry of Isaiah! From the beginning of his ministry, it is evident Isaiah perceived Who Jehovah was with all of His enduring personal attributes. This is obvious after studying the first five chapters of Isaiah's record. In chapter 6, however, Isaiah's awe and wonder of Jehovah reaches its zenith.

In this divine encounter, Isaiah discovered himself by way of a vision inside the throne room of Jehovah. With the death of a revered and powerful monarch and facing a challenging and uncertain, even threatening international crisis, Isaiah is forced to see Jehovah as the only real king and the only real hope for the nation. With His glory, sovereignty, holiness, and omnipotence made perfectly clear to the prophet, Jehovah proceeded to call for a human representative to be His ambassador to His people.

Isaiah accepted this challenge from the One on the throne. Jehovah equipped him for the work and outlined the task. The omniscience of Jehovah was apparent because He was able to foresee the outcome of Isaiah's ministry effort, even as He commissioned Isaiah for the undertaking.

The personhood of Isaiah's God is also clearly established in this throne room encounter. Isaiah encounters multiple divine beings, including multiple angels, and a single divine person he refers to as the Lord (Jehovah). Isaiah makes the multiplicity of angelic beings evident with phrases like "each one…" (Is. 6:2), "one cried to another…" (Is. 6:3), and "Then flew one…" (Is. 6:6). Similarly, Isaiah makes the singleness of the person of Jehovah clear with references to "the Lord" (Is 6:1, 8, 11, 12), "the Lord of hosts" (Is. 6:3, 5), and "the King" (Is. 6:5).

Historically, throughout the scripture, each of these were references to a single divine being. Moreover, in referring to his God, Isaiah speaks of "His train" (Is. 6:1) and "His glory" (Is. 6:3) and uses the pronoun *He* to introduce statements spoken by Jehovah (Is. 6:9,11).

The Lord, Who is sitting upon a throne in Isaiah's vision, speaks in Isaiah 6:8–13. He used two divine personal pronouns, *I* and *Us,* in His verbal exchange with Isaiah. This has led to some theological discussions regarding the singleness or multiplicity of Jehovah's divine person. The use of the pronoun *I* is consistent with the overwhelming view of Isaiah and his historical predecessors in Jewish history that Jehovah is a single divine person. Jehovah uses nearly 700 first person singular divine pronouns in reference to Himself in Isaiah's ministry account alone. The accounts of Abraham, Isaac, Jacob, Moses, Samuel, David, Elijah, Elisha, and others provide universal support of Isaiah's experience and recorded view.

So what theological conclusions should be drawn concerning Jehovah's use of the pronoun *Us,* when He issues His call to Isaiah (Is. 6:8)? That Isaiah unquestionably distinguished the presence of multiple divine beings in his vision, yet used only singular divine pronouns in reference to the One on the throne indicates that he did not perceive a multiplicity of persons in the being of Jehovah.

Through proper application of grammatical principles and proper contextual analysis, we can safely conclude that Isaiah did not perceive that Jehovah was more than one person.

The pronoun *Us* in Isaiah 6:8 has been variably interpreted. Some have suggested that it is an indicator of the the existence of multiple persons of the godhead. Others believe that it is a "royal plural" pronoun. Still others conclude that it confirms the fact that Jehovah took counsel with the angels in His divine decision making. Yet another interpretation is that it is simply a pronoun inclusive of all parties involved in the throne room interaction that was taking place, including the person of God. This final interpretation is most consistent with the internal evidence and best aligns with the entire body of evidence of the Bible.

At least two of the aforementioned possible interpretations of the use of the pronoun *Us* in Isaiah 6:8 can be dismissed immediately. As has been already mentioned, the idea of multiple persons in the godhead runs counter to the rest of the description of Jehovah in Isaiah's throne room scene. It also runs counter to what is documented of Isaiah's perception of Jehovah in the remainder of his written record. The idea of multiple persons in the godhead, indeed, also runs counter to what can be concluded about Jehovah from the encounters of Isaiah's predecessors in Jewish history. Examples of the use of royal plural pronouns are absent or diminishingly rare in biblical and other ancient literature to this point. Thus, this use of the pronoun *Us* is virtually impossible to either confirm or discredit; it is only a remotely possible alternative and should be abandoned if a more likely explanation is present. Thus, both of these explanations are easily dismissed.

The Apostle Paul would later declare that Jehovah does not counsel with others in His decision making but "does all things after the counsel of His own will" (Ephesians 1:11). This is consistent with the sovereignty Jehovah had consistently shown to Isaiah's predecessors. If this assessment is true, then Jehovah was not sending Isaiah to do a work that He and the other divine beings had determined was necessary. The most logical conclusion, and the one which is consistent with the entirety of biblical history, is that Jehovah used the pronoun *Us* as an inclusive pronoun. Jehovah, several angelic beings, and a human (Isaiah) were all present in the throne room of Jehovah described in Isaiah 6.

Jehovah, without taking counsel of the other attendees, has an agenda to get a message to the people of Judah. He inquires of those who are in attendance, "Whom shall I send?" and "Who will go for Us (Jehovah, the angels, and Isaiah)?" Isaiah is the logical representative of this gathering of agents. He volunteers to be the ambassador of Jehovah and the representative from the group. The singleness of the personhood of Jehovah as a divine being remains consistent with the entirety of scripture with this interpretation of Isaiah's vision.

Encounter three: Confronting King Ahaz (Is. 7:3–8:2)

Isaiah's third documented encounter with Jehovah occurred during the reign of Jotham's son, Ahaz. Unlike his fathers, Ahaz was an evil king. Before Ahaz, Judah had been ruled by four consecutive generations of good kings extending back to Joash (835–795 BC) and including Amaziah, Uzziah, and Jotham. Isaiah had witnessed at least a portion of the reigns of two of these good kings. Uzziah began to reign, independent of Amaziah, around 767 BC, and had known the security that resulted from living in a nation whose rulers governed through the principles of a covenant relationship with Jehovah. But now, a few years after the death of King Uzziah (Jotham being Uzziah's co-regent for many years), Judah's regional supremacy was being challenged by other nations while Judah was being led by a weak and evil leader, King Ahaz (see 2 Kings 16:10–18 and 2 Chronicles 18:2–4). Among the nations which formerly respected Judah—during the reign of Uzziah and were now a threat to Judah under Ahaz—were Israel (under King Pekah) and Syria (under King Rezin).

Assyrian archeological findings (The Nimrud Inscriptions) have confirmed Assyria's activity in Palestine during this period of history. The historical details of the confederacy of Israel and Syria against

Judah during the reign of Ahaz are recorded in 2 Kings 15:27–16:9. The solution of this weak and godless king of Judah for the crisis caused by the confederacy of Israel and Syria was to seek strength through relying on a confederacy of his own making. He forged a confederacy with the emerging world power, Assyria. This political climate was the setting of Isaiah's next divine encounter, and it took place in the mid-730s (~735 BC).

The God of Isaiah sent him to give courage and strength to King Ahaz and to instruct Ahaz not to pursue a confederacy with Assyria (Is. 7:3–7). Isaiah's God, historically, had not favored His people relying on outside sources to give them courage and strength; He was their strength and salvation. A classic example of this disposition of Jehovah and the consequences of ignoring it can be seen in the case of Asa's pursuit of a confederacy with Syria (1 Kings 15:18; 2 Chronicles 16:7–9) about 150 years earlier.

The same God, Who was God to Asa and Isaiah, was not in favor of Ahaz establishing a confederacy with Assyria. Jehovah challenged Ahaz, through Isaiah, to ask of Him a sign to confirm that He would protect Judah, that the efforts of Israel and Syria would fail, and that a confederacy with Assyria was unnecessary (Is. 7:11). When the faithless Ahaz refused to ask a sign, Jehovah's personal attributes of omnipotence and omniscience were demonstrated as He issued several prophecies.

Isaiah's concept of Jehovah as Israel's coming Messiah begins to take shape before the carefully observant eyes of students of history in this encounter between Isaiah and King Ahaz. Three memorable prophecies were issued in association with this encounter.

The first two prophecies were tied to Isaiah's family as observable confirmations of Jehovah's message. Isaiah's first messianic prophecy—given in this encounter—was ultimately among the most significant prophecies of the coming Messiah. This prophecy was that Jehovah would give Isaiah another son and the birth of this child would be an indication of Jehovah's presence with Judah to save the nation from its political and military enemies (Isaiah 7:14). The Messianic status of this prophecy, however, was confirmed by Matthew 1:22–23 (written about 60 AD). Besides indicating

Jehovah's presence with the nation of Judah in the days of Isaiah and Ahaz, this prophecy foretold the birth of Jehovah as a human child who would save His people from their sins.

The second prophecy was that within a decade of the conception of Isaiah's next son, both Syria and the northern kingdom of Israel would fall (Is. 7:14–16). It should not be overlooked that Isaiah's God, the Lord Himself (third person singular divine pronoun), would be the One Who gave this sign. To confirm the date of this prophecy, Isaiah had an official document witnessed by some key officials of the kingdom (Is. 8:1–2). The third prophecy was that a confederacy with Assyria would have significant negative ramifications for Judah as a nation (Is. 7:17–25). Once again, Assyrian archaeology confirms the significant destructive activity of Assyria in the land of Palestine contemporary with Isaiah's ministry.

Encounter four: Prophecy After the Birth of Maher-shal-al-hash-baz and Israel (Is 8:3–6,12)

Ahaz rejected the counsel of Isaiah and Jehovah and pursued a confederacy with Assyria (2 Kings 16:7–9). Isaiah and his wife conceived a son around 735 BC (Is. 8:3) whom they named Maher-shal-al-hash-baz which means "quick to plunder." The name was a prophetic statement that the Assyrian nation with which Ahaz had formed a confederacy would be quick to destroy the enemies of Judah.

After the birth of Maher-shal-al-hash-baz, Isaiah prophesied that while the child was still very young, Israel and Syria, the enemies of Ahaz, would be conquered by Assyria (Is. 8:3–4). Rezin of Syria, extra-biblical sources confirm, ruled between 754–732 BC. Isaiah reaffirms in this prophecy that, despite its apparent success in a short time span, this confederacy was not the will of Jehovah. It remained Jehovah's desire to be the One in Whom Judah trusted. There would be repercussions to the nation for their confederacy with Assyria (Is. 8:6–12).

Additional Messianic prophecies were issued, giving more insight into Isaiah's understanding of his God as Jehovah and future Messiah. The foretelling of the consequences of this confederacy and the associated Messianic prophecies connected to this fourth divine encounter of Isaiah and Jehovah further provide evidence of the long-ranged foresight (omniscience) of Isaiah's God.

Four Messianic prophecies were penned by Isaiah in association with his fourth historically documented encounter with Jehovah. After Jehovah told Isaiah not to join in with or celebrate the confederacy because of its offence to Him (Is. 7:12), Isaiah admonished the people to sanctify Jehovah and place their confidence in Him. He referred to Jehovah as a sanctuary and a rock of offence (Is. 8:13–15). The Messianic status of this admonition and prophecy was attested to by Matthew 21:43–44, Romans 9:33, and 1 Peter 2:8.

Isaiah used four third person singular divine pronouns referring to Jehovah in this admonition (Him [2], Himself, and He). Isaiah proceeds to tell the people that, as for his part, he will wait on Jehovah to provide deliverance and that as a result of the confederacy formed with Assyria, hardships would come upon the nation.

He follows this with a second Messianic prophecy, that the earthly ministry of Jehovah, the Messiah, would begin in the area that was going to be victimized by Assyria. This prophecy was given in Isaiah 9:1–2, and its Messianic status was confirmed by Matthew 4:13–17.

In the third Messianic prophecy in association with Isaiah's fourth encounter with Jehovah, Isaiah clearly prophesied the birth of Jehovah as a human child who would then rule as Messiah. The magnitude of this feat was so astounding that Isaiah concluded this prophecy by saying, "The zeal of the Lord of hosts will perform this" (Isaiah 9:6–7).

In this Messianic prophecy, the coming Messiah is called "Wonderful, Counsellor, The Mighty God, The everlasting Father, The Prince of Peace." The wonder of this feat itself qualified the One Who would perform it as "Wonderful." The title "Counsellor" was a reference to His legal or political authority as referenced by his association with a government, the throne of David, and His own kingdom, which He would rule with order and justice. It might also be translated purpose or plan and therefore refer to the fact that this Messiah was the purpose or plan of Jehovah, as confirmed by John 1:1–3.

"The Mighty God" was an equivalent to "The Mighty One of Israel," an expression used only by Isaiah in reference to Jehovah (Isaiah 1:24, 30:29). "The everlasting Father" was another divine title that originated with the prophetic ministry of Isaiah (9:6, 64:8) and is otherwise only found in the writing of Malachi (1:6) in the Old Testament. As "The Prince of Peace," he would rule a kingdom with boundless peace (Is. 9:7).

Each of these titles were to apply to the single divine eternal person, Whom Isaiah knew as God, and Who would be born as a human child according to this prophecy. Matthew 28:18–20 was a confirmation of the Messianic status of this extremely insightful and powerful prophecy.

The fourth and final Messianic reference associated with this one encounter between Isaiah and his God can be found in Isaiah 11:1–4, 11:10, and 12:2. This is a collection of prophecies all connected as one. They connect the coming Messiah to the Davidic line as Isaiah 9:6 had also done. In Isaiah 11:1–4, the Messiah would be "a rod out of the stem of Jesse and a branch growing out of his roots." In Isaiah 11:10, the Messiah would be "a root out of Jesse, a sign for the people, sought even by the Gentiles." In Isaiah 12:2, this Messiah, Israel's salvation, was the Lord Jehovah Himself. Taken together, these three passages communicate that the Messiah would be Jehovah, as an eternal person, while simultaneously being descendant from David as a human.

The personhood of Isaiah's God and the attributes of Jehovah are further testified to in this historically documented fourth encounter between Isaiah and Jehovah by the pronouns used in Isaiah's documentation and the expressions Isaiah applies to his divine associate. The prophet credits Jehovah with the words spoken in Isaiah 8:3–6, 8:12, 10:1–6, 10:12b, and 10:24–27. Jehovah used twelve first person singular divine pronouns when referring to Himself while speaking in these passages. Over two dozen third person singular divine pronouns are used by Isaiah in discussing Jehovah between the eighth and twelfth chapters of his writing. Moreover, besides the Messianic titles already discussed, the prophet refers to Jehovah as "the Lord of hosts" (eight times), "the Lord God of hosts" (two times), "the Light of Israel" (10:17), "Israel's Holy One" (10:17), "the Holy One of Israel" (10:20), and "the mighty God" (10:21).

Isaiah's God is a relationship-oriented God Who, though He brings judgment upon His followers when they transgress His covenant, remains a merciful provider willing to go to extreme measures to protect and provide for them. He extends His grace and mercy to all humanity through His Messianic manifestation.

Introduction to Isaiah's Burdens and the Insights These Burdens Reveal About Isaiah's God

The fourth encounter between Isaiah and Jehovah establishes the historical foundation for several of the "burdens" of Isaiah in the divine encounters that follow in his writings. The counsel given by Jehovah in each encounter and the prophecies spoken by Jehovah always point to the omnipotence, sovereignty, and loving provision of Jehovah for Judah. The historical backdrop of international turmoil and frenzied pursuit of international alliances to preserve Judah's national sovereignty is a pervasive theme throughout these burdens. This theme connects Isaiah's burdens with Judah's failure to simply live in covenant relationship with Jehovah and trust His provision for them because of this covenant relationship. The consequences of Judah's failure to keep covenant relationship with Jehovah are seen in Isaiah's burdens.

Through the record of the next eighteen encounters, it becomes clear that Jehovah would judge His people and even other nations for their failure to align themselves and their conduct with the person, the purposes and plans of the one true and living God. There is no safe refuge outside of Jehovah. There is no source worthy of allegiance or worthy to be relied upon besides Him.

In the sequence of encounters with Jehovah that follow Isaiah's encounter with King Ahaz, Isaiah pens what he terms *burdens* in which prophecies against various nations and people are pronounced. The Hebrew word translated *burden* in each of these proclamations is *massa*. It is variably translated load, lifting, or utterance. The historical inference is that Isaiah received these utterances from encounters with Jehovah, carried the load of the implications for various periods of time, and finally proclaimed that which Jehovah had given him. These prophecies were all likely issued between 735 and 701 BC. We will briefly discuss the historical significance of each of Isaiah's burdens and glean any specific insights about Isaiah's God in connection with each of these encounters.

Encounter five: The Burden of Babylon (Is. 13–14:28)

The first of Isaiah's burdens is a prophetic utterance against the nation that would ultimately be used by Jehovah to bring judgment upon Judah. One of the most remarkable things about this prophecy is that Babylon as a world power did not even exist at the time that Isaiah uttered this prophecy. During Isaiah's lifetime, Assyria was the great and fearful world power. The great city of Babylon was destroyed by the Assyrian king Sennacherib during his reign (705–681 BC). It was rebuilt by his son Esarhaddon (681–669 BC). The Babylonian Empire to which Isaiah made reference, ruled by Nabopolasser (626–605 BC), conquered Assyria around 612 BC (Is. 14:24–25). It was under the reign of Nebuchadnezzar II (605–562) that the Babylonian Empire would be used by Jehovah to punish sinful Judah and many other nations (Is. 13:6, 9, 13).

The judgment of Jehovah against this Babylonian Empire, proclaimed by Isaiah in this prophecy, was carried out by Darius the Mede in 539 BC (Is. 13:17–18, 14:21–23). Thus, Isaiah's prophecy, which was pronounced around 716 BC (Is. 14:28), predated the birth of this empire by about one hundred years and predated its final decline by about 200 years!

This prophecy is an astounding testimony to Jehovah's omnipotence, omniscience, and sovereignty. It declares unabashedly that He is the judge of all nations. In this encounter, the prophet repeatedly refers to Jehovah as the Lord of hosts (five times) as well as the Almighty (Is. 13:6) and the Most High (Is. 14:14). The time of Jehovah's judgment in this and the subsequent burdens or proclamations is referred to as "the day of the Lord" (Is. 6, 9, 13).

The personhood of this great judge of all the earth is clear from the fact that each time Jehovah spoke—as credited by Isaiah in 13:3, 11–13, 17–18, and 14:21–25—He used first person singular divine pronouns to reference Himself (nineteen in total). One third person singular divine pronoun is also used by Jehovah (Is. 13:13). All of the plans and purposes established by Jehovah will be carried out in the earth! They will occur in His time and for His glory.

> For the LORD of hosts hath purposed, and who shall disannul *it*? and His hand *is* stretched out, and who shall turn it back? (Is. 14:27)

Encounter six: The Burden of Palestine (Is. 14:29–32)

The prophecy regarding Palestine may have been issued around 722 BC. It was pronounced after the death of Shalmaneser V (the broken rod and serpent's root of Is. 14:29) and before the strength of Sargon II (the cockatrice and fiery flying serpent of Is. 14:29) was known in Palestine. Samaria and other parts of Palestine were besieged by Assyria under the leadership of Shalmaneser V. When he died, the inhabitants of Palestine thought this was a cause for celebration.

Jehovah, knowing the future, informs them that their judgment was not over because He, and not Shalmaneser V, was their judge and that more judgment and more suffering was yet to come. After the death of Shalmaneser V, Sargon II intensified Assyria's assaults on Palestine and Samaria, and other nations fell to Assyria in 722–721

BC. Zion (Jerusalem) would survive Assyria's assault on Palestine (Is. 14:32). Note the first person singular divine pronoun *I* spoken by Jehovah in Isaiah 14:30 and the reference to *His* people in Isaiah 14:32. In the midst of judgment, Jehovah again also shows Himself as a merciful person.

Encounter seven: The Burden of Moab (Is. 15–16)

This prophecy is issued during Assyria's attack on Palestine. It describes the swift and widespread destruction that occurs in Moab (Is. 15:1–8) and foretells the fact that more destruction is yet to come (Is. 15:9). The Lord gives instructions regarding some people who escape the ravaging of the land at the hands of the Assyrians (Is. 16:4) and forecasts the ultimate calamity of Moab within three years. This prophecy may well have been given at any time during the reign of Ahaz, even possibly during the same period when Shalmaneser V had laid siege to Samaria (approximately 725 BC).

It is well-documented that Samaria fell three years after this siege began. Moab may well have experienced the same fate as Samaria as prophesied by Is. 16:14. Jehovah made statements in Isaiah 15:9, 16:4, and 16:14 during this encounter with Isaiah. He used two first person singular divine pronouns *I* and *Mine* during these exchanges. His compassion toward Moab, despite His obligatory judgment upon them, is evinced by the tone of this proclamation by Isaiah.

Encounter eight: The Burden of Damascus (Is. 17)

Damascus was the capital of Syria. In this encounter, Isaiah speaks of the destruction that would come upon Syria, the nation that was confederate with Ephraim (Israel) against Judah. Several important titles describe Jehovah in this brief prophecy foretelling the destruction of Judah's enemies.

Jehovah is called the Lord of hosts (Is. 17:3), the Lord God of Israel (Is. 17:6), the Maker of man (Is. 17:7), the Holy One of Israel (Is. 17:7), the God of Israel's salvation (Is. 17:10), and the rock of Israel's strength (17:10). Part of the explanation for the destruction that was coming upon Israel was that as a people, they were not mindful of their God and their covenant relationship with Him.

Encounter nine: The Burden of Ethiopia (Is. 18)

Over a period of years, Assyria amassed conquest after conquest throughout Palestine and ultimately became a threat to Judah. When Assyria became a threat to Judah, the leaders of Judah considered a political alliance with Ethiopia and other African nations to protect the nation from the threat of Assyria.

Jehovah speaks against this consideration. Once again, He encourages national dependence upon Him instead of international alliances. Though He would allow Assyria a measure of success against His people, the ultimate containment of Assyria and dismantling of its threat would come at the discretion and through the intervention of Jehovah, not Ethiopia or other African nations. The prophet credits the words of Isaiah 18:4–6 to Jehovah, Himself. Jehovah uses four first person singular divine pronouns when referring to Himself in this passage. Jehovah is seen here to emphasize that He alone should be the provider, refuge, and protector of His people; after all, Jehovah is the Lord of hosts (Is. 18:7). His people continue, however, to look for ways to avoid the judgment that their loving God had pronounced on them early in Isaiah's ministry (Is. 1–5).

Encounter ten and eleven: The Burden of Egypt (Is. 19–20)

The initial prophecy of Isaiah 19 may be dated in the mid-720s BC, around the time of the fall of the northern kingdom of Israel to Assyria according to 2 Kings 17. Assyria's conquest of Egypt in 670 BC may well have been the historical event that ultimately fulfilled this prophecy. About the time that Sargon II took the northern kingdom of Israel, Assyria plundered much of Palestine, including Ashdod (Is. 20:1; 2 Kings 17:1–6). Israel, Judah, and other nations in Palestine looked to Egypt for an allegiance against the Assyrian Empire. Throughout this period, Isaiah protested this proposed alliance and set himself at odds with the people in so doing. Isaiah carried the burden or proclamations against an alliance with Egypt over many years.

Chapter 20 documents a historical event in the life of Isaiah, occurring around 712 BC. A revolt against Assyria by the Philistine city of Ashdod was summarily crushed as confirmed by archaeological evidences. Isaiah used this development and an embarrassing life demonstration (walking naked and barefoot) to deliver a strong message from Jehovah, proclaiming the futility of Judah's confidence in any alliance with Egypt or Ethiopia. The curious fondness of Israelites for their nation's former oppressors began during the Great Exodus (Exodus 14:11–12). This affinity became nationally systemic during the reign of Solomon (1 Kings 10:28–11:2) and continued throughout the ministry of Isaiah.

The Lord speaks in Isaiah 19:2–4, 19:25, 20:2, and 20:3–6. He uses seven first person singular divine pronouns to identify Himself. Jehovah again emphasizes in this prophecy that His people should look to Him alone for refuge. Six third person singular divine pronouns are used by the prophet in reference to Jehovah in this two-chapter long prophecy (Is. 19:1,16–22). The prophet uses the expression "the Lord of hosts" seven times in these two chapters when referring to Jehovah. Jehovah is the captain of the armies in which Judah should place their hopes.

Encounter twelve: The Burden of the Desert of the Sea (Is. 21:1–10)

Encounter thirteen: The Burden of Edom (Is 21:11–12)

Encounter fourteen: The Burden of Arabia (Is. 21:13–17)

The burden of the desert of the sea may be a reference to Assyria's destruction of Babylon in 689 BC. Merodach Baladan had opposed Assyria, and Sargon II had managed to conquer Babylon and displace him during the days of Hezekiah and Isaiah. Merodach Baladan survived Assyria's conquest of Babylon and continued to be a threat despite his displacement. Isaiah 21:1–10 may be a reference to Israel's consideration of Merodach Baladan and his forces as an ally in which they could place their confidence for support against Assyria.

Edom was a consistent ally for Assyria during Isaiah's ministry. Though Edom was a sister nation, it had repeatedly been unfaithful to Israel. Seeking an alliance with Edom was pointless (Is. 21:11–12).

Arabia, a nation that provided supplies to Palestine by way of merchantmen, was apparently another consideration for a military allegiance to fight against Assyria. The prophet Isaiah and his God warn that this is not a worthwhile pursuit either (Is. 21:13–17). Some scholars believe that these three prophecies occur later in Isaiah's ministry, probably between 704–701 BC.

The idea of the personhood of Jehovah presented by Isaiah in these three prophecies remains consistent with that which occurs throughout Isaiah's writings. There is only one solitary first person singular divine pronoun in the record of these burdens (Isaiah 21:2). However, divine titles including the Lord of hosts, the God of Israel, and the Lord God of Israel are also present, and their use is consistent with the idea of the personhood of Jehovah. Isaiah's ongoing message remains that Jehovah alone is the person to Whom the nation of Judah should look for refuge from the Assyrian threat.

Encounter fifteen: The Burden of the Valley of Vision (Is. 22)

The burden of the valley of vision and its associated prophecy were the product of an encounter between Isaiah and Jehovah during an Assyrian assault on Judah during the reign of Hezekiah. The prophecy was given between 704 and 701 BC, quite probably during the siege of 701 BC. The prophecy can be dated relatively precisely because Shebna and Eliakim are mentioned in it (Is. 22:15–25) and in the account of Assyria's siege on Jerusalem documented in Isaiah 36–37 (36:3,11,22, 37:2) and 2 Kings 18–19 (2 Kings 18:18).

Specifically, the political demotion of Shebna and the promotion of Eliakim is prophesied. Note that in Isaiah 22:15, Shebna is over the house, but in Isaiah 37:2, Eliakim is over the house.

The imagery in Isaiah 22:20–25 has led some to draw the conclusion that it is Messianic. The imagery used by Isaiah in recording this event invokes crisp scenes of the cross of Calvary. Twice in this prophecy, reference is made to "a nail fastened in a sure place" (Is. 22:23 and 22:25). Despite the imagery, the Messianic status of this prophecy cannot be confirmed by any direct reference made to it by the writers of the New Testament. Messianic or not, the God of Isaiah clearly identifies Himself as the originator of this prophecy.

Jehovah made His authorship of this prophecy quite evident. He used the first person divine pronoun *I* six times and called Eliakim "My servant" as He sent Isaiah to deliver the message of this prophecy to Shebna (Is. 22:15–25). Divine attributes that characterize Jehovah, including omniscience and omnipotence, are on display in this prophecy. The affairs of Shebna and Eliakim are judged by the Lord, because it is in His power to establish an individual. The psalmist aptly commented, "For promotion cometh neither from the east, nor from the west, nor from the south. But, God is the judge: He putteth down one, and setteth up another" (Psalm 75:6–7).

Encounter sixteen: The Burden of Tyre (Is. 23)

The final nation-specific prophecy from the prophet Isaiah in this series of prophecies was also contemporary with Assyria's siege on Jerusalem in Hezekiah's days. It was a prophecy concerning the future of Tyre. The Lord spoke in Isaiah 23:12–16 and foretold a lengthy period of trade restriction enforced by Assyria on Tyre, an eventual recovery of Tyre's international influence and trade, and the nation's ultimate decline. History confirms that from 700–600 BC, the commercial activity of Phoenicia was restricted by a series of Assyrian rulers. Babylon, under the rule of Nebuchadnezzar II, ultimately destroyed mainland Phoenicia in 572 BC. Moreover, the island of Tyre was famously conquered by Alexander the Great in 332 BC. Isaiah's God once again demonstrated that He was the Lord of hosts Who controlled and ordained judgment upon Tyre and all the honorable of the earth (Is. 23:9).

Encounter seventeen: Jehovah's Global Judgment with Mercy on a Remnant (Is. 24–27)

Isaiah is unrivaled in terms of the quantity and quality of his insights into the very distant future. The vision delivered to Isaiah in his seventeenth encounter with Jehovah is perhaps the one that peers deepest into the future with the greatest amount of detail about his God. It gives the person studying Isaiah's God a clear view of Jehovah as the window of time begins to close. This prophecy is yet to be fulfilled. It reveals Jehovah as the ultimate judge of the whole earth and paints a picture of the devastation coming upon the earth in the wake of Jehovah's ultimate judgment. Isaiah refers to this final judgment by Jehovah as "That Day" seven times in this vision (Is. 24:21, 25:9, 26:1, 27:1,2,12, 13).

In chapter 24, Isaiah gives a detailed picture of the coming judgment and desolation from which none who are outside of the protection offered by trusting in Jehovah will be spared (Is. 24:1–3). The prophet contrasts this destruction and desolation with the hope and peace that are the prize of those who trust in Jehovah (Is. 26). Throughout this vision, the prophet compares the sad state of the unbeliever with the comfort of the believer. The clear and ongoing focus is on the person of Jehovah and the worth of a covenant relationship with Him.

For instance, In Isaiah 25:6–9, Jehovah is the victorious refuge of all those who trust in Him. Here, Isaiah writes, "He will swallow up death in victory, and the Lord God will wipe away tears from off all faces; and the rebuke of His people shall He take away from off all the earth: for the Lord hath spoken it. And it shall be said in that day, Lo, this is our God; we have waited for Him, and He will save us: this is the Lord; we have waited for Him, we will be glad and rejoice in His salvation" (Is. 25:8–9).

On the other hand, in Isaiah 25:11, Jehovah is the inescapable hand of judgment upon those who oppose His purposes. Here, Isaiah writes, "And He shall spread forth His hands in the midst of them, as he that swimmeth spreadeth forth his hands to swim: and He shall bring down their pride together with the spoils of their hands."

What is striking about Isaiah 25 is not the obvious emphasis on the work and worth of Jehovah it contains; the prophet speaks of the Lord of hosts, the Lord God, God, and the Lord. This chapter leaps off the pages because while centering its focus on the divine person of Jehovah, it leaves no doubt about its reference to the coming Messiah, Jesus Christ.

The parallels between Isaiah 25:6–9 and Titus 2:12–14 are undeniable. Titus calls Him "the grace of God" and "the great God and our Savior, Jesus Christ." Isaiah tells us that "it shall be said in that day, Lo, this is our God; we have waited for Him, and He will save us: this is the Lord; we have waited for Him, we will be glad and rejoice in His salvation." The personhood of this single divine person, Who is Isaiah's God, is emphasized by the use of twelve third person singular divine pronouns in Isaiah 25. In all, in this vision (Is. 24–27), twenty-seven third person singular divine pronouns can be counted.

Jehovah's majesty and the reward of those who trust in Him are further emphasized in Isaiah 26:3–5. Isaiah's God is described as a strength to the poor, a strength to the needy in his distress, a refuge from the storm, and a shadow from the heat (Is 25:4). On the strength of these credentials, the prophet admonishes his listeners to "Trust in the Lord forever: for in the Lord Jehovah is everlasting strength" (Is. 26:4). It is Jehovah Who "will keep him in perfect peace, whose mind is stayed on Him" (Is. 26:3).

The credentials of Jehovah, including His omnipotence, are further laid out throughout chapter 26. This chapter concludes with a declaration of the boundless power of Jehovah by declaring that even physical death is no challenge for the divine person Who is Jehovah.

Isaiah 26:19 affirms the truth that Isaiah believed in a bodily or physical resurrection as attested by Paul (1 Corinthians 15:51–57; 1 Thessalonians 4:13–18). Why shouldn't Isaiah believe in a physical resurrection? Recent history testified of this reality. By the power of Jehovah, Elijah had raised the son of the widow of Zarephath around 860 BC (1 Kings 17:20–24). Through the power of this same God, Elisha had raised the only son of the Great woman of Shunem around 850 BC (2 Kings 4:31–37). These widely known events had occurred in the lives of Isaiah's fathers in prophetic ministry only a century beforehand. Their God was Isaiah's God. Their God's power was limitless. Moreover, the scope of the subject in this specific encounter between Isaiah and Jehovah had no boundaries. Shouldn't the life-giving power of Jehovah, one of His unique attributes in comparison to any other being—created or eternal—be displayed in That Day?

Throughout this vision, Isaiah depicts Jehovah as judge and savior. He is judge for those who fail to trust in Him. He is savior for those who place their trust in Him. Isaiah concludes this line of thought for this encounter in chapter 27. In 27:3–5, the words of Jehovah are recorded. Jehovah assures the hearer of the fact that He is worthy of trust and His purposes will be accomplished. Jehovah uses ten first person singular divine pronouns in this short passage. He confirms His personhood with the expression "I the Lord" (Is. 27:3). Isaiah does contextualize this end-time prophecy with Israel's imminent threat, eventual captivity, and ultimate restoration in Isaiah 27:12–13. Jehovah, though He is judge, is ever merciful as well.

Encounter eighteen:
First Woe (Is. 28)

Encounter nineteen:
Second Woe (Is. 29:1–14) and Third Woe (Is. 29:15–24)

Encounter twenty:
Fourth Woe (Is. 30–32)

Encounter twenty-one:
Sixth Woe (Is. 33)

Isaiah 28–33 records a series of divine encounters and the prophecies declared in association with these encounters. The first encounter in this series focused on Jehovah's judgment of Samaria (i.e., its fall to Assyria) and the lessons the rulers of Jerusalem could learn from the fate of Samaria and from Judah's misguided alignment with Assyria. During Isaiah's lifetime, the southern kingdom had first solicited the assistance of Assyria as an ally against the military allegiance of Syria and Samaria during the reign of Ahaz. The prophet warned Jerusalem's leaders against any confidence in this ally, assuring them that their Assyrian allies would not show them mercy any more than they had shown mercy to Judah's brothers in the northern kingdom (Is. 28:14–15). Instead of this "covenant with death and hell," the prophet expressed the heart of Jehovah, that His people would place their confidence in Him.

A messianic prophecy, as confirmed by Jesus in Matthew 21:42–44 and Mark 12:10–11 and by the Apostle Paul in Romans 9:33, is spoken by Jehovah in Isaiah's first divine encounter of this series. In this utterance, Jehovah speaks of some of the benefits Jerusalem could have if they would place their trust in the precious cornerstone and sure foundation He had laid in Zion. Jehovah contrasted this happy state to the unsavory fate associated with Jerusalem placing their confidence in foreign allies (Is. 28:16–19).

Judah's decision to act contrary to this prophetic counsel and to place its confidence in a wholly inadequate ally would force the hand of the Lord of hosts to act contrary to His desire. Instead of being their refuge, He would perform a strange act and allow His people to be consumed (Is. 28: 20–22). Jehovah's attributes as judge, covenant-keeper, protector, relationship-seeker, and merciful but jealous God are all evident in Isaiah's record of this divine encounter. The personhood of Jehovah is attested by the use of the first person singular divine pronoun *I* by Jehovah (Is. 28:16) and the third person singular divine pronouns *He* and *His* by the prophet (Is. 28:9,11,12, 21).

In a second divine encounter, Jehovah warns Jerusalem of pending judgment because of its hollow acts of worship of Him. Jehovah speaks in Isaiah 29:1–5 and contrasts the hollowness of the worship His people have offered overall for many years with the genuine worship, which David had conceived and practiced when he established Jerusalem as the nation's center of worship in 1000 BC (2 Samuel 6, 1 Chronicles 16). Jehovah expresses His dislike of worship that does not come from the heart but is ritualistic and empty (Is. 29:13–14). Jehovah used nine first person singular divine pronouns as He spoke to Isaiah in 29:1–5 and 29:13–14. Jehovah will judge His people for this indiscretion, but as is characteristic of Jehovah, He mixed His pronouncement of judgment with a message of mercy and hope. Jehovah expresses confidence in Jerusalem's ultimate repentance back to Him (Is. 29:22–24).

In Isaiah 29:22, the prophet calls Jehovah the Lord Who redeemed Abraham, reminding Jerusalem of Jehovah's relationship with Abraham over 1,200 years ago. Jehovah's relationship with Abraham had resulted in the land covenant that the people had enjoyed, despite their lack of faithfulness to Him. Jehovah uses two first person singular divine pronouns and the divine titles "the Holy One of Jacob" and "the God of Israel" in identifying Himself as He spoke at the conclusion of this divine encounter. The sincere desire of Jehovah for a covenant relationship with a people that love and honor Him cannot be missed in His conversation with the prophet in this encounter; nor can the distinct personhood of Jehovah that is evident be disputed.

Jesus referenced Isaiah 29:13–14 in Mark 7:6–7 when he chastised the hypocritical scribes and Pharisees during his earthly ministry. How intriguing that the precious cornerstone himself, the human expression of Jehovah, would reference this passage to communicate the unchanging heart of Jehovah 700 years after Jehovah had spoken these sentiments to the prophet Isaiah. Furthermore, right before his own eyes, Isaiah was seeing the fulfillment of the message he had received from Jehovah forty years earlier when he first accepted his call to prophetic ministry in the year that King Uzziah died (Is. 6:8–13). The people were blind and deaf, their understanding darkened, and they were facing impending consequences because of their rejection of Jehovah as their king.

When the Assyrian nation became a very present threat to Jerusalem, one political option was the formation of an alliance with Egypt. A strong political contingency favored this course of action because of the history and might of Egypt throughout the region. Jehovah, consistent with His history and personal attributes, voiced His discontent over the idea that His people were placing their confidence in an entity, personal or national, other than Him (Is. 30:1–2). He assured the prophet and the people that this pursuit would fail and that He alone was their hope (Is 30: 7–17). He emphasized the physical nature of Judah's proposed earthly alliance in comparison with Jehovah's supernatural person and power (Is. 31:1–3).

Jehovah ends His third encounter of this series, consistent with His character, with a vote of hope and confidence that His people would rest in their covenant relationship with Him and abandon their futile hope in other nations and other gods (Is. 31:7–9). That Jehovah is worthy of the privileged position He demands in the minds and hearts of His people is emphasized by His use of the divine titles "the Holy One of Israel," "the Mighty One of Israel," and "the Lord of hosts" throughout these divine proclamations. The divine personhood of Jehovah is strongly declared by the four first person singular divine pronouns and twenty-three third person singular divine pronouns that reference Him in this encounter.

In the next divine encounter in this collection, there is a divine proclamation against the Assyrians, particularly Sennacherib, because the Assyrians had threatened the national sovereignty of Judah. Because of Assyria's unprovoked hostility and threat against His people, Jehovah promised to defend His people against "the treacherous dealer" (Is. 33:10–13). Five first person singular divine pronouns are scattered through Jehovah's proclamation in this encounter. Isaiah uses the divine pronoun *Thyself* in reference to Jehovah as he elaborates on his anticipation of Jehovah's rescue of his people (Is. 33:3). He prophesied Judah's ultimate submission to divine protection in Isaiah 33:22, proclaiming, "For the Lord is our judge, the Lord is our lawgiver; the Lord is our king; He will save us."

Encounter twenty-two: Jehovah's Global Judgment with Mercy on a Remnant (Is. 34–35)

Jehovah's twenty-second encounter with Isaiah is reminiscent of the seventeenth encounter between these two persons. In His seventeenth encounter with Isaiah (Is. 24–27), Jehovah extrapolated comments about His purposes and judgment to a global scale and beyond the immediate historical timeframe. In like manner, in His twenty-second encounter with Isaiah (Is. 34–35), Jehovah used Judah's historically documentable national predicament—in this case, the siege by Assyria on Jerusalem—to declare what He would do to establish His purposes for Judah and on a global scale at the end of time. In his written record, Isaiah recites Jehovah's counsel and proposed solution to Judah's national crisis. But he goes further to reveal the person of Jehovah and to unveil the personal attributes of Israel's God on the global stage and beyond the immediate historical setting.

In Isaiah 34:5, Jehovah proclaims, "For My sword shall be bathed in heaven: behold, it shall come down upon Idumea, and upon the people of My curse, to judgment." Jehovah's encouragement to Isaiah inspires him. He writes, "Strengthen ye the weak hands and confirm the feeble knees. Say to them that are of a fearful heart, Be strong, fear not: behold, your God will come with vengeance, even God with a recompense; He will come and save you. Then the eyes of the blind shall be opened, and the ears of the deaf shall be unstopped. Then shall the lame man leap as an hart, and the tongue of the dumb sing: for in the wilderness shall waters break out, and streams in the desert" (Is. 35:3–6).

Two additional first person singular divine pronouns (Is. 34:5) and five third person singular divine pronouns (Is. 34:2,16, 35:4) are used in association with this divine encounter between Jehovah and Isaiah. Isaiah found encouragement in Jehovah's proclamation of the future judgment of the nations and His coming mercy upon His people.

Some believe Isaiah 35:4–6 to also be a messianic prophecy referencing the miracles that the Messiah would perform when he made his appearance. Jesus certainly opened the eyes of the blind, unstopped deaf ears, healed the lame, and made the dumb to speak during his earthly ministry. A host of New Testament references could be cited to confirm the messianic application of this prophecy in Isaiah's writing.

Encounter twenty-three: First Message to Hezekiah Concerning Sennacherib's Threat (Is. 37:6–7; 2 Kings 19:6–7)

The Assyrian Empire was allied with Judah under the reign of Ahaz. Assyria was a perpetual threat to Judah throughout the reign of Hezekiah. Ahaz had essentially hired the Assyrians as allies during his reign, because Israel and Syria were confederate against Judah at that time (730s–716 BC). During his reign, Hezekiah did a political 180-degree shift and withheld tribute from Assyria; this brought the fury of Assyria down on Judah. The tensions between Judah and Assyria came to a head a few years before the turn of the century, and Sennacherib sent a contingency to besiege and take Judah and Jerusalem.

Hezekiah built a system of underground water tunnels as a part of his defense strategy against this siege. The tunnels are modern-day evidence of the historicity of this biblical event. Assyrian archaeology and documents lend further confirmation attesting the success of the Assyrian assault on Judah, but notably omitting any report of the fall of Jerusalem (Sennacherib's Annals, Azekah Inscription). Isaiah records this historically documented Assyrian assault as the setting (Is. 36) for his next five encounters with Jehovah, each of which involves Jehovah using Isaiah as a messenger for matters that involve King Hezekiah (Is. 36–39).

After Rabshakeh, an Assyrian general, boasts of Assyria's superiority and threatens Hezekiah and Jerusalem, insulting the omnipotence of Jehovah in the process, Hezekiah sent messengers to seek counsel from Isaiah. Isaiah's message, from the mouth of Jehovah, is recorded in Isaiah 37:6–7. In it, Jehovah foretells the ultimate failure of Assyria to topple Jerusalem and prophesies the death of Sennacherib. Jerusalem does withstand this siege. The Assyrians are miraculously defeated that year, and Sennacherib is murdered in his own land twenty years later (681 BC). An Assyrian archaeological piece called the Lachish Relief describing Sennacherib's successes is consistent with the mention of Lachish in Isaiah 37:8. Jehovah used three first person singular divine pronouns in His response and words of encouragement to Hezekiah through the prophet Isaiah. Jehovah's response shows His omnipotence and His omniscience along with emphasizing His divine personhood.

Encounter twenty-four: Second Message to Hezekiah Concerning Sennacherib's Threat (Is. 37:21–35; 2 Kings 19:20–34)

This second encounter between Isaiah and Jehovah is a more detailed message of encouragement to Hezekiah after another round of diplomatic exchanges between Hezekiah's ambassadors and the ambassadors of Sennacherib. This time, Hezekiah takes the written threat of Rabshakeh into Solomon's Temple and prays to Jehovah. Jehovah sends Isaiah with a detailed answer in response to the threat and the prayer. In his response, Isaiah refers to Jehovah as "the Lord God of Israel," "the Holy One of Israel," and "the Lord of hosts."

These titles emphasize the value Jehovah places on His covenant relationship with His people and the power of Jehovah to protect His people. Each time the divine title "the Lord of hosts" is used, it is a reminder of the innumerable angelic armies that Jehovah revealed to Elisha's young student when the Syrian armies encamped against Elisha about 150 years earlier. Though Hezekiah was distressed, Elisha would have counseled him, "Fear not: for they that be with us are more than they that be with them" (2 Kings 6:16).

Through the mouth of Isaiah, Jehovah told Hezekiah, "[the king of Assyria] shall not come into this city, nor shoot an arrow there, nor come before it with shields, nor cast a bank against it. By the way that he came, by the same shall he return, and shall not come into this city. For I will defend this city to save it for Mine own sake, and for My servant David's sake" (Isaiah 37:33–35).

The personhood of Jehovah in this divine encounter is declared by the use of the pronoun *Whom* and fifteen first person singular divine pronouns. The words of Jehovah were brought to pass according to history and according to Isaiah 37:35–38. Something dramatic must have occurred to turn away a world superpower from the small city of Jerusalem. The unexplained overnight death of thousands in the Assyrian army as recorded by Isaiah's account would qualify for an explanation. The assassination of Sennacherib is an extra-biblically documented part of Assyrian history.

Encounter twenty-five: Proclamation of Death Upon Hezekiah (Is. 38:1; 2 Kings 20:1)

Encounter twenty-six: Hezekiah's Healing (Is. 38:4–8; 2 Kings 20:4–6)

At some point during Assyria's three year siege of Jerusalem, Hezekiah became very sick, and Jehovah sent Isaiah to the king to tell him that he would not recover from the illness. Hezekiah was shaken by this turn of events and again sought the intervention of the

God he had come to know as a loving, approachable, involved, miracle-working, relationship-oriented, omnipotent ruler and advocate.

Isaiah, Jehovah's prophet and intercessor, returned Jehovah's message to the king. Jehovah's response is significant because He demonstrated His approachability and His tendency to hear and answer the prayers of the righteous. Additionally, it revealed the personhood of Jehovah, His omnipotence, and His inclination to honor those in covenant relationship with Him.

Jehovah identifies Himself to Hezekiah as "the God of David, thy father." He uses the first person singular divine pronoun *I* six times in His exchange with Hezekiah through Isaiah in this encounter. By identifying Himself as He did, Jehovah was placing an emphasis on the relationship He had shared with David about three centuries before. This may have been intended to bring back to Hezekiah's mind the many times Jehovah had preserved the life of his ancestor, King David.

In a very practical way, and with a relevant historical precedent, Jehovah was providing reassurance to Hezekiah that He could also spare his life. Isaiah saw his God perform the miraculous healing of the king and the miraculous turning back of time as recorded by the sun dial of Ahaz. Hezekiah lived an additional fifteen years and may well have died the same year that Isaiah died, about 686 BC.

Encounter twenty-seven: Babylonian Captivity Prophesied to Hezekiah (Is. 39:5–7; 2 Kings 20:17–18)

The fifth and final in the series of divine encounters between Isaiah and Jehovah concerning Hezekiah occurred shortly after the Assyrian army retreated, not having conquered Jerusalem. A long-time foe of the Assyrian Empire, Merodach Baladan, sent ambassadors and a letter to King Hezekiah from Babylon. His pretense was that he was congratulating Hezekiah on his recovery from a grave illness. It is likely, however, that Merodach Baladan was attempting to establish an alliance with Jerusalem in light of what he perceived to be its defeat of the empire that had been and remained an aggressor and a threat against him. Hezekiah welcomed this proposed alliance as insurance against a future return of the Assyrians against Jerusalem.

This was an affront to Jehovah Who had just miraculously healed Hezekiah, extended his life, and defeated the formidable Assyrian Empire without any human intervention from international allies. After Hezekiah overextended his graciousness to these ambassadors from Babylon, demonstrating his continuing uncertainty about Jerusalem's future and lack of trust in Jehovah's protection, Jehovah sends Isaiah to reprimand the king. In His message to Hezekiah, Jehovah foretold the Babylonian captivity. This prophecy was spoken somewhere around 700 BC, about a century before the first captives were taken from Jerusalem into Babylon around 605 BC, and over a century before the fall of Jerusalem in 586 BC. Jehovah's omniscience and His divine attributes of being a judge but extending mercy even when issuing judgment are seen again on this occasion. The judgment Jehovah issued was not to come to pass in Hezekiah's days.

Introduction to Isaiah Part Two: Jehovah, His Character, His Servants, and His Salvation

The closing chapters of Isaiah's book contain the records of a series of sixteen divine encounters that reveal the depth of the insight the prophet achieved in understanding the nature of Jehovah over the course of decades of prophetic ministry. Jehovah began to deal with Isaiah during the reign of Uzziah and Jotham, possibly as early as 760–750 BC. Isaiah may have lived through the entire reign of Hezekiah which ended in 686 BC. Thus, the prophet's ministry may have spanned as much as three-quarters of a century.

From the early years of his ministry, Isaiah demonstrated a close relationship with Jehovah and showed his ability to hear from Jehovah, analyze the message of Jehovah, and accurately convey an interpretation of this message to its intended recipient(s). From Isaiah

6, it is evident Jehovah and Isaiah had a direct line of communication from the beginning of the prophet's ministry. However, from Isaiah's human perspective, the challenges of a decidedly evil king and a weakened nation threatened by increasingly hostile and powerful international foes resulted in many uncertainties in his mind about the purposes of Jehovah and how He would accomplish these purposes.

These experiences forced Isaiah to develop even greater intimacy with Jehovah and to probe for a more in-depth understanding of the purposes and plans of his God. The maturity of the prophet's insights and understanding are reflected in what scholars universally agree is a second distinct portion of Isaiah's writings. All sixteen of these encounters between Isaiah and his God likely occurred between 701 BC and 686 BC.

There is a solid justification for the argument that the latter portion of Isaiah's writing (chapters 40–66) is unique in comparison to the earlier chapters of his book. However, the cohesiveness of these two parts of the prophet's work is undeniable.

From the beginning of Israel's history as a nation, the events discussed in Isaiah 40–66 had been foretold. Idolatry and inconsistent or insincere worship of Jehovah were fatal national tendencies that plagued Israel from its birth as a nation.

In 1445 BC (Leviticus 26:14–45), and again in 1406 BC (Deuteronomy 28:15,36,47–68), Moses foretold the judgment that would befall God's chosen people if they violated their covenant relationship with Him. David had a passionate and sincere covenant relationship with Jehovah, but his son, Solomon, promoted idolatry within the nation as early as 970–930 BC.

Jeroboam institutionalized idolatry nationally in 930 BC within the northern kingdom. Elijah and Elisha, Isaiah's ministerial fathers, battled idolatry throughout their ministries (861–796 BC). From the beginning of his ministry, Isaiah contended with idolatry and insincere ritualistic worship. Over the course of Isaiah's prophetic ministry, Jehovah had repeatedly expressed His disapproval of the idolatry within the nation and the nation's apparent lack of confidence in His ability to protect and provide for them.

Isaiah had seen the northern kingdom judged because of the same sins Judah had perpetrated against Jehovah. Around 735–732 BC, Isaiah had warned the idol-worshipping King Ahaz to look to Jehovah and not an international confederacy for protection. In 725–722 BC, the prophet had seen the northern kingdom go into captivity under the Assyrian Empire. From 722–701 BC, Isaiah had lived with a people who were constantly threatened by Assyria and who were never confident in Jehovah's saving power. In 701 BC, Jehovah had miraculously delivered Judah, but the threat imposed by Assyria had forever changed the nation and the prophet.

The remainder of Isaiah's writings are the result of revelations given to him by encounters with Jehovah during the Assyrian threat and beyond. Isaiah gives the first hints of what is to come in the latter portion of his book when he prophesied the Babylonian captivity to Hezekiah around 701 BC (Isaiah 39:6–7). He then spent the remainder of his written work elaborating on the attributes of the divine person with Whom he had developed such a great intimate relationship through the hardships he had experienced over the course of his life. He further discusses the judgment, purposes, and plans of Jehovah for the nation and humanity as a whole. The short–ranged, mid–ranged, and long–ranged prophecies outlined in this portion of Isaiah's work are indisputably linked to the early portion of Isaiah's ministry, and even the early portion of Israel's history; there is no disconnect.

There are three divisions of the second part of Isaiah, each consisting of nine chapters. The first division covers Isaiah 40–48 and argues the supremacy and sovereignty of Jehovah. The second division of Isaiah Part Two consists of chapters 49–57 and outlines how Jehovah uses humanity as His servants to accomplish His will in history. Special attention is given to the use of a Messiah who would be the fleshly manifestation of Jehovah Himself. Because he is flesh, the Messiah is still a servant of Jehovah. The final division of Isaiah Part Two, Isaiah 58–66, is a comprehensive discussion of the incomprehensible salvation Jehovah offers to Israel and all of humanity.

Encounter twenty-eight: Prophecy of Restoration After Judgment and Messianic Prophecies (Is. 40)

Isaiah begins this second portion of his prophetic writings with a prophecy of peace after judgment. This is consistent with the nature of the God of Isaiah and his predecessors. Though God will judge those who live contrary to His will, He remains a compassionate person Who gives consolation or hope to those who are judged. Adam (Genesis 3:15), Noah (Genesis 8:21–22), David (2 Samuel 12:13; Psalm 32:1–5), and many others would testify to this divine attribute of Jehovah. Jehovah speaks in Isaiah 40:1,2,4,5, and 25. Three first person singular divine pronouns are used by Jehovah when He speaks during this divine encounter.

The prophet uses over thirty third person singular divine pronouns in reference to Jehovah throughout this encounter. Isaiah 40:3 is identified as a messianic prophecy in that at least three New Testament writers identify John the Baptist as the voice of him that crieth in the wilderness, "Prepare ye the way of the Lord, make straight in the desert a highway for our God" (Mark 1:2–3; Luke 3:4–5; John 1:23). If in fact John the Baptist was the voice of which Isaiah spoke, then Jesus Christ was "the Lord" and "our God."

The Lord and God Whom Isaiah knew from his previous experiences was the same person that he saw on the throne in Isaiah 6:1, but Isaiah was prophesying of His coming in flesh in this divine encounter. Isaiah makes this clearer in Isaiah 40:10–11 when he declares, "Behold, the Lord God will come, with strong hand, and His arm shall rule for Him: behold, His reward is with Him, and His work before Him. He shall feed His flock like a shepherd: He shall gather the lambs with his arm, and carry them in His bosom, and shall gently lead those that are with young."

In this encounter, the prophet completes his picture of Jehovah by calling Him "the Holy One," "the everlasting God," and "the Creator of the ends of the earth." The omnipotence and omniscience of Jehovah are acknowledged when the prophet says, "He fainteth not, neither is weary and there is no searching of His understanding."

Both Isaiah and Jehovah declare the unique status of the Holy One, asking rhetorically, "To whom can He be compared?" (Isaiah 40:18,25). Isaiah sees Jehovah as the God Who judges His people, yet will ultimately bring them back to full restoration by Himself, coming to complete the work necessary to bring about this restoration. Like a shepherd, Jehovah will come to nurse His flock to spiritual recovery.

Encounter twenty-nine: Courtroom Scene/ Judge Between Jehovah and Idol Gods (Is. 41)

Isaiah's next divine encounter is portrayed as a courtroom scene in which Judah was indicted, much like the scene which was presented in Isaiah 1. This time, however, the indictment is against the nations and their gods. In Isaiah 41:1–5, Jehovah challenges the nations to bring a case against Him for His judgment of the nations because of their worship of idol gods instead of Him. He identifies Himself as "I the Lord" and "I am He" as well as using the pronoun *Who* twice to indicate His personhood.

The pronoun *Us* in Isaiah 41:1 is communal, referring to the community that is gathered together for this discussion—Jehovah, Isaiah, and the nations and their gods. Isaiah circles back to Jehovah's challenge in Isaiah 41:22–24 and uses the pronouns *us* and *we* in a communal sense several times. The investigation yields the conclusion of the utter inadequacy of the gods of the nations in comparison to the God of Israel. While the nations have weak and inadequate gods, Israel's God is able to provide and protect His chosen people. Jehovah, "the Holy One of Israel," "I the Lord," "I the God of Israel," and "the King of Jacob" is sovereign and has no equal as declared through the investigation conducted in this courtroom scene.

Jehovah speaks for a majority of this encounter. He uses twenty-nine first person singular divine pronouns to identify Himself. The God of Moses Who declared Himself to be a jealous God in 1446 BC (Exodus 34:14) is the same person Who challenged the nations in this encounter with the prophet Isaiah. The challenge is issued because of the worship of idol gods instead of Jehovah. Jehovah is sovereign, omnipotent, omniscient, and omnipresent, and will judge those who live contrary to His word, His will, and His purpose for humanity.

Encounter thirty: Judgment and the Coming Servant of Jehovah-Messianic (Is. 42)

The omniscient Lord speaks with great anticipation of a special servant who will come in the future and bring forth a standard by which all of the nations, all of humanity, can be judged. Jehovah declared, "Behold, the former things are come to pass, and new things do I declare: before they spring forth I tell you of them" (Isaiah 42:9). He speaks of this human vessel as "My servant whom I uphold: Mine elect, in whom My soul delighteth" and says, "I have put My spirit upon him." The omnipotent God identifies Himself as, "God the Lord, He that created the heavens, and stretched them out; He that spread forth the earth...and giveth breath unto the people upon it," in Isaiah 42:4. He called Himself "I the Lord" and declared that He had called this special servant in righteousness.

Jehovah clearly distinguishes Himself from the humanity of this coming servant but in no way indicates a distinction in His eternal personhood from this servant. The nation of Israel is also referred to as the Lord's servant in this and the previous encounter (Is. 41:8,9, 42:19) clarifying that any flesh or human used by Jehovah for His purposes is considered a servant to Jehovah.

Regarding the coming Messiah, however, Jehovah speaks of giving this servant for a covenant of the people. Matthew leaves no question that this servant is the Lord Jesus Christ (Matthew 12:18–21). In Matthew 3:16–17, the spirit of Jehovah rests upon Jesus, and Jehovah proclaims that He is well pleased with him (Is. 42:1).

In Matthew 26:26–28, Jesus declares that He is establishing a new covenant by the shedding of his blood (Is. 42:6). In Jesus Christ, Jehovah came forth as a mighty man, no longer holding His peace, no longer refraining Himself, but destroying and devouring that which stood between Him and His servants (Is. 42:14–16). Jesus is the vessel Jehovah used to accomplish this incomprehensible task. He is servant, and later called son, to Jehovah. In all, Jehovah used thirty first person singular divine pronouns to refer to Himself in this encounter. Additionally, there are sixteen third person singular divine pronouns referencing Jehovah in Isaiah 42.

Encounter thirty-one: Jehovah's Supremacy and Israel, His Servant-Messianic Prophecy (Is. 43–44)

An examination of Isaiah 43–48 reveals that these chapters provide an undeniable link between several historical events involving Judah in Isaiah's day and the future of which Isaiah speaks in chapters 40–66. The Assyrian siege of Jerusalem around 701 BC (Isaiah 36–37:35) and Jehovah's miraculous deliverance of Jerusalem by a series of sudden events that led to the Assyrian army's retreat from Jerusalem (Isaiah 37:33–38) are among the connected historical events. The visitation to Hezekiah by political ambassadors from Merodach Baladan and Babylon (Isaiah 39:1–4) and Isaiah's prophecies concerning the Babylonian captivity (Isaiah 39:5–7) are also connected to the prophetic messages of Isaiah 40–66.

In Isaiah 40, after having proclaimed a future captivity to a people that had just endured a three-year siege by the most powerful nation of their times, the prophet speaks comfort concerning Jehovah's ultimate purposes for His people. In Isaiah 41, the justification for the indictment and judgment of the people by Jehovah is made. In Isaiah 42, it is made clear that Israel is Jehovah's servant and that any human instrument used by Jehovah is His servant, including something entirely new (Isaiah 42:9) that Jehovah would do. Jehovah Himself would come as a human vessel. His arrival would be marked by some obvious signs (Isaiah 42:1, 7). This fleshly vessel, also Jehovah's servant, would be the means of bringing deliverance to Israel and to all of humanity (Isaiah 42:2–6, 8). How could such a thing be possible? Jehovah proceeds in Isaiah 43–44 to explain His credentials for being able to pull off this incredible feat.

There are three primary ideas communicated by Jehovah to Isaiah in the divine encounter recorded in Isaiah 43–44. First, there is no one like Jehovah—He has all power and can do anything He chooses to do. Second, Jehovah chooses and uses any instrument He desires and calls the chosen instrument "His servant." Finally, Jehovah links Israel to Himself as a special servant, assuring them that He has the power to accomplish for and through His servant that which He has purposed.

In Isaiah 43:1–7, Jehovah speaks, saying that He chose the nation of Israel and would preserve them, though they would necessarily endure the judgment and captivity which was prophesied through Isaiah. In Isaiah 43:10–15, Jehovah reaffirms His unparalleled status, Israel's special position as His witnesses, and that He and they will remain linked, though they must endure the coming Babylonian captivity.

Isaiah 43:10–11 is of special significance. The prophet writes, "Ye *are* My witnesses, saith the LORD, and My servant whom I have chosen: that ye may know and believe Me, and understand that I *am* He: before Me there was no God formed, neither shall there be after Me. I, *even* I, *am* the LORD; and beside Me *there is* no saviour" (Is. 43:10–11). In this passage, Jehovah declares Israel's special status as His servant and His witnesses. He also establishes His status as the only person Who qualifies as God (*I* and *He*—note that both pronouns are singular) and savior ("I, even I am the Lord; and beside Me there is no savior"). He concludes this short speech (Is. 43:10–15) by identifying Himself as the Holy One of Israel, the Holy One, the creator of Israel, and Israel's King in addition to being Israel's savior and God.

Isaiah interjects his own reminder of Jehovah's past demonstrations of power in the ministry of Moses (1446–1406 BC) in Isaiah 43:16–17. But Jehovah interrupts this line of reasoning and concludes the former things are passed, and He is going to do a new thing (Isaiah 43:18–19). This is the new thing described in Isaiah 42, Jehovah will accomplish His purpose of salvation for Israel and humanity by becoming His own servant—fleshly vessel—and doing the necessary work. He explains that because of the nation's failure over the course of history, since its birth as a nation, to accomplish His purpose, He would save them and the rest of humanity from their transgressions.

In Isaiah 43:25–26, Jehovah challenges the hearers to accept His offer of redemption which He would personally obtain for them. Jehovah implores the people to consider His offer, saying, "Let us plead together." Jehovah's offer is incredible, indeed. Though history is littered with the crimes of Israel and humanity against the covenant relationship Jehovah has pursued with them, Jehovah offers, "I, *even* I, *am* He that blotteth out thy transgressions for Mine own sake, and will not remember thy sins" (Is. 43:25).

Isaiah 44 is a continuation of the same divine encounter which Jehovah began in the previous chapter. There is no one like Jehovah, and He chooses any vessel He likes as His servant. In Isaiah 44:6, Jehovah says, "I am the first, and I am the last: and beside Me, there is no God." The prophet makes it clear that the person making this proclamation is the Lord, the King of Israel, Israel's redeemer, and the Lord of hosts. These familiar titles have, throughout the book of Isaiah, made reference to the same person Whom Isaiah saw sitting on the throne after the death of Uzziah (Is. 6:1).

In Isaiah 44:9–20, there is a sense of indignation that any other gods could dare to be compared to this divine person Whom Isaiah has come to know. Isaiah is incredulous that Israel has insulted Jehovah by choosing to serve idols. However, Jehovah gives closure on this matter with Isaiah by reiterating that He has blotted out this transgression of His people (Is. 44:22).

Jehovah concludes this encounter by returning to the idea of His omnipotence and omniscience (Isaiah 44:24–27) and introduces the idea of another servant, Cyrus, who would be instrumental in the restoration of the nation after the Babylonian captivity was accomplished (Is. 44:28). The divine encounter recorded in Isaiah 43–44 contains ninety-one first person singular divine pronouns and seven third person singular divine pronouns in reference to Jehovah. This, in combination with the clear proclamations of Jehovah in Isaiah

43:10–11, 44:6, and 44:8 establish the personhood of Jehovah as God, Savior, Redeemer, and King without room for controversy.

Encounter thirty-two: Cyrus and Concerning the Coming Messiah (Is. 45)

Returning to the idea that Jehovah can use any instrument He chooses as His servant to accomplish His purposes, Isaiah 45 demonstrates that there is neither temporal, political, nor geographical boundaries limiting Jehovah's power. Over a century before the birth of Cyrus the Great (585–529 BC), Jehovah informs Isaiah that He will choose a foreign king to restore the nation of Israel after their time of captivity is accomplished (Isaiah 45:1–8). This divine encounter between Isaiah and Jehovah occurred between 701 BC and 686 BC.

Amazingly, Jehovah calls Cyrus by name (Is. 45:1–3) and proclaims what we now know as history that Cyrus would set Israel and other nations at liberty. The Cyrus Cylinder is an archaeological finding that confirms what Cyrus is known for historically—being a liberator and champion of human rights. How could Jehovah make such an accurate forecast a century before it occurred? He is the omniscient, omnipotent, sovereign God.

In this chapter, Jehovah emphasizes over and over again that He has no equal (Isaiah 45:5,6,18,21,22). In Isaiah 45:5, He says, "I *am* the LORD, and *there is* none else, *there is* no God beside Me…"

In Isaiah 45:6 it's, "That they may know from the rising of the sun, and from the west, that *there is* none beside Me. I *am* the LORD, and *there is* none else."

Isaiah 45:21 gives us, "*Have* not I the LORD? And *there is* no God else beside me; a just God and a Savior; *there is* none beside Me."

And again, in Isaiah 45:22, Jehovah says, "Look unto Me, and be ye saved, all the ends of the earth: for I *am* God, and *there is* none else."

Jehovah also emphasizes the idea of using other human vessels to accomplish His purposes. He has used Israel and will save Israel, and Israel will continue to be His servant. Finally, as confirmed by the Apostle Paul in Romans 14:11 and Philippians 2:10–11, in Isaiah 45:23–25, Jehovah inextricably links Himself with the human vessel (Jesus Christ), whom He will use as His servant to deliver humanity in a way not heretofore known.

In Isaiah, Jehovah declared that every knee would bow and every tongue swear to Him. But in Philippians, Paul confirms that every knee would bow and every tongue confess that Jesus Christ is Lord, to the glory of God the Father. Thus, Jesus receives the worship that Jehovah reserved for Himself and is inextricably identified with the Jehovah that Isaiah knew as a single divine person (Is. 6:1). In the divine encounter recorded in Isaiah 45, Jehovah uses forty-six first person singular divine pronouns along with the divine titles "God of Israel," "I the Lord," "Maker," "Holy One of Israel," "Lord of hosts," and "Savior." All of these titles are used to establish His personhood and His purpose of becoming His own servant. By becoming His own servant, Jehovah could accomplish a salvation that was larger than that which had been known in the past, one that would extend to all of humanity.

Encounter thirty-three: The Salvation of Israel's Remnant and the Supremacy of Jehovah (Is. 46)

No doubt, the hearers of Isaiah's prophecy concerning a coming captivity staggered at this idea, having just survived a multi-year siege by Assyria. Surely another hardship would be the end of the nation, they may have thought. Jehovah comforts His people through the prophet, reassuring them that a remnant would survive the coming hardships that were an inescapable eventuality. After all, Jehovah has the power to sustain His elect in any situation.

Jehovah had spoken to Isaiah concerning the Babylonian captivity around 716 BC (Isaiah 14:21–27). The message Jehovah communicated over a decade earlier was reiterated around 701 BC, after Hezekiah entertained the Babylonian ambassadors (Is. 39:5–7).

Jehovah sheds more light on this in Isaiah 46:10–11. He reassures His people, however, that this is His purpose (Is. 14:26–27, 46:11). The message of this encounter would best be received in the context of the fact that Jehovah is in complete control of all that befalls His chosen people and that He remains omnipotent (Is. 45:5, 9–11). Thus, in Isaiah 46:6, Jehovah rhetorically asks, "To whom will ye liken Me, and make *Me* equal, and compare Me, that We may be like?"

Then He asserts His omnipotence in Isaiah 46:9–11 with this proclamation, "Remember the former things of old: for I *am* God, and *there is* none else; *I am* God, and *there is* none like Me, Declaring the end from the beginning, and from ancient times *the things* that are not *yet* done, saying, My counsel shall stand, and I will do all My pleasure: Calling a ravenous bird from the east, the man that executeth My counsel from a far country: yea, I have spoken *it*, I will also bring it to pass; I have purposed *it*, I will also do it."

Jehovah uses twenty-seven first person singular divine pronouns in this extremely brief divine encounter with Isaiah and emphasizes that "I am God, and there is none else...there is none like Me."

Encounter thirty-four: Prophecy of the Future Judgment of Babylon (Is. 47)

In this encounter, the prophet turns his attention to the instrument that God would use to judge His own people. This instrument itself is subject to Jehovah and would ultimately be judged. This is an amazing prophecy because it prophesies the rise and fall of a world power long before the empire was even birthed. This encounter between Isaiah and Jehovah occurred between 701 BC and 686 BC.

The Babylonian Empire that ultimately took Judah into captivity beginning in 605 BC and toppled Jerusalem in 586 BC was established under the rule of Nabopolasser around 626 BC, at least sixty years after the death of the prophet. The judgment of Jehovah against the Babylonian Empire, initially proclaimed by Isaiah in 716–715 BC and reiterated in the encounter recorded in Isaiah 47, was carried out by Darius the Mede in 539 BC (Is. 13:17–18) and Alexander the Great in 332 BC (Is. 14:21–23). Thus, Isaiah's prophecy predated the final decline of the Babylonian Empire by a number of centuries. Only Jehovah, the Lord of hosts, the Holy One of Israel, could accurately forecast a historical event of this magnitude so far in advance.

Encounter thirty-five: The Omniscience of Jehovah (Is. 48)

This is Isaiah's final encounter in the first series of divine encounters that followed his prophecy of the Babylonian captivity to Hezekiah around 701 BC (Isaiah 39:5–7). In this final encounter, emphasis is again placed on the power of Jehovah to accomplish all of the prophecies detailed in connection with the judgment of God's chosen people for their failure to be effective as His representatives to lost humanity.

In Isaiah 48:1–6, emphasizing His omniscience, Jehovah reminds the hearers—Isaiah and, ultimately, the nation—that the current predicament of Israel was foretold centuries before the present. In 1445 BC (Leviticus 26:14–45), and again in 1406 BC (Deuteronomy 28:15,36,47–68), Moses foretold the judgment that would befall God's chosen people if they violated their covenant relationship with Him. Now, over 700 years later, the former things declared by Jehovah are a reality.

Based upon this evidence, the people are encouraged to listen to the new things Jehovah is declaring (Is. 48:6). Jehovah reiterates His credentials in His plea in Isaiah 48:12–13, "Hearken unto Me, O Jacob and Israel, My called; I *am* He; I *am* the first, I also *am* the last. Mine hand also hath laid the foundation of the earth, and My right hand hath spanned the heavens: *when* I call unto them, they, stand up together."

The prophet defends the credibility of his ministry, the prophecy concerning the coming of the Babylonian captivity, and his message of ultimate restoration after judgment in Isaiah 48:14–22. In Isaiah 48:15, Jehovah declares that He has spoken the word concerning the Babylonian captivity and it was inevitable. Jehovah stated, "I have brought him, and he shall make his way prosperous."

In Isaiah 48:16, after hearing the proclamation of Jehovah, the prophet declares that Jehovah sent him to deliver this message to those who would hear. The person Who sent Isaiah to deliver the message of the Babylonian captivity (Isaiah 39:5–7, 48:16) and ultimate deliverance (Isaiah 46–48) is the same person Who sent the prophet to the people after the death of Uzziah (Isaiah 6:1,8–13).

Jehovah, Israel's Redeemer and the Holy One of Israel, laments the disobedience of Israel to His laws and the necessary judgment that is forthcoming but beckons them to obedience to His will. The will of Jehovah that is their current reality includes captivity followed by restoration. As He had miraculously provided for His people in the past, He would do again. He would restore them after judgment.

The prophet records thirty-nine first person singular divine pronouns identifying Jehovah in this encounter and uses nine third person singular divine pronouns of his own in reference to God. As this first section of prophecies in the second part of Isaiah closes, it is instructive to recount the emphasis placed on the person and personal attributes of Jehovah. A myriad of divine titles have been used to identify and characterize Jehovah. These include:

1. Holy One
2. Everlasting God
3. Creator of the ends of the earth
4. Holy One of Israel
5. King of Jacob
6. I the Lord
7. I the God of Israel
8. God the Lord
9. Savior
10. Creator of Israel
11. King
12. King of Israel
13. Lord of hosts

14. Maker
15. Redeemer

Additionally, the Lord repeatedly makes claims like "I am God, and there is none else" or "I am the Lord, and beside Me there is no savior" or "There is no God beside Me… I know not any." Over 270 first person singular divine pronouns are spoken by Jehovah concerning Himself in these nine chapters. The omniscience, omnipotence, and sovereignty of Jehovah are repeatedly discussed. He is presented as judge and deliverer throughout this section of encounters.

An emphasis is made on the tendency of Jehovah to use human vessels to accomplish His purposes. Israel, Isaiah, and Cyrus are among the vessels depicted as servants of Jehovah in this series of encounters. A most revolutionary concept introduced and explained by Jehovah in the encounter in chapter 42, however, is the fact that in the future, He would use a servant in a way not previously done to accomplish a feat not previously witnessed by humanity. Jehovah would become His own servant and bring about salvation to humanity Himself. In the next series of encounters, Jehovah undertakes to reveal to the mind of Isaiah more details on how this inconceivable feat would unfold and what would be done through, to, and with this servant.

Encounter thirty-six: Messianic Prophecy Concerning Israel as Salvation to the World (Is. 49)

The second division of Isaiah Part Two records four divine encounters between Isaiah and Jehovah in chapters 49–57. These encounters all share the common theme of "servants used by Jehovah." Jehovah, because of His omnipotence, omniscience, and sovereignty, chooses any vessel He desires to accomplish His purpose(s) in the earth. Because His purposes are many and varied over the course of history, His vessels likewise are many and varied. Among the chief of the vessels used by Jehovah over the course of history has been the nation of Israel, God's chosen people from the days of Abraham

(2166–1991 BC). Isaiah is a servant of Jehovah, being used at this point in time to minister to the nation of Israel.

Chapter 49 is devoted to a divine encounter in which Isaiah and Jehovah discuss the significance of Israel as Jehovah's servant, Isaiah's role as a servant of Jehovah, and Jehovah's commitment to Israel as a people. Isaiah is the subject of the first portion of this discussion with Jehovah. Isaiah presents his perspective of his role as Jehovah's servant in Isaiah 49:1–2.

Jehovah confirms His selection of Isaiah and His presence with Isaiah in Isaiah 49:3. Isaiah expresses his frustration with the relative lack of success he has experienced in turning Israel to Jehovah (Isaiah 49:4–5). Jehovah had foreseen and foretold this result to His servant's ministry from the beginning (Isaiah 6:8–13) and comforts Isaiah in the present divine encounter (Isaiah 49:6, 8–11).

Isaiah 49:6 and Isaiah 49:10 also pertain to the work accomplished through the ministry of the Messiah—Jehovah's ultimate servant. The messianic status of these verses is confirmed by Paul and Barnabas in Acts 13:47 and the Apostle John in Revelation 7:16 respectively. Isaiah 49:14–26 is an exchange between Jehovah and Isaiah in which Jehovah extends His words of consolation to Israel, His servant, in light of the prophesied judgment coming upon them. Jehovah says, "Yet will I not forget thee" (Is. 49:15); and "I will contend with him that contendeth with thee, and I will save thy children" (Is. 49:25).

In this encounter, Jehovah is "the Redeemer of Israel," "the Holy One," "the Holy One of Israel," "I the Lord," "Savior," "Redeemer," and "the Mighty One of Jacob." He uses two dozen first person singular divine pronouns to identify Himself. The prophet uses nearly a dozen (ten, to be exact) third person singular divine pronouns when speaking of Jehovah. Jehovah is clearly seen as omnipotent, omniscient, sovereign, judge, and king. However, He is also a merciful person Who is mindful of those with whom He has a covenant relationship. This encounter is a fitting prelude to the next because the subject is Jehovah's servants (Isaiah and Israel), and an emphasis is placed on extending the possibility of covenant relationship to the Gentiles.

Encounter thirty-seven: The Redemption of Sinful Israel and Humanity—Messianic Prophecies (Is. 50–54)

Isaiah 50–54 is among the most significant written portions of Isaiah's ministry because of it's implications for Jews and Christians alike. In this divine encounter between Isaiah and Jehovah, the major theme is the redemption of Israel and of all of humanity as accomplished by Jehovah through the work of His servant, the Messiah. Jehovah begins this encounter with Isaiah by indicting Israel for its unfaithfulness in its covenant relationship with Him and asserting His ability to redeem His people (Is. 50:1–3). Isaiah spends the remainder of this brief chapter discussing the challenges He has faced among his people who have been hostile to his message from Jehovah (Is. 50:6) and the support that Jehovah has given him throughout his decades of ministry (Is. 50:4–5,7–9).

Isaiah 51 is a continuation of the previous chapter and involves the same divine encounter. Here, the prophet and Jehovah deal with the sins and redemption of the nation. In 51:2, Jehovah reminds the Israelites of their historical roots—the fact that Jehovah birthed the nation from the previously unfruitful marriage of Abraham and Sarah over 1,300 years ago (Gen. 12:1–5, 21:1-3). The prophet also alludes to Adam and Eve as historical figures when he speaks of Eden and the garden of the Lord.

In Isaiah 51:4–8, Jehovah speaks of the perpetual righteousness and salvation that He will bring by His own arm to any who will trust in Him, thereby demonstrating His goodness, mercy, and power to save (His omnipotence). Isaiah expresses confidence in the promised redemption of Jehovah based upon His record throughout history (Is. 51:9–11). Jehovah gives the hope of comfort in Isaiah 51:12–17, based upon His omnipotence as demonstrated by His acts throughout history. Jehovah cites His creation of the heavens and the earth, His deliverance of the Israelites from bondage, and His dividing of the sea to instill confidence in the prophet and the nation concerning the redemption He is promising to bring. These events of history are well-documented and firmly believed by Isaiah and the Israelites.

Portions of Isaiah 51:4–8 are quoted by the writer of Hebrews (Hebrews 1:10–11) in discussing the Son of God who is the express image of the person of Jehovah (Heb. 1:1-3). The Messiah has been seen as "the righteousness of Jehovah," "the salvation of Jehovah," and "the arm of Jehovah" as referenced in Jehovah's remarks in Isaiah 51:4–8. The connection of Isaiah 51:4–8 and Hebrews 1:10–11 is further substantiation for the fact that Jehovah identifies Himself with the coming Messiah as both His servant and a human manifestation of His divine person. The next chapter, which is a continuation of this same divine encounter, is a chapter devoted to transitioning to this idea in more detail.

The exchange between Isaiah and Jehovah concerning Jehovah's two servants, Isaiah and Israel, draws to a close in Isaiah 52, and a transition is made to a discussion of Jehovah's ultimate servant, the Messiah. Both the prophet (Isaiah 52:1–2,7–12) and Jehovah (Isaiah 52:3–6) encourage Israel to shake off the effects of sin and judgment and to look forward to redemption. For His part, Jehovah begins by saying, "Ye have sold yourselves for nought; and ye shall be redeemed without money."

Three times, Jehovah calls the people of Israel "My people" in His brief recorded comments. He promises redemption within the context of His knowledge of the complete history of His people by referencing their time in Egypt (before 1526 BC) and their recent Assyrian oppression (701 BC). Isaiah's hardships as Jehovah's servant may be the point of the comments made by Jehovah in Isaiah 52:13–14, which may be linked to Isaiah 20:3–6 and 50:5–7. However, these comments by Jehovah are also fitting closing remarks to this transition chapter, because some have interpreted these verses as being messianic in nature. While chapters 50–52 have been largely concerned with Jehovah's redemption of His servants Isaiah and Israel, the remainder of this encounter will focus in great detail on Jehovah's redemption of all of humanity by His servant, the Messiah.

As the Ethiopian eunuch discovered in the years shortly after the death, burial, and resurrection of Jesus Christ (Acts 8:26–40), the Old Testament chapter with the most comprehensive description of Jesus, the Messiah, and the work he would accomplish is

Isaiah 53. Amazing it is that this encounter between Isaiah and Jehovah took place about 700 years before the birth of Jesus! This chapter contains no less than five distinct messianic prophecies with the last coming directly from the mouth of Jehovah, according to the prophet Isaiah.

Isaiah begins this series of messianic prophecies by posing the critical question of how believable this amazing revelation could be—that is, the revelation that Jehovah would manifest Himself in flesh (the arm of the Lord) for the purpose of redeeming humanity. The prophetic description in Isaiah 53:2 spells out with clarity the fact that the Messiah, who is Jehovah, would be born like a regular human being and lead a relatively inconspicuous childhood life though he was God, even from his birth. Isaiah had made mention of the Messiah's Davidic ancestry in Isaiah 11:1–4, 11:10, and 12:2 decades earlier. The Apostle John makes an unmistakable association of the prophecy in Isaiah 53:1 with Jesus, the Messiah, in John 12:38–41. Notably, however, this same passage in John's gospel connects the prophecy in Isaiah 53:1–3 with the person, Jehovah, Who is encountered by the prophet in Isaiah 6:1–9.

The substitutionary death of the Messiah, Jehovah's servant, is a foundational truth of the Christian faith and is the next messianic prophecy in this critical chapter of Isaiah's writing. It is found in Isaiah 53:4–6. The Apostle Peter would later draw directly from Isaiah's prophecy when he discussed the work of Jesus on the cross in connection with the redemption of humanity (1 Peter 2:21–24).

Matthew, another eyewitness of Jesus's ministry and writer of the gospel according to Matthew, directly quoted Isaiah 53:4 while discussing a healing performed by Jesus, even before his death on the cross in Matt. 8:17. It is clear that the men who witnessed the life of Jesus Christ believed that he was the servant of Jehovah of whom the prophet Isaiah prophesied. The Apostle Paul, a chief architect of the doctrines of the Christian church, confirmed that the early church believed and taught that the person of God accomplished the work of salvation through His servant, the man, Christ Jesus. Paul declares, "For this *is* good and acceptable in the sight of God our Savior; who will have all men to be saved, and to come unto the knowledge of the truth. For *there is* one God, and one mediator between God and men, the man Christ Jesus; Who gave himself a ransom for all, to be testified in due time" (1 Tim. 2:3–6).

Isaiah foresaw that the Messiah would silently endure a trial in which he was accused falsely, judged unjustly, and condemned to death (Is. 53:7–8). In his gospel, Matthew remarked that Jesus did not defend himself during his trial before the chief priests and elders or before Pontius Pilate (Matthew 27:11–14). Philip also confirmed that the New Testament church applied Isaiah's prophecy to Jesus Christ when he interpreted this text for the Ethiopian eunuch in Acts 8:32–33.

In Isaiah 53:9, the prophet said of the Messiah "He made his grave with the wicked, and with the rich in his death; because he had done no violence, neither *was any* deceit in his mouth." Luke, the historian, carefully documented that Jesus was crucified on a cross hanging between two malefactors (Luke 23:32–41) and that his body was laid in the tomb of a wealthy pious man named Joseph (Luke 23:50–53). Peter again confirms the messianic application of this portion of Isaiah's prophecy (1 Peter 2:21–24).

Christ, the Messiah, suffered vicariously for our sins, and we vicariously experience the righteousness of God through his sufferings, according to 2 Corinthians 5:21. In this passage, Paul made the bold proclamation, "For he hath made him *to be* sin for us, who knew no sin; that we might be made the righteousness of God in him." This is a fulfillment of Isaiah's description of the work of the Messiah in Isaiah 53:10 (in combination with Is. 53:5).

The final words of Isaiah 53 (Is. 53:11–12), according to the prophet, were spoken directly by the mouth of Jehovah and are viewed as messianic according to Jesus in Luke 22:37 and Mark in Mark 15:28. Jehovah distinguishes Himself from the Messiah in that He calls him "My righteous servant" and declares, "I will divide him a portion with the great." Jehovah also proclaims the intercessory role of the Messiah in His redemption plan in that He would lay on the Messiah the iniquities of many.

Thus, in Isaiah 53, the Messiah is both God and man, a common claim of Christianity. The detail and the accuracy with which Jehovah and Isaiah describe the life and role of Jesus as the Messiah are nothing short of incredible. The foresight in this prophecy is indisputable evidence of the omniscience of Jehovah. The accomplishment of the feat of redemption by this mechanism is equally indisputable evidence of the omnipotence of Jehovah.

This encounter between Isaiah and Jehovah concludes in chapter 54 with a description by Jehovah and Isaiah of the magnitude of the salvation accomplished by the Messiah. The salvation and redemption provided through the ministry of the Messiah is extended to all of humanity, both Israel (Is. 54:6–12) and the gentiles (Is. 54:15–17). The person Isaiah knew as Jehovah accomplishes the work of redeeming Isaiah, Israel, and humanity by His own arm and not by the work of any other divine person. This is made obvious by Jehovah's use of seventy-two first person singular divine pronouns as He speaks throughout this multi-chapter encounter, focusing on the servants of Jehovah, their redemption, and His use of these servants. Though He is judge, He extends the ultimate in grace and mercy through His work as Messiah and demonstrates the extent to which He is willing to go to have a covenant relationship with those who desire to pursue this relationship with Him.

Encounter thirty-eight: The Sure Mercies of David— Messianic Prophecies (Is. 55)

Approximately 300 years before Isaiah's next encounter with Jehovah, Jehovah had established a covenant with David, Israel's great king and psalmist. David had the desire to build a house of worship for Jehovah. Jehovah, in response to David's genuine pursuit of an intimate relationship with Him, promised to make David's kingdom a perpetual kingdom with one of his descendants sitting on a perpetual throne (2 Samuel 7; 1 Chronicles 17). This was the great mercy extended by Jehovah to David. It was certain because it was established as a covenant between Jehovah and David.

In this encounter between Isaiah and Jehovah (Is. 55:1–4), Jehovah reveals the connection between the covenant He established with David around 997 BC and the suffering servant, the Messiah, of which He had spoken in His previous encounter with Isaiah (Is. 53). Through no sufficiency of their own, all who had the desire to pursue an intimate relationship with Jehovah would have access to the redemption described in His previous exchange with Isaiah. Jehovah would provide this redemption through the Messiah while simultaneously fulfilling His covenant with David by allowing the Messiah to be born of the line of David.

Of the identity of the Messiah, we have now learned that he would be a human instrument of Jehovah, and thus, "Jehovah's servant." He would be a fleshly or human extension of the eternal person, Jehovah, and thus, "the arm of the Lord." And he would be a descendant of David, thus fulfilling the covenant Jehovah had made with David and thus fulfilling the sure mercies of David.

During a speech to the Jews in a synagogue in Antioch in Pisidia, around 45 AD or so, Paul confirmed the connection between Jesus, the Messiah, and the prophecy spoken by Jehovah to Isaiah in this encounter (Acts 13:34).

The brilliance involved in connecting all of these things though one man, the Messiah, is otherworldly. It is beyond human intellect to conceive. Jehovah acknowledged this in Isaiah 55:8–11 saying, "As the heavens are higher than the earth, so are My ways higher than your ways, and My thoughts than your thoughts."

He goes on to assure the prophet that He would accomplish what He has spoken. His word is sure. Moreover, there may well be a connection between Jehovah's proclamations concerning His thoughts in Isaiah 55:9 and His word in Isaiah 55:11 and the Apostle John's teaching in John 1:1 and John 1:14 concerning the incarnate word of Jehovah. Of this, we are certain—Jehovah used thirteen first person singular divine pronouns in this exchange with Isaiah and thereby takes full credit as the person Who accomplishes the amazing work accomplished by His earthly appearance as the Messiah.

Encounter thirty-nine: Global Reach of Jehovah's Salvation— Messianic Prophecies (Is. 56–57)

In the last two chapters (Is. 56–57) of the second division (Is. 49–57) of Isaiah Part Two (Is. 40–66), Jehovah explains to the prophet how far and wide He plans to offer the unimaginable redemption plan He has detailed in the earlier encounters of this division. Jehovah explains in Isaiah 56:3–4 that no one should exclude himself from access and that anyone who chooses to take hold of *My* covenant is welcome.

Jews and Gentiles alike are all welcome, according to the Lord God, "which gathereth the outcasts of Israel" and proclaims, "Yet will I gather others to him, beside those that are gathered unto him" (Is. 56:8). Jesus made reference to this specific encounter between Isaiah and Jehovah (Is. 56:7) when he chastised the Jewish leaders of his day for implementing practices that effectively excluded people with limited financial resources. Because of pharisaical practices, some of Jehovah's people could not afford to take part in the worship services of Jehovah (Matt. 21:13; Mk. 11:17; Lk. 19:46).

Isaiah lamented the evil of men that negatively affect the access of others to Jehovah's redemptive plan (Is. 56:9–57:6). This encounter concludes as Jehovah confirms the sad state of the evil among his people but counters with the fact that He reaches out to them as well; they also have access to His redemption if they will have a contrite and humble spirit (Is. 57:7–21).

The interference of evil men will not thwart the plans of "the high and lofty One that inhabiteth eternity, whose name is Holy" (Is. 57:15). There will ultimately be redemption for all who choose Jehovah, but there is no peace to the wicked. Jehovah used thirty-five first person singular divine pronouns in His last encounter with Isaiah in the second division of Part Two of the book of Isaiah. In light of the supremacy of Jehovah, which was discussed in division one of Part Two of Isaiah, Jehovah concluded that "There is no peace to the wicked"—those who oppose Jehovah (Is. 48:22). In light of the magnificence of the redemptive plan and the vast inclusiveness of Jehovah's outreach, presented throughout the second division of Part Two of Isaiah, Jehovah concluded that "There is no peace to the wicked" (Is. 57:21).

Encounter forty: Jehovah is the Redeemer—Messianic Prophesies (Is. 58–59)

This divine encounter begins with Jehovah instructing Isaiah to declare to his people their sinful state and their empty, hypocritical, ritualistic worship toward Him. He is unimpressed by their religiosity, including their formality in fasting. These kinds of actions do not accomplish the purpose or plan of God. Jehovah offers a solution to His servant, Israel. If they will turn and truly seek the will of Jehovah, their covenant relationship will be restored, and He will be able to use them as "The repairer of the breach, The restorer of paths to dwell in." They will be His instruments of redemption to mankind (Isaiah 58:12).

In chapter 59, Isaiah adds, Jehovah has desired to use Israel for this purpose, not because of any inadequacy of Jehovah to accomplish this restoration of mankind without the help of Israel. The sins of Israel have prevented them from being used by Jehovah. Because of Israel's inadequacy in accomplishing the purpose of Jehovah, Jehovah Himself will be the repairer of the breach and the restorer of paths to dwell in.

According to Isaiah 59:16, Jehovah "saw that *there was* no man, and wondered that *there was* no intercessor: therefore His arm brought salvation unto Him; and His righteousness, it sustained Him." Jehovah confirmed Isaiah's assessment at the end of this encounter (Isaiah 59:20–21). Referencing Himself as the Redeemer, which is the equivalent of Isaiah's assessment in Isaiah 58:16, Jehovah says, "And the Redeemer shall come to Zion and unto them that turn from transgression in Jacob."

Paul quotes the words of Jehovah in this encounter during his dissertation concerning the redemption of Israel in Romans 11:26.

Isaiah used nineteen third person singular divine pronouns in reference to Jehovah in this encounter. Jehovah used thirteen first person singular divine pronouns to identify Himself. In total, in this encounter, thirty-two singular divine pronouns and the title "the Redeemer" clearly identify the person of Jehovah as the one Who would bring about salvation or redemption in Israel.

Encounter forty-one: Jehovah is the Light of the World— Messianic Prophecies (Is. 60)

This encounter simply builds on the previous encounter. Israel has proven itself inadequate for Jehovah's purpose of bringing humanity into fellowship with Him. Jehovah, as the Messiah, will restore Israel's glory and redeem mankind. The person of Jehovah is emphasized by the use of twenty first person singular divine pronouns and the divine titles "Holy One of Israel," "I the Lord," "Savior," "Redeemer," and "Mighty One of Jacob." Jehovah declares that He will be the light of Israel and the light of the world. The prophet prophesies the coming of the Messiah in verses 1–3 when he states "Arise, shine; for thy light is come, and the glory of the Lord is risen upon thee" and "...the Lord shall arise upon thee, and His glory shall be seen upon thee."

The Apostle Paul paraphrases this prophecy by Isaiah and equates Jesus with Jehovah in his letter to the Ephesians saying instead "...Christ shall give thee light." Jehovah closes His encounter with Isaiah, reiterating that He would be the light of His people. He declares, "The sun shall be no more thy light by day; neither for brightness shall the moon give light unto thee: but the LORD shall be unto thee an everlasting light, and thy God thy glory. Thy sun shall no more go down; neither shall thy moon withdraw itself: for the LORD shall be thine everlasting light, and the days of thy mourning shall be ended" (Is. 60:19–20).

John ends the writings of the New Testament, over a half century after the death, burial, resurrection, and ascension of Jesus

Christ, and after the death of all of the other original apostles, by reaffirming the message of Isaiah that Jesus is Jehovah and He will be the light of His people for eternity. John says this: "And the city had no need of the sun, neither of the moon, to shine in it: for the glory of God did lighten it, and the Lamb *is* the light thereof" (Rev. 21:23). It is a final confirmation that Isaiah's God, Jehovah, became the Messiah, Jesus, and redeemed humanity to Himself, becoming the light of the world.

Encounter forty-two: The Spirit of the Lord Will Rest on the Servant of the Lord (Is. 61–62)

This encounter between Jehovah and Isaiah is most notable, because Jesus read the messianic prophecy at the beginning of this encounter as he began his own earthly ministry (Luke 4:17–20). The messianic prophecy reads, "The Spirit of the Lord GOD *is* upon me; because the LORD hath anointed me to preach good tidings unto the meek; he hath sent me to bind up the brokenhearted, to proclaim liberty to the captives, and the opening of the prison to *them that are* bound; To proclaim the acceptable year of the LORD, and the day of vengeance of our God; to comfort all that mourn; To appoint unto them that mourn in Zion, to give unto them beauty for ashes, the oil of joy for mourning, the garment of praise for the spirit of heaviness; that they might be called trees of righteousness, the planting of the LORD, that he might be glorified" (Is. 61:1–3).

No doubt, Jesus was well aware of the fact that this prophecy spoke of the coming of the Messiah. Luke records that after Jesus read from the scroll of Isaiah, he closed the book and sat down. Having caught the attention of everyone in the synagogue, Jesus proclaimed, "This day is this scripture fulfilled in your ears," thus proclaiming himself to be the prophesied Messiah, the servant of Jehovah upon whom the Spirit of Jehovah rested.

Encounter forty-three (a): The Arm of the Lord Shall Bring Salvation—Messianic Prophecies (Is. 63–64)

The prophet Isaiah sees a battle scene in this encounter. The battle appears to be between the servant of Jehovah and the enemies of Jehovah. The servant of Jehovah, however, is the Messiah and therefore, Jehovah Himself. He describes Himself as, "I that speak in righteousness, mighty to save" (Isaiah 63:1).

The imagery in this encounter relies quite heavily upon the history of Israel and Jehovah. Edom, for instance, was perpetually at war with Israel. This struggle began even before the birth of Jacob (the father of Israel) and Esau (the father of Edom) around 2006 BC (Genesis 25:23–26). Jehovah's judgments and mercies toward Israel during the time of Moses (1446–1406 BC) are cited throughout this encounter. And Jehovah is compared to Abraham, the father of Isaac, the father of Jacob, the father of the twelve patriarchs to highlight His superior faithfulness to His children (Is. 64:16). Over the centuries, Israel has repeatedly violated Jehovah's trust, and judgment is imminent as Jehovah had revealed to Isaiah immediately after the Assyrian siege of Jerusalem (Is. 39:5–7).

Isaiah prays to Jehovah in light of Israel's history of failures and the judgment he has foreseen; he prays for Jehovah's mercy upon His people (Is. 64). In Isaiah 64:6, Isaiah acknowledges the woeful state of Israel, admitting to Jehovah that even the righteousness of Israel—and of every human, for that matter—is like filthy rags before Jehovah. Isaiah understood this personally, recalling his experience when he personally beheld Jehovah on His throne and understood his own pitiful sinful state in comparison (Is. 6). Isaiah recognizes the futility of the efforts of Israel and humanity to restore themselves to a right relationship with Jehovah.

It is in this context that Jehovah began this encounter by proclaiming that He alone was able to conquer the things that have warred against His people and their relationship with Him. He alone is mighty to save (Is. 63:1). Since there is none to help and none to uphold, the arm of the Lord brought the salvation He needed for His people. The arm of the Lord, we learned, is the Messiah of Jehovah, Jehovah Himself, born as a man to restore humanity to a right relationship with the Lord. Though he does not recite this passage, John wrote, "For this purpose the Son of God was manifested, that he might destroy the works of the devil" (1 Jn. 3:8).

A scene much like that depicted by Isaiah and Jehovah in Isaiah 63:1–6 is described by John in Revelation 19:11–21. In Isaiah, the man of war is Jehovah. In Revelation, the man of war is called "Faithful and True" (Rev. 19:11), "The Word of God" (Rev. 19:13), "The Almighty God" (Rev. 19:15), "King of Kings and Lord of Lords" (Rev. 19:16), and "The Great God" (Rev. 19:17). John sees this as a revelation of Jesus Christ, Jehovah our salvation. John's God is also Isaiah's God. Isaiah's God used over twenty first person singular divine pronouns to identify Himself during the encounter with Isaiah recorded in Isaiah 63–64. Isaiah uses an additional twenty-three third person singular divine pronouns in reference to Jehovah. Jehovah remains Father and Savior of His people throughout time.

Encounter forty-three (b): The Salvation of Jehovah Will Be Without Limits (Is. 65–66)

In response to the fervent prayer of Isaiah in the previous two chapters, Jehovah gives the rather lengthy speech documented in Isaiah 65–66 that concludes the prophet's record of his encounters with Jehovah. In His response, Jehovah contrasts Israel's rejection of Him and the empty worship offered by Israel with His acceptance by "a nation that was not called by My name."

Much of Jehovah's response focuses on the consequences of Israel's decisions and actions. Paul references Jehovah's response in this encounter during his dissertation concerning the redemption of Israel (Romans 10:19–20). Though He is disappointed by Israel's decisions and actions, Jehovah makes the point that He remains omnipotent, omnipresent, and sovereign. It is not He, but Israel that suffers from their erroneous decisions. Stephen refers to Jehovah's response in this encounter (Is. 66:1–2) during his lengthy recitation of Israel's history and his defense of his doctrine before the high priest in Acts 7:48–50. In essence, Jehovah makes the point—and Paul and Stephen refer to it—that ultimately, it is He Who will judge all of humanity, including Israel, and He will reward those who turn to Him and reject those who are obstinate.

Isaiah's final encounter demonstrates that Jehovah is "the God of truth," and the righteous judge Who is sovereign and makes all final decisions about who will have a relationship with Him beyond this life. Jehovah uses nearly eighty first person singular divine pronouns in His final comments in Isaiah 65–66 and closes with the final word on the relationship of humanity with Him. Jehovah boldly proclaims, "And it shall come to pass, *that* from one new moon to another, and from one sabbath to another, shall all flesh come to worship before Me, saith the LORD. And they shall go forth, and look upon the carcases of the men that have transgressed against Me: for their worm shall not die, neither shall their fire be quenched; and they shall be an abhorring unto all flesh" (Is. 66:23–24).

Summary and Conclusions

Isaiah's prophetic ministry began during the reign of one of Judah's great kings (Uzziah), and while the nation was a regional military powerhouse. He continued to be a mouthpiece for Jehovah during the reigns of a weak but righteous king (Jotham), and subsequently, a weak and evil king (Ahaz). His final years of ministry occurred during the reign of the great king Hezekiah, but during a time of great uncertainty and instability, as great and powerful international forces began to "take over the world" and threaten the future of God's people. It is in the context of this complex and changing historical backdrop that Isaiah's understanding of Jehovah is shaped. This covers a period of no less than fifty years and as many as seventy to seventy-five years.

Isaiah's first encounter with Jehovah predates the famous throne room encounter of Isaiah 6 by an undefined period of time. From the early days of his ministry, Isaiah understood that his people were unfaithful to Jehovah and that a time of judgment for their perpetual unfaithfulness in their covenant relationship with Jehovah was imminent (Isaiah 1–5). The decline of Judah's political and military influence after the death of Uzziah, and the uncertainty of their future on the international scene that ensued, most certainly impacted Isaiah's understanding of Jehovah and his insights regarding Jehovah's plans for his people.

The throne room encounter in Isaiah 6 is one of the most important documented encounters between Isaiah and his God, because it records a direct encounter in which Isaiah receives both visual and auditory input concerning the person of Jehovah. It occurred at a time when Isaiah was in great need of Jehovah's reassurance about his nation and his personal future. The awesomeness of the person Isaiah saw on the throne was overwhelming and life-changing. The encounter left Isaiah with a certainty about the omnipotence and omniscience of the One on the throne, Whom Isaiah called "the Lord of hosts," "the Lord" (Jehovah), and "the King." It also left Isaiah with a certainty about his own inadequacy and dependence upon Jehovah and the guiltiness and pending judgment of Judah.

Isaiah also left this encounter understanding the fact that Judah could only be reconciled to Jehovah by the divine intervention of Jehovah! The remainder of Isaiah's encounters with Jehovah and the understanding Isaiah develops over the next five decades of his prophetic ministry are built upon the foundation of Isaiah's second encounter with Jehovah.

During the reign of Ahaz (mid-730s–716 BC), from his position of being a politically well-connected and influential representative for Jehovah in Judah, Isaiah saw that the leaders and the nation were becoming less and less mindful of Jehovah. Isaiah's documented divine encounters during the reign of Ahaz reflect Judah's absence of godly direction, though the prophet repeatedly emphasizes Jehovah was the only hope for Judah's restoration. In the face of an uncertain future, the nation and its leaders were seeking help from international alliances. Meanwhile, Isaiah's God repeatedly spoke to the prophet concerning the inadequacy of these alliances. Jehovah asserted the fact that Judah and each of its proposed allies (Isaiah 13–23)—and for that matter all nations (Isaiah 24–27)—would ultimately be judged by Jehovah. While prohibiting Judah from placing their confidence in international alliances (Isaiah 8:12), Jehovah instead admonishes the nation to place their confidence in Him.

Consistent with Isaiah's understanding of Jehovah as Israel's only hope, the idea of the Messiah is established and begins to take shape from Isaiah's divine encounters unlike any prophet that predated Isaiah. It is initiated with what Jehovah communicated to Isaiah—and Jesus and his disciples later in history interpreted—as the prophecy of the virgin birth (Isaiah 7:14; Matthew 1:20–23) and Immanuel (God with us). In this same period of time, Isaiah begins to understand through his encounters with Jehovah that this coming Messiah would be the fulfillment of the Davidic covenant that had predated Isaiah by about three centuries (Isaiah 11–12).

Although Isaiah's overall experience as a spokesperson for Jehovah must have improved under the receptive leadership of Hezekiah, Judah's troubled relationship with Jehovah continued. The prophet continued to hear from Jehovah concerning judgments to come and the ultimate restoration of His fallen people that would follow these judgments. More prophecies of judgment occurred from 716 BC through the Assyrian siege of 704–701 BC and beyond (Isaiah 28–33, 34–35). Some extremely detailed historical information concerning the interactions between Jehovah, Isaiah, and Hezekiah are given in Isaiah 36–39. This is followed by what many scholars have labeled as Second Isaiah (Isaiah 40–66).

Second Isaiah, or Isaiah Part Two, is historically and conceptually intricately linked to First Isaiah (Isaiah 1–39). Judah's leadership—even its good leaders who have witnessed Jehovah performing the miraculous by destroying and dispersing the Assyrian army—never placed their hope completely in Jehovah. They continued to look elsewhere, despite witnessing the fall of the northern kingdom for this same spiritual infidelity. In response to this continued failure,

Jehovah prophesies the coming Babylonian captivity (Isaiah 39) and Israel's ultimate restoration by His handiwork alone (Isaiah 40–66).

Jehovah's encounters with Isaiah recorded in Second Isaiah—which cover a period from 701–686 BC—center around three broad subjects. First, Jehovah focuses on His supremacy in comparison to any gods, persons, or nations in which Judah might choose to place their trust (Isaiah 40–48). Secondly, Jehovah clarifies the concept of the Messiah as His servant and the means by which He would save His people (Isaiah 49–57). Finally, Jehovah develops conclusions regarding His judgment and the salvation He offers and Who will be the recipients of His judgment and His salvation (Isaiah 58–66).

The continuity of Isaiah's themes throughout his record of his divine encounters is apparent from an examination of each of the three broad subjects addressed in Second Isaiah. Jehovah's supremacy, His omniscience, His omnipotence, and His sovereignty are the subject of Isaiah 1, 6, and 40–48. Isaiah introduced the theme of Jehovah as Messiah during the reign of Ahaz but develops it fully in Isaiah 42 and 49–57. Isaiah 53 describes the human life of the Messiah, the servant of Jehovah, with exquisite accuracy. The Messiah is the child who is the descendant of David (Isaiah 7:12, 9:6, 11:1–4, 12:2, 53:1–2, 55:1–4), the servant of Jehovah (Isaiah 42, 53) and, Isaiah argues, he is also Jehovah, our judge and savior (Isaiah 1, 6, 9:6, 40–48).

Over the course of several decades and forty-three documented divine encounters, Isaiah develops a clear and consistent, yet progressive, understanding of the person he knows as Jehovah. Isaiah uses a formidable list of titles for Jehovah. The Lord of hosts, however, is an extremely commonly used title by the prophet. From the time Isaiah encounters Jehovah in the courtroom scene in Isaiah 1 and the throne room encounter in Isaiah 6, until Jehovah gives His last lecture to Isaiah regarding His judgment and restoration of His people, Isaiah sees Jehovah as a single divine person Who is sovereign, omnipotent, omniscient, a judge, savior, and seeker of covenant relationship with His people. Isaiah hears Jehovah use approximately 700 first person singular divine pronouns in reference to Himself. The prophet uses slightly more than 400 third person singular divine pronouns as he refers to his God.

Table 3.1 Isaiah's Encounters with Jehovah (Isaiah Chapters 1-39)

	Date BC	Subject of encounter	Reference	Divine titles, nouns and/or pronouns
		Early years of ministry		
1	Pre 740	Jehovah's case against Judah	Is. 1-5	Holy One of Israel, Lord of hosts, Mighty One of Israel FPSP-40, 3PSP-25
2	740	Throne room of Jehovah	Is. 6	King, Lord of hosts, FPSP-1, 3PSP-4, PLP-1
		Encounters during the reign of King Ahaz		
3	735-732	Isaiah confronts Ahaz	Is. 7:3-8:2	Lord God, Immanuel, FPSP-0, 3PSP-1
4a	735-732	Immanuel/Against alliances	Is. 8:3-6, 12	
4b	735-732	Assyrian-Israel dynamic	Is. 8-Is. 12	Lord of hosts, Wonderful, Counsellor, Mighty God, Prince of Peace, Everlasting Father, Light of Israel, Holy One, Holy One of Israel, FPSP-10, 3PSP-29
		Twelve Burdens of Isaiah		
5	716	Against Babylon	Is. 7:13-14:28	Almighty, Lord of hosts, Most High, FPSP-19, 3PSP-2
6	722	Against Palestine (Philistia)	Is. 14:29-32	FPSP-1
7	725	Against Moab	Is. 15-16	FPSP-2

8	735-725	Against Damascus	Is. 17	Lord of hosts, Lord God of Israel, Maker, Holy One of Israel, God of thy salvation, Rock of thy strength
9	720s	Against Ethiopia	Is. 18	Lord of hosts, FPSP-4
10-11	716-701	Against Egypt	Is. 19-20	Lord of hosts, FPSP-7, 3PSP-6
12-14	716-701	Against Babylon, Edom, Arabia	Is. 21	Lord of hosts, God of Israel, FPSP-1
15	716-701	Against corruption in Jerusalem	Is. 22	Lord of hosts, Lord God of hosts, Maker, FPSP-7, 3PSP-3
16	716-701	Against Tyre	Is. 23	Lord of hosts, 3PSP-3
17	716-701	Global judgment and mercy	Is. 24-27	Lord God of Israel, Lord of hosts, Lord Jehovah, Most Upright, FPSP-10, 3PSP-25
		Six Woes (Warnings) of Isaiah		
18	704-701	Against Samaria and Assyria	Is. 28	Lord (God) of hosts, FPSP-2, 3PSP-11
19	704-701	Against Judah	Is. 29:1-14 Is. 29:15-24	Lord of hosts, Holy One of Israel, the Lord Who redeemed Abraham, Holy One of Jacob, God of Israel, FPSP-11, 3PSP-1
20	704-701	Against Egypt	Is. 30-32	Holy One of Israel, Mighty One of Israel, Lord of hosts, FPSP-4, 3PSP-23
21	704-701	Against Assyria	Is. 33	Glorious Lord, lawgiver, judge, king, FPSP-6, 3PSP-3
22	704-701	Global judgment and mercy	Is. 34-35	FPSP-2, 3PSP-5

		Encounters during the reign of King Hezekiah		
23-24	704-701	Defense of Jerusalem	Is. 37	Living God, Lord God of Israel, Holy One of Israel, Lord of hosts, FPSP-15
25	701	Hezekiah's illness	Is. 38:1	
26	701	Hezekiah's healing	Is. 38:4-8	God of David, FPSP-6, 3PSP-5
27	701-700	Babylonian captivity prophesied	Is. 39:5-7	Lord of hosts

FPSP First person singular divine pronouns
3PSP Third person singular divine pronouns
PLP Plural divine pronouns

Table 3.2 Isaiah's Encounters with Jehovah (Isaiah Chapters 40-66)

	Date BC	Subject of encounter	Reference	Divine titles, nouns and/or pronouns
		The Supremacy of Jehovah		
28		Restoration after judgment	Is. 40	Holy One, Everlasting God, Creator of the ends of the earth, FPSP-3, 3PSP-31
29		Court case: Jehovah vs. idol gods	Is. 41	Holy One of Israel, King of Jacob, I the Lord, I the God of Israel, FPSP-29, 3PSP-3, PLP 1*
30		Judgment and Jehovah's servant	Is. 42	God the Lord, I the Lord, FPSP-30, 3PSP-16

31		Supremacy of Jehovah (none like Him)	Is. 43-44	Holy One of Israel, Savior, Holy One, King, Creator of Israel, King of Israel, Lord of hosts, FPSP-91, 3PSP-7, PLP-1
32		Cyrus and the Messiah (Jehovah's instruments of deliverance)	Is. 45	God of Israel, I the Lord, Maker, Holy One of Israel, Lord of hosts, Savior, FPSP-46, 3PSP-7
33		Jehovah's purpose in Judah's captivity	Is. 46	FPSP-27, 3PSP-1, PLP-1
34		Judgment of Babylon	Is. 47	Lord of hosts, Holy One of Israel, FPSP-6, 3PSP-1
35		The omniscience of Jehovah (Prophecy, purpose, process foretold)	Is. 48	God of Israel, Lord of hosts, Redeemer, Holy One of Israel, FPSP-39, 3PSP-9
		The Servant of Jehovah		
36		Israel as salvation to the world	Is. 49	Redeemer of Israel, Holy One, Holy One of Israel, I the Lord, Savior, Redeemer, Mighty One of Jacob, FPSP-24, 3PSP-10
37		Redemption (of Israel and the world)	Is. 50-54	God that divided the sea, Lord of hosts, God of Israel, Maker, Husband, Redeemer, Holy One of Israel, God of the whole earth, FPSP-72, 3PSP-18
38		Sure mercies of David	Is. 55	Holy One of Israel, FPSP-13, 3PSP-6

39		Global reach of Jehovah's salvation	Is. 56-57	The High and Lofty One that inhabiteth eternity, Holy, FPSP-35, 3PSP-3
		The Salvation of Jehovah		
40		Jehovah, the Redeemer	Is. 58-59	The Redeemer, FPSP-13, 3PSP-19
41		Jehovah, light of the world	Is. 60	Holy One of Israel, I the Lord, Savior, Redeemer, Mighty One of Jacob, FPSP-20, 3PSP-2
42		Spirt of the Lord on His servant	Is. 61-62	I the Lord, FPSP-6, 3PSP-11
43a		Arm of the Lord (past, present, future)	Is. 63-64	Savior, Father, FPSP-22, 3PSP-23
43b		Final judgment and salvation of Jehovah	Is. 65-66	God of truth, FPSP-79, 3PSP-10

All of the encounters in Isaiah 40-66 are written during or after the Assyrian siege of Jerusalem around 701 BC.

Isaiah died around 686 BC.

*Multiple other plurals appear in Isaiah 41. They are spoken by Isaiah, not Jehovah.

FPSP First person singular divine pronouns

3PSP Third person singular divine pronouns

PLP Plural divine pronouns

Table 3.3 Messianic passages in Isaiah

	Messianic prophecy reference	**New Testament prophetic confirmation reference**
	During the reign of Ahaz	
1	Is. 6.9	Jn. 12:38-41
2	Is. 7:14	Matt. 1:22-23
3	Is. 8:13-15	Matt 21:43-44, Rom. 9:33, 1 Pet. 2:8
4	Is. 9:1-2	Matt. 4:13-17
5	Is. 9:6	Matt. 28:18-20, Jn. 1:1-3
6	Is. 11:1-4, 11	Rom. 15:12
7	Is. 12:2	Matt. 1:20-21
	During the reign of King Hezekiah	
8	Is. 28:16	Rom. 9:33
9	Is. 40.3	Mk. 1:3, Lk. 3:4, 5, Jn. 1:23
10	Is. 40:10-11	Jn. 10
11	Is. 42:1-7	Matt. 12:18-21
12	Is. 43:11	Matt. 1:23
13	Is. 45:23-25	Rom. 14:11, Phil. 2:10-11
14	Is. 49:6	Acts 13:47
15	Is. 49:10	Rev. 7:16
16	Is. 53:1	Jn. 12:38-41
17	Is. 53:4-6	Matt. 8:17, 1 Pet. 2:24-25
18	Is. 53:7-8	Matt. 27:11-14, Acts 8:32-33
19	Is. 53:9	Lk. 23:32-41, Lk. 23:50-53, 1 Pet. 2:22
20	Is. 53:12	Mk. 15:28, Lk. 22:37
21	Is. 55:1-4	Acts 13:34
22	Is. 59:20-21	Rom. 11:26
23	Is. 60:1	Eph. 5:14
24	Is. 61:1-3	Lk. 4:17-20

References

The Holy Bible. 2010. *Authorized King James Version*. Nashville, TN: Holman Bible Publishers.

Wiersbe, Warren W. 2007. *The Wiersbe Bible Commentary: Old Testament*. Colorado Springs, Colorado: David C. Cook.

2009. *The Apologetics Study Bible for Students*. Nashville, TN: Holman Bible Publishers.

2008. *The Chronological Study Bible*. Nashville, TN: Thomas Nelson, Inc.

Baxter, J. Sidlow. 1966. *Explore the Book, Complete in One Volume*. Grand Rapids, MI: Zondervan Publishing House.

Robinson, Jeffrey S. 2014. *Satan as He Wants to Be Seen*. North Charleston, SC: CreateSpace Independent Publishing.

Lockyer, Herbert. 1973. *All the Messianic Prophecies of the Bible*. Grand Rapids, MI: Zondervan Publishing House.

Leston, Stephen. 2011. *The Bible in World History*. Urichsville, OH: Barbour Publishing Inc.

4

Encountering the God of Isaiah's Contemporaries in Prophetic Ministry

Isaiah was the most prominent and influential prophet of Jehovah during the eighth century BC. However, biographical accounts reveal that several other men had encounters with Jehovah during this period and were commissioned by Jehovah to communicate messages to Judah, Israel, and even other nations of people. Each of these men who were Isaiah's contemporaries in prophetic ministry had unique encounters and relationships with Jehovah. They each served in a unique capacity in a consistent theme of Jehovah's overall plan to reach out to humanity. The relationship of each of these prophets with Jehovah offered some additional insights into the person of the God of Israel.

Isaiah's prophetic contemporaries included Jonah, Amos, Hosea, and Micah. Through Jonah's biography, Jehovah's compassion for humanity in the world beyond the borders of His chosen people is highlighted. Jehovah used His relationships with Hosea and Amos to reach out to the people of the northern kingdom while Isaiah was ministering in Judah.

The narrative of Hosea's life demonstrated Jehovah's love for Israel in a very literal sense and communicated Jehovah's heartfelt message concerning His relationship with His people. Amos was a commoner in every sense of the word but was called by Jehovah from the fields of a city of Judah to the people of the northern kingdom to deliver powerful and unpopular messages of indictment and judgment during a time of national peace and prosperity.

Micah was Isaiah's ministerial contemporary in the land of Judah. While Isaiah's ministry was in the high political society of Jerusalem, however, Micah's ministry was in the small towns of the remainder of the southern kingdom. Micah's message was more like that of Isaiah than any of Isaiah's other prophetic contemporaries. All four of these men, their ministries and messages, and the unique insights their relationships yield concerning the person of Jehovah will be examined briefly.

The most significant extra-biblical confirmations of the period of history in which these men lived and prophesied come from Assyrian archaeological findings and Assyrian historical documents. These historical references abound. Assyrian rulers who reigned during the lifetimes of these prophets included Adad-Nirari III, Tiglath-Pileser III, Shalmaneser V, Sargon II, and Sennacherib.

Assyria was not a world power at the beginning of the eighth century BC, but it would emerge as one before the century ended. Many of the prophecies of Isaiah and his contemporaries predate Assyria's assent to the status of being a world power. These prophecies reveal Jehovah's foreknowledge of Assyria's future and His plan to use this part of human history for His personal purposes involving His people and, ultimately, the world.

Both Israel (the northern kingdom) and Judah (the southern kingdom) experienced periods of renewed political influence and economic prosperity in the first half of the eighth century. Israel's resurgence as a regional power and the period of prosperity it enjoyed during the early part of the eighth century occurred under the reign of Jerobaom II (792–751 BC). Jonah, Hosea, and Amos each ministered to Israel during the reign of Jeroboam II.

Three decades after the death of Jeroboam II, Israel was overrun by Assyria. Under the reigns of Uzziah (790–740 BC) and Jotham (740–722 BC), Judah enjoyed the same resurgence of regional power and prosperity that Israel experienced under Jeroboam II. While Isaiah prophesied during the reigns of Uzziah, Jotham, Ahaz, and

Hezekiah, Micah did not prophesy during the reign of Uzziah but did so during the reigns of the other three aforementioned kings of Judah. Interestingly, some of the leaders of Judah in the days of Jeremiah (around 588 BC) specifically referenced the impact of Micah's ministry during the days of Hezekiah (Jeremiah 26:16–19), and not the ministry of Isaiah.

Syria was a political force that both Israel and Judah had to reckon with during this century, before the rise of Assyria. Syria was led by Benhadad III and Rezin, who were the son and grandson, respectively, of Hazael. Hazael had been anointed king by Elijah around 858 BC (1 Kings 19:15) and commissioned to begin his reign by Elisha around 840 BC (2 Kings 8:7–15).

Several other events occurred outside of the middle east during the same historical timeframe as the ministries of Isaiah and his prophetic ministry contemporaries. The eastern Zhou Dynasty of China was established during this era. The period of the Greek city-state began. In fact, the first Olympic games were held in Greece in 776 BC. Homer may have written *The Iliad* and *The Odyssey* during this time. The city of Rome was formed from a group of villages in Italy, and the first Greek colony in Italy was founded.

Each of Isaiah's four prophetic contemporaries—Jonah, Amos, Hosea, and Micah—are unique personalities with unique backgrounds and unique ministries. Each had a unique relationship with the same divine person they each knew as Jehovah. Jehovah showed remarkable consistency in His character traits across His relationships and His many encounters with these very different men through their very different prophetic ministries. Let's discuss Isaiah's contemporaries as they emerged chronologically.

Jonah: Jehovah's Prophet to Assyria

Jonah is the first of Isaiah's contemporaries to emerge. He is the son of Amittai and can be firmly placed in history during the reign of Jeroboam II (792–751 BC) according to 2 Kings 14:23–29 and Jonah 1:1. He lived during the latter portion of the reign of Jehoash of Israel, the father of Jeroboam II, and was likely a voice of Jehovah to both of these evil but strong kings of Israel. Although Jeroboam II was an evil king, Jehovah used the ministry of Jonah to encourage and strengthen him to help the people of Israel who had seen their political and economic status severely crippled by Syrian assaults under the leadership of Hazael (841–796 BC). Jonah saw the nation recovering economically and, once again, increasing its political and military influence in the region.

The scripture does not expressly link Jonah to any knowledge of the prophetic ministry of Joel who prophesied to Judah sometime between 860 BC and 830 BC. Nonetheless, Jonah may well have been aware of the word from Jehovah recorded in Joel 2:1–11 and its implication that a northern army (the rising nation of Assyria) would be God's instrument of punishment for Judah and Israel.

Knowledge of this prophecy and its implications would certainly have impacted Jonah's willingness to deliver any prophetic word that he received from Jehovah to Assyria. We know nothing else of Jonah's background, but we can deduce that he was a strong-willed, influential, and persuasive prophet who understood the power of his ministry and the character of his God.

Jonah's biographical account of his encounters with Jehovah includes at least ten verbal exchanges or deliberate acts of intervention by Jehovah in the prophet's life. Under Jeroboam II, Jonah was beginning to see or hoping to see his nation recover from decades of Syrian assaults.

In His first recorded message from Jehovah, Jonah is instructed by God to go to Nineveh to preach repentance to a nation that might come against his people in the future (Jonah 1:2) and impede this economic and political recovery. Jonah did not agree with the mind of Jehovah and set out in the opposite geographical direction away from Nineveh.

In His second recorded encounter with Jonah, Jehovah intervened directly in the prophet's life, sending a storm to interrupt Jonah's travel plans to bring Jonah back in line with His divine will and purpose (Jonah 1:3–16).

In His third encounter and His second direct intervention, Jehovah sent a great sea creature to the ship's vicinity in time to swallow the wayward prophet after he was cast into the sea by his desperate and frightened shipmates (Jonah 1:17). Though he had deliberately rebelled against the plan of God, Jonah knew that Jehovah was merciful and he prayed to Jehovah in the midst of his crisis from the blackness of the belly of a great fish (Jonah 2:1–9). Compassionate Jehovah heard Jonah's prayer and caused the fish to beach himself and vomit Jonah out on dry land (Jonah 2:10).

In His second direct verbal message to Jonah, Jehovah again commissions Jonah to carry a message of repentance to Nineveh (Jonah 3:2). Understanding now that he cannot resist the will of Jehovah, Jonah hastily commits to carrying out the will of his God (Jonah 3:3–10). Because of the power and influence of Jonah's ministry, Nineveh receives the message of Jehovah, repents, and is spared the imminent judgment of which Jonah prophesied. Jonah understood the nature of the person he served and was somehow displeased that Jehovah had extended the grace and mercy consistent with His nature to a people that might someday come against his beloved nation (Jonah 4:1–2).

In another act of grace and mercy and to teach and mature His prophet, Jehovah poses a rhetorical question to Jonah (Jonah 4:4) and then proceeds to show him through three additional deliberate acts of intervention why his judgment was again flawed (Jonah 4:3–9). Jonah's biographical account of his encounters with Jehovah end with a verbal exchange in which Jehovah enlightens him about the error of his judgment concerning the extension of Jehovah's grace and mercy to a gentile nation (Jonah 4:10–11).

Several things are evident about the person Jonah knew as Jehovah. Jehovah was well-known as the king and judge of Israel. However, Jonah's biography reveals that He is the judge of all the earth, including non-Hebrew nations. Jonah learns that Jehovah's grace and mercy—because they are a part of the nature of Jehovah (Jonah 4:2)—are also extended to other members of the human family (Jonah 3:10). Jehovah has expectations for people and will judge those who fail to meet His expectations (Jonah 1:2–4), though He is ever merciful (Jonah 4:10–11). Jehovah's omnipotence, omnipresence, and omniscience are on display for Jonah to witness. Jehovah was the God of heaven, which hath made the sea and the dry land (Jonah 1:9). He prepared a great fish to swallow up Jonah (Jonah 1:17) and spake to the fish to vomit out Jonah upon the dry land (Jonah 2:10). He was aware of Jonah's whereabouts at all times and aware of the state of the Assyrians who were far removed from Jonah and Israel. He prepared the gourd that gave shelter to Jonah (Jonah 4:6), the worm that caused the gourd to wither (Jonah 4:7), and the wind and sun that beat down upon Jonah in the absence of the gourd (Jonah 4:8). All these interventions helped Him plant seeds of instruction into the life of one of His children, Jonah.

Each time Jehovah used a divine personal pronoun in reference to Himself when He spoke to Jonah (Jonah 1:2, 3:2, 4:11), the divine pronoun was a first person singular divine pronoun. The person Jonah knew as Jehovah was an omnipotent, omnipresent, and omniscient person Who imposed His expectations upon people and judged them when they failed to meet these expectations. At the same time, He was gracious, merciful, and kind, and extended opportunities for redemption to those who transgressed their relationship with Him.

Amos: Jehovah's Plumb Line Prophet

Amos probably preached to Israel during the decade between 770–760 BC. His written work clearly defines the historical time frame during which the prophet Amos ministered. He lived in Judah during the reign of Uzziah (790–740 BC) but was sent by Jehovah to prophesy to Israel during the reign of Jeroboam II (792–751 BC). Amos also mentioned the house of Hazael and the palaces of Benhadad; probably Benhadad III, son of Hazael. Thus, he links his life and times to extra-biblical historical markers.

The plumb line vision that Amos received from Jehovah caused friction between Amos and Jeroboam II and his emissary, Amaziah (Amos 7:7–17), the priest of Bethel. Despite the valiant and courageous ministries of Elijah (861–851 BC) and Elisha (851–796 BC), the northern kingdom had continued to be plagued by the idolatry that started with Jeroboam I in about 930 BC (1 Kings 12:26–33) and expanded to include Baal worship under Ahab and Jezebel (874–853 BC). The kind, patient, loving, and merciful Jehovah had endured the insolence and unfaithfulness of His chosen people for centuries at this point. A measure of judgment was imminent and included the earthquake to which Amos makes reference that occurred after his prophecy was issued.

Jehovah's selection of Amos for His prophetic word to Israel at this time was notable for two reasons. First, Amos was not from the northern kingdom, but from a small city in Judah called Tekoa (Amos 1:1). To the people of the northern kingdom, Amos was somewhat of an outsider.

Secondly, Amos had no political or priestly clout of his own. He was merely a lowly shepherd and farmer from a little village in Judah (Amos 7:14–15). By sending a nobody, from nowhere, who had no personal agenda or prejudice, who confirmed Jehovah's previous messages in a fresh way, Jehovah removed all possibility for any misdirected concepts about the source and authenticity of His message to Israel.

The record of the ministry of Amos can be easily divided into three sections, and he reports a dozen and a half personal encounters with his God. The first seven divine encounters between Amos and Jehovah were communicated to Amos's audience as indictments and judgments of other people in surrounding lands. In a succession of public speeches over a brief but undefined period of time, Amos proclaimed Jehovah's indictments and the consequent judgments of Damascus (1:3–5), Gaza (1:6–8), Tyre (1:9–10), Edom (1:11–12), Ammon (1:13–15), Moab (2:1–3), and even Judah (2:4–5). It is time-worthy to at least mention that the judgment of which Jehovah spoke concerning the palaces of Jerusalem was not a reference to the Assyrian confrontations because these did not succeed in toppling Jerusalem. Amos's prophecy, in this instance, was a reference to the Babylonian captivity that occurred at the hands of Nebuchadnezzar, beginning around 606 BC. This took place over 150 years after the prophecy of Amos.

No doubt, this first series of prophecies of Jehovah through the ministry of Amos endeared the unlikely prophet to his target audience and got their attention. Amos, no doubt, makes sure that his hearers understand that the messages he is delivering are from Jehovah. There are eighteen first person singular divine pronouns and one third person singular divine pronouns referencing Jehovah across these first seven encounters between Jehovah and Amos. Amos delivers Jehovah's messages and words directly to the people of the northern kingdom.

The second group of messages Amos received from Jehovah, which he communicated to his now rapt audience, were directed at God's people in the northern kingdom of Israel. Jehovah delivers these messages to Amos over the course of four divine encounters. First, Jehovah presents His case against Israel. He then issues the impending judgment of His people followed by His lamentation for His lost relationship with them. He concludes this series by declaring the inevitable punishment for their transgressions. His plea, through the ministry of Amos, was for the return of His people to a faithful relationship with Him.

Amos delivers the message of each of these four divine encounters to the people. In the first of these four messages—Amos's eighth divine encounter overall—Jehovah informs the Israelites that their pending judgment is for moral and ethical injustices perpetrated by them during their recent period of political and economic prosperity. He assures them of their vulnerability and His omnipotence by referencing historical occurrences, of which they are familiar, including the Great Exodus of 1446 BC (Amos 2:10) and their conquest of the land of promise beginning in 1406 BC (Amos 2:9). Then He reminds them of His patience in the face of their sins against Him since that time in history (Amos 2:11–13). Judgment, He declares, is now imminent (Amos 2:14–16).

Lest the Israelites should invoke their "special" status in the eyes of Jehovah against the message of Amos, the next encounter addresses their abuse of their privileged relationship with Jehovah as another reason for the impending judgment (Amos 3:1–15). The devastation that Israel would experience from the coming judgment, the Assyrian invasion of the northern kingdom, is described very graphically in Amos 3:11–13. History confirms that in 722–721 BC (at least thirty to fifty years after Amos's prophecy), Israel was literally dismantled by the Assyrians. Amos was certain of the fact that Jehovah had revealed this message to him (Amos 3:7).

In his third encounter of this series of four encounters with Jehovah, Amos is informed that Israel's failure to respond to the previous interventions of Jehovah on their behalf was yet another contributing factor to their impending judgment (Amos 4:1–13). Previous famines (4:6), droughts (4:7–8), natural disasters, and disease (4:9–10) are cited as Jehovah's attempts to correct and draw His people back into fellowship with Him. The famine of Elisha's days, the plague of locusts of Joel's days, the invasions of Israel by the Syrians, and the destruction of Sodom and Gomorrah are all possible historical references intended by Jehovah and His prophet in this encounter. Amos makes it clear that Jehovah had a hand in Israel's history and that it was His tool to draw them. The omnipotence of Jehovah is testified to by the use of the phrase "God of hosts" (3:13, 4:13) and by Amos's description of Jehovah in Amos 4:13. Amos confidently proclaimed, "For, lo, He that formeth the mountains, and createth the wind, and declareth unto man what *is* His thought, that maketh the morning darkness, and treadeth upon the high places of the earth, The LORD, The God of hosts, *is* His name."

In his final encounter in the second series of messages to Israel (Amos 5–6), Amos communicates Jehovah's lamentation for the judgment that is coming upon Israel. Jehovah's plea is for Israel to return to a truly faithful relationship with Him, instead of the insincere worship that has characterized their past (Amos 5:21–26). The Assyrian captivity is once again foretold in Amos 5:27 and 6:14. Five times in this last encounter, Amos refers to Jehovah as "the God of hosts" (5:14, 5:16, 5:27, 6:8, 6:14). There are forty-four first person singular divine pronouns used by Jehovah in reference to Himself in this series of four divine encounters with Amos. Seven third person singular divine pronouns are also noted.

The third section of the book of Amos informs us of seven additional encounters between Jehovah and Amos. One of these is a confirmation of Amos's call to the prophetic ministry. Amos refers to this past encounter to vindicate his ministerial purpose when he is confronted by Amaziah, the priest of Bethel (7:15). It is noteworthy that Amos considered his ministry a personal call from a personal God to His chosen people; Jehovah used the first person singular divine pronoun *My* when He called Amos. A second message from Jehovah in this third section of Amos was a message to Amaziah concerning his personal judgment and the certainty of Israel's judgment and is recorded in Amos 7:16–17.

The remaining five divine encounters documented by Amos were visions sent from Jehovah and included the vision of the grasshoppers destroying the land (7:1–3), a consuming fire within Israel (7:4–6), a plumb line or standard of righteousness against which Israel would be compared to reveal its departure from Jehovah's righteous standards (7:7–9), a basket of summer fruit (8:1–14), and a vision of Jehovah standing upon the altar (9:1–5).

In the final vision, the character of Jehovah that has been seen across millennia is again seen. He desires an intimate relationship with His people. However, He has a standard of conduct that He requires of those with whom He is in relationship. When these standards are not met, judgment will follow. However, as He issues forth judgment, Jehovah always incorporates a word of hope because the judgment is not for the purpose of punishment so much as it is for the purpose of eventually restoring the relationship to the pure and intimate level He desires. Thus, in Amos 9:1–5 and 9:7–10, Jehovah speaks of the coming judgment of Israel.

But in Amos 9:11–15, the words of Jehovah through His prophet, Amos, speak of the restoration of God's people to their land. Jehovah used twenty-four first person singular divine pronouns to reference Himself in this final vision. History confirms that Cyrus the Great gave a proclamation that allowed the people of Israel to return to their homeland a few decades before the end of the sixth century (around 539 BC).

Amos had a very well documented personal understanding of the person he knew as Jehovah. In his own words, Amos says this concerning Jehovah, "For, lo, He that formeth the mountains, and createth the wind, and declareth unto man what *is* His thought, that maketh the morning darkness, and treadeth upon the high places of the earth, The LORD, The God of hosts, *is* His name" (Amos 4:13).

In Amos 9:5–6, Amos continues, "And the Lord GOD of hosts *is* He that toucheth the land, and it shall melt, and all that dwell therein shall mourn: and it shall rise up wholly like a flood; and shall be drowned, as *by* the flood of Egypt. *It is* He that buildeth His stories in the heaven, and hath founded His troop in the earth; He that calleth for the waters of the sea, and poureth them out upon the face of the earth: The LORD *is* His name."

Jehovah's plea to His people gives additional insight into the character of Jehovah as understood by the prophet Amos. The sovereignty and compassion of the relationship-oriented God of Amos is demonstrated when Jehovah says to the house of Israel, "Seek ye Me, and ye shall live" (Amos 5:4).

The fact that He expects a standard of conduct from those who live in covenant relationship with Him and that He has a genuine disdain for anything that separates His people from Him is evidenced by Jehovah's words in Amos 5:21–27. In this passage, Jehovah says, "I hate, I despise your feast days, and I will not smell in your solemn assemblies. Though ye offer Me burnt offerings and your meat offerings, I will not accept *them*: neither will I regard the peace offerings of your fat beasts. Take thou away from Me the noise of thy songs; for I will not hear the melody of thy viols. But let judgment run down as waters, and righteousness as a mighty stream. Have ye offered unto Me sacrifices and offerings in the wilderness forty years, O house of Israel? But ye have borne the tabernacle of your Moloch, and Chiun, your images, the star of your god, which ye made to yourselves. Therefore will I cause you to go into captivity beyond Damascus, saith the LORD, whose name *is* The God of hosts."

The person Amos knew as Jehovah was omniscient, omnipotent, omnipresent, and sovereign. He was relationship-oriented. He had expectations of those with whom He entered into relationship and judged them when they refused to walk in these standards. Yet, He was a kind and merciful person. The personhood of Jehovah is declared by the use of a hundred first person singular divine pronouns and nearly two dozen third person singular divine pronouns in the eighteen divine encounters recorded in the written work of Amos.

Hosea: Jehovah's Prophet to His Unfaithful People

Like the ministry of Amos, Hosea's prophetic ministry was directed to the northern kingdom. As opposed to Amos, however, this was Hosea's home. One might say that Hosea was more personally connected to the people of the northern kingdom and had more emotional investment in ministering to the people of the northern kingdom. His ministry began near the end of the reign of Jeroboam II who was the last ruler of the dynasty Jehovah promised Jehu after he overthrew Ahab.

God had promised this dynasty of four generations to Jehu for his obedience in eradicating the house of Ahab out of Israel around 841 BC (2 Kings 10:30). Since Hosea's ministry paralleled at least a portion of the reigns of Uzziah, Jotham, Ahaz, and Hezekiah in the southern kingdom, it probably began shortly before 750 BC and extended over thirty to forty years because Hezekiah became king of Judah around 716 BC.

The ministry of Hosea was unique. Not long after the stinging rebukes of Amos were delivered, Jehovah sent Hosea to live out the pain He was personally experiencing because of His love for Israel and their perpetual unfaithfulness to Him. Adultery and sexual immorality were known to be highly offensive to the God of Israel. Therefore, it is especially unique that Jehovah called Hosea to live out a prophetic ministry and personal life that exposed the prophet to the pain of this sin. The purpose of Hosea's life and ministry was to communicate a very personal message to the chosen people of Jehovah in a very personal and intimate way. Only a very personal God, through very clear and personal encounters, could induce a devout man like Hosea to do what He did for the purpose of helping Jehovah reach out to His chosen people.

Hosea's ministry speaks volumes about Hosea as a man, but it also speaks volumes about the God with Whom Hosea had a personal relationship. Hosea's God is emphatically a relationship-oriented, patient, kind, forgiving person Who relentlessly pursues the people who are the object of His affection.

Hosea's book can be divided into several parts. The first chapter of Hosea 1 contains the first four distinct encounters between Hosea and Jehovah. This section of Hosea gives details about Hosea's personal life and links Jehovah to the past, present, and future of the northern kingdom. For instance, the name of Hosea's first child, Jezreel (Hosea 1:4–5), was also the name of the place where the members of the house of Ahab were killed by Jehu and his accomplices (2 Kings 9:30–37, 10:11). Despite Jehovah's faithfulness to His promise to Jehu, neither Jehu nor his successors ultimately led the northern kingdom back to the worship of Jehovah. Though Israel was now experiencing a measure of prosperity under Jehu's dynasty during the rule of Jeroboam II, they continued to be unfaithful to Jehovah as a nation.

The second section of Hosea contains chapters 2-4 and has three more encounters between Jehovah and Hosea. The encounters in this section demonstrate that though Judah and Israel are guilty of spiritual infidelity, Jehovah still desires to have them return to the faithful relationship of Him as their God. In His fifth encounter with Hosea, Jehovah implores His people to return to Him (Hosea 2). In His sixth encounter with the prophet, Jehovah implores him to live out this message by going to buy the freedom of his estranged wife who has returned to the bondage of her sinful lifestyle (Hosea 3). The remainder of this section focuses on the misconduct of Jehovah's people and His indictment against them (Hosea 4).

The remainder of the book of Hosea contains very emotional messages that their divine lover, Jehovah, wants to communicate to their hearts and minds to ultimately affect their return to a faithful relationship with Him. The encounter in chapter 5 and the beginning of chapter 6 is about Jehovah's warnings to His wayward people of Judah and Israel and His plea for them to repent at long last (Hosea 5:1–6:3).

A subsequent encounter and message covers the remainder of chapter 6 and extends through chapter 8 and reveals Jehovah's lament over the unfaithfulness of His people and concludes with the addition of His verdict against them (Hosea 6:4–8:14). The remainder of Hosea's writing details five encounters between Jehovah and Hosea (Hosea 9:1–14:9). Four of these last five encounters focus on Jehovah's reasons for ultimately punishing His people, Israel.

In His final encounter with Hosea, Jehovah issues a promise of restoration to His people once they return to Him (Hosea 14:4–8). This is consistent with the character of Jehovah throughout history. Though He is just and righteous in His judgment, He is compassionate and merciful and gives hope to His people in the face of this judgment. For Hosea, Jehovah is the divine person Who called him into his prophetic ministry.

Jehovah required the sacrificial lifestyle that Hosea lived out. But this lifestyle was also fueled by Hosea's love for a woman who was perpetually unfaithful to him. As was paralleled by Hosea's decades long experience with Gomer, Jehovah endured the unfaithfulness of the people of Israel for centuries; yet, He continued to pursue a covenant relationship with them. Insights into the character of the divine person Who called Hosea and Who was experiencing the same relationship challenges with the object of His affection that Hosea endured because of his love for Gomer are given by multiple key verses throughout Hosea's written work.

The most pervasive personal attribute of Jehovah portrayed through the life of Hosea and taught by Jehovah through the ministry of Hosea was the fact that Jehovah is a person of love. The love of Jehovah is taught in more than one way. In Hosea 11:1, Jehovah very pointedly states, "When Israel *was* a child, then I loved him, and called My son out of Egypt."

This statement by Jehovah bluntly professes His love for Israel, but it is also messianic, and thus alludes to His love for all of humanity. Other passages in Hosea (Hosea 3:5, 13:14) may also have messianic implications; but Hosea 11:1 is the most definitive messianic statement contained in Hosea's writings.

Matthew confirms the messianic nature of Hosea 11:1 by citing it while informing us of the fact that the parents of Jesus spent some time in Egypt when Jesus was an infant and a toddler to avoid

Herod's murderous plot against their son (Matthew 2:15). This portion of Jesus's life was then foretold approximately 750 years before his birth. It was through the life of Jesus that Jehovah would display His greatest act of love and His most compelling and complete act of relationship restoration for all of humanity.

Hosea 11:1–9 was also a historical reference to Jehovah's longstanding love for and commitment to Israel and Judah. In 1446 BC, Jehovah had "called His son" out of Egypt in what was known as the Great Exodus (Exodus 4:22–23). Hosea's love for Gomer is a beautiful demonstration of the power of a husband's love for his wife and, in this way, powerfully demonstrates the love Jehovah has for His people.

Jehovah's love is like the love a husband has for his bride. However, this is not the relationship Jehovah uses to depict His intimate love for His people in the passage in Hosea 11:1–9. Jehovah's love for His people is also like a father's love for his child. Jehovah uses this picture of His relationship with His people to communicate His message in this passage.

A parental love relationship leads the parent to protect and provide for the object of His love. Demonstrating this aspect of parental love, in Hosea 11:3–4, Jehovah says, "I taught Ephraim also to go, taking them by their arms; but they knew not that I healed them. I drew them with cords of a man, with bands of love: and I was to them as they that take off the yoke on their jaws, and I laid meat unto them."

As the love of a parent disciplines his children to direct them toward positive ultimate outcomes, so the love of Jehovah caused Him to discipline Israel in an effort to move them toward positive goals He envisioned for them. One of these goals was for them to enter into a more intimate fellowship with Him, but they resisted, according to the assessment of Jehovah in Hosea 11:7, which reads, "And My people are bent to backsliding from Me: though they called them to the most High, none at all would exalt *Him*." To His dismay, Israel has continued to go away from Jehovah.

While Jehovah is full of love, throughout history, He has consistently required that the object of His love would live a lifestyle governed by an awareness of and an appreciation for their covenant relationship with Him. Throughout history, there were consequences when Jehovah's people did not regard the standards He expected from them as the objects of His affections. The personality of Hosea's God was consistent with this historical pattern of Jehovah.

In Hosea 4:6, Jehovah said, "My people are destroyed for lack of knowledge: because thou hast rejected knowledge, I will also reject thee, that thou shalt be no priest to Me: seeing thou hast forgotten the law of thy God, I will also forget thy children." These comments, made by Jehovah during His seventh encounter with Hosea are also consistent with His attribute of being a just and righteous judge Who has expectations of His people and will ultimately demand recompense for transgressions against His covenants.

Hosea understands that Jehovah is a righteous judge. This personal attribute is depicted by Jehovah during his thirteenth encounter with Hosea when He says, "I will meet them as a bear *that is* bereaved *of her whelps*, and will rend the caul of their heart, and there will I devour them like a lion: the wild beast shall tear them" (Hos. 13:8). Hosea 13 contains a historical reference to Israel's sins against Jehovah but also gives a justification for His judgment of Israel's ongoing transgressions against Him. Jehovah loves them, but He must judge unrelenting unrighteousness.

In Jehovah's eleventh encounter with Hosea, Jehovah also delivers warnings of the imminent judgment of His people for their continued spiritual infidelities and unfruitfulness. In Hosea 9:10–12, Jehovah says, "I found Israel like grapes in the wilderness; I saw your fathers as the first ripe in the fig tree at her first time: *but* they went to Baalpeor, and separated themselves unto *that* shame; and *their* abominations were according as they loved. *As for* Ephraim, their glory shall fly away like a bird, from the birth, and from the womb, and from the conception. Though they bring up their children, yet will I bereave them, *that there shall* not *be* a man *left*: yea, woe also to them when I depart from them!"

Jehovah reaches back to 1408–1406 BC, to Israel's unfaithfulness at Baalpeor (Numbers 25) for a historical citing of how long He has endured the sinfulness of Judah and Israel. For over 700 years at the time of Hosea's ministry, God's chosen people had been unfruitful as His ambassadors to the rest of humanity to bring the rest of humanity into a covenant relationship with Him. Jehovah's verdict against them is just. Hosea can only accept the verdict of Jehovah as seen in Hosea 9:17.

Throughout history, the choice of experiencing Jehovah as a God of love or a righteous judge has been contingent upon the choices of His people. Armed with this knowledge about the character of Jehovah, Hosea admonished his countrymen after his eighth encounter with Jehovah, "Come, and let us return unto the LORD: for He hath torn, and He will heal us; He hath smitten, and He will bind us up. After two days will He revive us: in the third day He will raise us up, and we shall live in His sight. Then shall we know, *if* we follow on to know the LORD: His going forth is prepared as the morning; and He shall come unto us as the rain, as the latter *and* former rain unto the earth" (Hos. 6:1–3). If the people of God continue to choose to pursue a path that violates their covenant relationship with Him, He will ultimately judge them. Hosea's God is a God of love, but He is also Israel's judge.

Hosea's God is also Israel's one and only true king. Historically, Israel has sought after others to rule over them and to provide them protection. During His thirteenth encounter with Hosea, Jehovah admonishes Israel, "I will be thy king: where *is any other* that may save thee in all thy cities? and thy judges of whom thou saidst, Give me a king and princes? I gave thee a king in Mine anger, and took *him* away in My wrath" (Hos. 13:10–11). Jehovah does not want Israel to look to another person to provide for them, protect them, or rule over them.

Hosea's predecessors and contemporaries alike saw Jehovah as a lone acting personal agent or divine person Who acted on behalf of His people. Moses professed this understanding when he shared his teachings concerning Jehovah to the new generation of Israelites at the closing of his time as their leader (Deut. 4:35, 4:39). In 1406 BC, Moses taught that Jehovah wanted Israel to know that He was God alone and the only source of their provision. Isaiah, Hosea's contemporary, agreed with the understanding and professions of Moses (see Isaiah 6:1, 43:11, 44:6, 45:5–6).

For Hosea, this was evident when Jehovah proclaimed, "Yet I *am* the LORD thy God from the land of Egypt, and thou shalt know no god but Me: for *there is* no saviour beside Me" in Hosea 13:4. Jehovah continues this theme of being one and acting as the redeemer or rescuer of His people in Hosea 13:14 when He says, "I will ransom them from the power of the grave; I will redeem them from death: O death, I will be thy plagues; O grave, I will be thy destruction: repentance shall be hid from Mine eyes."

He further emphasizes His position as Israel's redeemer in His final encounter with Hosea and His final message to His people through Hosea. In Hosea 14:4–8, Jehovah says, "I will heal their backsliding, I will love them freely: for Mine anger is turned away from him. I will be as the dew unto Israel: he shall grow as the lily, and cast forth his roots as Lebanon. His branches shall spread, and his beauty shall be as the olive tree, and his smell as Lebanon. They that dwell under his shadow shall return; they shall revive *as* the corn, and grow as the vine: the scent thereof *shall be* as the wine of Lebanon. Ephraim *shall say*, What have I to do any more with idols? I have heard *him*, and observed him: I *am* like a green fir tree. From Me is thy fruit found."

Hosea's God, like Adam's God so long ago (Genesis 3), gives hope in the midst of handing out judgment for the sin's committed against Him that He justly must punish. During Hosea's final two encounters with Jehovah, Jehovah is careful not to let Hosea's ministry conclude without a message of hope. Though judgment is just, righteous, and certain, Hosea's God is a compassionate and kind divine person Who will ultimately restore His people to their land and to a right relationship with Him.

Hosea also sees Jehovah as "the living God" (1:10), "the Most High" (7:16), "the Holy One" (11:9), "Israel's Maker" (8:14), and "the Lord God of hosts" (12:5). There are approximately 200 singular divine pronouns referencing the person Hosea encounters throughout his ministry and knows as Jehovah. Hosea's God uses 168 first person singular divine pronouns in reference to Himself during His conversations with Hosea, which Hosea then records in his written documentation. Hosea certainly understood that Jehovah was the omnipotent, omniscient, omnipresent, sovereign, compassionate judge of Israel and Judah. Hosea knew Him to be a personable God Who understood and felt the emotion of love, the pain of rejection, and the anger that follows betrayal. Hosea's God had the will to provide for and protect an unfaithful spouse, though this may be undeserved.

Micah: Jehovah's Salvation Plan; a Shorter Version for the Common People of Judah

The fourth and final ministerial contemporary of Isaiah is the prophet Micah. Micah lived and prophesied under the same four kings of Judah that Isaiah encountered during his ministry (Micah 1:1; Isaiah 1:1). While Isaiah prophesied mostly to the political elite and the royal and priestly lines in Jerusalem, Micah carried the same message from the same God to the commoners of Judah and Samaria. He was, after all, from the small town of Moresheth, several miles removed from the big city of Jerusalem.

Micah lived to see Assyria capture and enslave Judah's brethren in Samaria in 722 BC. His hometown of Moresheth may well have been among the casualties that fell to Assyria during the Assyrian assault on Judah near 700 BC. The historical setting of Isaiah's ministry is the setting in which Micah also prophesied, but while Isaiah was a political insider, Micah was an average citizen of Judah, outside of the security of the walls of the big city of Jerusalem.

The message of Jehovah that Isaiah communicated through over forty encounters and wrote about within sixty-six chapters in our Bible, Micah communicated in three documented divine encounters recorded in only seven chapters. Micah's ministry, message, and his God are best understood in direct comparison with the more comprehensive written work of Micah's contemporary, Isaiah.

In the first divine encounter in Micah, Jehovah's case against Judah and Israel is outlined and the judgment proclaimed. The second divine encounter lays out the coming restoration of Jehovah's people and proclaims the coming of a Messiah promised by Jehovah.

In Micah's third encounter with Jehovah, Jehovah reaffirms the guilt of His people and the fact that His punishment of the people is justified but also highlights the deliverance that is afforded them because of the nature and character of their God.

The first encounter between Jehovah and Micah resembles a courtroom scene. Micah 1:2 reads, "Hear, all ye people; hearken, O earth, and all that therein is: and let the Lord GOD be witness against you, the Lord from His holy temple." In this scene, which covers the first three chapters of Micah, Jehovah presents His case against Judah and Israel and issues a verdict and judgment against His chosen people. The judge is the same person Who Isaiah saw sitting upon a throne, high and lifted up, and His train filled the temple (Isaiah 6:1). The presentation very strongly parallels that described by Isaiah in Isaiah 1:1–4 and Isaiah 41:1–29.

In Isaiah 1:2, the prophet introduces the presider with, "Hear, O heavens, and give ear O earth; for the Lord hath spoken." In Isaiah 41:1, the presider Himself, the Lord, brings the court proceedings to order by saying, "Keep silence before Me, O islands; and let the people renew their strength: let them come near; then let them speak." He addresses everyone in the courtroom as a collective body as He concludes His introduction with, "Let Us come near together to judgment."

In Jehovah's first encounter with Micah, He sequentially pronounces judgment upon Israel (Micah 1:5–7) and then upon Judah (1:15–16). The judgment upon Israel, prophesied during the decade of 740–730 BC, was accomplished with Assyria's capture of Samaria around 722–721 BC. The judgment upon Judah was accomplished with the Babylonian captivity over 100 years later, around 606–586 BC.

Jehovah made the same prophetic proclamations concerning Israel (Isaiah 10:1–5) and Judah (Isaiah 13–14, 39:5–7) through the ministry of Isaiah in Jerusalem during Micah's lifetime. The list of accusations for which Jehovah issues His judgment are detailed in chapters 2 and 3 of Micah. They include covetousness, fraud, selfishness, unrighteousness, and unfaithfulness to the words of the law of Jehovah.

It is interesting again that Isaiah addresses these issues in a real life case study in his "burden of the valley of vision." Isaiah proclaims Jehovah's judgment upon Shebna, an unrighteous treasurer in Jerusalem, who was demoted and replaced by Eliakim, according to Isaiah 22:1–25. There are thirteen first person singular divine pronouns used by Jehovah referring to Himself in this first divine encounter in the book of Micah. Seven third person singular divine pronouns are also recorded.

Consistent with His character and His trend as far back as when He pronounced judgment during the lifetime of Adam and Eve in the Garden of Eden (Genesis 3), in His second encounter with Micah, Jehovah gave a word of hope and encouragement to those with whom He had a relationship in the midst of issuing judgment for their wrongdoings. Micah's record of Jehovah's message of hope to Judah and Israel during his day is recorded in Micah 4–5.

Jehovah begins this message of hope by foretelling a time when many nations would seek Him and He would teach them His ways and they would walk in His paths (Micah 4:1–2). The person of Whom Jehovah was speaking is seen as the God of Jacob (4:2) and is, as the context of the encounter demonstrates, also the prophesied Messiah.

Micah calls Him the judge of the people (4:3) and the Lord of hosts (4:4). Jehovah proclaims His role in the restoration of His people in His next comments (4:6–7). Considering the significant calamity caused by Assyria in his lifetime and the Babylonian captivity which he understood that Jehovah would allow (4:8–11), Micah could only hope and believe that Jehovah had a purpose and plan that would ultimately result in restoration.

Micah sees this entire process as foreknown in the mind of Jehovah and refers to it as the counsel and the thoughts of the Lord (4:12). The words of Jehovah that follow (4:13–5:2) are a prophetic battle cry for His people and a messianic proclamation. The people of Judah would be restored after the Babylonian captivity. But on a grander scale, Jehovah's people, which included the people of many nations (4:1–2), would be united under a single ruler who would be born in Bethlehem (5:2). It is this Messiah, this ruler, this governor of the people who would come forth out of Bethlehem of whom Matthew believed Jehovah was speaking during this conversation with Micah (Micah 5:1–2; Matthew 2:1–6). This process, already formulated in all its details and glory in the mind of Jehovah from everlasting (Micah 5:2 and Revelation 5:1–8), was also prophesied in much greater detail by Isaiah in Micah's days.

Isaiah identifies this coming Messiah using a variety of descriptors and divine titles. First, He identifies this Messiah as the child born of a virgin (Isaiah 7:14). The Messiah is also the arm of the Lord who would grow up as a tender plant (allusions to a life as a human child; Isaiah 53:1–2). Isaiah also describes him as a child born unto the nation of Israel who would be called Wonderful, Counsellor, the mighty God, The everlasting Father, and The Prince of Peace (Isaiah 9:6).

In Isaiah 42 and 53, he is the one who would minister to the needs of Jehovah's people. In Isaiah 46:9–13, 55:8–11, the Messiah is the embodiment of the higher thoughts, higher words, and higher purpose of Jehovah. Matthew's contemporary and another student under the Messiah himself, John the Apostle, agreed with this assessment according to John 1:1 and 1:14. Jesus was the Messiah, the culmination of the prophecy of Micah and Isaiah, and the human embodiment of the thoughts and purposes of Jehovah Who would come to save humanity.

Micah 5:3–9 is Micah's understanding of the things that the coming Messiah would accomplish in the process of the promised restoration of Judah and Israel. Jehovah confirms the coming judgment of His people and of the nations He would use to punish His people in Micah 5:10–15. The Messiah of whom Micah and Jehovah spoke in Micah 4–5 is the same Messiah of whom Isaiah wrote in Isaiah 7, 8, 9, 11, 12, and 40–57.

In Jehovah's closing comments in this second encounter with Micah, as He had done in Micah 4:6–7, Jehovah equates Himself with this Messiah. Though the functions described and the things accomplished by the person of whom Jehovah speaks in Micah 5:10–15 are those of the Messiah, Jehovah used the first person singular divine pronoun *I* to describe this person eight times in these closing remarks. He used the divine pronoun *I* four times in Micah 4:6–7. There are an additional four first person singular divine pronouns used in Micah 4:13–5:2. Micah's Messiah is Jehovah, yet he will come forth as a human born in Bethlehem.

Micah writes about a third encounter with Jehovah. It is his final encounter with Jehovah and its message very closely resembles what Isaiah describes in Isaiah 58–66. It reaffirms the guilt of the nation and the fact that the coming judgment is quite justifiable. It concludes with a message that the ultimate deliverance of Jehovah's people is the result of the tremendous mercy that has been characteristic of Jehovah throughout history.

Micah's account of this third encounter, like the first encounter in Micah, is presented as a courtroom scene. It begins with all of creation being called to witness Jehovah's case (6:1–2). Jehovah then speaks and calls upon history to substantiate His case. He testifies of the Great Exodus of 1446 BC and Israel's sin at Baalpeor in 1407 BC as evidence for Israel's sins (Micah 6:3–5; Numbers 22–25). With this evidence, in the courtroom setting at the close of Micah, the guilty party speaks of how it might redeem itself (Micah 6:6–7), and Micah resigns himself and the nation to the state of guiltiness. Jehovah's verdict is justified in the eyes of Micah (6:8–9). Jehovah reinforces the fact that His verdict is righteous in Micah 6:10–16.

In the final chapter of Micah, he laments the coming judgment upon Israel and Judah (7:1–13) and appeals to Jehovah (7:14). Jehovah answers Micah's prayer with a promise of mercy and redemption (7:15–16), and Micah rejoices in Jehovah's promise as the record of this final encounter with Jehovah concludes (7:17–20). In Micah's ministry, as in the ministry of Isaiah, just as the guilt of God's people is indisputable and judgment is certain, so is the deliverance of God's people certain. It is the direct result of the grace and mercy of Jehovah which will be manifest through the coming of the Messiah in the future.

Summary and Conclusions

From the beginning of human history, Jehovah demonstrated a determination to pursue a relationship with humanity. When the people with whom Jehovah entered into relationship transgressed, Jehovah would issue the consequences of judgment, while at the same time extending a word of hope for them in the midst of their judgment. During the eighth century BC, Jehovah spoke to the people of Israel and Judah, and even people outside of the nation of the Hebrews, using five major prophets.

Isaiah was the most prominent prophet of this century. However, in chronological order of their appearance on the stage of time, Jonah, Amos, Hosea, and Micah also had encounters with Jehovah during this century. Each of these prophets left a record of their divine encounters in the Bible. Jonah had about ten documented encounters with Jehovah and found Jehovah to be a gracious and merciful person beyond what Jonah himself considered necessary or advantageous.

Amos, the shepherd of Judah who became a prophet to Israel, had about eighteen documented encounters with Jehovah and understood Jehovah to be a just and righteous judge Who judged nations for their failure to adhere to the standards of righteousness that He established. Hosea lived his calling like no other prophet and, through about fourteen reported divine encounters with Jehovah, focused on the unfaithfulness of Israel and Judah to the covenant relationship Jehovah had pursued with them over centuries. Micah's ministry was a brief replica of the message of Jehovah to Judah through Isaiah. Micah's ministry, however, primarily addressed Jehovah's people outside of the city of Jerusalem, while Isaiah ministered largely within the walls of the big city.

When combined, Isaiah's contemporaries recorded forty-five divine encounters with the divine person they each knew as Jehovah. The record of Jehovah speaking to these men is filled with more than 300 first person singular divine pronouns used by Jehovah when referring to Himself. Over eighty 80 third person singular divine pronouns are used by these prophets in reference to the person they all knew as Jehovah.

This divine person was consistently seen as a God Who had endured the transgressions of His people against Him and would judge humanity for these breaches but would offer hope while issuing the promise of judgment. Their God, like the God of their contemporary, Isaiah, spoke a great deal concerning the Assyrian and Babylonian captivities of Israel and Judah. But He also spoke of the coming Messiah who would be His instrument of securing a hope and restoration that exceeded the comprehension and the scope of the Hebrews as a people and extended to the whole of humanity.

Table 4.1 Outline of Jonah's encounters with Jehovah

	Description	Reference	FPSP	3PSP
	Jehovah's first call to Jonah: consequences of Jonah's rebellion			
1	Jehovah commissions Jonah	1:1–2	1	
2	Jonah's rebellion, Jehovah sends a storm	1:3–16		
3	Jehovah prepares a Great fish to intervene	1:17		
	Jonah's prayer from the deep	2:1–9		1
4	Jehovah preserves and rescues Jonah	2:10		
	Jehovah's second call to Jonah: benefits of Jonah's obedience			
5	Jehovah speaks to Jonah a second time	3:1–2	1	
	Jonah's submission to Jehovah's will and result	3:3–10		4
	Jonah's disapproval of Jehovah's mercy	4:1–3		
	Jehovah's attention to Jonah's personal understanding of His character			
6	Jehovah questions Jonah's response	4:4		
7-9	Jonah sulks, and Jehovah intervenes three times (gourd, worm and sun and east wind)	4:5–8		
10	Jehovah and Jonah the experience; Jehovah is shown righteous and Jonah unrighteous	4:9–11	1	

The name of Jehovah appears twenty-six times in Jonah.
Jonah refers to Jehovah as "the God of heaven" (1:9).
2 Kings 14:23–29 identifies Jonah and places him in the historical time frame when Jeroboam II was king in Israel (792–751 BC).
Tiglath-Pileser III was probably not the ruler of Assyria when Jonah preached there.
FPSP First person singular divine pronouns
3PSP Third person singular divine pronouns

Table 4.2 Outline of Amos' encounters with Jehovah

	Subject	Reference	FPSP	3PSP
	Jehovah's judgments against other nations given to Amos			
1	The judgment of Damascus	1:3–5	3	
2	The judgment of Gaza	1:6–8	4	
3	The judgment of Tyre	1:9–10	2	
4	The judgment of Edom	1:11–12	2	
5	The judgment of Ammon	1:13–15	2	
6	The judgment of Moab	2:1–3	3	
7	The judgment of Judah	2:4–5	2	1
	Jehovah's judgment of Israel's Northern Kingdom delivered by Amos			
8	Judgment of Israel for moral and ethical injustices	2:6–16	7	
9	Woe for abuse of privileged relationship with Jehovah	3:1–15		
9a	Jehovah	3:1–2	3	
9b	Amos	3:3–8		3
9c	Jehovah	3:9–15	3	
10	Woe for Israel's failure to respond to earlier divine interventions	4:1–13		
10a	Amos	4:1–2		1
10b	Jehovah	4:3–12	15	
10c	Amos	4:13		3
11	Amos' lamentation, plea, and critique of Israel's insincere responses to Jehovah's calls			
11a	Jehovah	5:3–4, 10–12, 16–17, 21–27	13	
11b	Jehovah	6:8, 14	3	

	The vindication and the visions of Amos' ministry			
12	Vision of grasshoppers	7:1–3		1
13	Vision of consuming fire	7:4–6		
14	Vision of plumb line	7:7–9	4	2
15	Amos encounters Amaziah, the priest of Bethel (a)	7:11–17		
16	Amos encounters Amaziah, the priest of Bethel (b)	7:15	1	
17	Vision of the summer fruit	8:1–14		
17a	Jehovah	8:2, 3, 7, 9–12	9	
17b	Amos	8:1–2, 4–6, 8, 13–14		1
18	Vision of God at the altar	9:1–15		
18a	Jehovah	9:1–4, 7–15	24	
18b	Amos	9:1, 4–6		6

Divine titles: God of hosts (3:13, 4:13, 5:14, 5:16, 5:27, 6:8, 6:14, 9:5). Amos 4:13 is notable for its lengthy description and attributions to God.

FPSP First person singular divine pronouns

3PSP Third person singular divine pronouns

Table 4.3 Hosea's encounters with Jehovah

	Event	Reference	FPSP	3PSP
	Jehovah orders Hosea's personal life to parallel His relationship with Israel			
1	Instructed to marry Gomer	1:2		
2	Naming of Jezreel	1:4-5	2	
3	Naming of Loruhamah	1:6-7	3	
4	Naming of LoAmmi	1:9-11	4	
5	Jehovah implores Judah and Israel to return to Him	2:1-23	38	
6	Instructed to buy Gomer's freedom	3:1-5		1

	Hosea's indictment against his people	4:1		
7	Jehovah's indictment against Judah	4:2-19	11	
	Jehovah's messages to His people through Hosea's ministry			
8a	Jehovah's warning to Judah and Israel	5:1-3	3	
	Hosea elaborates	5:4-9		3
8b	Jehovah continues His warnings	5:10-15	11	
	Hosea's plea for Judah and Israel to repent	6:1-3		8
9a	Jehovah laments the unfaithfulness of His people	6:4-7:4	13	1
	Hosea's commentary	7:5-6		
9b	Jehovah interjects	7:7	1	
	Hosea's commentary	7:8-11		1
9c	Jehovah's lament continues; verdict added	7:12-8:14	12	1
10	Hosea speaks of judgment to come	9:1-9		3
11a	Jehovah addresses Israel's unfruitfulness	9:10-16	10	
	Hosea elaborates on Israel's unfruitfulness	9:17-10:8		1
11b	Jehovah addresses consequences of unfaithfulness	10:10-11	4	
	Hosea's commentary	10:12-15		1
12a	Jehovah's parental love for His son	11:1-9	21	1
	Hosea on parental discipline	11:10		2
12b	Jehovah on parental discipline	11:11	1	
13	Hosea recalls his people's history of deceitfulness	11:12-12:8		4
A	Jehovah's continued reaching for His people	12:9-10	3	
	Hosea on the righteousness of Jehovah's judgment of Israel	12:11-14		2
B	Jehovah on His righteousness in judging Israel	13:1-14	19	
	Seeing judgment, Hosea implores Israel to repent	13:15-14:3		1
14	Jehovah promises restoration after Israel returns	14:4-8	7	
	Hosea's conclusion	14:9		

Divine titles: Living God (1:10) Most High (7:16), Maker (8:14), Holy One (11:9), Lord God of hosts (12:5)
FPSP First person singular divine pronouns
3PSP Third person singular divine pronouns

Table 4.4 Outline of Micah's three encounters with Jehovah

	Description	Reference	FPSP	3PSP
	Encounter one: Court convened/The case against Judah and Israel	**1-3**		
1	Jehovah is presented as judge of His people	1:1–4		3
2	Jehovah proclaims judgment on Israel	1:5–7		4
3	Micah laments Jehovah's judgment of Israel	1:8–9		
4	Micah laments Jehovah's judgment of Judah	1:10–14		
5	Jehovah proclaims judgment on Judah	1:15–16		1
6	The case against Jehovah's detailed and discussed	2–3		
6a	Covetousness and fraud	2:1–2		
6b	Jehovah proclaims judgment	2:3	1	
6c	Unfaithfulness to the words and law of Jehovah	2:4–6		
6d	Jehovah proclaims judgment	2:7–9	4	1
6e	Micah elaborates	2:10–11		
6f	Jehovah proclaims judgment and restoration	2:12	3	
6g	Micah elaborates	2:13		
6h	Selfishness and unrighteousness of leaders	3:1–4		3
6i	Jehovah proclaims judgment	3:6–7		
6j	Micah distinguishes himself and elaborates	3:8–12		

	Encounter two: Restoration and the Messiah promised	**4–5**		
1	Jehovah describes the worldwide impact of Messiah	4:1–2		3
2	Micah elaborates on Messiah's impact	4:3–5		1
3	Jehovah describes Zion's benefit from Messiah	4:6–7	4	
4	Micah describes Zion's state before Messiah comes	4:8–12		2
5	Jehovah describes Zion's state after Messiah comes	4:13	3	
6	Micah describes Messiah' struggle, suffering	5:1		
7	Jehovah foretells birth of Messiah	5:2	1	
8	Micah elaborates of Messiah and Zion with Messiah	5:3–9		
9	Jehovah equates Himself with Messiah by role	5:10–15	8	
	Encounter three: A reaffirmation of national guilt, justified punishment and ultimate deliverance because of Jehovah's mercy and character	**6–7**		
1	All creation called to witness Jehovah's case	6:1–2		2
2	Jehovah uses His history with Israel as witness	6:3–5	6	
3	Israel's guilt and inability to redeem itself	6:6–7		1
4	Micah justifies Jehovah verdict	6:8–9		1
5	Jehovah reinforces the righteousness of His verdict	6:10–16	5	
6	Micah laments the coming judgment of Israel and Judah	7:1–13		4
7	Micah's prayer to Jehovah	7:14		
8	Jehovah's response to Micah's prayer	7:15–16	1	
9	Micah rejoices in Jehovah's promised redemption and Mercy	7:17–20		7

Divine titles in Micah: God of Jacob (4:2), Lord of hosts (4:4), Lord of the whole earth (4:13), the High God (6:6).
Messiah is judge and ruler of Israel from everlasting (5:1–2).
FPSP First person singular divine pronouns
3PSP Third person singular divine pronouns

References

The Holy Bible. 2010. *Authorized King James Version*. Nashville, TN: Holman Bible Publishers.

Wiersbe, Warren W. 2007. *The Wiersbe Bible Commentary: Old Testament*. Colorado Springs, Colorado: David C. Cook.

2009. *The Apologetics Study Bible for Students*. Nashville, TN: Holman Bible Publishers.

2008. *The Chronological Study Bible*. Nashville, TN: Thomas Nelson, Inc.

Leston, Stephen. 2011. *The Bible in World History*. Urichsville, OH: Barbour Publishing Inc.

Encountering Jehovah and His Seventh Century Prophets (Nahum, Zephaniah, Habakkuk)

The major events in world history during the seventh century BC, with only a couple of notable exceptions, involved the activities of Assyria and Babylon. The notable exceptions were the developments in Greece and Japan.

In Greece, the Second Messenian War took place between 650–630 BC, ultimately contributing to Sparta's development into a military city-state. Meanwhile, the Athenians produced a constitution around 620 BC in an attempt to stabilize their city-state. In the Far East, the Empire of Japan was established under its first emperor around 660 BC.

During this century, the Assyrian Empire continued the aggressive imperialism that had characterized this new world power throughout the previous century.

Assyria continued to expand under the leadership of Sennacherib's son, Esarhaddon (681–669 BC), and grandson, Ashurbanipal (668–626 BC). The greatest memories of Esarhaddon are that he rebuilt the city of Babylon, which had been destroyed by his father, and that he began Assyria's conquest of Egypt, which Sennacherib was unable to accomplish. The greatest contributions of Ashurbanipal, Assyria's last great king, were the conquest of No-Amon (known as Thebes to Greek and Roman historians) and the development and ultimate preservation of a vast library that he accumulated. His library contained copies of books from conquered people throughout the Assyrian Empire. Ironically, the neo-Babylonian Empire was born in this century and ultimately replaced Assyria as the next great world power.

Jehovah, the God of Israel, patiently endured the repeated transgressions of His chosen people against His desired covenant relationship with them for centuries. He finally permitted the northern kingdom of Israel to be overrun by the Assyrian Empire during the eighth century BC (722–721 BC). The Assyrian Empire ruled the people of Palestine mercilessly for a century. The Babylonian Empire, with the help of the Medes and the Scythians, overthrew the Assyrian Empire (609 BC) and ultimately became the new oppressors of the people of the southern kingdom of Israel (Judah) near the end of the seventh century BC (606 BC).

Judah's failure to learn from the consequences that befell Israel for its transgressions against Jehovah coupled with Judah's continued transgressions against Jehovah's desired covenant relationship with them led to their eventual fall to the Babylonian Empire (586 BC). The kings of Judah, during the lifetime of the prophets to be discussed presently, would have been Manasseh (697–642 BC), Amon (642–640 BC), and Josiah (640–609 BC). Assyria's merciless handling of God's chosen people, along with its other social and spiritual misconduct, led to its own judgment and its eventual demise. During the seventh century, three prophets of Jewish history left records that continue to give us insights into the person Whom Israel knew as God.

Nahum, Zephaniah, and Habakkuk wrote concerning Jehovah's judgment of Assyria, Judah, and Palestine, and the rise and fall of the Babylonian Empire during the seventh century BC. From their records, we learn about the messages they received and the person they knew as God. Nahum was the earliest of these three prophets. His writings focus on the judgment of the mighty Assyrian Empire and the fall of its capital city, Nineveh. Zephaniah writes concerning the coming judgment of various countries during this century including Judah and other people of the land of Palestine. Habakkuk deals with the rise and fall of the next world power, Babylon, and its role as the new aggressor against God's chosen people. The writings of each prophet enlighten the reader about the interactions each man had with Jehovah and the personal attributes of this divine person as understood by the prophet.

Encountering the God of Nahum, the God Who Terminated the Great Assyrian Empire

During a period of prosperity in Judah and Israel, somewhere between 792 and 751 BC (2 Kings 14:25), Jehovah had sent the prophet Jonah to the great city of Nineveh, the capital of the Assyrian Empire, with a warning of judgment for their transgressions (Jonah 3:4). This intervention by Jehovah had resulted in the preservation of Nineveh. Jehovah said He would later use Assyria to discipline His own people of Israel and Judah (Isaiah 10:5–6; Amos 5:27, 6:8, 7:9). Assyria accomplished the work of Jehovah but allowed its overzealousness and ungodly tendencies to drive it to perpetrate unacceptable atrocities against Jehovah's people. A century after rescuing Nineveh by His words of instruction to them and His heart of compassion toward them (Jonah 3–4), Jehovah sent another prophet to the capital of Assyria, the prophet Nahum.

Nahum brought the message of Nineveh's ultimate destruction. Little is known about Nahum. He establishes that he was from a city of Judah named Elkosh (Nahum 1:1). He prophesied sometime after the fall of No-Amon in 663 BC (Nahum 3:8) and before the fall of Nineveh in 612 BC. The final collapse of Assyria occurred in 609 BC. Because he did not bother to mention the name of the king of Judah in his writing, it is believed that Nahum prophesied under Manasseh and/or Amon and not under the righteous King Josiah. This places Nahum's ministry between 660–640 BC, 100 to 150 years after Jonah had delivered his prophecy to Nineveh.

Nahum's message is the message that Jonah would love to have delivered but could not because the time was not yet right. While Jonah was unaware of this fact, in His omniscience, Jehovah foreknew that Nineveh had not yet committed the crimes that would justify the magnitude of the judgment He would one day bring upon the Assyrian Empire. The time had now come, and Nahum delivered the prophecy of the utter destruction of Nineveh and the Assyrian Empire that would come to pass thirty to fifty years later.

Nahum's Message was most succinctly stated by Jehovah in Nahum 3:7 when Jehovah declares, "And it shall come to pass *that* all they that look upon thee shall flee from thee, and say, Nineveh is laid waste: who will bemoan her? Whence shall I seek comforters for thee?" The prophet gives the details of the destruction of Nineveh and Assyria in the verses after Jehovah's proclamation (Nahum 3:8–19).

Nahum's understanding of the person of Jehovah is established right from the beginning of his short book (1:2–9). He proceeds to record the words that Jehovah spoke to him in Nahum 1:12–14, 2:13, and 3:5–7. An evaluation of these passages gives a very clear picture of Whom Nahum perceived Jehovah to be as a person. Several attributes of Jehovah are lauded at the beginning (Nahum 1:2–9). Nahum's God is all-powerful, all knowing, patient, good, and kind. He is a judge and exacts vengeance with a fury against those who oppose His will or corrupt His will. He is a preserver of those who trust in Him. The very forces of nature are at His disposal to accomplish His will in the earth.

In His first statements to Nahum, Jehovah demonstrates that He is judge of all the earth, referencing His judgment upon Israel and Judah by means of the Assyrians and His judgment upon the Assyrians that was shortly to come (Nahum 1:12–14). Jehovah uses five first person singular divine pronouns in this proclamation. Jehovah's second proclamation of judgment against Assyria is found in Nahum 2:13 and contains three first person singular divine pronouns. A third proclamation against Nineveh and Assyria is spoken by Jehovah in Nahum 3:5–7 and begins like Nahum 2:13, "Behold, I am against thee, saith the Lord of hosts." This proclamation contains five additional first person singular divine pronouns.

Nahum's perception of the person of God is made apparent by his use of seventeen third person singular divine pronouns in describing Jehovah. In addition, Nahum's God uses thirteen first person singular divine pronouns in reference to Himself when Nahum records His words. Jehovah is the preserver of Nahum's people, the judge of the enemies of Nahum's people and the omnipotent, omniscient, sovereign, faithful, kind, good, relationship-oriented God of Israel.

Encountering the God of Zephaniah; Jehovah's Final Judgments Upon Palestine

Compared to his immediate prophetic predecessor (Nahum), Zephaniah leaves more historical information about himself. Historians generally agree that Zephaniah was a descendant of the good king, Hezekiah, who had ruled Judah prior to the evil reigns of Manasseh and Amon. Contrary to the prophet Nahum, Zephaniah dates his ministry by naming the king of Judah during his time. The good king, Josiah (640–609 BC), the great-grandson of Hezekiah, ushered in a period of spiritual restoration (2 Chronicles 34–35) after decades of idolatrous practice which was unprecedented in the southern kingdom (2 Chronicles 33; 2 Kings 21). During the national revival under Josiah, the book of the law of Moses, written between 1446–1406 BC, was unearthed and used as a guide by Judah's leaders (2 Chronicles 34:14–21; 2 Kings 22:8–10).

After recovering the book of the law, Josiah sought the counsel of the prophetess Huldah concerning the fate of the people of Judah. Huldah prophesied Jehovah's ultimate judgment of Judah that would be poured out after the death of King Josiah (2 Chronicles 34:22–28; 2 Kings 22:14–20). The prophecy of Zephaniah likely took place during the same time that Jehovah spoke to Josiah through the prophetess Huldah. Zephaniah's ministry is a detailed confirmation of the prophecy that Huldah gave Josiah. Zephaniah gives a detailed word of judgment against Judah in Zephaniah 1. He gives prophecies against the enemies of Judah in Zephaniah 2. In Zephaniah 3, he gives a final admonition for the people to place their confidence and trust in Jehovah.

The earliest part of Jeremiah's ministry was also contemporary with the ministry of Zephaniah. The ministries of both prophets were instrumental in spurring the great revival of Judah that took place under Josiah. Second Chronicles 34:3, 34:8, and 34:16–28 are very useful in placing Zephaniah into a historical timeframe. He certainly prophesied after 640 BC and before 620 BC. Zephaniah may well have been one of the last of Jehovah's prophets sent to Judah before Babylon began its invasions of Judah.

Assyria's global influence declined while Babylon's ascension to world power unfolded during Zephaniah's lifetime. Recall that the neo-Babylonian (Chaldean) Empire was birthed under Nabopolassar in 626 BC, Nineveh was destroyed in 612 BC, and Assyria collapsed for good in 609 BC.

A significant majority of Zephaniah's written work is a record of the actual words of Jehovah. Thus, a very good understanding of the person of Jehovah is gathered from reading Zephaniah. Zephaniah's God is the just Lord (Zephaniah 3:5) and the King of Israel (Zephaniah 3:15) Who is in the midst of His people and Who foretells the coming day of judgment, referred to as "the day of the Lord."

Jehovah speaks to or through Zephaniah in Zephaniah 1:2–6, 1:8–10, 1:12–13, 1:17, 2:5, 2:8–9, 2:12, 3:6–13, and 3:18–20. In chapter 1, Jehovah speaks concerning the judgment of Judah and the reasons for this judgment. Judah's idolatry and spiritual unfaithfulness are among the chief reasons given (1:2–6). Their sinfulness had gone without severe punishment for so long because of the patience of Jehovah that they had begun to doubt that punishment would ever come (1:12). Therefore, Jehovah promised that judgment was indeed coming (1:17).

In chapter 2, Jehovah turns His attention to the judgment of other nations, including Philistia (2:4–5), Moab and Ammon (2:8–9), Ethiopia (2:12), and Assyria (2:13–15). Nahum's ministry notes conclude with Jehovah's justification of His judgments (3:6–7), His admonishment of His people to place their confidence in Him, even in the face of judgment (3:8–13) and His word of hope for their ultimate restoration (3:18–20).

Jehovah uses forty-five first person singular divine pronouns in reference to Himself when He speaks during His encounter with Zephaniah. Zephaniah uses twenty-three third person singular divine pronouns when he speaks of Jehovah. The day of the Lord is referenced in Zephaniah 1:7, 1:14, 2:2, 3:11, and 3:16. Zephaniah certainly understands Jehovah to be the divine person Who dwells in the midst of His people, knows and judges their sinfulness, but advocates for them and preserves them against their enemies. He will ultimately bring them as a people to the state of their greatest fulfillment.

One can grasp Zephaniah's concept of the person of Jehovah by reading the following verses in his prophecy:

> I will also stretch out Mine hand upon Judah, and upon all the inhabitants of Jerusalem; and I will cut off the remnant of Baal from this place, *and* the name of the Chemarims with the priests; And them that worship the host of heaven upon the housetops; and them that worship *and* that swear by the LORD, and that swear by Malcham; And them that are turned back from the LORD; and *those* that have not sought the LORD, nor enquired for Him. (Zeph. 1:4–6)
>
> The just LORD *is* in the midst thereof; He will not do iniquity: every morning doth He bring His judgment to light, He faileth not; but the unjust knoweth no shame. (Zeph. 3:5).
>
> The LORD thy God in the midst of thee *is* mighty; He will save, He will rejoice over thee with joy; He will rest in His love, He will joy over thee with singing. (Zeph. 3:17)

Encountering the God of Habakkuk, the God Who Gave Rise to the Great Babylonian Empire

In 609 BC, King Josiah died an untimely death at the hands of Pharaoh Necho II and the Egyptians when he intercepted and challenged them as they were on their way to assist the Assyrians who were being attacked by the Babylonians (2 Kings 23:28–30; 2 Chronicles 35:20–27). After defeating Josiah's army, the Egyptians proceeded on but did not arrive in time to help prevent the overthrow of Assyria. As they were returning to Egypt three months later, Pharaoh Necho II and his forces deposed Jeohohaz, the son of Josiah, and placed his brother, Jehoiakim, on the throne of Judah.

Josiah's revival ended with his death, and once again, Judah descended into transgressions against their covenant relationship with Jehovah (2 Chronicles 36; 2 Kings 24:31–37). The Assyrians, oppressors of Judah for over a century since the days of King Ahaz (730–716 BC), were replaced by yet another instrument of Jehovah's judgment—the Babylonians. Just as the Assyrians had taken the people of the northern kingdom from their land in 722–721 BC, Jehovah foretold that the Babylonians would remove the people of the southern kingdom from their land. He spoke this prophecy to Isaiah around 701 BC (Isaiah 39:5–7) and again to King Josiah around 622–621 BC (2 Kings 23:27). Babylonian documents corroborate the details of the biblical setting in which Habakkuk has his encounters with Jehovah.

Habakkuk's contribution to history is a documentation of a timeless controversy that men have had with Jehovah. Habakkuk's interactions with Jehovah, documented in his short book, center around the fact that Jehovah, sovereign that He is, sometimes uses "less righteous people" to exact a measure of judgment upon a people that are—in their own eyes—at the very least, "more righteous" (Habakkuk 1). Habakkuk saw the flames of spiritual revival initiated during the reign of Josiah beginning to be extinguished.

Unrighteousness and godlessness were on the rise in Judah, and evil seemed to be gaining an upper hand on good among Habakkuk's people. He sought his God's intervention. Jehovah revealed His plan to use a new instrument of judgment against His people, the Babylonians. Incredulous at this idea, Habakkuk wondered how Jehovah could allow such a people to oppress His own people. Jehovah's response to this "perceived injustice" is recorded in Habakkuk 2.

Despite his contention with the plans and methods of Jehovah, which he admittedly does not understand, Habakkuk understands that he must submit himself and his requests to the divine person with Whom he has this conflict. In chapter 3, Habakkuk accepts the counsel, the heart and historical reputation of Jehovah. He ultimately finds peace in the face of the challenges and unfortunate developments that Jehovah reveals to him. Habakkuk's writing expresses this contention and concludes with a prayer to Jehovah and a statement of confidence and hope in Jehovah.

Habakkuk's descriptions of Jehovah in 1:12–13, 3:3–16, and 3:17–19 give us the best insight into how he perceived Jehovah. According to Habakkuk 1:12–13, Jehovah is everlasting, pure, a judge, holy, and one person. This understanding is the basis upon which Habakkuk can rationally tolerate Jehovah's decision to use the unrighteous Chaldeans as instruments against the people of Judah.

In Habakkuk 3:3–16, the prophet recalls the person and works of Jehovah in history as he basks in his awe of God. Most of the references in these verses are to the God of Moses and the Israelites during the time of the Great Exodus, the wandering in the wilderness, and the initial entry into the land of promise from 1446–1406 BC. The prophet is particularly awed by the historical appearance of Jehovah at Sinai (Habakkuk 3:3–4; Exodus 19:16–20; Deut. 33:2) and the power that Jehovah showed during the crossing of the Red Sea (Habakkuk 3:15; Exodus 14:21–22).

Because of Jehovah's person, power, and purpose throughout history, Habakkuk sees Him as a preserver in Whom he can place his trust as he faces the challenges of the future according to Habakkuk 3:17–19. Habakkuk uses twenty-three third person singular divine pronouns in describing Jehovah. Jehovah speaks in Habakkuk 1:5–11 and 2:2–19. He uses two first person singular divine pronouns in reference to Himself.

The most memorable verses of Habakkuk are 2:2–4 and 3:17–19. In Habakkuk 2:2–4, the prophet records the following: "And the LORD answered me, and said, Write the vision, and make *it* plain upon tables, that he may run that readeth it. For the vision *is* yet for an appointed time, but at the end it shall speak, and not lie: though it tarry, wait for it; because it will surely come, it will not tarry. Behold, his soul *which* is lifted up is not upright in him: but the just shall live by his faith."

In this commonly quoted verse, Jehovah informs Habakkuk that the invasion of Judah by the Chaldeans of which He had spoken in Habakkuk 1:5–11 would assuredly take place, and soon, and that the prophet should proclaim it and record it. He then counsels Habakkuk that in the face of this distressing development—as with any unsavory or unfortunate occurrence in the life of a person in relationship with Jehovah—he should always rely upon his faith in the person, purpose, and power of Jehovah as a source of strength and encouragement.

Habakkuk 3:17–19 says, "Although the fig tree shall not blossom, neither *shall* fruit *be* in the vines; the labour of the olive shall fail, and the fields shall yield no meat; the flock shall be cut off from the fold, and *there shall be* no herd in the stalls: Yet I will rejoice in the LORD, I will joy in the God of my salvation. The LORD God *is* my strength, and he will make my feet like hinds' *feet*, and he will make me to walk upon mine high places."

This passage, which is the record of Habakkuk's conclusion concerning the controversy that he has with Jehovah, reveals that the prophet, after considering the whole matter, has decided that confidence in Jehovah is well-placed, regardless of life's circumstances.

Summary and Conclusions

In the eighth century BC, the captivity of the northern kingdom of Israel became a historical reality. In the seventh century BC, the judgment of the nation that was used by Jehovah to discipline Israel, the subsequent judgments of Judah and other nations within the land of Palestine, and the rise of the Babylonian Empire would become the staples of history. Jehovah speaks of these historical eventualities to the prophets Nahum, Zephaniah, and Habakkuk.

Nahum's writing reads like a single encounter between him and Jehovah in which three proclamations against the mighty Assyrian Empire are given. Jehovah is God and judge of the mighty Assyrians. Zephaniah was sent by Jehovah to assure Judah that after their partial, obviously ineffective, judgment would become a completed work similar to that which befell their brethren of the northern kingdom. To Habakkuk, the final prophet of this century, it was revealed that the Babylonians would be the instrument by which Jehovah would exact His final judgment upon His wayward children.

Over the course of this century, through at least four encounters with three prophets, and through the use of sixty first person singular divine pronouns and fifty-two third person singular divine pronouns, Jehovah is declared to be the Holy One. Consistent to His character, He is the judge of all mankind. He is the omniscient, omnipotent, sovereign, relationship-oriented God Who is the preserver of His people, though His righteous judgment demands consequences for their transgressions against Him.

Table 5.1 The God of Nahum, the God Who terminated the great Assyrian Empire

Description	Reference	FPSP	3PSP
Jehovah as the One Who will destroy Nineveh	1:1–9		17
Nahum describes evil Assyria	1:10–11		
Jehovah speaks of Judah's rescue from evil Assyria	1:12–14	5	
Nahum predicts the fall of Nineveh	1:15–2:12		
Jehovah's actual words against Nineveh	2:13	3	
Nahum justifies the judgment of Nineveh	3:1–4		
Jehovah's verdict against Nineveh	3:5–7	5	
Nahum describes Nineveh's destruction	3:8–19		

Divine titles: Jealous (1:2), The Lord of hosts (2:13)
FPSP First person singular divine pronouns
3PSP Third person singular divine pronouns

Table 5.2 The God of Habakkuk, the God Who gave rise to the great Babylonian Empire

Description	Reference	FPSP	3PSP
Habakkuk's complaint against Judah (First prayer)	1:1–4		
Jehovah foretells Judah's judgment (captivity)	1:5–11	2	
Habakkuk's complaint about God's methods and God's choices (Second prayer)	1:12–17		
Habakkuk waits for an answer from Jehovah	2:1		1
Jehovah's response to Habakkuk's complaint	2:2–19		
Habakkuk's worship of Jehovah (Third prayer)	2:20–3:19		17

Divine titles: Holy One (1:12, 3:3), Mighty God (1:12), the Lord of hosts (2:13)
FPSP First person singular divine pronouns
3PSP Third person singular divine pronouns

Table 5.3 Encountering the God of Zephaniah, the final judgment of Palestine

Description	Reference	FPSP	3PSP
Jehovah judges Judah for syncretism	1:1–6	7	1
Zephaniah comments	1:7		2
Jehovah judges Judah for social injustices	1:8–10	2	
Zephaniah comments	1:11		

Jehovah judges Judah for apathy	1:12–13	1	1
Zephaniah comments	1:14–16		
Jehovah judges all sin	1:17	1	
Zephaniah comments	1:18		2
Zephaniah comments about Philistia	2:1–5		1
Jehovah's judgment of Philistia	2:5	1	
Elaboration on the judgment of Philistia	2:6–7		
Jehovah's judgment of Moab and Ammon	2:8–9	5	
Elaboration on the judgment of Moab and Ammon	2:10–11		2
Jehovah's judgment of Ethiopia	2:12	1	
The judgment of Assyria	2:13–15		3
Zephaniah speaks concerning Babylon	3:1–5		4
Jehovah's judgment of Babylon	3:6–13	20	1
Zephaniah speaks concerning Judah's restoration	3:14–17		5
Jehovah's final words of consolation	3:18–20	8	

Divine titles: the Lord of hosts (2:9, 10), the God of Israel (2:9), The Just Lord (3:5), the King of Israel (3:15)
FPSP First person singular divine pronouns
3PSP Third person singular divine pronouns

References

1999. *The King James Bible Commentary.* Thomas Nelson Publishers.

2007. *The Wiersbe Bible Commentary: Old Testament.* David C. Cook.

Baxter, J. Sidlow. *Baxter's Explore the Book.*

1973. *All the Messianic Prophecies of the Bible.* The Zondervan Corporation.

2011. *The Bible in World History.* Barbour Publishing.

Encountering the God of the prophets of Judah's Captivity (Jeremiah, Ezekiel, and Daniel)

Jeremiah, Ezekiel, and Daniel each lived during the fall of Jerusalem to the mighty Babylonian Empire in 586 BC. Each of these men had a number of encounters with the same divine person they all knew as Jehovah. Books of the Bible bearing their names enumerate each man's encounters with Jehovah and give a fairly comprehensive understanding of how each man perceived Jehovah. The encounters of Jeremiah, Ezekiel, and Daniel with Jehovah cover nearly a century of Jewish history, extending from 627 BC to 537 BC.

The world of the people of Israel and Judah changed forever with the rise of the Assyrian Empire. Much of the history of the people of Israel during this time can be confirmed by extra-biblical references in Assyrian literature and archaeology and was discussed in previous chapters. Israel, the northern kingdom, fell at the hands of the mighty Assyrian Empire around 722–721 BC. Judah, the southern kingdom, having failed to learn from Jehovah's judgment upon the northern kingdom, met its demise about one hundred and forty years later at the hands of the Neo-Babylonian Empire that supplanted the Assyrian Empire. The historicity of the persons and events documented within the pages of the Bible that were contemporary with this epoch of history can also be firmly established by extra-biblical references.

The history of the Neo-Babylonian Empire is preserved in the Babylonian Chronicles. The Babylonian Chronicles are a series of archaeological findings with inscriptions that detail the activities of the Chaldean kings that ruled during the century in which Babylon took Judah into captivity. The historicity of several significant biblical events and characters are established by these important extra-biblical inscriptions.

In 609 BC, Judah had fallen into the hands of the Egyptians after the death of King Josiah at the Battle of Megiddo (2 Kings 23:28–37; 2 Chronicles 35:20–27). Egyptian and Assyrian sources confirm this historical event. Jeremiah and Daniel both directly or indirectly reference Nebuchadnezzar's subsequent conquest of Pharaoh Necho II and his armies at the Battle of Carchemish and the initial capture of some of Judah's people in 605 BC.

The Battle of Carchemish is the major historical event mentioned in the Babylonian Chronicles that ties to the biblical event referenced in Jeremiah 46:1–12, Daniel 1:1–7, 2 Kings 24:1–4, and 2 Chronicles 36:5–8. Daniel and the three Hebrew boys (Daniel 1–3) were among Nebuchadnezzar's captives taken in 605 BC.

When Judah rebelled against Nebuchadnezzar, a second Babylonian invasion occurred in 598–597 BC. This invasion is the subject of Jeremiah's writings in Jeremiah 24, 27, 29, 50, and 51. Ezekiel and Jeconiah were among the captives taken by Nebuchadnezzar in this invasion. The Babylonian Chronicles make reference to Jeconiah and the rations afforded him by Nebuchadnezzar, thus confirming his historicity extra-biblically. The Bible references the events of this second invasion in 2 Kings 24:5–19 and 2 Chronicles 36:9–10.

A third Babylonian siege and invasion of Judah led to the ultimate fall of Judah to the Babylonians and the seventy-year captivity of which Jeremiah prophesied in Jeremiah 25:1–14. This final siege occurred between 588–586 BC and is chronicled in several chapters of Jeremiah including 31–34 and 37–42. The writers of 2 Kings 24:20–25:7 and 2 Chronicles 36:11–21 also capture this historical event which is confirmed by extra-biblical documentation in the Babylonian Chronicles.

One final piece of archaeological evidence confirming the historicity of Jeremiah is the clay bullae which have been found that belonged to his friend and scribe, Baruch. These clay bullae bear the inscription of Baruch. Jeremiah makes mention of Baruch in Jeremiah 36 and 45.

The historicity of the Great King Nebuchadnezzar, which was questioned at one time, is now an unquestionable fact of history. Daniel emerges as a person, prophet, and writer as a captive of the Great King Nebuchadnezzar. Ezekiel's encounters with Jehovah all occur as a captive under this same historical figure, Nebuchadnezzar.

Other significant historical figures and events were contemporary with the experiences and writings of Jeremiah, Daniel, and Ezekiel. The rise of the classical Greek city-states of Sparta and Athens occurred during the lifetime of Jeremiah, Daniel, and Ezekiel. Pythagoras, a Greek mathematician of "Pythagorean Theorem" fame, was probably born around 570 BC. Siddhartha Gautama, born a prince, eventually abandoned his royal inheritance and set out to achieve a state of inner peace called nirvana. Once he achieved this state, he became known as Buddha and was the father of the well-known religion of Buddhism. Buddha was born around 563 BC. The famous Chinese philosopher, teacher, and politician known as Confucius was born on September 28, 551 BC. He taught a code of moral and ethical behavior to be implemented in the daily lives of all people of all social ranks to live a good, useful, and harmonious existence. The Babylonian Empire under King Nebuchadnezzar, the Greek city-states, Pythagoras, Buddha, and Confucius were all contemporary with Jeremiah, Daniel, and Ezekiel.

Jeremiah, Daniel, and Ezekiel each encountered a divine person they all called Jehovah. Jeremiah had over sixty encounters with Jehovah. All of his encounters occurred in Jerusalem and Egypt during the final years and eventual fall of Judah. Daniel likely knew of Jeremiah before he was taken captive by Nebuchadnezzar's armies. Daniel encountered Jehovah while living in a foreign country, far removed from Jeremiah. Ezekiel also writes of his encounters with

Jehovah while living in a foreign country into which he was taken captive by the Babylonians.

Each of these three men, however, describes a divine person Whose attributes are the same and are consistent with the God Whom their fathers had described. Thus, the understandings and perceptions about Jehovah are consistent among the prophets who lived during Judah's captivity and among men who were spread across a wide geographical area during the same historical era. Importantly, the attributes of the Jehovah of these men are also consistent with those described in the encounters of the prophets who preceded them.

Encountering Jehovah with Jeremiah

Jeremiah was probably the son of Hilkiah, the high priest that found the book of the law that ignited the national revival that occurred under Josiah (2 Kings 22:8–13). He was contemporary with Huldah, the prophetess (2 Kings 22:14–20). He was probably familiar with—if not contemporary with—the ministries of Zephaniah and Habakkuk which may have concluded just before his birth or during his early years. Approximately sixty years after the death of the great prophet Isaiah who had prophesied the coming Babylonian captivity around 700 BC (Isaiah 39:5–7), Jehovah called Jeremiah.

Jeremiah can be characterized as an initially unwilling spokesman for Jehovah, called to a ministerial post that was inconsistent—at least in Jeremiah's own mind—with his character. As Jeremiah's life experiences would bear out, his ministry was also consistently distasteful and unacceptable to the audience to which Jehovah sent him. Jeremiah's ministry grieved him. The judgment that his people suffered because of their unwillingness to accept his divinely inspired counsel also grieved him. He was a meek and sensitive young man with a heart for his people. He was called to a challenging and confrontational ministry in a final effort to turn their hearts to Jehovah before an inevitable and harsh judgment was released upon them for their centuries of transgressions against their covenant relationship with Him.

To accomplish his ministry, Jeremiah had to know Jehovah intimately, know Jehovah's voice, understand Jehovah's character, and trust Jehovah's omniscience, omnipotence, and sovereignty, knowing that He was able to accomplish all that He spoke to him. Jeremiah had over sixty direct encounters with Jehovah beginning during the reign of Josiah and ending after Judah fell into the seventy-year period of captivity to Babylon which Jehovah had foretold. Let's examine Jeremiah's encounters with his God.

Eight encounters during the revival under Josiah:

1. *Jeremiah's call at Anathoth/The rod of the almond tree (1:4–12).*
2. *Jeremiah's call at Anathoth/The seething pot (1:13–19).*
3. *Jeremiah sent from Anathoth to Jerusalem (2:1–3).*
4. *Jeremiah's initial message to Jerusalem (2:4–3:5).*
5. *Jeremiah's specific initial message to Israel (3:6–4:2).*
6. *Jeremiah's specific initial message to Judah (4:3–5:4).*
7. *Jeremiah's message to the great men of Jerusalem (5:5–31).*
8. *Jeremiah's message to the children of Benjamin (6:1–30).*

Jeremiah's first eight historically documented encounters with Jehovah occurred during the reign of Judah's last good king, Josiah (2 Kings 22:1–23:28; 2 Chronicles 34:1–35:19). Jeremiah's first two encounters were Jehovah's call and subsequent confirmation of His call to Jeremiah to serve as His prophet. Like Moses in 1446 BC (Exodus 3:1–4:17), Jeremiah was reluctant to embrace his call and offered several excuses before accepting his commission after Jehovah offered His reassurances (Jeremiah 1:4–10).

Integral to the ministry that Jehovah had for Jeremiah was the message that if they rejected revival at this time, judgment was imminent. In these first two encounters, Jehovah's message to Jeremiah of the impending judgment upon Judah was illustrated by two visions. One vision was of a rod of an almond tree and the second was of a seething pot. Both visions communicated the fact that the nation of Babylon was waiting to spring into military action as Jehovah's instrument of judgment against His chosen people (Jeremiah 1:11–19).

After the gravity of his prophetic message had simmered in his spirit long enough, Jeremiah's third encounter with Jehovah was his actual launching into his primary prophetic ministry field, Jerusalem (Jeremiah 2:1–3). In these three initial divine encounters, Jehovah used twenty-two first person singular divine pronouns in reference to Himself. Jeremiah used two third person singular divine pronouns in reference to Jehovah. It is apparent that Jeremiah believes that he is encountering a divine person—the same person Who had called Moses, the human author of the once lost and now recovered written law. The freshly recovered law of Moses was the founding document upon which the covenant relationship of Jehovah with Israel and Judah was based.

Jeremiah begins his prophetic ministry around 627–626 BC. His next five historically documented divine encounters are likely only a small sample of the messages Jehovah prompted him to deliver during the national revival under King Josiah. In Jehovah's fourth recorded encounter with Jeremiah, He questions the reason for Judah's abandonment of their covenant relationship with Him throughout history since the time of His initial rescue of the nation from enslavement by Egypt (Jeremiah 2:5–8).

Despite being aghast by the nation's abysmal and offensive choice to abandon Him, the fountain of living waters, to pursue broken cisterns that can hold no water (idol gods), Jehovah pleads with the nation to return into their covenant relationship with Him (Jeremiah 2:9–13). Jeremiah's God is a compassionate and forgiving person Who seeks to preserve His covenant relationship with His chosen people but Who will judge those who opt to live in transgression in defiance of His pleas. For the remainder of this encounter (Jeremiah 2:4–3:4), Jehovah reminds Jeremiah—and through him, He reminds the people—that He has endured this covenant violation repeatedly and had His pleas repeatedly rejected (see Jeremiah 2:9, 13, 32). In Jeremiah 3:5, Jeremiah wonders how much longer Jehovah can endure this mistreatment.

In His fifth encounter with Jeremiah, Jehovah reminds Jeremiah (and, through him, the people) of the northern kingdom's transgressions and judgment. This is an attempt by Jehovah to stir His people to learn from this recent example of the ultimate consequences for rebellion against covenant relationship (3:6–10). The mercy, compassion, and heart of Jehovah for relationship is clearly seen by His words in Jeremiah 3:12,14,15, and 19. Jehovah refers to Himself as a husband and a father and to His people as His family. He remains willing to restore the covenant relationship and forgive them if they will return to Him (3:22, 4:1). An undetermined amount of time passes as Jeremiah continues his plea to the people on behalf of Jehovah; but the people fail to respond to Jeremiah's message.

In His sixth encounter with Jeremiah, Jehovah declares the inevitability of His judgment upon Judah (see Jeremiah 4:3–6,12,27–28). Still, Jehovah displays His mercifulness (4:27). In Jeremiah's desperate attempt to evade Jehovah's judgment, he turns to communicate a message from Jehovah to the leaders, the great men of Jerusalem (5:4–31). Jehovah's seventh message to Jeremiah is wasted upon them.

The nature of Jeremiah's God is evinced in 5:18,22,24–25. He is merciful. He is the good and sovereign ruler over the "forces of nature" that result in the abundant life Judah takes for granted. Yet another message to another segment of the population goes unheeded in Jehovah's eighth encounter with Jeremiah (Jeremiah 6). No doubt, these are only a small representation of Jehovah's messages to Judah during the national revival under Josiah.

The five messages that Jeremiah received from Jehovah during Josiah's national revival and documented for the record of history give a great deal of information about the character of Jeremiah's God. While conveying these messages, Jehovah used approximately 100 first person singular divine pronouns referring to Himself. Ten third person singular divine pronouns are littered throughout these five encounters. Instead of being the capricious, vindictive, judgmental person of which He is often accused by the uninformed (Christian and non-Christian alike), Jeremiah's God is a patient, kind, merciful, divine person. He has sought the good of His covenant people for centuries and continues to call them to covenant relationship.

Ultimately, however, He releases them to experience the consequences of their transgressions. He knows the consequences of their choices but respects their free will to choose a consequence He has foretold about 800 hundred years before Jeremiah's ministry began (Deuteronomy 31:16–21).

In the course of Jeremiah's call and the early years of his ministry under the reign of King Josiah, Jeremiah heard Jehovah use over 120 first person singular divine pronouns in reference to Himself. A dozen third person singular divine pronouns are also present in the record of history during this part of Jeremiah's ministry. Jeremiah, who was reluctant to be Jehovah's spokesperson for a ministry of judgment and confrontation, learns over these early years that Jehovah is the sovereign, omnipotent, omniscient ruler of the earth. However, he also comes to understand that Jehovah is a divine person Who is full of mercy, kindness, long-suffering, and patience. He comes to see how Jehovah has endured hundreds of years of relationship transgressions against Himself by His chosen people. In the early part of his ministry, Jeremiah witnesses that Jehovah is still trying to call His people back to the covenant relationship that He desires to share with them.

Six encounters around the death of Josiah, the capture of Jehoahaz, and during the early reign of Jehoiakim:

9. *Lament for Josiah and Jehoahaz, early instructions to Jehoiakim (22:1-17).*
10. *Early instructions to Judah under Jehoiakim (26:1-6).*
11. *Temple sermon under Jehoiakim (7:1-8:3).*
12. *Aftermath of Temple sermon (26:7-30).*
13. *To the men of Judah concerning the covenant (11).*
14. *Jehovah counsels Jeremiah concerning His delayed fulfillment of Judah's judgment (12).*

After Josiah's death in the Battle of Megiddo in 609 BC (2 Kings 23:29–37; 2 Chronicles 35:20–36:4), Jeremiah saw the beginning of the end for Judah. He lamented the death of a king that was supportive of Jehovah's mission to turn the hearts of the nation back to Him and began to instruct a new king and an increasingly hardhearted nation. The tone of Jeremiah's ministry began to harden after nearly two decades of pleading with the people to turn back to Jehovah.

Jeremiah's next six encounters with Jehovah occur between 609 BC and 605 BC. In one of these encounters, Jehovah gives instructions about the continued lamenting over the death of Josiah and the deportation of Jehoahaz. Then, over a series of encounters, Jehovah addresses the indiscretions of the new king, Jehoiakim, and the increasingly godless nation.

Jehovah's ninth encounter with Jeremiah occurred at least three to six months after the Battle of Megiddo. Josiah was dead. Jehoahaz had been captured and enough time had passed so that Jehoiakim's predisposition as monarch could be assessed (Jeremiah 22:10–12). Jeremiah lamented the death of Josiah (2 Chronicles 35:25), as did the nation of Judah. Jehovah instructed Jeremiah to tell Jehoiakim not to lament Josiah or Jehoahaz any longer but to live righteously or face imminent judgment (Jeremiah 22:1–17). Jehovah's tenth encounter with Jeremiah is a command to give a separate but similar message to the people at the beginning of Jehoiakim's reign (Jeremiah 26:1–6).

Jeremiah's famous temple sermon (Jeremiah 7:1–8:3) is a complex and pivotal message that was given shortly after these two encounters. Jehovah's instructions to Jeremiah concerning this sermon comprise the eleventh historically documented encounter between the two persons. The people of Judah are instructed to amend their ways with a promise of restoration if they do (7:3–7). Judgment is promised if they refuse (7:8–15). The most stinging verse in this encounter between Jehovah and Jeremiah is Jehovah's instruction to Jeremiah to refrain from even praying for the people because He would not hear this prayer as judgment was imminent (7:16). Moreover, Jehovah spoke to Jeremiah of the futility, even the travesty of Judah's sacrifices to Him and to idols; He was never concerned about sacrifices. Obedience and a covenant relationship were His desires from the beginning (7:22–23,31). The Temple sermon is strikingly similar to the message Samuel spoke to Saul around 1028 BC after the slaughter of the Amalekites (1 Samuel 15:22). A brief probing into the Temple sermon will prove instructive from a historical perspective.

As Jehovah prepares Jeremiah to deliver the Temple sermon, He makes some important teaching points and gives some historical references to the prophet. Jehovah establishes that behaviors consistent with His covenant are essential for those in covenant relationship with Him. Lip service alone, with the expectation of receiving the benefits of covenant relationship, is a misguided undertaking (7:6–11). By mentioning Shiloh, Jehovah makes reference to the fall of the northern kingdom which had occurred about 100 years previously in 722–721 BC (7:12–15). This was a historical fact, not a mere allegory. This reference also connects the delivery of the Temple sermon with the next event in Jeremiah's life, the rebellion of the people against Jeremiah with an intent to kill him (26:7–30).

Jehovah also made a historical reference to His time with Israel at Sinai in 1446 BC (Exodus and Leviticus). The primary purpose of His encounters with them at that time was not to establish rituals of sacrificial worship, but principles of covenant relationship (7:21–26). When accusations and threats were levied against Jeremiah after he delivered the Temple sermon, one defense of Jeremiah by those who opposed the move to punish him for the words he spoke during the sermon was a historical reference to Micah.

Micah had prophesied during the days of Hezekiah, during the eighth century BC (Jeremiah 26:18 and Micah 1:1). Ahikam, the son of Shaphan advocated for Jeremiah at this time. Shaphan had served alongside Hilkiah, the father of Jeremiah, and there was possibly some allegiance between Ahikam and Jeremiah because of the close relationships of their two families. Having escaped punishment, Jeremiah continued the work of ministry he had been given by Jehovah.

Jeremiah's thirteenth encounter with Jehovah occurred not long after the aforementioned threatening encounter with the leaders of Judah. This time, Jehovah instructed Jeremiah to review the words of the covenant and speak to the people of Judah to encourage them to obey the covenant, to remind them of how their fathers had also transgressed the covenant, and to inform them of the consequences of continued transgression of the covenant (Jeremiah 11).

As he had done in the Temple sermon (7:16), Jehovah instructed Jeremiah not to pray for the people because He would not hear this prayer (11:14). That this encounter followed the Temple sermon (Jeremiah 7) and the subsequent death threats upon Jeremiah (26:7–24) is clear, because in 11:19, Jeremiah describes the death threats. In Jeremiah 11:20, Jeremiah prays to Jehovah for help, and in Jeremiah 11:21–23, Jehovah answers Jeremiah's prayer with a proclamation of judgment upon his persecutors.

In a subsequent encounter, Jeremiah expressed his gratitude for God's care of him, but he questioned Jehovah's delay in judgment upon the wrongdoers of Judah. In Jeremiah 12:5, Jehovah counseled Jeremiah that neither he nor the people were quite ready for the next phase of judgment, because "If thou hast run with the footmen, and they have wearied thee, then how canst thou contend with horses?" Jehovah assures Jeremiah that though judgment is delayed, at this point it is certain as is restoration after judgment.

During the earliest part of Jehoiakim's reign, Jeremiah had six historically documented encounters with Jehovah. All of these encounters were instructional in nature. Jehovah gave instructions to Jeremiah and, through Jeremiah, to the people of Judah as well. While Jeremiah heeded the instructions given by Jehovah, the people of Judah were not necessarily as receptive to Jehovah's messages through the prophet.

Jeremiah experienced persecution as a result of being Jehovah's messenger and grew impatient with the fact that the judgment of which Jehovah spoke seemed to be ever in the future and never in the present. Jeremiah did not foresee that the first wave of invasions by the Babylonians was less than a year in the future, and neither he nor the people were really ready for what was to come.

Through these encounters, we can see that Jehovah is omniscient, omnipotent, sovereign, patient, and kind. Though judgment is coming, Jehovah permits it to come with some sense of timing that considers the ultimate good of His chosen people. Jehovah's concern for His people is evinced by this consideration. His concern for His prophet is also demonstrable. In these six encounters, during the earliest part of Jehoiakim's reign, Jehovah used 108 first person singular divine pronouns. Six third person singular divine pronouns are seen in this portion of the historical account of Jeremiah's ministry.

Jeremiah's remaining encounters with Jehovah before Babylon's first invasion of Jerusalem:

15. *Certifying the first Babylonian invasion of Jerusalem (8:4-10:16).*
16. *Jeremiah sent to get a linen girdle (13:1-2).*
17. *Jeremiah sent to hide the linen girdle at Euphrates (13:3-5).*
18. *Jeremiah sent to recover the linen girdle (13:6-7).*
19. *Jeremiah's receives the message concerning the linen girdle (13:8-14).*
20. *Jeremiah pleads for mercy (13:15-27).*
21. *Jeremiah sent to the potter's house (18:1-2).*
22. *The message of the potter and the clay (18:5-11).*
23. *Judah's judgment and Jeremiah's persecution for preaching (18:13-23).*

During the next year or so, Jeremiah's ministry begins to crescendo as the imminence of the Babylonian invasion bears down upon the people of Judah. While Jeremiah does not know when this invasion will occur, his divine counselor, Jehovah, is omniscient and is well-aware. A series of nine divine encounters between Jeremiah and Jehovah occurred between 606 BC and Nebuchadnezzar's first invasion of Jerusalem in 605 BC. The first of these, though a separate encounter, can hardly be distinguished from Jehovah's encounter with Jeremiah in preparation for the Temple sermon. This encounter is recorded in Jeremiah 8:4–10:16.

In 8:7, Jehovah expresses to Jeremiah how Judah's responses to Him are contrary to the natural course of things. In 8:11, Jehovah declares that though false prophets have spoken peace over Judah, the good feeling that resulted from these false proclamations will be short-lived.

Sensing the nearness of Jehovah's judgment because of his relationship with Jehovah, Jeremiah lamented the state of his people. It is with this sense of inescapable judgment that Jeremiah records one of his most famous sayings of the period before Nebuchadnezzar's first invasion. In Jeremiah 8:20–22, Jeremiah says, "The harvest is past, the summer is ended, and we are not saved. For the hurt of the daughter of my people am I hurt; I am black; astonishment hath taken hold on me. Is there no balm in Gilead; is there no physician there? Why then is not the health of the daughter of my people recovered?" It is a lament of Judah's failure to respond to Jehovah's calls for repentance, Judah's failure to respond to Jehovah's presence and desire to heal and restore the nation.

As this fifteenth encounter between Jehovah and Jeremiah goes on, Jehovah describes for Jeremiah the destruction and judgment coming on Judah. Jeremiah expresses his dread repeatedly (9:4–6,10,18–21). Jehovah rejects Judah's smugness for being His chosen nation of people, instead telling Jeremiah to convey a message of national judgment and individual responsibility for relationship with the Lord. In Jehovah's words can be found the fact that He is loving and kind; yet, He is also a righteous judge.

Throughout history, this completeness of Jehovah as a person—the ability to judge righteously and impartially, independent of His relationship with the party being judged—has been demonstrated. On this occasion, Jehovah says, "Let not the wise man glory in his wisdom, neither let the mighty man glory in his might, let not the rich man glory in his riches: But let him that glorieth glory in this, that he understandeth and knoweth Me, that I am the LORD which exercise lovingkindness, judgment, and righteousness, in the earth: for in these things I delight," saith the LORD (Jer. 9:23–24 KJV).

Jehovah further explains that the basis of His coming judgment upon His chosen people and others among humanity is the fact that they have chosen to walk in their human desires rather than seeking to pursue the spiritual relationship He has desired and pursued with them. He describes this as a state of uncircumcision. Uncircumcision is such a concise and descriptive expression. It reflects the fact that a degree of fleshly response is natural, expected, and acceptable. This humanness was created in man by God from the beginning. It is the excesses of the flesh that a person—or a nation—that desires a spiritual relationship with Jehovah is expected to lay aside. Failure to rid itself of the excesses of the flesh had brought Judah to the brink of judgment (Jeremiah 9:25–26).

Finally, after Jeremiah had received his instructions from Jehovah during their fifteenth encounter, he conveyed the message to the people as recorded in Jeremiah 10. In his message to the people, Jeremiah focused on Judah's incomprehensible decision to settle for the worship of idol gods instead of pursuing a relationship with Jehovah. This message gives tremendous insight into Jeremiah's perception of the person of Jehovah. He calls Jehovah not just the King of Judah, but the "King of nations" (Jeremiah 10:7). He recognized the sovereignty of Jehovah saying, "There is none like unto thee" (Jeremiah 10:8). He calls Jehovah the "True God," the "Living God," and the "Everlasting King" (Jeremiah 10:10).

In the mind of Jeremiah, these titles for Jehovah were well-earned based upon His works in creation—something Jeremiah considered factual. In Jeremiah 10:12–16, Jeremiah says this concerning Jehovah: "He hath made the earth by His power, He hath established the world by His wisdom, and hath stretched out the heavens by His discretion. When He uttereth His voice, there is a multitude of waters in the heavens, and He causeth the vapours to ascend from the ends of the earth; He maketh lightnings with rain, and bringeth forth the wind out of His treasures. Every man is brutish in his knowledge: every founder is confounded by the graven image: for his molten image is falsehood, and there is no breath in them. They are vanity, and the work of errors: in the time of their visitation they shall perish. The portion of Jacob is not like them: for He is the former of all things; and Israel is the rod of His inheritance: The LORD of hosts is His name."

Over the next year, before He allowed Nebuchadnezzar's first invasion of Jerusalem in 605 BC, two object lessons were used by Jehovah to express how He felt about His relationship with Judah and their transgressions against Him. The object lesson of the marred linen girdle required five encounters between Jeremiah and Jehovah. These are recorded in Jeremiah 13.

Jeremiah 13:11 is a concise summary of the message of Jehovah through this object lesson. It conveys Jehovah's initial expectations of His chosen people, the intimacy with which He perceived His relationship with them and their utter disrespect for His plans and purposes. The actions of the people of Judah, known by Jehovah before He initiated this relationship and borne out by history time and again, drew this conclusion by Jeremiah: "Can the Ethiopian change his skin, or the leopard his spots? Then may ye also do good, that are accustomed to doing evil" (Jer. 13:23, KJV). Though their actions were not going to change and judgment was therefore certain, Jeremiah pleaded on their behalf with Jehovah.

Jehovah gave Jeremiah one further object lesson concerning His relationship with Judah and the judgment that was coming upon them. This famous object lesson is recorded in Jeremiah 18 and required three additional divine encounters between Jeremiah and Jehovah. Jeremiah was sent to observe a potter work. During his observations, Jeremiah received a message from Jehovah. The message from Jehovah is recorded in Jeremiah 18:5–11 and is simply "O house of Israel, cannot I do with you as this potter? saith the LORD. Behold, as the clay is in the potter's hand, so are ye in mine hand, O house of Israel" (Jer. 18:6, KJV).

The nation rejected Jehovah's object lessons and persecuted Jehovah's messenger, Jeremiah (18:18). Jeremiah, in the midst of another series of persecutions for his preaching, turns his praying against the people (18:19–23).

The messages of Jehovah certifying the coming of the first Babylonian invasion of Judah and the two object lessons given to help the people understand what was going to soon come upon them transpired over several months before Nebuchadnezzar's first invasion of Jerusalem in 605 BC. These messages involved nine divine encounters between Jeremiah and Jehovah. Jehovah used fifty-four first person singular divine pronouns during these encounters with Jeremiah. There are no less than eighteen third person singular divine pronouns referencing Jehovah during these months leading up to Nebuchadnezzar's invasion in 605 BC.

CHAPTER SIX

Encountering Jehovah Surrounding Babylon's First Invasion of Jerusalem

When he became king of Judah, Jehoiakim was initially subservient to the Babylonians. He later rebelled against Nebuchadnezzar with some reassurances from Egypt. In 605 BC, the Babylonians reasserted their authority over him. They invaded Jerusalem and took many of its people captive. Daniel and the three Hebrew boys were among those taken captive in Babylon's first invasion of Jerusalem. Events pertaining to this piece of history are the subject of 2 Kings 24:1–4, 2 Chronicles 36:5–8, and Daniel 1:1–7.

Jeremiah has two encounters with Jehovah which address the accompanying fates of Philistia (Jeremiah 47) and Egypt (Jeremiah 46:1–12) during this incursion by Nebuchadnezzar. The span of time from Nebuchadnezzar's first invasion of Jerusalem until his second invasion was very trying for Jeremiah. During most of this period of great hardship, Jehoiakim continued to be Judah's king. Jeremiah's ministry became increasingly despised by Jehoiakim and the people of Judah. Including the prophecies concerning Egypt and Philistia, Jeremiah had sixteen documented encounters with Jehovah relating to Babylon's first invasion of Jerusalem.

Jeremiah was in hiding at the time that he had his next five divine encounters after the prophecies against Philistia and Egypt. In Jeremiah 36:2–3, after Nebuchadnezzar's 605 BC invasion, Jeremiah is instructed to write the words spoken to him by Jehovah since the beginning of his prophetic ministry in a scroll. Baruch, Jeremiah's scribe, performed this task at Jeremiah's request. Baruch read this scroll in the temple (Jeremiah 36:5–8).

Jeremiah 25:1–10 seems to look forward to additional hardships upon Jerusalem at the hands of Nebuchadnezzar and may have occurred while Jeremiah was still in hiding, and Baruch was reading Jeremiah's scroll in his stead. After reading the scroll in the temple, Baruch then read it to other audiences including the princes (Jeremiah 36:11–32). The king ultimately had Jeremiah's scroll burned because its contents were so reprehensible to him in pronouncing the ultimate demise of his kingdom. In his twenty-eighth encounter, Jeremiah is instructed to write another scroll to replace the one destroyed by the leaders of Judah. Jehoiakim's demise is also addressed. Jehovah gave Jeremiah words of encouragement for Baruch in his twenty-ninth encounter with Him (Jeremiah 45).

It would be unthinkable that Jeremiah would be unaffected emotionally by the burden of his ministry and the social and political opposition against him. In fact, he is so burdened by the weight of his ministry that his petition to Jehovah in Jeremiah 15:10–21 reads very much like the petition and burden of Job over a millennium before him (see Jeremiah 15:10, 15–18, and Job 3). It also resembles the petitions of Moses in 1445 BC (Num. 11:14-15) and Elijah in 858 BC (1 Kings 19:4).

After speaking to Jeremiah to give words of reassurance to Baruch (Jeremiah 45), Jehovah has to encourage His prophet who is strained under the weight of the ministry given to him (Jeremiah 15:11–14 and 19–21). He tells Jeremiah, "I am with thee to save thee;" and, "I will cause the enemy to entreat thee well in the time of evil and in the time of affliction." We see this divine proclamation fulfilled when Jerusalem falls in 586 BC (Jeremiah 40:1–5).

With Jehovah's encouragement, Jeremiah came out of hiding (Jeremiah 15:19–21, 36:5) and commenced his prophetic ministry against the people of the distressed kingdom of Judah. Jeremiah 14:1–15:9 is a record of Jehovah's encounter with Jeremiah in which He instructs Jeremiah to prophesy of more war and famine in Judah (Jeremiah 14:2–6, 15:1–9).

This portion of the scriptural account of history is particularly heart wrenching because Jeremiah, the victim of persecution at the hands of his fellow Judeans, pleads through his own tears as he intercedes in prayer for them (Jeremiah 14:7–10,13,17–22). Jehovah, Who has been a lover of His people over the centuries and has pursued intimate fellowship with them for generations, responds to Jeremiah's intercession during their conversation by telling him, "Pray not for this people for their good. When they fast, I will not hear their cry; and when they offer burnt offering and an oblation, I will not accept them: but I will consume them by the sword, and by the famine, and by the pestilence" (Jer. 14:11–12).

No doubt, Jehovah is saddened by the fact that His relationship with His chosen people has come to this point. He reaches back in His memory to recall great men of Israel's past who had responded to His calls for intimate fellowship and uses them as examples to Jeremiah. He tells Jeremiah, "Though Moses and Samuel stood before Me, yet My mind could not be toward this people: cast them out of My sight, and let them go forth" (Jer. 15:1).

This conversation between Jeremiah and Jehovah takes place between 604 and 599 BC. This is about 440 years after Samuel's heartfelt intercessions before Jehovah for His people around 1045–1040 BC (1 Samuel 8) and about 840 years after Moses's intercession for the nation at Sinai in 1446 BC (Exodus 32:7–15). Jehovah remembers these great men by name to Jeremiah and tells him that even these legendary men of Israel could not prevent the judgment that Judah had chosen by their actions over the centuries. As He had done in two separate conversations with Jeremiah in 609 BC (Jeremiah 7:16, 11:14), Jehovah again reluctantly dissuades the prophet from interceding on the behalf of His people (Jeremiah 14:11).

Jeremiah's instructions to prophesy the doom and destruction coming on Judah are continued in his next encounter with Jehovah. In Jeremiah 16:1–17:18, Jeremiah is instructed to speak of the ultimate fall of Jerusalem and captivity of Judah. In this, Jeremiah's thirty-second divine encounter, he is told not to marry because of the heartbreak he would experience as a father and husband watching his family endure the coming hardships (Jeremiah 16:2). At this point, Jeremiah has come to understand the love, compassion, goodness, and kindness of Jehovah and knows that the evil that is coming is not a reflection of Jehovah being evil. The coming doom and captivity is a reflection of Judah's rejection of the peace, lovingkindness, and mercies (16:5) of the Lord of hosts and the God of Israel (16:9). Jehovah reiterates these points in this conversation with Jeremiah (16:9–13).

True to His pattern over the course of history, Jehovah attaches a ray of hope to His verdict of judgment (16:14–15). Jeremiah and his status as one in intimate fellowship with Jehovah is distinguished from the nation as a whole during this conversation. Through his hardships, and in the face of the coming destruction, Jeremiah has chosen to place his confidence in Jehovah, the person Whom he calls "my strength, my fortress, and my refuge in the day of affliction" (16:19). Jehovah says to Jeremiah, "Cursed be the man that trusteth in man, and maketh flesh his arm, and whose heart departeth from Jehovah... Blessed is the man that trusteth in Jehovah, and whose hope Jehovah is" (17:5–7).

It is during this conversation, around 604–599 BC, that Jehovah makes the oft-quoted statement, "The heart is deceitful above all things, and desperately wicked: who can know it? I the Lord search the heart, I try the reins, even to give every man according to his ways, and according to the fruit of his doings" (17:9–10).

Being reminded of this, yet feeling the burden of oppression by his people, and a burden to not see his people go into captivity, Jeremiah asks Jehovah, the hope of Israel and the fountain of living waters (17:13), for His help (17:12–18).

Not long after this, Jeremiah has his thirty-third encounter with Jehovah. In this encounter, Jehovah sends him to preach against Judah's disregard of the Sabbath day while standing at the gate of the city (17:19–27). Next, Jehovah sends Jeremiah to offer wine to the Rechabites (35:1–2), knowing well of the integrity and faithfulness of this family to the commission which they received from Jonadab, the son of Rechab (35:4–11). From this encounter and the refusal of the Rechabites to transgress their covenant, Jehovah gave Jeremiah his next lesson to teach the men of Judah. This family was faithful and obedient to their father. Judah was unfaithful and disobedient to their father, the God of hosts, the God of Israel (35:16). These events were recorded as Jeremiah's thirty-fourth and thirty-fifth encounters with Jehovah.

Jeremiah then proceeds to lament the fact that there is an abundance of false prophets in Judah (23:9–10). Jehovah makes clear during this thirty-sixth encounter with Jeremiah His disdain for the prophet who claims to speak for Him when He has not spoken to them. Repeatedly, He tells Jeremiah, "I am against them," and He proclaims their coming judgment for misleading His people. Identifying Himself as the One Who is the only source of truth,

Jehovah used forty first person singular divine pronouns during this single exchange with Jeremiah.

During this same time frame of approximately five years (604–599 BC), Jeremiah was also sent to Tophet to preach a sermon concerning the broken vessel to the elders among the people and the priests (Jeremiah 19). In this object lesson, Jeremiah is instructed to take the vessel and break it to illustrate how the ways of the nation and the relationship of the nation to Jehovah are broken because they have worshipped idol gods and even sacrificed their young to these idols.

During his fifty-five-year reign between 697–642 BC, Manasseh had led the people to the deepest level of idol worship in the history of Judah (2 Kings 21:1–18). Manasseh's son, Amon, maintained the idolatrous practices of his father (2 Kings 21:18–22; 2 Chronicles 33:20–25). Jehovah's promise of judgment for the transgressions that occurred in the days of Manasseh (2 Kings 21:11–15) was going to be fulfilled in the days of Jeremiah in 586 BC.

Pashur, chief governor in the Temple, was getting fed up with the ongoing antagonistic prophetic ministry of Jeremiah. He used his political influence to try to put a stop to Jeremiah's work. He had Jeremiah imprisoned, according to Jeremiah 20. In Jeremiah's thirty-eighth encounter with Jehovah, Jehovah condemned the actions of Pashur and spoke of the coming destruction which Pashur did not believe would come (20:4–5).

Jeremiah is distraught by this turn of events. He had come out of hiding at the beckon of Jehovah and preached the messages of Jehovah, only to now find himself imprisoned for his obedience and his messages. During this imprisonment, sometime between 604 and 599 BC, Jeremiah uttered the famous confession, "Then I said, I will not make mention of Him, nor speak any more in His name. But His word was in mine heart as a burning fire shut up in my bones, and I was weary in forbearing, and I could not stay" (20:9). In the years just before 600 BC, Jehovah gave a final rebuke and admonishment of Jehoiakim and Jeconiah (22:18–30).

After Babylon's first assault on Jerusalem in 605 BC and before the second invasion in 597 BC, Jeremiah had sixteen historically documented encounters with Jehovah. His messages were perceived as unpatriotic, even heretical, by the people in general and by the people in positions of power in particular. This caused great resistance against his ministry. At one point, Jeremiah went into hiding and had to have Baruch deliver his messages for him. After coming out of hiding and boldly preaching, Jeremiah found himself imprisoned.

The weight of this unpopular ministry weighed heavily upon Jeremiah. However, Jeremiah found that he could not refrain from speaking the words of his Lord, his counselor, and his divine friend, Jehovah. Jeremiah's relationship with Jehovah was too valuable and his confidence in the person and promises of Jehovah were too strong to let him walk away from his commission. Jeremiah did not doubt the identity of the person he represented. He was the God of Moses and the God of Samuel. He was the maker of heaven and earth. He was the savior of Israel. He had used nearly 200 first person singular divine pronouns during the sixteen divine encounters with Jeremiah over the eight years between the first and second invasions by the Babylonians. Nineteen third person singular divine pronouns were used in reference to Jehovah in this phase of Jeremiah's ministry.

Encountering Jehovah During Nebuchadnezzar's Second Invasion of Judah

Jehoiakim and his son, Jehoiachin (a.k.a. Jeconiah), were eventually deposed from the throne of Judah by Nebuchadnezzar. Mattaniah (a.k.a. Zedekiah) was placed on the throne in their stead in 597 BC. The turbulent ending of the reign of Jehoiakim and the brief reign of Jehoiachin with their replacement by Zedekiah is recorded in 2 Kings 24:5–19 and 2 Chronicles 36:9–10. Five of Jeremiah's encounters with Jehovah occur during the time surrounding Nebuchadnezzar's second invasion of Judah. Three additional encounters occur after this invasion and before the beginning of the final three-year siege that ended in the fall of Jerusalem.

Jeremiah's ministry and his encounters with Jehovah around the time of Nebuchadnezzar's second invasion of Jerusalem are documented in Jeremiah 24–25, 27–29, and 48–51. Jeremiah's vision of the the two baskets of figs in front of the temple, the subject of Jeremiah 24, constituted his fortieth encounter with Jehovah. Interestingly, Jehovah's message to Jeremiah was that the good figs represented the captives taken by Nebuchadnezzar in 597 BC (including Ezekiel the prophet). He would preserve them and not the people that remained in Jerusalem after the second invasion.

Scholars believe that Jeremiah 27 deals with the reign of Zedekiah, though the name of Jehoiakim appears in 27:1 because of a translational error. In this encounter, Jeremiah's forty-first, Jehovah instructs Jeremiah to urge five gentile kings to submit to Nebuchadnezzar whom He called "My servant" (27:6). Jehovah promised destruction to the nation(s) that refused this mandate (27:8) and preservation to the nation(s) that obeyed (27:11). Zedekiah is also encouraged to be submissive to Nebuchadnezzar (27:12–22).

Later that same year, another prophet named Hananiah publicly challenged Jeremiah's assertion that Judah would go into captivity for a period of seventy years. Jeremiah had made this assertion based upon his twenty-seventh encounter with Jehovah—about the time of Nebuchadnezzar's first invasion of Jerusalem (Jeremiah 25:11).

During the second invasion, Jeremiah said that Jehovah declared that the people would serve Nebuchadnezzar, his son, and his son's son (Jeremiah 27:7). Hananiah, however, encouraged the people, saying that Jehovah had informed him that the power of the Babylonians would be broken within two years and the captives would return home (Jeremiah 28:2–4,11). Jeremiah, knowing the truth of the word he had received from Jehovah and that this was incompatible with the words being spoken by Hananiah, expressed his hope for the truth of Hananiah's prophecy. Then Jehovah spoke to Jeremiah, confirming His word to Jeremiah and informing him that Hananiah would soon die. Hananiah died within about two months of his last recorded false prophecy (28:17).

Jeremiah also sent at least two letters to the captives taken from Jerusalem to Babylon during the invasion of 597 BC. These letters were inspired by encounters with Jehovah. In the letter inspired by Jeremiah's forty-third divine encounter (29:1–29), Jehovah tells

Jeremiah to write that He (Jehovah) had ordained the captivity and that they should settle in for a long captivity. They were to build houses, plant gardens, marry, have children, and pray for the peace of the land, because they would be there seventy years (29:10). Jehovah goes on to explain the purpose and merit of the captivity and His intentions in allowing the captivity. In His explanation, Jehovah makes the oft-recited statement, "For I know the thoughts that I think toward you, thoughts of peace, and not of evil, to give you an expected end. Then shall ye call upon Me. And ye shall seek Me, and find Me, when ye shall search for Me with all of your heart" (29:10–13).

Jeremiah's second letter is the result of his forty-fourth divine encounter (29:30–32). It is a denouncement of Shemaiah, one of the false prophets among the captives. Through Jeremiah, Jehovah decries the false prophets among the captives who promise a shorter captivity than Jehovah has told Jeremiah the people would endure before restoration is granted. In these five encounters with Jeremiah, Jehovah uses seventy-three first person singular divine pronouns to reference Himself. Jeremiah, through these encounters, sees this divine person as omniscient, omnipresent, omnipotent, merciful, thoughtful, kind, and concerned. However, he understands as well that Jehovah is a God Who judges those who transgress His will and His purposes.

Three additional divine encounters between Jeremiah and Jehovah are documented before the final three-year siege of Jerusalem by Nebuchadnezzar, which began in 588 BC. In the first, the future judgment of Babylon is foretold. This encounter and the details of this judgment are recorded in Jeremiah 50 and 51. This prophecy, made between 597 and 590 BC, was fulfilled when Cyrus the Great toppled the Babylonian Empire around 539 BC. The judgment of other countries of Palestine is foretold in Jeremiah 48–49. The judgment of Judah and other nations is prophesied in Jeremiah 25:15–38.

The prophetic nature of these three additional divine encounters makes the fact that there are nearly 100 (ninety-three by my count) first person singular divine pronouns spoken by Jehovah about Himself of no surprise. Thirty-seven third person singular divine pronouns are also present in these chapters. The omnipotence and omniscience of Jeremiah's God are on full display in the foretelling of the judgments of nations, years before the judgments are fulfilled.

So from the time of Nebuchadnezzar's second invasion of Jerusalem in 597 BC to the beginning of Babylon's final siege of Jerusalem in 588 BC, Jeremiah had eight encounters with Jehovah. There are 170 first person singular divine pronouns and thirty-seven third person singular divine pronouns that are documented in these eight encounters.

Encountering Jehovah During Babylon's Third Siege of Jerusalem

In 588 BC, Nebuchadnezzar began a three-year siege of Jerusalem. This final siege was Judah's inescapable judgment because of the nation's continued insolence against Jehovah, despite His perpetual call to repentance and relationship. Judah's persistent national hope in the face of Nebuchadnezzar's formidable forces was fueled by false prophets who told the people of Judah what they wanted to believe and not the words of Jehovah concerning their fate against mighty Babylon.

Jerusalem would fall to Babylon in 586 BC. The temple and the king's palace would be raided and desecrated, and the people of the land would see the utter destruction of their city. Jeremiah had preached this from the inception of his prophetic ministry in 627 or 626 BC. But when it became palpable and the process was prolonged over the course of three years, one can only imagine the impact it had on Jeremiah.

With his own eyes, Jeremiah could see Jehovah's words becoming reality and his beloved people and city being decimated. The details leading up to and describing the siege and the fall are documented in 2 Kings 24:20–25:3 and 2 Chronicles 36:11–21. During this siege, there are fourteen encounters between Jeremiah and the divine person he had come to know personally and intimately. But even before these encounters, Jeremiah had already learned that he could absolutely depend upon the truth of the words spoken by Jehovah.

In the first of these fourteen encounters, recorded in Jeremiah 10:17–25, you can detect Jeremiah's dread as the reality of the imminent final demise of Jerusalem sets in. He expresses his feeling of grief and hurt in Jeremiah 10:19 and the hurt of Jehovah in Jeremiah 10:20–22. Knowing the futility of his prayer, Jeremiah pleads for mercy anyway in Jeremiah 10:23–25. King Zedekiah, whose false prophets had inspired his rebellion against Nebuchadnezzar, prompting this siege, asked Jeremiah to inquire concerning Jehovah's intervention on their behalf. Jeremiah 21 contains the record of Jehovah's response during His forty-ninth encounter with Jeremiah.

Jeremiah 21:9 places Jehovah's definitive response foretelling the defeat of Zedekiah and Jerusalem at the beginning of the siege. There are a dozen first person singular divine pronouns referencing the person of Jehovah in His response. Zephaniah and Pashur delivered Jeremiah's message from Jehovah to Zedekiah. Later, after Jeremiah's fifty-first divine encounter, Jeremiah personally delivered Jehovah's final warning of inevitable defeat to Zedekiah (Jeremiah 34:1–7). He gives some pretty specific details of the circumstances of his capture.

At some time, preceding Jeremiah's final face-to-face warning to Zedekiah, Zedekiah and the great men of the city transgressed a covenant they had personally made to proclaim liberty to their servants in agreement with the mosaic law. This was the final recorded breach of the law by wicked Zedekiah before the fall of Jerusalem. It is recorded in Jeremiah 34:8–22.

Jehovah had sent Jeremiah to confront the king after this transgression. That was Jeremiah's fiftieth divine encounter. Jehovah uses his fifty-first divine encounter with Jeremiah to issue a final warning to Zedekiah (Jeremiah 34:1–7). Rejecting the inevitability of Jerusalem's defeat by Babylon, Zedekiah had secured the backing of Egypt with temporary success. In his fifty-second encounter with Jehovah, Jeremiah is informed of the futility of the help obtained from the Egyptians and of the eventual judgment of Egypt

(Jeremiah 46:13–28). In his fifty-third encounter, he is told that the relief obtained by Egypt's intervention will be short-lived (Jeremiah 37:1–15).

Jehovah called Himself "The King" and The Lord of hosts," in contrast to Zedekiah's ally who could only give him a temporary reprieve (Jeremiah 46:18). For his unpatriotic ministry and messages during the siege, Jeremiah was imprisoned during the temporary retreat of Babylon from Jerusalem (Jeremiah 37:11–15). Jeremiah hears from Jehovah during this imprisonment (37:17), his fifty-fourth divine encounter.

Jeremiah's fifty-fifth divine encounter is of particular interest. It also occurs during his imprisonment in the midst of the siege on Jerusalem between 588–586 BC. Though he is experiencing personal hardship at this time, Jeremiah can hear the message of hope Jehovah delivered to him concerning the future of His people, Israel. This message is recorded in Jeremiah 30–31. It contains three of the five specific messianic prophecies that we know of, which Jehovah spoke to Jeremiah.

During this encounter, Jehovah spoke of the restoration of His people after the captivity (30:3). In Jeremiah 30:9, Jehovah tells Jeremiah that a day will come when His people "shall serve the Lord their God, and David their king, whom I will raise up unto them." Surely, He was not speaking of an earthly resurrection of David, but instead, He was referencing the coming of the Messiah and the fulfillment of the Davidic covenant which He established around 1000 BC according to 2 Samuel 7:5–16 and 1 Chronicles 17:4–14.

David was overwhelmed by Jehovah's kindness toward him and penned Psalm 2, 16, and 110 as he pondered Jehovah's promise. It is this same promised Messiah to whom Jehovah referred when He spoke to Jeremiah of David, their king, whom Jehovah would raise unto His chosen people. Nearly 600 years after Jeremiah's fifty-fifth encounter with Jehovah, this king was born. The slaughter of male Hebrew children perpetrated by Herod around the time of the birth of the prophesied Messiah was also foretold by Jehovah to Jeremiah during this encounter while Jeremiah was in prison (see Jeremiah 31:15 and Matthew 2:16–18).

The tenderness of Jehovah toward His people is especially notable during this message of hope. Jehovah says, in Jeremiah 30:17, "I will restore health unto thee, and I will heal thee of thy wounds..."

In Jeremiah 31:3, Jehovah says, "Yea, I have loved thee with an everlasting love: therefore with lovingkindness have I drawn thee."

In Jeremiah 31:9 He says, "I am a father to Israel, and Ephraim is My firstborn."

And Jeremiah 31:20 reads, "Is Ephraim My dear son? Is he a pleasant child? For since I spake against him, I do earnestly remember him still: therefore My bowels are troubled for him; I will surely have mercy upon him."

The final messianic prophecy spoken by Jehovah to Jeremiah during His fifty-fifth encounter with him is found in Jeremiah 31:31–34. Here, Jehovah says, "Behold, the days come, saith the LORD, that I will make a new covenant with the house of Israel, and with the house of Judah: Not according to the covenant that I made with their fathers in the day that I took them by the hand to bring them out of the land of Egypt; which My covenant they brake, although I was an husband unto them, saith the LORD: But this shall be the covenant that I will make with the house of Israel; After those days, saith the LORD, I will put My law in their inward parts, and write it in their hearts; and will be their God, and they shall be My people. And they shall teach no more every man his neighbor, and every man his brother, saying, Know the LORD: for they shall all know Me, from the least of them unto the greatest of them, saith the LORD: for I will forgive their iniquity, and I will remember their sin no more."

The new covenant of which Jehovah spoke was established in the shed blood of the Messiah according to Matthew 26:28 and Acts 20:28, and its messianic nature is confirmed by the writer of Hebrews (see Hebrews 8:8–13). Nearly seventy first person singular divine pronouns are spoken by Jehovah as He communicated this message of hope and these three messianic prophecies to Jeremiah in 588–587 BC.

A rare plural divine pronoun is spoken by Jehovah in this interaction with Jeremiah and should be addressed. In Jeremiah 30:4–7, the plural divine pronoun *We* is spoken.

> And these are the words that the LORD spake concerning Israel and concerning Judah. For thus saith the LORD, "We have heard a voice of trembling, of fear, and not of peace. Ask ye now, and see whether a man doth travail with child? wherefore do I see every man with his hands on his loins, as a woman in travail, and all faces are turned into paleness? Alas! for that day is great, so that none is like it: it is even the time of Jacob's trouble; but he shall be saved out of it." (Jer. 30:4–7, KJV)

It appears that Jehovah is making note of the fact that the people of Israel and Judah had refused to embrace the ultimate judgment He had been proclaiming through His prophets for centuries. They were smug in their status of being His chosen people, despite their refusal to walk according to His expectations. They had no apparent fear of Jehovah's judgment. Now that the fulfillment of His prophecy was actually coming to pass, both they and Jehovah could witness their fear of His great judgment which would be accomplished before their ultimate restoration. The fact that this single plural divine pronoun referenced Jehovah and others and not a plurality within the godhead is certain, because there are nearly seventy first person singular divine pronouns spoken in reference to Jehovah during this encounter. The obvious emphasis is on His singularity as a person. Moreover, Jeremiah used five third person singular divine pronouns in reference to the divine person with Whom he is speaking in Jeremiah 30–31, indicating that he believes he is speaking to a single individual.

Jeremiah's fifty-sixth, fifty-seventh, and fifty-eighth encounters with Jehovah are recorded in Jeremiah 32 and show Jeremiah's well-founded confidence in the omniscience of Jehovah. Jeremiah remained imprisoned at the time that Jehovah forewarned him that he would receive a proposition to buy some land (Jeremiah 32:1–8). Jeremiah purchased the land and officially and publicly certified his purchase (32:9–12). This was a public display of his confidence in Jehovah's word that the land of Judah would one day be inhabited again after the captivity was fulfilled.

Jeremiah instructed Baruch to take the evidence of his purchase and preserve it (Jeremiah 32:13) as he had been instructed by Jehovah (Jeremiah 32:14–15). Jeremiah commences to pray to Jehovah after having been obedient and purchasing the land from his uncle. Concerning the restoration of Judah, which the Lord promised after the Babylonian captivity was accomplished, some of this was difficult for Jeremiah to comprehend, though he trusted Jehovah's omniscience and omnipotence. Jeremiah rehearsed Jehovah's great works of history as he reassured himself and spoke with Jehovah (see Jeremiah 32:17–23).

To address the uncertainties in Jeremiah's mind, in Jeremiah 32:27, Jehovah posed the rhetorical question to His prophet, "Behold, I am the Lord, the God of all flesh: is there anything too hard for me?" Jehovah proceeds to tell Jeremiah once again that He would allow the captivity to occur and restore the people and the land afterwards. He used thirty-nine first person singular divine pronouns in this discourse with Jeremiah.

Another message of hope and restoration was delivered in Jeremiah's fifty-ninth encounter with Jehovah, which also occurred during Jeremiah's imprisonment around 587 BC. Jeremiah writes about this encounter in chapter 33. Because of the frailty of his humanity and oppressiveness of the ongoing siege by Babylon, one can imagine that Jeremiah needed repeated words of encouragement. Jehovah gave that to Jeremiah in this encounter. He reassures Jeremiah that if he calls, He will answer and show him great and mighty things (33:3). Jehovah reassures Jeremiah that He will, indeed, restore health and an abundance of peace and truth to His people (33:6). He proclaims that He will cleanse them and pardon their sins against Him (33:8). He then announces the fourth messianic prophecy which He gave to Jeremiah during his ministry.

In Jeremiah 33:14–15, He mentioned the coming of the Branch of righteousness that He would cause to grow up unto David to execute judgment and righteousness in the land. The messianic nature of this statement by Jehovah is attested by His reference back to the establishment of the Davidic covenant (see Jeremiah 33:16–21; 2 Samuel 7; 1 Chronicles 17; Psalm 2, 110). Jehovah's dedication to the concept of covenant and His faithfulness to keep His covenants is strongly evident during this particular encounter. He makes reference to His covenant concerning the laws of the physical universe, His covenant with David, His covenant with Abraham, Isaac, and Jacob, and His covenant with the house of Israel as He concludes His comments to Jeremiah (33:21–26). Thirty-five first person singular divine pronouns are spoken by Jehovah in this encounter with Jeremiah, reinforcing that He is a covenant-keeping, relationship-oriented person.

The final messianic prophecy given to Jeremiah by Jehovah is a reiteration of Jeremiah 33:15 because it references the righteous Branch and King that would be raised unto David (Jeremiah 23:5). However, it goes further in clarifying that this King would be Jehovah, The Lord Our Righteousness (Jehovah-Tsidkenu), according to Jeremiah 23:6. Thus, in this sixtieth divine encounter with Jeremiah, Jehovah alludes to the fact that He would be intimately connected, one with the righteous Branch of David that would come in the future.

During Jeremiah's final encounter with Jehovah during the siege and before the fall of Jerusalem, he is in the dungeon. He was still imprisoned for his perceived treason in prophesying the fall of Jerusalem (Jeremiah 38:1–6). He had been sorely mistreated because of his ministry, though he was extended a measure of relief because of the intervention of Ebedmelech the Ethiopian (Jeremiah 38:7–13). His divine encounter came after the greatly distressed king of Israel, Zedekiah, secretly sought his counsel.

Zedekiah was desperately seeking a remedy to the siege that did not include his surrender or the destruction of the city. Jehovah's answer, through Jeremiah, did not provide that remedy. Once again, Zedekiah was told that his only solution was to surrender to Babylon;

any other response would end in the destruction of the city (Jeremiah 38:18–19, 22–23). Zedekiah refused to heed this counsel, and the city was overthrown in 586 BC.

The final siege of Jerusalem by Nebuchadnezzar began in 588 BC and ended in 586 BC, extending over the course of three years. Jeremiah found himself imprisoned during a significant portion of the siege. His prophetic message was unpopular, even perceived as unpatriotic and treasonous. He had fourteen encounters with Jehovah documented during the siege. Over 200 first person singular divine pronouns and eleven third person singular divine pronouns can be found in the biblical account of Jeremiah's divine encounters during the siege.

Jeremiah's experiences during the siege inform us that he understood Jehovah to be an omniscient, omnipotent, omnipresent, and sovereign person. Though He allowed the threats and destruction that came on Jerusalem as a result of their transgressions, He cared deeply for the nation. However, He set a greater value on the ultimate outcome of a covenant relationship with His chosen people that would extend beyond the time of Judah's judgment.

Encountering Jehovah During the Fall of Jerusalem and Jeremiah's Lamentations

The fall of Jerusalem in 586 BC remains one of the most painful and memorable events in Jewish history. The historicity of this event is confirmed in the Bible and in extra-biblical sources alike. 2 Kings 25:4–7, 2 Chronicles 36:17–21, and Jeremiah 39–42 and 52 provide extensive details of this historic event. Also, the book of Lamentations gives insight into Jeremiah's emotional burden as he witnessed the destruction that befell his beloved city. While Daniel and Ezekiel were Jeremiah's contemporaries, only Jeremiah, among the men who penned biblical history, witnessed the full scope of this calamity firsthand. He saw the spiritual revival that began during the reign of Josiah and the progressive decline ending in destruction and captivity twenty-three years after Josiah's death.

The biblical record identifies two occasions when Jehovah spoke to Jeremiah during the fall of Jerusalem and its immediate aftermath. In one, Jehovah gives Jeremiah some words to share with Ebedmelech. In the second, Jeremiah's sixty-third divine encounter, he is instructed to give counsel to the remnant in Jerusalem not to abandon their city in favor of Egypt. Sixteen first person singular divine pronouns and two third person singular divine pronouns are present in Jeremiah's divine encounters after the fall of Jerusalem.

During this time, King Zedekiah is blinded and taken captive by the Babylonians as Jehovah had said to Jeremiah during the siege. Ebedmelech is rewarded by Jehovah for his kindness to His prophet (Jeremiah 39:16–18). Jeremiah is rewarded and released by the Babylonians. Nebuzaradan, the captain of Nebuchadnezzar's army, delivered a message from Jehovah to Jeremiah as recorded in Jeremiah 40:2–3. Gedaliah was made governor of the land. A contingent of the remnant of people in Jerusalem decided to defect from the desolate city and relocate to Egypt. Jehovah admonished them to stay in Jerusalem and, again, they did not obey Him (Jeremiah 42:9–21).

Jeremiah's emotional distress after the fall of Jerusalem in 586 BC can be ascertained by even a casual reading of the book of Lamentations. What is most poignant in this book, however, is the fact that Jeremiah's perception of Jehovah is not bitter or negative after judgment is poured out on his beloved city. Instead, Jeremiah retains a very lofty view of Jehovah. Jeremiah's perception of Jehovah at this time is best summarized in Lamentations 3:17–26.

> And Thou hast removed my soul far off from peace: I forgat prosperity. And I said, "My strength and my hope is perished from the LORD: Remembering mine affliction and my misery, the wormwood and the gall. My soul hath them still in remembrance, and is humbled in me. This I recall to my mind, therefore have I hope. It is of the LORD'S mercies that we are not consumed, because His compassions fail not.

> They are new every morning: great is Thy faithfulness. The LORD is my portion, saith my soul; therefore will I hope in Him. The LORD is good unto them that wait for Him, to the soul that seeketh Him. It is good that a man should both hope and quietly wait for the salvation of the LORD." (Lam. 3:17–26)

No new encounters between Jeremiah and Jehovah are recorded in Lamentations. However, Jeremiah's perception of the presence and person of Jehovah is unmistakable. Jeremiah used ninety-one third person singular divine pronouns to reference the person he knew as God and Who remained his friend, his hope, and his source of strength in this very difficult time, even after the fall of Jerusalem.

Jeremiah's Last Encounters with Jehovah

Scholars still dispute when Jeremiah's final encounters with Jehovah occurred. The latest proposed date is 569 BC, nearly twenty years after the fall of Jerusalem. The final two divine encounters of Jeremiah and Jehovah are documented in Jeremiah 43–44 and entail prophecies concerning Egypt and the people of Israel who have settled in Egypt. At the end of his ministry (Jeremiah 43:9–13, 44:2–14) as at the beginning (Jeremiah 1:5–19), Jeremiah encounters God as a divine person Who speaks to him directly. Jehovah gives Jeremiah clear directives concerning Who He is and what His instructions are for him as Jeremiah speaks on His behalf. Jeremiah's God is an omniscient, omnipotent, omnipresent, sovereign person Who seeks a covenant relationship with people and Who has expectations of those whom He encounters. In the final two encounters, twenty-nine first person singular divine pronouns are spoken by Jehovah regarding Himself.

CHAPTER SIX

Jeremiah: Summary and Conclusions

Of the three major prophets of Judah's era of captivity, Jeremiah was the only one who lived in Jerusalem and personally witnessed the demise of his beloved city and of the southern kingdom to the bitter end. Jeremiah was born into a priestly family. His father was the Hilkiah that found the book of the law (the book of Moses) that was the document that Josiah zealously referenced as the basis for Judah's final revival before the Babylonian captivity occurred. This physical document and the God Who authored this document and gave it to Moses over 800 years before He called Jeremiah were critical influences during Jeremiah's formative years before he began his prophetic ministry.

Jeremiah's first personal encounter with the divine person Who authored the book of the law came in 627 BC when Jehovah called him to be a prophet to Judah and to the nations. In His call of Jeremiah, Jehovah revealed Himself as a sovereign, omniscient, and omnipotent person. Twenty first person singular divine pronouns were used by Jehovah in reference to Himself in His call of Jeremiah. Through the messages that Jehovah gave him to preach over the next eighteen years, Jeremiah came to understand some additional things about the character of Jehovah. He was also a compassionate relationship-oriented God Who had pursued a covenant relationship with Judah over the centuries, only to have them reject His pursuit of them and to bring upon themselves a certain judgment because they refused to walk in covenant relationship with Him. Jehovah used over 120 first person singular divine pronouns during His conversations with Jeremiah during the reign of Josiah.

With the death of Josiah and the spiritual decline that followed, Jeremiah found himself and his people facing imminent judgment. He preached several messages of imminent judgment including the Temple sermon, the sermon of the marred linen girdle, and the sermon of the potter and the clay between 609 and 605 BC when Babylon took the first captives from Judah, including Daniel. Over 160 additional first person singular divine pronouns were spoken by Jehovah to Jeremiah during this brief period of only half a decade.

To Jeremiah, Jehovah was yet the strong loving father and husband Who foresaw Judah's judgment and called His chosen people back from the brink of this destruction. They refused to hear. Despite being persecuted for preaching Jehovah's unpopular messages to the nation, Jeremiah continued to deliver His messages until Nebuchadnezzar invaded Jerusalem again in 597 BC, taking a second group of captives including Ezekiel and King Jeconiah. Jehovah used over 180 first person singular divine pronouns in His sixteen encounters with Jeremiah between the first and second invasions of Jerusalem by Nebuchadnezzar.

Before the three-year siege of Jerusalem by Babylon began in 588 BC, Jeremiah had eight more historically documented encounters with Jehovah. During this time, Jehovah used 168 more first person singular divine pronouns in reference to Himself. He pronounced judgment upon the people left in the city of Jerusalem, the surrounding countries in the land of Palestine, and the country of Babylon itself, while giving words of instruction to His chosen people concerning their captivity.

During the siege, Jeremiah encountered Jehovah as a God of judgment fulfilled and a God Who foresaw the restoration of His people. He spoke of this coming restoration and something greater than the mere restoration of Judah. He spoke concerning the accomplishment of the ultimate purpose of restoring fellowship between Himself and lost humanity. He spoke concerning the coming Messiah during the siege. Jehovah also sustained and encouraged His persecuted prophet during this time. Jehovah used over 200 first person singular divine pronouns in fourteen encounters with Jeremiah during the siege.

Jeremiah continued to interact with Jehovah even after Jerusalem fell in 586 BC. Four final encounters between Jeremiah and Jehovah are found in the record of history, including the immediate aftermath of the fall and the years thereafter. Jeremiah heard Jehovah use forty-five first person singular divine pronouns in reference to Himself during the final years of his prophetic ministry. As he lamented the fall of Jerusalem, Jeremiah used nearly 100 third person singular divine pronouns in reference to his God and confidant.

In all, Jeremiah's ministry spanned nearly seven decades and included sixty-five documented encounters with Jehovah. Jehovah used approximately 885 first person singular divine pronouns in identifying Himself as a divine person to Jeremiah. Almost 200 third person singular divine pronouns are also used in reference to Jehovah as we read the historical record of Jeremiah's encounters with Him. Without dispute, Jeremiah, the weeping prophet, understood Jehovah to be a sovereign, loving, relationship-seeking, covenant-keeping person Who knew the future, inhabited lands far and near simultaneously, and had all power. Jeremiah also understood that Jehovah had expectations of conduct He upheld for His chosen people and that He allowed His people to make their own choices regarding living according to those expectations. There were consequences if His people did not choose to live out these standards. Jehovah, though He saw the consequences and had the power to squelch their free will, thus preventing their calamity, would not usurp their ability to make personal choices.

Encountering Jehovah with Ezekiel

Judah's second prominent prophet during its time of captivity under Babylon was Ezekiel. As previously noted, Ezekiel was taken captive during Babylon's 597 BC invasion of Jerusalem along with Jeconiah whose captivity is clearly confirmed by the Babylonian Chronicles. Ezekiel's historically documented encounters with Jehovah all occur while he is captive in Babylon. As previously noted, all of Jeremiah's encounters with Jehovah occur while he is in Jerusalem or Egypt. None of Ezekiel's encounters with this divine person of history take place while he is physically present in Jerusalem. As a point of historical reference, Ezekiel would have been a relative contemporary to Pythagoras, Buddha, and Confucius along with Daniel and Jeremiah.

Ezekiel's nearly three dozen documented encounters with Jehovah tend to have a more metaphysical character about them than the encounters between Jeremiah and Jehovah. The reasons for this difference are not immediately clear since Ezekiel's God is the same person as Jeremiah's God. The difference may have been somehow consequent to the fact that during his historically documented divine encounters, Ezekiel and the people to whom he prophesied were not physically present in Jerusalem, the city that he associated with the presence of Jehovah. Lacking a physical connection to the city where he understood that the presence of his God rested, the prophet's connection with Jehovah had to take on a more spiritual or, for want of a better term, metaphysical nature.

Despite having heard Jeremiah prophesy a seventy-year period of captivity around the time Nebuchadnezzar had taken his first captives from Jerusalem in 605 BC (Jeremiah 25:1–14), this second group of captives, to whom Ezekiel was tasked to minister, believed their captivity would be short-lived. Through His encounters with Ezekiel, Jehovah seems to undertake to impress upon the captives several critical messages:

1. His presence extends beyond the borders of Jerusalem and permeates the earth and the heavens;
2. their judgment is certain, it is justified, and it is prolonged; and
3. His favor upon them continues and their ultimate restoration is equally certain.

Though there are several types of encounters documented in his book, what is unique about Ezekiel is that a disproportionate number of encounters between him and his God are described as visions. As personal, spiritual, and intellectual experiences, these encounters cannot be verified by any sources external to Ezekiel. However, Ezekiel seemed to have had the foresight—almost as a defense of the veracity of his encounters with Jehovah—to place his encounters into a historical context by meticulously dating his visions.

In the examination of Ezekiel's encounters, only a limited focus will be placed on the content of the visions. A greater focus will be placed on distinguishing each encounter, the date of the encounter, the historical setting of each encounter, and the attributes of Jehovah as a person that are made apparent through Ezekiel's encounters with Him.

Ezekiel's encounters before the final Babylonian siege of Jerusalem:

593 BC Ezekiel's call (1–7)

1. *First vision: Jehovah and His glory (1–3:15).*
2. *Second vision and call to be a watchman (3:16–27).*

   Instructions for Ezekiel's enactments:

   A) *Siege of Jerusalem (4:1–17).*
   B) *Fall of Jerusalem (5:1–17).*

3. *Prophecy against idolatrous nation (6:1–14).*
4. *Final judgment of Jerusalem foretold (7:1–27).*

Ezekiel was taken captive along with Jeconiah in 597 BC during Babylon's second invasion of Jerusalem. He was thirty years old (Ezek. 1:1) and had been in captivity for approximately five years (Ezek. 1:2) when he had his first historically documented encounter with Jehovah. In this fantastic maiden divine encounter, Ezekiel saw the glory of Jehovah and received his call to the prophetic ministry. Some scholars have dated this encounter at July 31, 593 BC, based on documentation by Ezekiel, 2 Kings 24:10–16, 2 Chronicles 36:9–10, and Babylonian chronicles. The river that Ezekiel describes as the setting may have been Nebuchadnezzar's royal canal, a river project completed on the backs of the captives and undertaken to connect the Euphrates River and the Tigris River.

While Ezekiel and his fellow Judean captives were working on this river project, Ezekiel had the dramatic vision and series of encounters with Jehovah documented in the first seven chapters of the book that bears his name. These seven chapters can easily be divided into a distinct initial vision that personally introduced Jehovah to Ezekiel and three subsequent encounters that launched the prophet into his ministerial work. All of these encounters occurred within the span of one year.

The initial vision, the focus of Ezekiel 1:1–3:15, is full of characters and events that stretch the human imagination and challenge Ezekiel's abilities of description. Here, Ezekiel describes four living creatures with four faces (a man, an ox, a lion, and an eagle) and four wings and a wheel in the middle of a wheel in the heavens above him. These creatures were, it is important to note, beneath the feet of a superior divine being Who sat on a throne above them. Ezekiel's comprehension of Jehovah, the person sitting on the throne (Ezek. 1:26–28), is not unlike that described by Isaiah around 740 BC (Isaiah 6:1–10) when Isaiah was called to the prophetic ministry. No doubt, this Jehovah is also the person Who passed by Elijah in 858 BC and reassured him and gave him direction during a crisis point in his prophetic ministry (1 Kings 19:9–18). No doubt, this Jehovah is also the person Who passed by Moses and reassured him and gave him direction—allowing him to see His glory—during a crisis point in his leadership of the fledgling nation of Israel in 1446 BC (Exodus 33:12–23).

It is instructive to note the pronouns that reference the person of Jehovah in the encounters of each of these prophets. There are two third person singular divine pronouns referencing Jehovah in Ezekiel 1:27. There are three third person singular divine pronouns referencing Jehovah in Isaiah 6:1, 3, and 9. There are the two first person singular divine pronouns spoken by Elijah's Jehovah in 1 Kings 19:18. And twenty-one first person singular divine pronouns were used by Jehovah in reference to Himself as He spoke to Moses in Exodus 33:12–23.

Ezekiel's vision of the person of Jehovah is consistent with that of each of his predecessors. The omnipotence, omnipresence, omniscience, and sovereignty of Jehovah, which is on display in this magnificent experience of Ezekiel, is consistent with the manifestations of Jehovah's presence experienced by prophets over millennia of time.

After revealing Himself as the Almighty (Ezek. 1:24), the God of the heavens (Ezek. 1:26–28) and Jehovah Elohim/the Lord God (Ezek. 2:4), Jehovah displays toward Ezekiel the personal, intimate, relationship orientation that has characterized His relationship with His messengers over time. Much like He had done in His call of Jeremiah (Jeremiah 1:5–10), Jehovah gives Ezekiel his call, his mission, and reassurance of His divine presence and support when opposition should arise against his ministry in the future (Ezek. 2:1–3:11). Jehovah used sixteen first person singular divine pronouns in reference to Himself during this initial encounter with Ezekiel. That Ezekiel experienced Jehovah as a single person, though other divine beings are simultaneously encountered, is evinced by his use of thirteen third person singular divine pronouns in reference to Jehovah during this first encounter. Throughout the rest of his ministry, Ezekiel refers back to this first grand encounter with Jehovah as foundational to his understanding of the person of Jehovah.

It took Ezekiel a week to digest his first mind-expanding, intellectually, spiritually, and emotionally revolutionary encounter with Jehovah (Ezek. 3:15). After allowing him time to digest the initial experience, Jehovah bestowed on Ezekiel the role and title "Watchman" and explained the accompanying responsibilities (Ezek. 3:17–21). As a part of this encounter, Ezekiel briefly sees the glory of the Lord a second time (Ezek. 3:22–24). Some very specific instructions from Jehovah to Ezekiel follow (Ezek. 3:22–27).

After his initiation into the prophetic ministry, Ezekiel receives instructions that involve the enactment of the fate of Jerusalem to the captives in Babylon. At this time, the captives still retained some false hope of a quick and miraculous restoration without the prolonged captivity that Jeremiah had prophesied a decade earlier (Jeremiah 25:1–14). Jehovah gave Ezekiel detailed instructions to perform literal physical enactments of the siege of Jerusalem (Ezek. 4) and the fall of Jerusalem (Ezek. 5) during this second divine encounter. These enactments would take the balance of the next year to complete (Ezek. 4:4–6). There are fifty-six first person singular divine pronouns spoken by Jehovah during His second encounter with Ezekiel.

Of special note, during this encounter, Jehovah introduced an expression to Ezekiel—"I the Lord"—that He would repeat nearly two dozen times in the ears of Ezekiel over the course of the two decades of Ezekiel's prophetic ministry. This expression emphasized to Ezekiel the sovereignty of the person, Jehovah. This specific expression is used only once by Jehovah during Jeremiah's ministry (Jeremiah 17:10). The expression "I the Lord" is used thirteen times by Jehovah in conversations with Moses; seven of these are recorded in the book of Leviticus alone. Jehovah says, "I the Lord" fourteen times in conversations with Isaiah. In Jehovah's encounters with Ezekiel, He first used this expression in 5:13, 5:15, and 5:17. He proceeded to use this expression twenty-two times over the course of thirty-four encounters with Ezekiel. Thus, in His first two encounters with Ezekiel, Jehovah asserted unequivocally in the mind of the young prophet that He was the sole sovereign of all of heaven and earth.

Ezekiel's third and fourth divine encounters also occurred in 593 BC and are documented in chapters 6 and 7. In chapter 6, Jehovah laments that the sacred land of Jerusalem has been filled with the practice of idolatry by the people with whom He has a covenant relationship. During this encounter with Ezekiel, Jehovah instructs Ezekiel to prophesy the judgment that would come upon the land for this transgression. Throughout chapter 6, He emphasized the covenant relationship orientation that He has demonstrated from the beginning of His dealings with humans and His faithfulness to His promises. Judah's judgment for idolatry was a fulfilment of the promise He had made to Moses and Israel in 1446 BC (Leviticus 26:14–46). Jehovah had restated this to Moses in 1406 BC at the close of Moses's ministry to the nation (Deut. 31:16–21).

As Jehovah gave instructions to Ezekiel to speak the words of prophecy against idolatrous Judah, which were now soon to be fulfilled, He introduced another expression to His conversations with Ezekiel—"I am the Lord" (Ezek. 6:7,10,13,14). This expression is used more commonly by Jehovah than "I the Lord" and dated back to His encounters with Abraham (Genesis 15:7) around 2081 BC. Jehovah had used this expression during conversations with Jacob, Gideon, Moses, Isaiah, and Jeremiah as well in years past. With the exception of Moses, however, this expression never enjoyed much frequency of use by Jehovah, according to the record of history, before His encounters with Ezekiel. Jehovah used this expression once in His encounters with Jacob (Gen. 28:13) and once during His encounters with Gideon (Judges 6:10).

"I am the Lord" is recorded three times in the entire ministry of Jeremiah (Jer. 9:24, 24:7, and 32:27). To the prophet Isaiah, Jehovah says, "I am the Lord" ten times, according to Isaiah's documentation. Moses documents seventy-one uses of the divine title "I am the Lord" in the five books he authored. Forty-five of these occurrences are in the book of Leviticus alone. Only Moses surpasses Ezekiel in this regard. Sixty-seven times during His encounters with Ezekiel, Jehovah was noted to say "I am the Lord" beginning with Ezekiel 6.

In chapter 7, the final judgment of Judah is foretold. The expression "I am the Lord" is stated an additional three times in this chapter (Ezek. 7:4,9,27). It is unfortunate that it took the judgment of Jehovah upon His covenant people in order that they would understand His sovereignty. History bears out the fact that all will come to know His sovereignty; some by accepting His love and mercy and walking in covenant relationship with Him, others by experiencing His judgment.

Forty-five first person singular divine pronouns litter the remarks of Jehovah in the two chapters documenting His third and fourth encounters with Ezekiel. In all, 117 first person singular divine pronouns are spoken by Jehovah in reference to Himself during His first four encounters with Ezekiel. In the context of Ezekiel's initial vision of the one on the throne (Ezek. 1:26–28), these first person singular divine pronouns point to the fact that Ezekiel experienced Jehovah as one divine person. The personhood of Jehovah is further substantiated by Jehovah's use of the divine expressions "I the Lord" and "I am the Lord" during these early encounters with Ezekiel. As noted, throughout the remainder of Ezekiel's prophetic ministry, Jehovah often uses these divine expressions to describe Himself.

592 BC

5. *Third vision: Temple abominations (8–12:7).*
6. *Instructions for enactments about exile and prophecy against false prophets (12:8–13:23).*

7. *Prophecy against idolatrous elders among exiles (14:1–11).*
8. *Noah, Daniel, and Job; righteous individuals (14:12–23).*
9. *Parable of the vine tree (15).*
   Parable given (15:1–5).
   Parable interpreted (15:6–8).
10. *Parable of the adulterous wife (16).*
11. *Parable of the two eagles (17).*
    Parable given (17:1–10)
    Parable interpreted (17:11–24)
12. *The proverb of the sour grapes (18) and divine lamentation for Israel's princes (19).*

In the fall of the next year (September 592 BC according to Ezekiel 8:1), Ezekiel had another vision; this was his fifth encounter with Jehovah. The characters in this vision were likely persons with whom Ezekiel had lived and worked in Jerusalem in his role as priest before he was taken into captivity (Ezek. 8:11). The divine person Who had called Ezekiel into prophetic ministry just over a year previously was Ezekiel's chief narrator and correspondent (see Ezek. 1:26–28, 8:2–4, and 10:1). Their meeting took place during a supernatural visitation back to the Temple in Jerusalem to see the abominations that had been perpetrated against Jehovah. These abominations had alienated Jehovah from His temple and His covenant people.

A series of egregious acts of idolatry (spiritual adultery), both overt and covert, are witnessed by Ezekiel during this vision. The perpetual acts of idolatry and spiritual adultery are presented as the reason that the glory of Jehovah, Who chooses to separate Himself from unclean acts and unclean people, abandons His temple. The sequential steps of Jehovah's departure from His temple can be traced through Ezek. 8:4, 9:3, 10:4, 10:18–19, and 11:22–23. Jehovah is careful to reiterate in this vision that because Judah had failed to recognize Him as their covenant-keeping God in response to His kindness and His merciful relationship with them, they were going to know Him as God through judgment.

Twice during this vision, He commented, "And Ye shall know that I am the Lord" (Ezek. 11:10,12). Jehovah also used a total of thirty-seven first person singular divine pronouns in reference to Himself throughout this vision. Twenty-three third person singular divine pronouns also appear in the historical documentation of this encounter (Ezek. 8:1–12:7).

That evening, the same day that Ezekiel had his third vision, Jehovah gave him instructions regarding another enactment (Ezek. 12:1–7). This enactment prompted questions among the exiles and, the following morning, Ezekiel had another encounter with Jehovah during which he received instructions on how to answer these questions (Ezek. 12:8–16). Ezekiel received instructions for a series of additional enactments, teachings, and prophecies to deliver to the exiles during this—his sixth—divine encounter (Ezek. 12:8–13:23).

The message of these enactments, teachings, and prophecies is clear—the time of judgment is now. Jehovah had decided that He would no longer be taken for granted by His covenant people and that they would no longer be deceived by their false prophets. Among the forty-three first person singular divine pronouns spoken by Jehovah during this encounter with Ezekiel are seven additional times that He declared, "I am the Lord" (Ezek. 12:15,16,20,25, 13:9,21,23).

Ezekiel's next five divine encounters also transpire during 592 BC and are prophecies, parables, and a proverb dealing with the fact that, at this time, the final judgment of Jerusalem is a foregone conclusion in the mind of Jehovah. Ezekiel's seventh encounter with Jehovah occurs when he is confronted by several of the elders of Israel who were among the exiles in Babylon. Jehovah begins this encounter with Ezekiel by expressing His disdain for the audacity shown by these men in presuming to confront Him (Ezek. 14:3). The omniscience of Jehovah is displayed in this encounter. Just as He had revealed to Ezekiel the secrets of the imaginations of the leaders in the temple in Jerusalem during Ezekiel's third vision (Ezek. 8:12), so Jehovah knows and reveals the secrets of the imaginations of the elders that confronted Ezekiel in Babylon (Ezek. 14:1–5). These elders had committed the transgression of idolatry in their hearts; but Jehovah knows the secrets of the heart and judges accordingly (Jer. 17:10).

He tells Ezekiel that He will judge a man's worthiness based upon His omniscient survey of the heart. Jehovah again identifies

Himself using the expressions "I the Lord" (Ezek. 14:4,7,9) and "I am the Lord" (Ezek. 14:8). To remove any doubt concerning His identity in this specific encounter with Ezekiel, Jehovah used three dozen first person singular divine pronouns to identify Himself.

In His next encounter with Ezekiel, Jehovah elaborates further on His assertion that He will judge each individual according to his own character and righteousness. In making this assertion, Jehovah referenced three notable human historical figures as examples of righteous men. In doing this, Jehovah—and Ezekiel—validates the historicity of these men. Scholarly discussions periodically surface in which a pivotal issue is whether Noah and/or Job were fictional characters, simply used to teach lessons about life principles. Neither Ezekiel nor Jehovah seem to accept any attempt to fictionalize these men. In this conversation, they speak of Noah, Daniel, and Job as if they are, in fact, real persons and examples of righteous men (Ezek. 14:14,20).

Ezekiel's ninth encounter with Jehovah is an extremely brief encounter. In this encounter, Jehovah used a parable of a vine tree to convey the message that He would judge the nation of Israel. According to Jehovah, the sovereignty He exercised in this judgment is substantiating evidence that "I am the Lord" (Ezek. 15:6–7).

Ezekiel's tenth divine encounter is recorded in chapter 16. In contrast to the previous encounter, this encounter contains a very lengthy parable and elaboration by Jehovah to Ezekiel. In this encounter, Jehovah graphically depicts Jerusalem as an adulterous wife and tells the prophet to teach the people how their sins—past and present—are perceived by Him. First, Jehovah described how He unilaterally decided to set His affection upon Israel. He rescued them from a lowly state and developed them into a nation of repute (Ezek. 16:6–14). Several attributes of Jehovah are evident in His description. He is sovereign. He unilaterally chose Israel; for no merit of its own. He is omnipotent. He rescued the nation by the mere power of His word. It was the power of His command for them to "live" that created the status they once enjoyed as a powerful nation.

According to Ezekiel 16:6, Jehovah declared, "And when I passed by thee, and saw thee polluted in thine own blood, I said unto thee when thou wast in thy blood, Live; yea, I said unto thee when thou wast in thy blood, Live." It should not be overlooked that He is compassionate, seeing beyond superficial appearances, and addressing the need of the object of His affection. He is covenant and relationship-oriented.

The passion of Jehovah for His relationship with Israel is best seen in Ezekiel 16:8–9 where Jehovah continues, "Now when I passed by thee, and looked upon thee, behold, thy time was the time of love; and I spread my skirt over thee, and covered thy nakedness: yea, I sware unto thee, and entered into a covenant with thee, saith the Lord GOD, and thou becamest mine. Then washed I thee with water; yea, I throughly washed away thy blood from thee, and I anointed thee with oil."

In the remainder of this chapter, beginning with verse 15, Jehovah describes the betrayal He has endured at the hands of His beloved people, Israel. He is careful in laying out His case to Ezekiel—and through him to the exiles—to establish that the transgressions and betrayals have occurred generation after generation, including the present generation of Israelites. Jehovah concludes this encounter with a word about the certainty of His judgment and the assurance of His mercy through restoration after His judgment is accomplished. It is not the vindictiveness of Jehovah that has brought about the judgment of Israel, but the covenant-breaking lawlessness of the nation. It is not the righteousness of the nation that will cause the restoration of their covenant relationship with the God of heaven, but their covenant-minded, loving, relationship-oriented God will restore them.

In Ezekiel 16:59–62, Jehovah explains, "For thus saith the Lord GOD; I will even deal with thee as thou hast done, which hast despised the oath in breaking the covenant. Nevertheless I will remember My covenant with thee in the days of thy youth, and I will establish unto thee an everlasting covenant. Then thou shalt remember thy ways, and be ashamed, when thou shalt receive thy sisters, thine elder and thy younger: and I will give them unto thee for daughters, but not by thy covenant. And I will establish My covenant with thee; and thou shalt know that I am the LORD."

This message, which Ezekiel received directly from the mouth of Jehovah, is graphic. It lays out Jehovah's history with the nation and, through it, His case against Judah. It demonstrates, emphatically, the personal stock Jehovah has invested in His relationship with His chosen people. It demonstrates many of the attributes of Jehovah that have been seen over the course of history. It refutes the false notion that Jehovah is a vindictive God of judgment and fire and brimstone waiting to pounce on helpless men. Instead, it eloquently lays out the case for His mercy, compassion, patience, goodness, and kindness. Nonetheless, it makes clear that He has an expectation for the conduct of His chosen people toward Him and that there are consequences for their rejection of these standards. Jehovah used sixty first person singular divine pronouns in this tenth encounter with Ezekiel as He speaks of His past, present, and future relationship with Judah.

In another encounter in 592 BC—Ezekiel's eleventh overall—Jehovah uses a parable or riddle involving two eagles (Ezek. 17:1–10). After laying out the riddle, Jehovah proceeds to decipher it for His prophet so that Ezekiel can teach the people (Ezek. 17:11–24). It is a prophetic statement by Jehovah regarding the international dynamics between Babylon, Egypt, and Judah. Babylon is Jehovah's current instrument of judgment. Judah will be judged using this instrument. Egypt is an interference and will be judged as well. Sixteen first person singular divine pronouns are used by Jehovah as He delivers and explains this parable of the two eagles to Ezekiel. Twice, in this encounter, Jehovah used the expression "I the Lord" (Ezek. 17:21,24).

Ezekiel's final encounter with Jehovah in 592 BC is arguably the most famous of the seven encounters that transpired during that year of ministry. The princes of Israel were perpetuating a misleading and malicious attack on the character of Jehovah using a proverb concerning the consumption of sour grapes. This proverb and its implications were confronted head-on in the encounter between Ezekiel and Jehovah documented in Ezekiel 18 and 19. Chapter 19 provides insight into the population perpetuating this falsehood, while chapter 18 gives Jehovah's response concerning this accusation against Him.

The accusation against Jehovah by the leaders is that they are being punished for crimes that their fathers had committed against Jehovah and that they are a generation of innocent victims of the sins of their forefathers (Ezek. 18:2,25,29). Jehovah spends the balance of chapter 18 explaining that each individual is accountable for his own choices and will be judged accordingly. Jehovah explains that even past choices by an individual will not prevent them from benefiting from a change of heart that leads to righteous choices in the present. Jehovah then implores Judah through this encounter with Ezekiel to turn and live because He takes no pleasure in the death of the transgressor; He would prefer that they obey and live.

Along with Ezekiel 18:2, verses 23 and 30–32 provide the most succinct summary of this divine encounter in which Jehovah used fourteen first person singular divine pronouns in reference to Himself as He enlightens the mind of His prophet in response to this false accusation.

> "Have I any pleasure at all that the wicked should die? saith the Lord GOD: and not that he should return from his ways, and live?" (Ezek. 18:23)
> "Therefore I will judge you, O house of Israel, every one according to his ways, saith the Lord GOD. Repent, and turn yourselves from all your transgressions; so iniquity shall not be your ruin. Cast away from you all your transgressions, whereby ye have transgressed; and make you a new heart and a new spirit: for why will ye die, O house of Israel? For I have no pleasure in the death of him that dieth, saith the Lord GOD: wherefore turn yourselves, and live ye." (Ezek. 18:30–32)

591 BC

God rejects the consultation of Israel's elders (20–23).

13. *Israel's rebellion: Jehovah's case (20).*
14. *The sword of judgment (21).*
15. *Jerusalem's indictment (22).*
16. *Two evil sisters: a parable (23).*

Almost a year goes by before the next historically documented confrontation between the elders of Judah and the God of Israel (Jehovah) through His prophet (Ezekiel). This confrontation occurs in the fall of 591 BC (Ezekiel 20:1) and is recorded in Ezekiel 20–23. It is documented as a series of exchanges between Ezekiel and Jehovah, explaining Jehovah's response to this new confrontation. Jehovah explains to the prophet why Judah will be judged and how they have violated His covenant relationship with them. What emerges is a picture of the impenitence of Judah, despite its transgressions against Jehovah. There are over 200 first person singular divine pronouns spoken by Jehovah in identifying Himself during this series of four encounters. Jehovah begins by explaining that He will not be brought into judgment by Judah or its leaders concerning this matter (Ezekiel 20:3). Jehovah's response to Ezekiel can be best understood when broken down into a chapter by chapter analysis.

Each of the four encounters focuses on one encounter between Ezekiel and Jehovah. Chapter 20 is the foundational chapter of Jehovah's response and lays out the case of Israel's rebellion. Chapter 21 speaks of the sword of Jehovah's judgment for this rebellion. Chapter 22 is Jehovah's indictment against His people. And the final chapter makes Jehovah's case through a parable about two evil sisters. The two sisters figuratively represent the northern and southern kingdoms of Israel, both of which violated their covenant relationships with Jehovah and deserved the judgment that came upon them.

588 BC

Judgment of Palestine proclaimed (24–25).

17. *Prophecy against Judah: Boiling pot parable (24).*
18. *Prophecy against Ammon (25:1–7).*
    Prophecy against Moab (25:8–11).
    Prophecy against Edom (25:12–14).
    Prophecy against Philistia (25:15–17).

The final siege of Jerusalem and Nebuchadnezzar's assault that resulted in the conquest of Judah and Palestine began in 588 BC. Ezekiel 24–25, Ezekiel's documentation of his seventeenth and eighteenth divine encounters, contains prophetic statements from Jehovah to Ezekiel concerning the ultimate outcome of this military campaign by Babylon. Thus, in January 588 BC (Ezekiel 24:1), Jehovah spoke to Ezekiel and foretold the conquest of Judah, Ammon, Moab, Edom, and Philistia. The parable of the boiling pot was used in chapter 24 as a visual of the fact that the "fullness of time" for Judah's ultimate collapse had come.

In these two chapters, Jehovah used forty-five first person singular divine pronouns to identify Himself. In Ezek. 24:7, Jehovah assured the prophet that "I the Lord have spoken it: it shall come to pass, and I will do it; I will not go back, neither will I repent; according to thy ways, and according to thy doings, shall they judge thee."

Throughout the remainder of this encounter, Jehovah repeatedly states that the judgment of Judah and Palestine was coming and by these judgments, the observers would "know that I am the Lord" (Ezek. 24:24,27, 25:5,7,11,17). Jeremiah was present in Jerusalem during Babylon's siege of 588–586 BC. He twice confirmed the date of the beginning of this siege as documented by Ezekiel's divine encounter (Jer. 39:1–3, 52:4–6). The writer of 2 Kings also confirms Ezekiel's date (2 Kings 25:1–3). Ezekiel's God here demonstrated His omniscience, omnipotence, omnipresence, and sovereignty.

The eighteen encounters between Ezekiel and Jehovah, before the final siege of Jerusalem by Babylon, establish an understanding of Ezekiel's perception of the person of Jehovah. Ezekiel had a grand view of Jehovah. He was a divine person Who sat above the heavens and intervened on the earth. He spoke directly to the prophet and was able to transport the prophet in time and space in order to enlighten the mind of the prophet. He was patient, kind, loving, and merciful.

Yet, He was a God of judgment, and the time of judgment had come for Judah. He was a God of relationship. Ezekiel was in relationship with this God. Judah had transgressed its relationship with this God throughout the course of history, and the time of His judgment upon them had come. Jehovah used 365 first person singular divine pronouns in His eighteen encounters with Ezekiel, prior to the final Babylonian siege of Jerusalem. The first encounter took place in 593 BC. The last of these eighteen encounters between Jehovah and Ezekiel took place in January 588 BC.

I. Ezekiel's encounters during the final Babylonian siege of Jerusalem

587 BC

19. *Judgment of Egypt proclaimed (29:1–16).*
20. *Judgment against Pharaoh by Jehovah (30:20–26).*
21. *Assyria as an example for Egypt (31).*

During the three-year period of Babylon's final siege on Jerusalem, Ezekiel, who was living in Babylon, had a series of four encounters which were distinctly different than the encounters which he had experienced with Jehovah before the final siege. In His encounters with Ezekiel up to this time, the historical record reveals an exclusive focus by Jehovah, mainly on Judah, but to a limited extent, also on the neighboring countries in Palestine. Judah was the subject of Jehovah's conversations with Ezekiel in chapters 1–24. In chapter 25, Jehovah gave proclamations that, if they came to pass, would establish Him as God over the land of Palestine.

Beginning in 587 BC, Jehovah broadens the focus of His revelations to Ezekiel to include the nations outside of Palestine that had military and political interactions with Judah. Through this series of encounters, Jehovah was proclaiming Himself to be ruler over all the kingdoms on earth. The kingdoms that were considered the seats of political and military power during this era were not exempt from the sovereign rule of Jehovah. Though Judah was under siege and threatened by the kingdoms of men, Jehovah, the prophet would understand, was truly omnipotent, omniscient, omnipresent, and sovereign in all the earth.

The series of four encounters between Jehovah and Ezekiel that dealt with Jehovah's judgment of countries outside the land of Palestine occurred over a period of several months (about thirteen months) during the early portion of Babylon's three year siege of Jerusalem. The first of these encounters, Ezekiel's nineteenth historically documented encounter with Jehovah, occurs in January 587 BC (Ezek. 29:1). In this encounter, Jehovah gives Ezekiel a prophecy declaring the futility of Egypt's support for Judah against the military campaign of Babylon (Ezek. 29:1–16).

In 588 BC, Jehovah had spoken a similar warning to Jeremiah, the prophet living in Jerusalem during the final siege, in His fifty-second encounter with Jeremiah (Jer. 46:13–28). In His encounter with Jeremiah, Jehovah used eleven first person singular divine pronouns. In this very similar encounter with Ezekiel, Jehovah used eighteen first person singular divine pronouns. In the encounter with Ezekiel, three times Jehovah declared that the result of His judgment upon Egypt would be that they shall know that "I am the Lord" (Ezek. 29:6,9,16).

Not quite four months later, at the end of April 587 BC, Ezekiel had his twentieth historically documented encounter with Jehovah (Ezek. 30:20). In the brief record of this encounter (Ezek. 30:20–26), Ezekiel records an additional confirmation that Jehovah would not allow Egypt to prevent Babylon from successfully conquering Jerusalem. Jehovah was the person Who ultimately determined Judah's future, not Pharaoh. Jehovah used thirteen additional first person singular divine pronouns in this encounter. Two more times during this brief follow-up encounter with Ezekiel, Jehovah stated that the Egyptians would know that "I am the Lord" (Ezek. 30:25,26).

About two months later, in June 587 BC, no doubt, as Ezekiel is continuing to prophecy the downfall of Jerusalem and the futility of the hope of his people in Egypt's help, Jehovah spoke again to reassure His prophet of the accuracy and the certainty of His prophetic message (Ezek. 31:1). In this encounter, Jehovah directed the attention of His prophet to the pages of history which testified to His power to bring to pass that which He had declared prophetically. Jehovah compared Egypt of 587 BC to Assyria, which had been the great world power during the time of Isaiah's ministry (740–686 BC). God had used Assyria to humble the rebellious northern kingdom of Israel in 722 BC. When Assyria was lifted up in its own sight, Jehovah prophesied, through the ministry of Isaiah (Is. 13–14, specifically 14:24–25), that Assyria would be destroyed. In 612 BC, Nabopolasser, Nebuchadnezzar, and the Babylonians defeated the great Assyrian empire.

It is instructive to note that Jehovah compares the loftiness of Assyria—an earthly empire—to the trees of the Garden of Eden (Ezek. 31:8–9). Eden, in the minds of Jehovah and of Ezekiel, was an actual geographical location in the history of the earth. If mighty Assyria had fallen to Babylon, an event that had occurred during Ezekiel's childhood and during the lifetime of many of the captives who were in exile with Ezekiel, was it so amazing that Jehovah could thwart the interventions of Egypt using this same Babylon, His current instrument of judgment?

Jehovah declared to His prophet that He would deliver mighty Egypt into the hands of "the mighty one of the heathen" and "the terrible of the nations" (Ezek. 31:11–12). The cataclysmic collapse of Egypt's efforts and of Pharaoh, the leader of Egypt, are described by Jehovah in Ezekiel 31:13–18. The slaughter of the Egyptians and the subsequent disarray of its reigning Pharaoh are described in epic fashion, using phrases that are nostalgic of the early catastrophes that befell humankind when they resisted the will of Jehovah. Jehovah used nine more first person singular divine pronouns in this, His twenty-first encounter with Ezekiel. After the twenty-first encounter between Jehovah and Ezekiel, the case against Egypt is closed for the present.

586 BC

22. *Judgment of Tyre and Sidon by Jehovah (26–28).*

The fantastic descriptive phrases used by Jehovah to declare His judgment upon the nations that resist His will, as recorded by Ezekiel, continued throughout the remainder of Babylon's final siege on Jerusalem. Jehovah's prophecy against Tyre and Sidon, the subject of Ezekiel's twenty-second encounter with Jehovah, is a topic of intense theological discussion. Some of these discussions are fueled by scholarly interpretations of the descriptive phrases Jehovah chooses in His declaration of judgment upon Tyre and Sidon in this encounter. The encounter is recorded in Ezekiel 26–28. It took place in early 586 BC (Ezek. 26:1) during the final stages of the collapse of Jerusalem. The resistance of Jerusalem against Babylon had been broken at this point.

In the prophecy proclaimed in this encounter between Jehovah and Ezekiel, the downfall of Phoenicia (Tyre and Sidon) at the hands of Babylon (Ezek. 26:7) is forecast. Jehovah warned that the demise of Jerusalem was not a cause for the inhabitants of Tyre to celebrate, as now Nebuchadnezzar, the instrument of Jehovah's judgment, would turn his attention to their nation and "they shall know that I am the Lord" (Ezek. 26:6). Furthermore, the destruction of Tyre was certain, according to Jehovah, because "I the Lord have spoken it" (Ezek. 26:14). In Ezekiel 27, the prophet is instructed to lament the fall and the great losses of Tyre at the hand of Babylon.

The theologically controversial portion of this encounter, and the subject of great debate in Christianity for decades, is found in Ezekiel 28. From a historical perspective, it is clear that in this portion of His twenty-second encounter with Ezekiel, Jehovah is prophesying the demise of the leader of Tyre as He had previously prophesied the demise of the leader of Egypt (compare Ezek. 31:11–12 with Ezek. 28:7–10). The grandness of the fall of the king of Tyre (Ezek. 28:12–19) is described in terms similar to those used to describe the fall of Pharaoh, the king of Egypt (Ezek. 31:13–18).

Interestingly, such lofty descriptive imagery was also used by Isaiah around 715 BC when he prophesied the demise of the king of Babylon (Is. 14), a prophecy which was still yet to be fulfilled. What the leaders of each of these nations had in common that warranted such a grand description of their demise was that they each dared to exalt their will above the will of Jehovah. Each time, Jehovah was reassuring His prophet that His will was supreme and that no earthly ruler could prevent Him from accomplishing His will.

A further theological interpretation has become entrenched in the doctrines of the Christian church, however, suggesting that these passages are also descriptive of Jehovah's expelling of Satan from the heavenly realm prior to the creation of man. Confirming or debunking this additional theological interpretation is beyond the scope of this manuscript and has been adequately investigated by other writers.

The historical interpretation of Ezekiel's twenty-second encounter with Jehovah is without debate. In this encounter, Jehovah used thirty-four first person singular divine pronouns in reference to Himself, three times also emphasizing that by His acts of judgment Phoenicia would know that "I am the Lord" (Ezek. 28:22,24,26). Overall, in Ezekiel's four divine encounters that occurred during the final siege of Jerusalem and before Babylon captured the city, Jehovah used sixty-four first person singular divine pronouns in identifying Himself to his prophet.

II. Ezekiel's encounters after the final Babylonian siege of Jerusalem

585 BC

News of the fall of Jerusalem reaches Ezekiel (33:21–39:29).

23. *The fall of Jerusalem declared (33:21–33).*
24. *Unjust shepherds and unjust sheep (34).*
25. *Judgment of Seir by Jehovah (35).*
26. *A message of restoration to the land of Israel (36).*

Two messages of restoration to the nation of Israel (37)

27. *Fourth vision: The valley of dry bones (37:1–14).*
28. *The miraculous fusion of two sticks (37:15–28).*
29. *Prophecy concerning Gog and Magog (38–39).*

The next ten historically documented encounters between Ezekiel and Jehovah occur in 585 BC. This series of encounters begins just before the word of the fall of Jerusalem reaches the ears of Ezekiel (Ezek. 33:21–23) in January 585 BC. Jehovah continues to convey harsh messages of judgment in this series of encounters with Ezekiel. However, as has been consistent with His pattern in pronouncing judgments upon His chosen people, He does not leave them hopeless and in despair; in 585 BC, Jehovah begins also to speak to Ezekiel of Israel's restoration after their judgment has been accomplished.

The seven encounters between Ezekiel and Jehovah that include Ezekiel's fourth vision contain 230 first person singular divine pronouns spoken by Jehovah in reference to Himself. Ezekiel leaves a record of these seven encounters in Ezekiel 33:21–39:29. In the first of these seven encounters, Jehovah reveals to Ezekiel the fall of Jerusalem (Ezek. 33:21–33). In the second encounter, He discusses His judgment upon Israel's shepherds—spiritual leaders in Judah—who have misused their spiritual office and have not fulfilled their spiritual duties, instead using their office for personal gain (Ezek. 34:1–16). He goes on in this second of the seven encounters to speak of His judgment upon the elite social class of Jerusalem for their injustices against the people of the lower socioeconomic groups (Ezek. 34:17–21).

The first of Jehovah's extremely rare references in the book Ezekiel concerning the earthly ministry of the Messiah is made in Ezekiel 34:22–31. Here, Jehovah declares that He will judge between cattle and cattle—higher and lower socioeconomic status people (Ezek. 34:22). He goes on to say that He will set up one shepherd over His people, someone whom He calls "my servant David" (Ezek. 34:23). This is an unmistakable reference to the descendant of David, promised when Jehovah established the Davidic covenant around 997 BC (2 Samuel 7:1–16; 1 Chronicles 17:1–14).

Among the prophets that preceded Ezekiel, Isaiah gave the most detailed description of this coming Messiah. Isaiah wrote about this Messiah around 700 BC (see Isaiah 55:1–4 and Isaiah 40–48). In this, His twenty-fourth encounter with Ezekiel, Jehovah states, "I the Lord will be their God and My servant David a prince among them" (Ezek. 34:24). Thus, Jehovah makes a distinction between Himself and this earthly descendant of David.

This assertion is consistent with the fact that Jehovah as an eternal divine person is descendant to none. At the same time, it is not inconsistent with the eventual Christian teaching that the Messiah was both God and man. That which was human in the Messiah was a descendant of David, while the divine person residing in the Messiah was Jehovah.

While Ezekiel 34:23–24 is consistent with Jehovah's mindfulness of the Davidic covenant, Ezekiel 34:26 is a reminder of Jehovah's faithfulness to the Abrahamic covenant. This covenant was first made around 2091 BC. In the Abrahamic covenant, Jehovah promised to bless the whole world through the seed of Abraham (Gen. 12:1–5, 22:18). In regard to the promise which He made to Abraham, Jehovah spoke of showers of blessing to Ezekiel. The Messiah of whom Ezekiel wrote in Ezekiel 34 is the fulfillment of both the Davidic covenant and the Abrahamic covenant.

The third in this series of seven encounters between Ezekiel and Jehovah is a message of judgment for the land of Seir, the descendants of Esau. The inhabitants of Seir, like the people of Tyre and Sidon (Ezek. 26–28), celebrated the fall of Jerusalem to Babylon. In this encounter, documented in Ezekiel 35, there are twenty-five first person singular divine pronouns. Jehovah uses the expression "I am the Lord" (Ezek. 35:4, 9, 12, 15) while declaring the judgment that is coming on the people of Seir. By the judgment that He brings upon Seir, Jehovah proclaims, "they shall know Him."

This encounter is followed by a series of three consecutive encounters in which Jehovah speaks to Ezekiel of the restoration of Israel. First, Jehovah instructs Ezekiel to prophesy concerning the restoration of the land of Israel (Ezek. 36:1–15). He then proceeds, in the same encounter, to prophesy of the restoration of the people of Israel (Ezek. 36:16–38). What is most interesting about Jehovah's conversation with Ezekiel in chapter 36 is Jehovah's allusion to a time when the spirit of Jehovah would live inside of men and direct the lives of men through this intimate relationship. This promise of Jehovah is essentially the same promise that Jehovah spoke to Jeremiah about three years previously, in 588 BC (Jer. 31:31–34).

In Ezekiel 36:25–27, Jehovah declares, "Then will I sprinkle clean water upon you, and ye shall be clean: from all your filthiness, and from all your idols, will I cleanse you. A new heart also will I give you, and a new spirit will I put within you: and I will take away the stony heart out of your flesh, and I will give you an heart of flesh. And I will put My spirit within you, and cause you to walk in My statutes, and ye shall keep My judgments, and do them." This promise is Jehovah's second messianic reference to Ezekiel.

The writer of Hebrews repeated Jehovah's words to Jeremiah (and by proxy, His message to Ezekiel) approximately thirty years after Jesus instituted the new covenant and birth the Christian church (Hebrews 8:10–12). Joel first mentioned this concept of the indwelling spirit of Jehovah within His people around 835 BC (Joel 2:28–32). Jehovah's words to Jeremiah and Ezekiel were later confirmations of Jehovah's intentions to foster an internal change in His future followers that would empower them to live out their covenant relationship with Him.

The encounter between Jehovah and Ezekiel, in which Jehovah addresses this internalization of His covenant relationship with His people, contains fifty-six first person singular divine pronouns alone. He concludes this encounter by saying that through this future process, He would cause Israel to know that "I am the Lord" (Ezek. 36:38). In fact, the expressions "I the Lord" (Ezek. 36:36) and "I am the Lord" (Ezek. 36:11,23,38) show up five times in this encounter.

Ezekiel 37 records two encounters between Jehovah and the prophet Ezekiel. These two encounters are number five and six of the series of seven encounters that began in January 585 BC. The twenty-seventh encounter between Ezekiel and Jehovah is the fifth of the series of seven encounters. This encounter is Ezekiel's well-known vision of the valley of dry bones. Ezekiel describes his experience of the vision in Ezekiel 37:1–10 and Jehovah's interpretation of the vision in 37:11–14. The message of the vision—the restoration of a lifeless and scattered nation of people—is resounding. The means by which the restoration of Jehovah's people is going to be accomplished, according to Jehovah, is through the power and person of Jehovah—"I am the Lord" and "I have spoken it" (Ezek. 37:6,13,14).

In Ezekiel's twenty-eighth encounter with Jehovah (Ezek. 37:15–28), Ezekiel describes the miraculous fusion of two sticks while he held them together in his hand (Ezek. 37:17). The miracle of the fusion of these two sticks is accomplished through the power and person of Jehovah, like the restoration of life to the dry bones in the vision that preceded this encounter. The miraculous fusion of the sticks represented the reunion of the northern and southern kingdoms into one unified nation (Ezek. 37:18–19).

The third and final reference in the book of Ezekiel that can be interpreted as having messianic significance is found at the end of this twenty-eighth encounter (Ezek. 37:24). Here again, Jehovah speaks to His prophet of "David My servant" who, in the future, would be king and shepherd over His people. He goes on to say that this David would be their prince forever and that He (Jehovah) would make an everlasting covenant with His people. This clearly links the person and work of Ezekiel's Messiah with Jeremiah's Messiah (Jer. 23:7–8, 30:9, 31:31–34, 33:14–15), Isaiah's Messiah (Isaiah 55:1–4, Isaiah 40–49), and David's descendant (2 Samuel 7:1–16; 1 Chronicles 17:1–14).

Jehovah concludes this encounter by saying to Ezekiel that through His fulfillment of these incredible promises of restoration among His people, the heathen would know that "I the Lord" sanctify Israel (Ezek. 37:28). Jehovah used seventy-two first person singular divine pronouns between the three combined messages of restoration documented in Ezekiel 36:16–37:28.

Ezekiel's final encounter with Jehovah that is included in the series of seven documented in Ezekiel 33:21–39:29 is a prophetic message from Jehovah concerning His judgment on Gog and Magog.

Discussions concerning the possible eschatological significance of this prophecy by Jehovah continue to this day. Even today, the historical identity of Gog and Magog remain unclear. Thus, some have concluded that the characters and places mentioned in this encounter are figurative and not literal.

What we know is that in this encounter with Ezekiel, Jehovah used sixty-seven first person singular divine pronouns, thus making it abundantly clear that it is the divine person, Jehovah, Who is giving this revelation to Ezekiel. Through this description, Jehovah makes clear both His defense of His people and the hopelessness of those who would fight against Him and His people. Five times in this single encounter, Jehovah states that through His victory over Gog and Magog, others would know "I am the Lord" (Ezek. 38:23, 39:6,7,22,28).

30. *Lamentation for Pharaoh (32:1–16).*
31. *Lamentation for Egypt (32:17–32).*
32. *The watchman, the wicked, and the way of the Lord (33:1–20).*

Jehovah's next two encounters with Ezekiel in 585 BC, documented in Ezekiel 32, took place during the month of March. Both of these encounters, which are separated by only two weeks (Ezek. 32:1,17), are prophecies against Pharaoh and Egypt. Encounters nineteen, twenty, and twenty-one had addressed the subject of the judgment of Egypt and Pharaoh in 587 BC. At that time Jehovah had made an elaborate case for why the people of Judah should not place their hope in Egypt and Pharaoh. Now, two years or so later, and after the fall of Jerusalem to Babylon, Jehovah temporarily reopens His case against Egypt and Pharaoh.

Yet again, Jehovah emphasizes that through Egypt's calamity at the hands of Babylon, they shall know that "I am the Lord" (Ezek. 32:15). These two encounters have a combined twenty-five first person singular divine pronouns referencing the person of Jehovah.

In His final historically documented encounter with Ezekiel in 585 BC, Jehovah revisits the theme of the watchman. This is a theme He had placed on Ezekiel's prophetic ministry and a title He had placed upon Ezekiel from the outset—recall Ezekiel's second encounter with Jehovah in 593 BC (Ezek. 3:16–27). Now, eight years and over thirty encounters later, and after Ezekiel had seen that many of the judgments which Jehovah had instructed him to prophesy had actually come to pass, Jehovah reminds the prophet of the responsibilities of his office as a watchman (Ezek. 33:7–9).

According to Jehovah, it is not the responsibility of the watchman to turn the people. The response of the people to the message of Jehovah through the watchman is the responsibility of the people who hear the message (Ezek. 33:12–16). Neither Jehovah nor His messenger can be blamed for the consequences of the evil choices of those who refuse to change in response to Jehovah's admonitions (Ezek. 33:11,17–20). Though one is judged because of his choices, Jehovah the compassionate God makes it clear that "I have no pleasure in the death of the wicked" (Ezek. 33:11).

In His second encounter with Ezekiel in 593 (Ezek. 3:16–27), Jehovah had used eleven first person singular divine pronouns to identify Himself. In this final encounter with Ezekiel in 585 BC, Jehovah used twelve first person singular divine pronouns in reference to Himself. The divine personhood of Jehovah is clear to Ezekiel, after nearly a decade of interacting with Him.

573 BC

Fifth vision: Temple restoration

33. *Temple and priesthood restored (40–48).*

More than a decade after his last historically documented encounter with Jehovah (Ezek. 32:17) and two decades after his first (Ezek. 1:2), Ezekiel has another vision. This vision, Ezekiel's thirty-third encounter with Jehovah, occurs in 573 BC and is documented in the last nine chapters of his book (Ezek. 40–48). In September 592 BC, during Ezekiel's third vision and fifth encounter with Jehovah, Jehovah had taken Ezekiel back to Jerusalem to witness the defiling of His temple at the hands of the priests that remained there while Ezekiel was living among the captives in Babylon (Ezek. 8:1–12:7). Because of the abominable idolatrous practices that were rampant in the temple, the glory of God (His presence among His people) had been relocated outside of the temple and outside of the city in sequential steps (Ezek. 8:4, 9:3, 10:4, 10:18–19, 11:22–23).

Now, nearly twenty years later, in April 573 BC, Jehovah gives Ezekiel a new vision in which the temple is restored, His relationship with the priesthood is restored, and the presence of the Lord returns to the temple. The person of Jehovah is undeniable in this new vision of Ezekiel. In Ezekiel 40:1–2, the prophet says that the hand of Jehovah brought him to a mountain outside of Jerusalem. An angelic being escorts and interacts with Ezekiel intermittently throughout this vision. Ezekiel took an extensive tour of the restored city and the restored temple according to Ezekiel 40–42. Then, the glory of Jehovah that had left the temple and the city in Ezekiel's vision in 592 BC returned to the city and the temple in the vision he had in 573 BC (Ezekiel 43:1–6).

The vision of the return of the glory of God to the temple is associated with a lengthy interaction between Jehovah and the prophet (Ezekiel 43:7–46:18). The relationship-oriented God begins this exchange by declaring His intention to live in the presence of His people forever and the circumstances necessary for this to occur. In Ezekiel 43:7–9, Ezekiel records the initial remarks made by Jehovah as they begin the dialogue that follows the return of the glory of God to the temple. He writes, "And He said unto me, Son of man, the place of My throne, and the place of the soles of My feet, where I will dwell in the midst of the children of Israel forever, and My holy name, shall the house of Israel no more defile, neither they, nor their kings, by their whoredom, nor by the carcasses of their kings in their high places. In their setting of their threshold by My thresholds, and their post by My posts, and the wall between Me and them, they have even defiled My holy name by their abominations that they have committed: wherefore I have consumed them in Mine anger. Now let them put away their whoredom, and the carcasses of their kings, far from Me, and I will dwell in the midst of them forever."

After many details of the restored temple and the restored covenant relationship between Jehovah and His people are given, Jehovah concludes this vision by saying that the restored city, the place of His residence among His people, would bear His name. It would be called Jehovah-shammah—the Lord is there (Ezek. 48:35).

Nearly sixty first person singular divine pronouns are used by Jehovah during this lengthy and detail-filled vision. Interestingly, there were sixty singular divine pronouns referencing Jehovah in the temple vision that had taken place in 592 BC. Thirty-seven first person singular divine pronouns were used by Jehovah in the vision in 592 BC. Twenty-three third person singular pronouns were used in that vision which had preceded Ezekiel's vision of restoration by nearly two decades.

The vision recorded by the Apostle John around 95–100 AD bears striking resemblances to Ezekiel's vision of the restored temple and Jehovah's restored fellowship with His people. Revelation 21 and 22 contain John's rendition of the restored temple and God's restored fellowship with His people. Like Ezekiel, John describes viewing the new Jerusalem from a high mountain (Ezek. 40:2; Rev. 21:10). As was the case in Ezekiel's vision in 573 BC, in John's vision, the new temple is the place where Jehovah fellowships with His people (Ezek. 48:35; Rev. 21:3). Both men see a single throne occupied by a single divine person Who pursues an intimate relationship with His people that will last throughout eternity (Ezek. 1:26–28, 43:7, 48:35; Rev. 21:5–8, 22:1–4). Thus, John confirms the expectation that Jehovah will ultimately have an everlasting relationship with His chosen people.

571 BC

34. *Babylon's wages (29:17–30:19).*

Ezekiel's final documented encounter with Jehovah occurred two years later in April 571 BC (Ezek. 29:17). This encounter apparently took place after Nebuchadnezzar and the Babylonians had not only routed Judah, they had defeated Tyre and the Phoenicians

(Ezek. 29:18) as Jehovah had ordained in 586 BC (Ezek. 26–28). In this final documented encounter between Ezekiel and Jehovah, Jehovah promised to give Nebuchadnezzar some additional conquest over Egypt as remuneration for the service he rendered against haughty Tyre.

According to Josephus, the siege of Tyre by the Babylonians lasted thirteen years, ending with the conquest of the mainland in 573 BC, two years before this final encounter between Ezekiel and Jehovah. Thus, the foundational conditions for this final encounter can be established based upon extra-biblical historical information. This final encounter, covered in Ezekiel 29:17–30:19, contains twenty-four first person singular divine pronouns spoken by Jehovah in reference to Himself. Jehovah also used the expressions "I am the Lord" (Ezek. 29:21, 30:19) and "I the Lord" (Ezek. 30:12) in this final encounter; expressions which He used commonly across the decades long ministry of Ezekiel beginning in 593 BC (Ezek. 5:15,17, 6:7,10,13,14, 7:4,9,27).

Ezekiel: Summary and Conclusions

Ezekiel's ministry began in 593 BC in the fifth year of his captivity in Babylon. It was not nearly as long as the ministry of Jeremiah but covered just over two decades nonetheless. He had nearly three dozen encounters with Jehovah including multiple visions, several parables and prophecies, and a number of instructions to conduct enactments as object lessons witnessed by his fellow Judean exiles in Babylon. Jehovah spoke approximately 1,000 first person singular divine pronouns over the course of Ezekiel's ministry, clearly establishing His personhood in the mind of this prophet.

The visions experienced by Ezekiel establish the omnipresence, omnipotence, and omniscience of his God. The parables and prophecies testify of Jehovah's omniscience and omnipotence. Jehovah's interactions with Ezekiel and the content of Jehovah's conversations regarding His chosen people are a testament of His covenant relationship orientation as a person. Ezekiel's record contains more first person singular divine pronouns referencing Jehovah than any other writer of the Old Testament. It also contains a remarkable number of divine titles like "I the Lord" and "I am the Lord." These facts establish the undeniable truth that Ezekiel perceived Jehovah to be a true divine person and not a theological concept or fictional character.

Encountering Jehovah with Daniel

Daniel was contemporary with both Jeremiah and Ezekiel. Jeremiah began his prophetic ministry around 627 BC. Ezekiel was taken captive into Babylon during Babylon's second invasion of Jerusalem around 597 BC and began his prophetic ministry in 593 BC. Daniel, on the other hand, was taken captive during Babylon's first recorded invasion of Jerusalem around 605 BC. He stepped into his unique role in Jehovah's ministry to humanity between 605 and 602 BC.

Daniel's ministry began during the same period of time as the ministries of Jeremiah and Ezekiel but was a much more far-reaching ministry than that of either of his prophetic contemporaries. Jeremiah's ministry was centered in Jerusalem but may well have also extended to Egypt while continuing to focus on the people of Judah. The ministry of Ezekiel was addressed to the captives of Judah who were exiles in Babylon. Ezekiel's ministry extended over a period of approximately two decades, it's records ending in 571 BC. The ministry of Daniel had a much broader focus than the ministries of his contemporaries; also, it extended over a period of seven decades, an extremely lengthy time period.

Daniel's experience with Jehovah was similar in many ways to that of Joseph, the son of Jacob, who lived around 1900–1800 BC and was referred to by his brothers as "this dreamer" (Gen. 37:19). Dreams were the vehicles Jehovah used to launch Joseph's ministry and direct his paths. Jehovah used dreams to provide insights into Joseph's personal future and the future in general (Gen. 37:20, 40:5–8, 41:1,14–16).

Between 605 BC and 537 BC, some 1,300 years after Jehovah had dealt with Joseph through dreams, He relied primarily on this mode of communication once again throughout the course of the profound prophetic ministry of Daniel. Just as there are no direct verbal communications from Jehovah in the record of His dealings with Joseph, so there is no record of any words spoken directly by Jehovah in His communications with Daniel. Nonetheless, the interventions of Jehovah are clear, and the dealings of Daniel and others with Jehovah are unmistakable. Furthermore, the character of Jehovah is evident throughout the book of Daniel.

The attributes that Jehovah demonstrated in His interactions with Daniel are consistent with those He demonstrated in His interactions with Daniel's ministerial contemporaries and Daniel's ministerial predecessors. This validates that He is the same divine person known by other men of Israel's history.

The record found in the book bearing the name of the prophet Daniel shares eleven events that give insight into the character of Jehovah. Peering through chronological lenses, these encounters can be grouped into three distinct time frames:

1. Encounters during the reign of Nebuchadnezzar,
2. Encounters in Babylon after the reign of Nebuchadnezzar, and
3. Encounters during the reign of the Medes and the Persians.

Encounters during the reign of Nebuchadnezzar:

1. *605 BC Jehovah's intervention permits Daniel's captivity (1:1–7).*
2. *603 BC Jehovah's intervention positions Daniel among his captors (1:8–21).*
3. *603 BC Revelation of Nebuchadnezzar's dream of the great image (2:1–49).*
4. *603 BC Shadrach, Meshach, and Abednego in the furnace (3:1–30).*

5. *569 BC Interpretation of Nebuchadnezzar's final dream (4:1–37).*

The first two encounters of Daniel with Jehovah are inferred, albeit scripturally supported. In Daniel 1:1–2, Daniel reports that in the third year of the reign of Jehoiakim (609–598 BC), Jehovah gave Jehoiakim into the hands of Nebuchadnezzar. History records that this event occurred in 605 BC. From Daniel's perspective—a perspective reconfirmed in Daniel 9:4–14—this invasion, and therefore his captivity, was an intervention by Jehovah in the national life of Judah and in the personal life of Daniel (Dan. 1:2–4). This, therefore, constitutes the first personal divine encounter that Daniel recognizes in his record of history.

The second intervention of Jehovah in the life of Daniel is the favor Jehovah allowed Daniel to have with his captors (Dan. 1:9–14). It was this favor that allowed Daniel to pursue and fulfill the desire of his heart to not defile himself with the king's meat. Jehovah's intervention and Daniel's heart also worked together to position Daniel within the kingdom of Babylon for the decades of ministry which were to follow (Dan. 1:8,17–21).

Daniel's third encounter with Jehovah is the first direct encounter between Daniel and Jehovah recorded in his historical account. This encounter took place during the second year of Daniel's captivity, 603 BC (Dan. 2:1), while he and his three close companions—Hananiah, Mishael, and Azariah—were still in their initial three years of training in Babylon (Daniel 1:4–6). Around 1900–1800 BC, Jehovah had given a dream to Pharaoh while Joseph was a captive in Egypt and had given the interpretation of the dream to Joseph, thereby creating an opportunity for him to be promoted to a position of influence in Egypt (Gen. 41). Similarly, in 603 BC, Jehovah gives Nebuchadnezzar a dream, and then He gives Daniel, a captive in Babylon, the interpretation of the dream, thereby positioning Daniel for promotion within the kingdom of Babylon. Daniel's experience, however, differs from that of Joseph.

While Pharaoh was able to recall the details of his dream to Joseph, Nebuchadnezzar can remember neither the dream nor can he provide an interpretation or understanding of his dream. In both cases, Jehovah demonstrated His omniscience. Each is reminiscent of when Jehovah revealed to Elisha the strategic plans of the king of Syria against the king of Israel around 848 BC (2 Kings 6:8–11). Even the thoughts of the mind are not hidden from the omniscient God of Israel.

The circumstances surrounding Daniel's first historically detailed encounter with Jehovah (his third encounter overall) are described in Daniel 2:1–16. Throughout his decades of ministry, Daniel established himself as a man of prayer; the crisis in 603 BC was the first historical encounter in support of this assessment of the prophet Daniel.

Daniel and his close friends called a prayer meeting to seek the intervention of Jehovah during their crisis (Dan. 2:17–18). Jehovah answered this prayer and revealed both the details of Nebuchadnezzar's dream and the interpretation of its meaning (Dan. 2:19). Daniel's perception of the person of Jehovah is clearly recorded in his account of this encounter. Daniel sees Jehovah as the omnipotent, omniscient, and sovereign God of heaven, yet an approachable, personable, and caring God of relationship (Dan. 2:17–18,27–30). In Daniel 2:17–26, he describes Jehovah as "the God of heaven," the possessor of all knowledge, wisdom and power, and the one Who dispenses these positions and gifts to people and nations at His sovereign discretion.

Emphasizing his understanding of Jehovah as a person, Daniel used seven third person singular divine pronouns and the pronoun *Who* in reference to his God in Daniel 2:20–23. He referenced Jehovah as "the God of heaven" three more times as he made his presentation to Nebuchadnezzar in Daniel 2:27–45. He also used the title "the great God" along with yet two more third person singular divine pronouns (Dan. 2:29,38). Daniel sees the revelation of Nebuchadnezzar's dream as an act of compassion and personal concern from Jehovah to him and his three friends because of their relationship with Him and because of Jehovah's concern for their well-being (Dan. 2:17–23,30,36).

The length of time into the future that Jehovah foretells through Nebuchadnezzar's dream is nothing short of astounding. According to Daniel's interpretation and the annals of history, Nebuchadnezzar's dream (Dan. 2:31–35) foretells the eventual fall of Babylon (Dan. 2:37–38), the rise and fall of the Medes and the Persians (Dan. 2:39), the rise and fall of Greece (Dan. 2:39), the rise and fall of the Roman Empire (Dan. 2:40–43), and the birth, pervasiveness, and persistence of the kingdom of God in Jesus Christ, the Messiah (Dan. 2:44–45).

According to Daniel, this kingdom of God in Christ would be born during the reign of Rome. Daniel interpreted the dream of Nebuchadnezzar in 603 BC. Babylon fell to the Medes and the Persians in 539 BC. The Persian Empire was conquered by Alexander the Great and the Grecians in 330 BC. Rome conquered Greece around 63 BC. Rome was the great world power during the time of the birth of Christianity around 30 AD. So Nebuchadnezzar's dream in 603 BC foretold events over 600 years in the future with an amazing degree of detail and precision.

Great minds throughout the course of history have validated the historical accuracy of Nebuchadnezzar's dream and Daniel's interpretation thereof. Herodotus (484–425 BC), a noted Greek historian, writes of some of this history in *The Histories*. Flavius Josephus (37–100 AD), a highly regarded Jewish scholar and historian during the days of the Roman Empire, gave several details concerning the historical content addressed by Nebuchadnezzar's dream in *Antiquities of the Jews*. Isaac Newton (1643–1727 AD) wrote an entire manuscript called *Observations Upon the Prophecies of Daniel*, which contained chapters devoted to the historical content in Nebuchadnezzar's dream and Daniel's interpretation. Many other scholars throughout history have confirmed the historicity of the dream and the historical accuracy of its content. Students of the Bible today continue to accept time-tested interpretations of this dream of Nebuchadnezzar. The historicity of this event cannot be questioned without questioning the intellect and rationale of many great minds throughout the course of history.

Another crisis occurred not long after Nebuchadnezzar had this dream, Daniel (and his associates) interpreted it (Dan. 2:17–19,30,36) and Daniel, Hananiah, Mishael, and Azariah were promoted in Babylon (Dan. 2:46–49). While Daniel served as an elite advisor in the court of the king, his three associates were made rulers throughout the various domains of Babylon. The king commissioned the building of a large statue for his subjects to worship (Dan. 3:1–5).

The crisis arose when Daniel's associates, who were committed to the tenets of Judaism handed down since 1446 BC (Exodus 20:1–5), refused to comply with the king's commandment to bow before the idol he had erected, and their stance was communicated to Nebuchadnezzar (Dan. 3:7–12). When Nebuchadnezzar confronted them, their response gave insight into their views concerning Jehovah. It is apparent that they perceived Jehovah to be the same divine person Whom Moses had encountered and Who had given the mandates recorded in Exodus 20.

In their minds, He was the same God Who had delivered their fathers out of the hands of the Egyptians and had divided the Red Sea, allowing them to cross over on dry ground (Exodus 14–15). They were convinced, based upon their understanding of Jehovah and the omniscience and omnipotence for which He was known, that He saw their predicament and was able to deliver them from the judgment of Nebuchadnezzar if they remained faithful to His covenant (Dan. 3:16–18). Their concept of the person of Jehovah is confirmed by the use of the pronouns *Whom* and *He* in Daniel 3:17.

It is possible that the fiery furnace into which they were cast was one of the brick kilns or furnaces used by the Babylonians to melt down metals for the many major building projects for which Nebuchadnezzar is well-known. The three Hebrew boys were subjected to this punishment because of their refusal to submit to the king's mandate which would have been a transgression against their covenant relationship with Jehovah.

While being cast into this brick kiln should have meant certain death for the three servants of Jehovah, the king discovered that Daniel's associates were unhurt by the fire. Furthermore, another human figure is seen accompanying them as they walked around in the fire. It is Nebuchadnezzar, the polytheistic non-Jehovah worshipper, who commented that the fourth person looked like the son of God (Dan. 3:25). He later acknowledged, probably after consultation with Jehovah's servants, that the fourth person was an angel dispatched by Jehovah to protect them because of their faithfulness to Jehovah's covenant (Dan. 3:28).

It is also instructive that Nebuchadnezzar—again possibly due to the input of Shadrach, Meshach, and Abednego—used three third person singular divine pronouns and the pronoun *Who* in reference to their God, "the most high God." In light of this intervention of Jehovah into the affairs of men, Nebuchadnezzar can only conclude that "there is no other God that can deliver after this sort" (Dan. 3:29).

Daniel may have served in the court of Nebuchadnezzar for as many as three decades when Nebuchadnezzar had a second pivotal dream experience. Nebuchadnezzar again required the services of Daniel, who was more mature now, to give an interpretation of the second troubling dream. Some scholars believe that this may have taken place around 570–569 BC. The date is unimportant in this encounter. The important fact in this encounter is that Nebuchadnezzar's dream predicted his eventual short-lived deposing from his throne and his eventual restoration. Jehovah gave the dream to Nebuchadnezzar and gave the interpretation to Daniel (Dan. 4:19–27).

While this dream and the events that unfolded afterward are not validated by extra-biblical documentation directly, a case can certainly be made to validate them. Nebuchadnezzar's experience can be described as a case of boanthropy. Transient cases of mental disturbance and identity crises, like that described concerning Nebuchadnezzar, can be found throughout history. The modern psychiatric literature has reported cases of lycanthropy—people who believe they are a werewolf—as recently as the 1900s. It is not far-fetched at all to believe that a human could conceive of himself as a cow and behave in a manner consistent with Daniel's description of Nebuchadnezzar.

Daniel counseled the king on how to respond to the dream. The king conducted himself in a manner contrary to the counsel of Daniel and suffered the psychiatric break that Daniel foretold (Dan. 4:24–27). In his interpretation of Nebuchadnezzar's dream, Daniel again confirms his view of the person of Jehovah when he calls Him "the most High" and uses the pronoun *He* in reference to Him (Dan. 4:24–25).

Nebuchadnezzar used similar terminology to describe Jehovah as "the King of heaven" and "the Most High" after recovering his mental faculties and his throne (Dan. 4:34–37). There are eight third person singular divine pronouns in Nebuchadnezzar's final description of Daniel's God.

In all, the five encounters of Jehovah with humanity described by Daniel during the reign of Nebuchadnezzar occurred over about thirty-five five years and contain nearly thirty third person singular divine pronouns referencing Jehovah. Two of these encounters are inferred but scripturally supported. Two of these encounters involved Jehovah giving a dream to the ruler and giving the interpretation of the dream to Daniel. The fifth encounter did not involve Daniel, but instead involved his close associates and fellow Jehovah worshippers, Hananiah, Mishael, and Azariah.

In all of these encounters, the person Daniel knew as Jehovah demonstrated His sovereignty, omniscience, and omnipotence as well as the fact that He is a covenant-oriented, personable, approachable, relationship-minded God.

Encounters in Babylon after the reign of Nebuchadnezzar:

6. *553 BC Daniel's vision of the four great beasts (7:1–28).*
7. *551 BC Daniel's vision of the ram and the goat (8:1–27).*
8. *539 BC The hand writing on the wall (5:1–31).*

Nebuchadnezzar was king of the Babylonian Empire for over four decades (605–562 BC), having succeeded his father, Nabopolasser (626–605 BC). Just over two decades after the death of its greatest king, the Babylonian Empire fell to the Medes and the Persians (539 BC). Nebuchadnezzar had two children, Evil-Merodach (son) and Nitocris (daughter). Over the twenty-three-year period after the death of Nebuchadnezzar, the reins of Babylon passed through the hands of his son, Evil-Merodach (562–560 BC), his son-in-law,

Neriglissar (560–556 BC), his grandson, Labashi-Marduk (556 BC), another son-in-law, Nabonidus (556–539 BC), and another grandson, Belshazzar (553–539 BC).

Neriglissar, Labashi-Marduk, Nabodidus, and Belshazzar are all linked to Nebuchadnezzar through his daughter, Nitocris. Neriglissar and Nabonidus were each married to Nitocris in succession. Labashi-Marduk was the son of Neriglissar and Nitocris. Belshazzar was the son of Nabonidus and Nitocris. Belshazzar, Babylon's final king, was a co-regent with Nabonidus who was absent from Babylon for long stretches during his reign.

In 553 BC, without actually vacating his throne, Nabonidus, it is believed, moved away for a lengthy stay. While the lineage of the Babylonian Dynasty is difficult to piece together and is a compilation from multiple, sometimes conflicting sources, there is certainly extra-biblical evidence to support the royal lineage presented in this document. Information from the Babylonian Chronicles, the Nabonidus Cylinder and references in *The Histories* by Herodutus contributed to the construction of this royal lineage.

The historical perspective of the lineage of the Babylonian Dynasty which I support is consistent with the prophetic proclamation of Jehovah to Isaiah in 716 BC concerning Nebuchadnezzar and Babylon. Isaiah 14:22 records that Jehovah proclaimed, "For I will rise up against them, saith the LORD of hosts, and cut off from Babylon the name, and remnant, and son, and nephew, saith the LORD."

In this prophecy, which was proclaimed 177 years before the fall of Babylon, Evil-Merodach and Nitocris would be the remnant, while Belshazzar would be the son of the remnant. Jehovah, in his omniscience, foretold the demise of Nebuchadnezzar, Evil-Merodach, Nitocris, and Belshazzar before they were born. Jehovah had given a similar supporting follow-up prophecy in 597 BC during an encounter with the prophet Jeremiah (Jer. 27:6–7). The prophecy in Jeremiah predated the demise of the Babylonian Empire by nearly sixty years and reads, "And now have I given all these lands into the hand of Nebuchadnezzar the king of Babylon, My servant; and the beasts of the field have I given him also to serve him. And all nations shall serve him, and his son, and his son's son, until the very time of his land come: and then many nations and great kings shall serve themselves of him."

This proposed lineage being true also brings understanding to the insight which the queen, Nitocris, was able to give to the perplexed and frightened king, Belshazzar, at his last feast (Daniel 5:9–12). Nitocris had witnessed the wonders of dream interpretation performed by Daniel (Daniel 2 and 4) during the reign of her father, Nebuchadnezzar, before the birth of her son, Belshazzar. She had lived to observe some of the life and ministry of Daniel and was able to give counsel concerning Daniel to her son.

> Then was king Belshazzar greatly troubled, and his countenance was changed in him, and his lords were astonied.
>
> Now the queen, by reason of the words of the king and his lords, came into the banquet house: and the queen spake and said, "O king, live forever: let not thy thoughts trouble thee, nor let thy countenance be changed:
>
> There is a man in thy kingdom, in whom is the spirit of the holy gods; and in the days of thy father light and understanding and wisdom, like the wisdom of the gods, was found in him; whom the king Nebuchadnezzar thy father, the king, I say, thy father, made master of the magicians, astrologers, Chaldeans, and soothsayers;
>
> Forasmuch as an excellent spirit, and knowledge, and understanding, interpreting of dreams, and shewing of hard sentences, and dissolving of doubts, were found in the same Daniel, whom the king named Belteshazzar: now let Daniel be called, and he will shew the interpretation. (Dan. 5:9–12 KJV)

It was during the reign of Belshazzar that Daniel had his next three historically documented encounters with Jehovah.

Jehovah's Fifth Intervention in Daniel's Life (Daniel 7)

The sixth divine encounter in Daniel, Jehovah's fifth intervention in the personal life of Daniel, was Daniel's first personal prophetic vision. On two previous occasions, once around 603 BC and once around 569 BC, Jehovah had revealed to Daniel the interpretations of the dreams of Babylon's greatest king, Nebuchadnezzar. After the death of Nebuchadnezzar, there is no record of divine encounters until the first year of the reign of Belshazzar. In this year, 553 BC, Jehovah gives His prophet his own prophetic dream.

The interpretation of Daniel's dream from 553 BC is largely consistent with the dream that Nebuchadnezzar had in 603 BC, some fifty years earlier. Daniel's dream predates the fall of Babylon by fourteen years and foretells the rise and fall of two of the kingdoms that would succeed the Babylonian Empire. The head of gold from Nebuchadnezzar's dream (Dan. 2:31–35,38) and the lion in Daniel's dream (Dan. 7:4) were prophetic representations of the Babylonian Empire which was conquered by the Medes and the Persians in 539 BC.

The kingdom of the Medes and the Persians, the breast and arms of silver in Nebuchadnezzar's dream (Dan. 2:31–35,39), was represented by a bear in the dream Jehovah gave to Daniel (Dan. 7:5). A third kingdom arose after this in both dreams. This third sequential kingdom which arose was the kingdom of Greece. Greece was the great world power from 330–63 BC and was represented by the belly and thighs of brass in Nebuchadnezzar's dream (Dan. 2:31–35,39), and the leopard in Daniel's (Dan. 7:6).

At this point, the dreams of Nebuchadnezzar and Daniel take divergent paths. While Nebuchadnezzar's dream reveals the next kingdom in historical succession after the fall of Greece, the Roman Empire, Daniel's dream becomes apocalyptic at this point. The fourth beast in Daniel's dream appears to be representative of the political setting before the God of heaven issues a final judgment upon humanity.

Daniel initially describes Jehovah as the God of heaven (Dan. 2:18,19,37,44). In the polytheistic world of Babylon, Daniel's God became known, however, as "the Most High God" or simply "the Most High." Daniel's perspective of the personhood of the God of heaven does not deviate from that which had been held from the beginning of human history.

Adam had experienced Jehovah as a single person walking in the garden of Eden and before Whom he stood for judgment after he disobeyed His commandment. This is demonstrated by the use of first person singular pronouns in Genesis 3:1–19.

Abraham had experienced Jehovah as a single person when he intervened before Him for evil Sodom and Gomorrah (Genesis 18:17–33). This is demonstrated by Jehovah's use of fifteen first person singular divine pronouns in reference to Himself during this particular conversation.

Throughout his 139 encounters with Jehovah, Moses heard Jehovah use nearly 700 first person singular divine pronouns in reference to Himself. Moreover, when Moses was permitted to see the glory of Jehovah, a single person passed by him as indicated by the account in Exodus 33:18–23.

In 740 BC, Isaiah saw One sitting on a throne, Whose glory filled the temple (Isaiah 6).

Jeremiah knew Jehovah as the divine person Who had given the law to Moses and Who had called him to ministry and promised to be his support when he met opposition (note the twelve first person singular divine pronouns spoken by Jehovah in His initial call of Jeremiah in Jer. 1:4–12).

In 593 BC, Ezekiel saw Jehovah sitting on a throne above the firmament over the heads of the four living creatures (Eze. 1:26–28) and heard Him speak to him and give him a call to the prophetic ministry.

And in 553 BC, Daniel saw this same Jehovah sitting on a throne in the first dream that he reports personally having received from the Lord. The title that Daniel gives to the person Whom he sees is unique to Daniel's writing. Daniel calls Him "the Ancient of Days" (Dan. 7:9,13,22). Daniel describes Him with seven third person singular divine pronouns in these verses of scripture. He is the same person Daniel had known as "the Most High" during the reign of Nebuchadnezzar (Dan. 7:18,22,25,27).

Finally, it is instructive to note the description of Israel's Messiah in the writings of Daniel and to compare Daniel's Messiah with the person Isaiah described as Messiah 150–200 years earlier. In the vision which Daniel saw in 553 BC, the Messiah is seen as "One like the Son of man" Who appears before "the Ancient of Days," riding on the clouds of heaven. This Messiah is given dominion, glory, and an everlasting kingdom from among all the nations of the earth (Dan. 7:13–14).

The "One like the Son of man" (Dan. 7:13) correlates seamlessly with "the stone cut out of the mountain without hands" (Dan. 2:34–35,44–45) described by Daniel in his interpretation of Nebuchadnezzar's dream in 603 BC. The kingdom of "the One like the Son of man" is the same kingdom" set up by the God of heaven which shall never be destroyed" seen in Nebuchadnezzar's dream (Dan. 2:44, 7:14). While "the one like the Son of man" is clearly distinct from "the Ancient of Days" in Daniel's vision (Dan. 7:13), his kingdom is the same as that set up by "the God of heaven" (Dan. 2:44). This kingdom is described as a kingdom given to "the people of the saints of "the Most High, Whose kingdom is an everlasting kingdom" (Dan. 7:27).

The ruler of this everlasting kingdom is seen as a single divine ruler ("Him" in Daniel 7:27). The person Who is the ruler of the everlasting kingdom of Nebuchadnezzar's dream and Daniel's vision is "the Ancient of Days," "the God of heaven," "the Most High," and "One like the Son of man" who would come one day in the future. Daniel's Messiah, therefore, was currently "the Ancient of Days," but in the future would come as "One like the Son of man." This is exactly the Messiah described by Isaiah in his much more comprehensive description between 740 BC and 686 BC. The writings of Isaiah make a comprehensive case that Jehovah, Daniel's "Ancient of Days," is the coming Messiah.

During his prophetic ministry, Isaiah introduced the theme of Jehovah as Messiah around 735 BC (Is. 7:12–14) but developed it fully between 701–686 BC (Isaiah 42, 49–57). While Daniel simply describes the Messiah as "One like the son of man," Isaiah described him more comprehensively as the child who would be a descendant of David (Isaiah 7:12, 9:6, 11:1–4, 12:2, 53:1–2, 55:1–4). Daniel, in the extremely limited record of his interpretation of Nebuchadnezzar's dream, describes the Messiah as "the stone cut out of the mountain" and the instrument by which Jehovah would birth His everlasting kingdom within the earth (Dan. 2:34–35,44–45).

Isaiah more comprehensively describes the process by which the Messiah, as the servant of Jehovah, would establish the everlasting kingdom of Jehovah (Isaiah 42, 53). Additionally, however, Isaiah's writings convincingly develop the idea that the coming Messiah is Jehovah, our judge and savior (Isaiah 1, 6, 9:6,40–48).

In Daniel's vision, the "One like the Son of man" is given the kingdom; it is his kingdom. However, all the subjects of the kingdom serve and obey "the Most High" (Dan. 7:13–14,27). In his writings, Isaiah recorded these words spoken by Jehovah, "I have sworn by Myself, the word is gone out of My mouth in righteousness, and shall not return, That unto Me every knee shall bow, every tongue shall swear" (Is. 45:23).

The Apostle Paul brought ultimate clarity to the vision of Daniel and the proclamation of Jehovah to Isaiah when he wrote, "That at the name of Jesus every knee should bow, of things in heaven, and things in earth, and things under the earth; And that every tongue should confess that Jesus Christ is Lord, to the glory of God the Father" (Phil. 2:10–11).

From 735–686 BC, Isaiah developed a fairly comprehensive message concerning the coming Messiah. In 603 BC, Daniel began to see this coming Messiah. Fifty years later (553 BC), Daniel's understanding is further clarified. By the end of his ministry, Daniel will study this topic, including the writings of Isaiah, and will receive one of the greatest messianic revelations recorded in history.

Jehovah's Sixth Interaction with Daniel (Daniel 8)

Daniel's next divine encounter is his second personally experienced vision. While he described the encounter in 553 BC as "a dream and visions of his head upon his bed" (Dan. 7:1), he is clearly awake throughout this encounter in 551 BC and describes it simply as a vision (Dan. 8:1–2). This encounter, which occurs two years after Daniel's first dream/vision, is connected to the previous experience. This encounter has its own unique significance among Daniel's encounters, however.

With amazing precision, Daniel received a divine revelation of the demise of the kingdom of the Medes and the Persians and the rise and reign of the kingdom of Alexander the Great and his successors and their relationship to the people of Israel. Daniel described this vision in Daniel 8:2–14 and the interpretation in Daniel 8:19–26. An examination of the history that transpired between 539 BC and 63 BC testifies to the incredible foreknowledge of Daniel's God, the person to Whom Daniel would no doubt credit his dream and the interpretation.

Daniel described the expansion of the kingdom of Media and Persia under Cyrus the Great (Dan. 8:3–4,19–20) as a ram with two horns. Cyrus the Great conquered Babylon in 539 BC over a decade after Daniel's vision, and his kingdom proceeded to grow strong as foretold. Alexander the Great conquered the Medes and Persians in 330 BC as pictured by the goat that subdued the ram in this vision which Daniel experienced in 551 BC, two centuries prior to Alexander's conquests (Dan. 8:5–8,21).

In 323 BC, the kingdom of Alexander the Great was subdivided into four kingdoms (Dan. 8:22). According to history, the four divisions were ruled by Ptolemy (Egypt), Seleucas (Syria and Asia Minor), Lysimachus (Thrace), and Cassander (Macedonia and Greece proper) and their successors.

Out of one of these kingdoms, Daniel accurately described the rise of Antiochus IV Epiphanes (175–163 BC), a Seleucid ruler. Furthermore, Daniel described a very specific event in which Antiochus IV Epiphanes defiled the temple of Jehovah by offering a pig on an altar therein to Zeus, a Greek God. History records that Antiochus IV Epiphanes indeed carried out this travesty on December 14, 168 BC. The Maccabean Revolt was intricately connected to this act of desecration by the Greek ruler. These events in Jewish history were foretold nearly 400 years in advance of their documented occurrence (Dan. 8:9–13) and testify to the omniscience and sovereignty of Daniel's God. Furthermore, the care with which Jehovah's messenger attends to Daniel throughout this vision is indicative of the level of care and the relationship-mindedness of Jehovah toward Daniel. Jehovah has been known throughout history to possess this caring relationship-oriented mindset.

Daniel's Seventh Divine Encounter (Dan. 5)

On the night of the conquest of Babylon by the Medes and the Persians, Daniel had his final encounter with Jehovah under the Babylonian Empire. In this encounter, like the two with Nebuchadnezzar, Daniel was Jehovah's interpretive mediator to a Babylonian ruler. Belshazzar was the grandson of Nebuchadnezzar. His mother, Nitocris, was the daughter of Nebuchadnezzar. She knew well of the two dreams Nebuchadnezzar had received from Jehovah, both of which had been interpreted by Daniel. Though she may not have been a practicing believer of Jehovah, she had witnessed His manifestations of omnipotence and omniscience. She understood the basis for the claims of Jehovah being sovereign. No doubt, she had related some of this information to her son, the resident ruler.

Belshazzar was certainly not ignorant of Who the God of Israel was and of the things He valued. It is for this reason that Belshazzar's feast, in 539 BC, was such an affront to Jehovah. Jehovah interrupted this feast with a supernatural manifestation—the fingers of a man's hand appeared and wrote a message on the wall (Dan. 5:5).

Based upon her knowledge that Jehovah had given Daniel the ability to interpret two of her father's dreams years ago, Nitocris advised the king to seek out Daniel to assist in interpreting the meaning of the writing on the wall (Dan. 5:10–12). Daniel's presentation before Belshazzar is recorded in Daniel 5:18–28. Daniel confirms what may well have been previously described by Nitocris—that Nebuchadnezzar had been temporarily deposed as king because of his haughtiness against Jehovah (Dan. 5:18–21). Daniel upbraids Belshazzar because of his transgression against "the Most high God," "the Lord of heaven" (Dan. 5:22–23). He then predicts the demise of the kingdom of Babylon by reading the message communicated by Jehovah through the handwriting on the wall (Dan. 5:23).

Daniel's God, through this encounter, once again demonstrated His omnipotence, omniscience, and sovereignty.

> "The Most High rules in the kingdom of men,
> and gives the kingdom to whomsoever He will."
> (Dan. 4:32)
> "Those that walk in pride He is able to abase."
> (Dan. 4:37).

Daniel used five third person singular divine pronouns to reference "the Lord of heaven," "the Most High God," Whose message he interpreted to wayward Belshazzar on the final night of his reign as king of Babylon. Daniel was made the third ruler in the kingdom, behind Nabonidus and Belshazzar (Dan. 5:29).

Encounters during the reign of the Medes and the Persians:

9. *539 BC Daniel's prayer and atonement (Messiah) (9:1–27).*
10. *538 BC In the Lion's den (6:1–28).*
11. *537 BC Earthly kingdom transitions and history (10:1–12:13).*

The similarities between Jehovah's method of communication with Daniel between 605–537 BC and His communication with Joseph between 1900–1800 BC was previously noted. Both were dreamers and interpreters of dreams. Daniel can certainly rightfully assume a position, with Joseph, among the great men in Israel's history.

The studious manner of Daniel is reminiscent of historical characters like Moses (1526–1406 BC), Solomon (970–930 BC), Isaiah (740–686 BC), and Jeremiah (627–539 BC). When one understands that many of the psalms attributed to Israel's great psalmist, King David (1035–970 BC), were in fact prayers from David to his God, David can be seen as a great prayer warrior. With this possible exception, none of the great men of Israel's history rival the prophet Daniel with regards to his reputation as a man of prayer.

In 605 BC, when faced with the challenge of being transitioned into an important role under a heathen king, Daniel's commitment to prayer and fasting and his relationship with Jehovah were shown to be his greater priority (Daniel 1:8,17). During his three years of apprenticeship in Babylon, around 605–603 BC, Daniel's prayer life positioned him to hear the voice of Jehovah, preserving his life, promoting him within the kingdom, and giving him his first insights into the future rise and fall of nations on earth and the future of the kingdom of his God (Dan. 2:16–23,31–45).

Prayer, consultation with Jehovah, was likely what occupied Daniel during the hour that he was contemplating the king's second dream before receiving an interpretation of this dream which may have occurred in 569 BC, over thirty years later (Dan. 4:19,24). As we shall see in short order, the final three encounters recorded in the book of Daniel were distinctly and directly connected with Daniel's prayer life and were associated with dreams and visions. It is also very reasonable to conclude that the dreams and visions recorded in Daniel 7 (553 BC) and 8 (551 BC) were the result of Daniel's prayer life. Daniel's ministry and his relationship with Jehovah was predicated upon Daniel's prayer life. We will conclude our examination of history according to Daniel and the perspective concerning Jehovah found in Daniel by examining these final three encounters between Daniel and Jehovah.

Daniel's Prayer of Forgiveness for Israel; Jehovah's Response (Dan. 9)

At some point later in the same year that the Babylonian Empire was conquered by the Medes and the Persians (539 BC), Daniel was struck—through facts obtained by his research of existing documents—by the fact that seventy years had passed since Judah had been invaded by Babylon. Jeremiah, Daniel discovered, had been informed by Jehovah that the captivity would last seventy years (Jer. 25:11–14, 29:10–11). At the end of seventy years, Jehovah had promised to intervene in favor of His chosen people. With the fall of Babylon, Daniel must have been convinced that the words of Jehovah to Jeremiah were about to be fulfilled and he set out to seek Jehovah for His mercies upon the nation of captives (Dan. 9:1–20).

Daniel's written account concerning this prayer lends significant insight into his perception of Jehovah. Besides referencing Jehovah by His name eighteen times in this account, Daniel also calls Him "the great and dreadful God" (Dan. 9:4). Daniel does not see Jehovah as an angry vengeful God, but a righteous judge Who allowed Israel to suffer the consequences of violating her covenant relationship with Him (Dan. 9:5–6). Daniel prayed to the divine person he believed had established a covenant relationship with his predecessors at least as far back as the time of Moses in 1446 BC (Exodus 20).

What had befallen Daniel's nation was directly related to their violation of their covenant with Jehovah (Leviticus 26). Daniel's prayer was to the divine person Whom he perceived to be relationship-oriented, merciful, and forgiving (Dan. 9:9,19). Daniel's concept of Jehovah as the same person Who had given the law to Moses is emphasized by the fact that he used fourteen third person singular divine pronouns in reference to Jehovah in his account of his intercessory prayer to Jehovah on behalf of Judah toward the end of the seventy years of captivity Jeremiah had written concerning. In answer to Daniel's intercessory prayer in 539 BC, Jehovah sent one of His messengers, Gabriel, to speak with Daniel. Gabriel begins his conversation with Daniel by emphasizing the relationship-oriented nature of Jehovah, telling Daniel that he is "greatly beloved." Daniel cannot help but understand that Jehovah is a touchable, approachable, personable God.

Through Gabriel, Jehovah proceeded to give Daniel one of the most precise messianic prophecies in the historical record. Scholars acknowledge that a week can represent a period of seven years in Jewish writings. Daniel is told that seven plus sixty-two weeks, or sixty-nine weeks, would transpire between the time that the commandment went forth to restore and rebuild Jerusalem and the days of Israel's Messiah. Moreover, he is informed that Messiah would be cut of at the end of these days. The Messiah would not be cut off for himself, according to Gabriel. Sometime thereafter, the rebuilt city and sanctuary would once again be destroyed.

Archaeological evidence, the Cyrus Cylinder, confirms that Cyrus the Great gave a decree, around 539–538 BC, liberating many of the people who had been displaced under the inhumane governance of the Babylonian Empire. Ezra 7:11–26 contains the words of a letter from Artaxerxes I (465–424 BC) in which he gives a commandment concerning the restoration and rebuilding of Jerusalem and the temple. The commandment from Artaxerxes was issued around 458–457 BC.

If the sixty-nine weeks of which Gabriel spoke began at this time, then the crucifixion of Jesus Christ, which took place around 27–30 AD, took place around the end of the prophesied sixty-nine weeks (7 times 69 equals 483 years). Within a generation after this, the Romans destroyed Jerusalem and desolated the temple again. Thus, Daniel was given exquisite details by Jehovah through His messenger, Gabriel, about the death of Messiah and the destruction of the restored temple long before these events transpired.

This prophecy predated the commandment from Artaxerxes by eighty-two years. It predated the death of the innocent man, Jesus Christ, who was a sacrifice for the sins of humanity by over 560 years. It predated the destruction of Jerusalem and its temple by the Roman emperor, Titus, by over 600 years. Daniel's God, through this recorded prophecy, left an indisputable and magnificent record of His omniscience, omnipotence, and sovereignty.

> Seventy weeks are determined upon thy people and upon thy holy city, to finish the transgression, and to make an end of sins, and to make reconciliation for iniquity, and to bring in everlasting righteousness, and to seal up the vision and prophecy, and to anoint the most Holy.

> Know therefore and understand that from the going forth of the commandment to restore and to build Jerusalem unto the Messiah the Prince shall be seven weeks, and threescore and two weeks: the street shall be built again, and the wall, even in troublous times.
>
> And after threescore and two weeks shall Messiah be cut off, but not for himself: and the people of the prince that shall come shall destroy the city and the sanctuary; and the end thereof shall be with a flood, and unto the end of the war desolations are determined. (Dan. 9:24–26)

The sacrificial death of Jesus, according to Christianity, certainly fulfills the prophecy described by Gabriel. It was the final and complete atonement for transgressions against Jehovah, for the reconciliation of humanity to Jehovah, and to make men righteous in the eyes of a righteous judge and God. And as Isaiah had afore confirmed between 701 and 686 BC, Jesus died not for his own crimes, but for our transgressions (Is. 53).

In the Lion's Den (Dan. 6)

The fact that Daniel was not a Babylonian but was one of the captives in the Babylonian Empire may have been instrumental in preventing his death at the hands of the Medes when they conquered Babylon in 539 BC. Whatever the reason for his survival, Daniel survived the fall of Babylon and rapidly became established within the political hierarchy of the Medes.

Darius the Mede established a political network to create accountability and stability within his new government. He favored Daniel in his political appointments. This resulted in some animosity from other political leaders in the relatively young kingdom, and they conspired to have Daniel destroyed. They understood, however, that because of Daniel's integrity and his commitment to Jehovah worship, their conspiracy would only be successful if they used Daniel's commitment to his covenant relationship with Jehovah against him and for their objectives.

Daniel's relationship with Jehovah and his need to talk with Jehovah daily was the tool that his detractors used against him, hoping for his demise. Daniel was sentenced to death in the den of the lions for praying to Jehovah after an edict was established forbidding prayer to anyone other than Darius for a period of thirty days.

Jehovah—the faithful, loving, relationship-oriented God of Israel to Whom Daniel directed his prayers—intervened on Daniel's behalf and preserved him in the den of the lions. Jehovah showed that He was an omnipotent, omniscient, sovereign God by preserving His beloved servant. Daniel's view of the person of his God, Jehovah, is recorded when he responds to a despondent king who thought Daniel had surely fallen prey to the lions overnight.

Before the king left Daniel for the night, he had expressed hope in Daniel's God, stating to Daniel, "Thy God Whom thou servest continually, He will deliver thee" (Dan. 6:16). When he returned in the morning after Daniel's sentence was carried out, Darius cried out, hoping against hope, "O Daniel, servant of the living God, is thy God, Whom thou servest continually, able to deliver thee from the lions" (Dan. 6:20)?

Acknowledging the successful intervention of his God on his behalf, Daniel responded from the lion's den, "My God hath sent His angel, and hath shut the lions' mouths, that they have not hurt me: forasmuch as before Him innocency was found in me; and also before thee, O king, have I done no hurt" (Dan. 6:22). Two third person singular divine pronouns are present in Daniel's reply. The decree proclaimed by Darius the Mede in the wake of this notable even contains five additional third person singular divine pronouns in reference to the God of Daniel, Whom Daniel presumably spoke of to the king (Dan. 6:26–27).

Daniel's Final Vision of Earthly Kingdoms and Human History (Dan. 10–12)

In 537 BC, Daniel went on an extended—three weeks—fast, praying to Jehovah (Dan. 10:1–3). The purpose of this extended fast and Daniel's pursuit of Jehovah on this occasion is not revealed in the biblical account. While he was on the shore of the Tigris River, three days after concluding this time of prayer and fasting, however, Daniel had one of the most comprehensive visions documented in his historical record.

Gabriel, who had delivered the messages to Daniel in 551 BC (Dan. 8:1,16) and 539 BC (Dan. 9:21–23), delivered this final message to Daniel (Dan. 10:11, 11:1–2). As he had done two years earlier, Gabriel addressed Daniel with the endearing title of "greatly beloved" (Dan. 9:23, 10:11, 10:19). This title, as previously stated, is not only reflective of the regard Jehovah has for His servant, Daniel (see also Ezek. 14:14,20), it is reflective of the relationship-oriented caring nature of Daniel's God. Gabriel proceeds to inform Daniel that he had come to give him prophetic insight into the future of the people of God (Dan. 10:13).

The omniscience, omnipotence, and sovereignty of Jehovah are all prominently emphasized by the detail and precision displayed by the prophetic revelations given to Daniel in 537 BC. The number of historical characters accurately described in this final prophecy received by Daniel is mind-numbing. No less than a dozen characters who would later be revealed as real people in the course of history are mentioned in Daniel 11. An extremely abbreviated discussion of these figures of history is undertaken in this manuscript.

In Dan. 11:2, mention is made of four kings of Persia after Cyrus. The four kings that immediately followed Cyrus in succession included Cambyses (529–522 BC), Pseudo-Smerdis (522–521 BC), Darius I Hystapes (521–486 BC), and Xerxes I (486–465 BC). It is incorrect to interpret this prophecy to suggest that only four kings would succeed Cyrus in Persia before Greece conquered the Persians.

Instead, Daniel was to understand that the fourth king would really stir up the Persians against the Grecians and fuel the conflict which would ultimately end with the Grecians conquering the Persians. There is substantial extra-biblical historical documentation of the Greco-Persian wars. At least seven more kings ruled Persia after Xerxes I, the last being Darius III, before Alexander the Great conquered this empire in 330 BC. The details concerning the history of the empire of Greece, received by Daniel in his divine encounter of 551 BC (Dan. 8)—extremely detailed on its own merit—are enlarged upon in Daniel 11.

The kings of the south in Daniel 11 are the kings of Egypt, the Ptolemy division of Alexander's divided kingdom. Some specific historical details are foretold regarding four Ptolemy rulers in this final prophecy received by Daniel. Ptolemy I Soter (305–282 BC) is the subject of Dan. 11:5. He founded the Ptolemaic dynasty which outlasted all of the other dynasties that were formed from the division of the kingdom of Alexander the Great.

Details concerning the life of Ptolemy II Philadelphus (282–246 BC) are contained in Dan. 11:6. Daniel 11:7–9 discusses Ptolemy III Eurgetes (246–222 BC). His military campaign against the Seleucid kingdom is described in this vision. The downturn of rule of the Ptolemies under Ptolemy IV Philopater (222–205 BC) and thereafter is described in Dan. 11:10–19.

The kings of the north are the rulers of Syria, the Seleucid division of Alexander's divided kingdom. The activities and identities of the Seleucid rulers are described alongside their Ptolemaic contemporaries in this final prophecy received by Daniel. Seleucus I Nicator (306–281 BC) was contemporary with Ptolemy I Soter and established the Seleucid empire in the time span covered in Dan. 11:5. The marriage of Antiochus II Theos (261–246 BC), the third Seleucid ruler, to Berenice, the daughter of Ptolemy II Philadelphus, is described in Dan. 11:6. Seleucus II Callinicus (246–226 BC) was the son of Antiochus II Theos and his first wife, Laodice, conceived after he reunited with her, after his union with Berenice was dissolved. Callinicus ruled during the time discussed in Dan. 11:7–9. Though he experienced some challenges and defeats as well, Anthiochus III (223–187 BC) was able to strengthen the Seleucid kingdom during his reign as alluded to in Dan. 11:10–19. Details of his demise are also insinuated in the vision described to Daniel by Gabriel. The vicious and oppressive antics of Antiochus IV Epiphanes (175–164 BC) against the Hebrews are described in Dan. 11:21–35.

This gives us over a dozen individuals and a myriad of other historical details which are accurately foretold to Daniel by his God or an agent of his God! The prophecies concerning these individuals predate their arrival on the stage of history by as many as 360 years! The foreknowledge of Daniel's God is like that of no other person in history! This final divine encounter for Daniel concludes with an apocalyptic turn (Dan. 11:36–12:13), just as the prophecies in 553 BC (Dan. 7:19–28) and 539 BC (Dan. 9:27) had concluded. Daniel's God is referenced during this final prophecy as "Him that liveth forever" (Dan. 11:7).

Daniel: Summary and Conclusions

Daniel is a teenager when he is taken into captivity in Babylon in 605 BC. Even his captivity is attributed to the intervention of Jehovah in his life. Throughout a ministry that extends over nearly seven decades, Daniel's life is marked by his experiences with Jehovah through dreams, visions, and his prayer life. Jehovah gives Daniel the interpretation for two dreams by Nebuchadnezzar.

Daniel interprets the mysterious handwriting on the wall for Belshazzar, the last king of Babylon. Additionally, Daniel has three prophetic dreams or visions of his own which reveal short and long-term and even apocalyptic information with great accuracy. Finally, Daniel has an intercessory prayer answered and faced a potentially life-endangering encounter with lions because of his commitment to his covenant-relationship with Jehovah.

In all, there are eleven divine encounters in Daniel; ten of these are directly related to the ministry of Daniel. The other divine intervention involved Daniel's three teenaged Jewish colleagues while Daniel was in the king's court.

Jehovah does not speak directly in Daniel's historical accounts; however, He is referenced by over sixty third person singular divine pronouns. The name of Jehovah appears sparingly in Daniel's book. A significant number of these references occur in Daniel's account of his prayer to Jehovah in 539 BC (Dan. 9). Other divine titles for Jehovah in Daniel's writings include "the God of heaven," "the Lord of heaven," "the Great God," "the Ancient of Days," "the Most High" and "the Most Holy." And along with Isaiah and Micah, Daniel gives one of the most specific messianic prophecies recorded in the old testament. Daniel's understanding of the person of Jehovah and his encounters with Jehovah are a source of inspiration for Christians of all ages to aspire to know his God.

The Prophets of Judah's Captivity: Summary and Conclusions

Judah, the southern kingdom of Israel, was officially overthrown by Babylon in 586 BC. However, Babylon's first incursion into Judah occurred with the death of Josiah in 609 BC. Daniel and his three colleagues—Hananiah, Mishael, and Azariah—were among the captives taken to Babylon in 605 BC. Ezekiel was among the captives taken in 597 BC. Jeremiah was among those who were left in Jerusalem throughout the final years of the demise of the southern kingdom, never actually being taken captive by the Babylonians, rather being under their oppressive rule while remaining in his home country.

These three prophets were the writers of four of the five books categorized as the books of the major prophets. Each encountered Jehovah during the seventy-year captivity period which Jehovah foretold to Jeremiah. Each prophet documents numerous personal encounters with the same divine person they all knew as Jehovah. Jehovah's attributes are consistent throughout His encounters with these three prophets.

Jeremiah documents about sixty-five encounters with Jehovah beginning in 627 BC and extending over six or seven decades. He hears Jehovah use nearly 900 first person singular divine pronouns in reference to Himself over the course of his relationship with Him.

Including the book of Lamentations, Jeremiah's writings contain a couple hundred third person singular divine pronouns in reference to Jehovah as well.

Daniel is taken captive in 605 BC and this is when he first writes of his encounters with Jehovah. He documents ten personal encounters with Jehovah over the course of a relationship with Him extending over about seventy years. Daniel also documents an amazing encounter between Jehovah and Hananiah, Mishael, and Azariah which does not involve Daniel himself. Unlike his ministerial contemporaries, Daniel never records any words spoken directly from the mouth of Jehovah, and so there are no first person singular divine pronouns in his book. However, from the presence of over sixty third person singular divine pronouns in his record, it is easy to conclude that Daniel sees Jehovah as a single divine person, just like Jeremiah and Ezekiel.

That Daniel is aware of Jeremiah and his relationship with Jehovah—as a prophet of Jehovah—is evinced by his reference to the writings of Jeremiah in 539 BC (Dan. 9:2). While Jeremiah is prophet to Judah's homeland, Daniel is a prophet in Babylon and subsequently in Media and Persia, and Jehovah reveals to him far-reaching insights concerning the rise and fall of kingdoms far beyond Judah and far beyond the historical time period in which he and his ministerial contemporaries live. Daniel is clearly the most widely influential of the three major prophets. In fact, Jehovah makes a direct reference to Ezekiel concerning Daniel in two of His encounters with Ezekiel (Ezek. 14:14,20, 28:3). Daniel seems to be highly regarded by Jehovah in the eyes of Ezekiel.

Ezekiel, the third of the prophets of Judah's captivity, was taken captive into Babylon in 597 BC and has no position of power within the kingdom of his captives. Ezekiel is the voice of Jehovah to the common people among the displaced captives. Ezekiel documents only thirty-four encounters with Jehovah over a much shorter period than his two ministerial contemporaries.

Several dramatic visions and multiple prophecies concerning the people of Judah, the captives, and other nations and people during his lifetime are revealed to Ezekiel by Jehovah. Among the three prophets—Jeremiah, Ezekiel, and Daniel—Ezekiel's writing is the one most densely populated with divine pronouns referencing the person they all knew as Jehovah. In only thirty-four encounters over only twenty-two years (593–571 BC), Ezekiel attributes approximately 1,000 first person singular divine pronouns to Jehovah in reference to Himself.

In total, in the writings of Jeremiah, Ezekiel, and Daniel, which cover a historical period from 627–537 BC, nearly 100 years, almost 1,900 first person singular divine pronouns are spoken by Jehovah in reference to Himself. Over 300 third person singular divine pronouns are spoken in reference to this same divine person during this historical period. All three of these prophets experienced Jehovah, even during a period of judgment upon the nation of Judah as an omnipotent, omniscient, omnipresent, sovereign God Who was approachable, covenant-minded, relationship-oriented, kind, and merciful.

These attributes of Jehovah were, therefore, consistent within their historical time frame and consistent with the God Whom the fathers of the nation of Israel had known for centuries before Jeremiah, Ezekiel, and Daniel. Moreover, the Messiah of whom these prophets foretold was consistent with the Messiah of the prophet Isaiah who had given an extremely detailed description of Israel's Messiah at least several decades before these prophets were even born.

Table 6.1 Encountering the God of Jeremiah

	Date BC	Description	Reference	FPSP	3PSP
	640-609	**Revival under reign of Josiah**	2 Kings 22:1-23:28 2 Chron 34:1-35:19		
1	627	Call at Anathoth: Rod of almond tree	Jer. 1:4-12	12	1
2	627	Call at Anathoth: Seething pot	Jer. 1:13-19	8	
3	627	Sent from Anathoth to Jerusalem	Jer. 2:1-3	2	1
4	627	Josiah's revival: Message to Jerusalem	Jer. 2:4-3:5	29	5
5	627	Josiah's revival: Message to Israel	Jer. 3:6-4:2	25	2
6	627	Josiah's revival: Message to Judah	Jer. 4:3-5:3	12	1
7	627	Josiah's revival: Great men of Jerusalem	Jer. 5:4-31	17	2
8	627	Josiah's revival: Children of Benjamin	Jer. 6:1-30	16	
	609-605	**Death of Josiah, capture of Jehoahaz and early reign of Jehoiakim**	2 Kings 23:29-37 2 Chron 35:20-36:4		
9	609	Lament for Josiah, Jehoahaz and early instructions to Jehoiakim during his reign	Jer. 22:1-17	6	
10	609	Early instructions to Judah under Jehoiakim	Jer. 26:1-6	10	
11	609	Temple Sermon under Jehoiakim	Jer. 7:1-8:3	42	
12	609	Aftermath of Temple Sermon	Jer. 26:7-30		4
13	609-605	To men of Judah concerning the covenant	Jer. 11	24	1

14	609-605	Jehovah counsels Jeremiah concerning His delayed fulfillment of Judah's judgment	Jer. 12	26	1
	606-605	**The middle of the reign of Jehoiakim**	2 Kings 24:1-4 Chron 36:5-8		
15	606-605	Referencing the Temple Sermon, Jehovah certifies the (first) Babylonian invasion	Jer. 8:4-10:16	22	16
16	605	Sent to get a linen girdle	Jer. 13:1-2		
17	605	Hide the linen girdle at Euphrates	Jer. 13:3-5		
18	605	Recover the linen girdle	Jer. 13:6-7	1	
19	605	The sermon of the linen girdle	Jer. 13:8-14	8	
20	605	Jeremiah pleads for mercy	Jer. 13:15-27	5	2
21	605	Sent to potter's house	Jer. 18:1-2	2	
22	605	Sermon of the potter and the clay	Jer. 18:5-11	13	
23	605	Judgment for rejection of this sermon	Jer. 18:13-17	4	
		Jeremiah persecuted for preaching	Jer. 18:18-23		
	605	**Babylon's first invasion of Jerusalem**	2 Kings 24:1-4 2 Chron 36:5-8		
	605	Daniel and others taken to Babylon	Daniel 1:1-7		
24	605	Judgment of Philistia	Jer. 47		
25	605	Judgment of Egypt	Jer. 46:1-12	1	3
26	605-604	Jeremiah's scroll read in the Temple	Jer. 36:1-10	4	1
27	605-604	Declaration of 70 years of captivity	Jer. 25:1-14	12	1
28	605-604	Jeremiah's scroll read in the Palace	Jer. 36:11-32	3	
29	605-604	Jeremiah reassures Baruch	Jer. 45	6	

30	605-604	Jehovah reassures Jeremiah	Jer. 15:10-21	11	
31	604-599	Prophesy of coming famine and war	Jer. 14:1-6, 10, 11, 12, 14-18 and 15:1-9	33	1
32	604-599	Prophesy of Judah's fall and the captivity	Jer. 16:2, 4-18, 20-22 Jer. 17:1-11	26 7	1
33	604-599	Message in the gates of Jerusalem	Jer. 17:19-27	4	
34	604-599	Sent to the Rechabites	Jer. 35:1-2		
35	604-599	Lesson from the Rechabites	Jer. 35:3-19	13	
36	604-599	Against false prophets	Jer. 23:9-40	40	7
37	604-599	Sermon at Tophet with the broken vessel	Jer. 19:1-13, 15	15	
38	604-599	Persecution/imprisonment by Pashur	Jer. 20:1-18	4	3
39	602-599	Later rebuke of Jehoiakim and Jeconiah	Jer. 22:18-30	7	
	597	**Nebuchadnezzar's second invasion of Judah** Ezekiel and Jeconiah among the captives	2 Kings 24:5-19 2 Chron 36:9-10		
40	597	The vision of the two baskets of figs	Jer. 24	16	
41	597	Zedekiah and five gentile kings urged to submit to Babylon	Jer. 27	16	
42	597	Confronted by Hananiah in the king's court	Jer. 28	8	
43	597	First letter to the exiles in Babylon	Jer. 29:1-29	31	
44	597	Second letter to the exiles in Babylon	Jer. 29:30-32	4	

45	597-590	Prophecy of Babylon's future judgment	Jer. 50, 51	46	28
46	597-590	Judgment of countries of Palestine	Jer. 48:1-49:39	40	4
47	597-590	Judgment of the nations including Judah	Jer. 25:15-38	7	5
	588-586	**Babylon's third siege of Jerusalem**	2 Kings 24:20-25:3 2 Chron 36:11-21		
48	588	Judah's captivity imminent (during siege)	Jer. 10:17-25	7	
49	588	Message to Zedekiah through Pashur	Jer. 21:1-14	12	
50	588	Zedekiah's final transgression judged	Jer. 34:8-22	16	
51	588	Final warning to Zedekiah	Jer. 34:1-7	2	
52	588	The futility of Egypt's help foretold	Jer. 46:13-28	11	
53	588	Egyptian aided relief is only temporary	Jer. 37:1-15	2	1
54	588	Jehovah speaks to Jeremiah in prison	Jer. 37:16-21		1
55	587	Message of hope (while imprisoned)	Jer. 30-31	67	5
56	587	Instructed to buy a field	Jer. 32:1-8	2	
57	587	Evidence of purchase recorded in history	Jer. 32:9-25		1
58	587	The field bought, the message of the fiel	Jer. 32:26-44	39	
59	587	Message of restoration	Jer. 33	35	3
60	587	Messianic prophecy	Jer. 23:1-8	9	
61	587	Jeremiah in the dungeon	Jer. 38		
	586	**The fall of Jerusalem**	2 Kings 25:4-21 2 Chron 36:17-21 Jer. 39-42, 52		

62	586	Words for Ebedmelech the Ethiopian	Jer. 39:16-18	5	
63	586	Advising the remnant to not go to Egypt	Jer. 42	11	2
	586	Book of Jeremiah's lamentations			91
	569	**The end of Jeremiah's life in Egypt**	Jer. 43, 44		
64		Jeremiah's final prophecy against Egypt	Jer. 43:8-13	4	
65		Jeremiah's final prophecy against the people of Israel in Egypt	Jer. 44:1-30	25	4

Jeremiah was born around 648 BC, lived in Jerusalem and Egypt during the captivity and may have died in Egypt.

FPSP First person singular divine pronouns

3PSP Third person singular divine pronouns

PLP The divine plural pronoun, "We" in Jer. 30:5 references Jehovah and Jeremiah as they both perceive the situation being discussed figuratively.

Divine titles in Jeremiah

Lord of hosts, Fountain of living waters, Balm in Gilead, Physician, King of nations, True God, Living God, Everlasting king, Portion of Jacob, God of hosts, Father, Great and mighty God, Faithful witness, King, Holy One of Israel, Most High, Redeemer

Messianic references and allusions in Jeremiah include: Jer. 23:7–8, 30:9, 31:15, 31:31–34, 33:14–15

In Lamentations

"I am the Lord" occurs three times, "I the Lord" occurs once

Messianic titles: A righteous branch, David their king, Branch of Righteousness
"The Lord"—Jehovah name equivalent—occurs forty-four times

Table 6.2 Encountering the God of Ezekiel

	Dates BC	Description	Reference	FPSP	3PSP
		Encounters before the final Babylonian siege of Jerusalem			
1	593	Ezekiel's call	1–7	117	16
		First vision: Jehovah and His glory	1–3:15	16	13
2		Second vision and call to be a watchman	3:16–27	11	1
		Instructions for Ezekiel's enactments			
		Siege of Jerusalem	4:1–17	6	2
		Fall of Jerusalem	5:1–17	39	
3		Prophecy against idolatrous nation	6:1–14	20	
4		Final judgment of Jerusalem foretold	7:1–27	25	
5	592	Third vision: Temple abominations	8–12:7	37	23
6		Instructions for enactments about exile and prophecy against false prophets	12:8–13:23	43	
7		Prophecy against idolatrous elders of exiles	14:1–11	19	
8		Noah, Daniel and Job; righteous individuals	14:12–23	17	
9		Parable of the vine tree Parable given Interpretation given	15 15:1–5 15:6–8	8	

10		Parable of the adulterous wife	16	60	
11		Parable of the two eagles Parable given Interpretation given	17 17:1–10 17:11–24	16	
12		The proverb of the sour grapes and a divine lamentation for Israel's princes	18 19	14	
	591	God rejects consultation of Israel's elders	20–23	205	1
13		Israel's rebellion: Jehovah's case	20	119	
14		The sword of judgment	21	24	1
15		Jerusalem's indictment of Israel	22	33	
16		Two evil sisters: a parable	23	29	
	588	Judgment of Palestine proclaimed	24–25	45	
17		Prophecy against Judah: Boiling pot parable	24	16	
18		Prophecy against Ammon	25:1–7	10	
		Prophecy against Moab	25:8–11	3	
		Prophecy against Edom	25:12–14	9	
		Prophecy against Philistia	25:15–17	7	
		Encounters during the final Babylonian siege of Jerusalem			
19		Judgment of Egypt proclaimed	29:1–16	18	
20	587	Judgment against Pharaoh by Jehovah	30:20–26	13	
21	587	Assyria as an example for Egypt	31	9	
22	586	Judgment of Tyre and Sidon by Jehovah	26–28	34	
		Encounters after the final Babylonian siege of Jerusalem			

	585	News of fall of Jerusalem	33:21–39:29	230	6
23		The fall of Jerusalem declared	33:21–33		
24		Unjust shepherds and unjust sheep	34		
25		Judgment of Seir by Jehovah	35		
26		A message of restoration to the land of Israel	36		
		Two messages of restoration to the people of Israel	37		
27		Fourth vision: The valley of dry bones	37:1–14		
28		Miraculous fusion of the two sticks	37:15–28		
29		Prophecy concerning Gog and Magog	38–39		
30	585	Lamentation for Pharaoh	32:1–16	2	
31	585	Lamentation for Egypt	32:17–32	2	
32		The watchman, the wicked and the way of the Lord	33:1–20	12	
33	573	Fifth vision: Temple restoration Temple and priesthood restored	40–48	57	7
34	571	Babylon's wages	29:17–30:19	24	

FPSP First person singular divine pronouns
3PSP Third person singular divine pronouns
Divine titles in Ezekiel:

Spirit, Almighty, Glory of the Lord, God of Israel, Spirit of the Lord, Spirit of God, Holy One

"I the Lord" occurs twenty-two times
"I am the Lord" occur sixty-seven times
"The Lord", the name of Jehovah, appears 434 times in Ezekiel
Messianic references in Ezekiel: 34:23–24, 36:26–27, 37:26–28
Some key chapters of Ezekiel: 1, 8, 16, 18, 20, 33, 34, 36, 37

Table 6.3 Encountering the God of Daniel

	Dates BC	Description	Reference	3PSP	Other divine titles/pronouns/ nouns
1	605	Jehovah's intervention permits Daniel's captivity	1:1–7		
2	603	Jehovah's intervention positions Daniel among his captors	1:8–20		
3	603	Revelation of Nebuchadnezzar's dream of the great image	2:1–49	9	God of heaven, Great God, God of gods,
4	603	Shadrach, Meshach, and Abednego in the fiery furnace	3:1–30	4	the most high God, God of Shadrach, Meshach and Abenego
5	569	Interpretation of Nebuchanezzar's dream of the tree hewn down	4:1–37	15	the most High
6	553	Daniel's vision of the four great beasts	7	8	Ancient of days, the most High
7	551	Daniel's vision of the ram and the goat	8		
8	539	The hand writing on the wall	5	5	the most high God
9	539	Daniel's prayer and atonement (Messiah)	9	14	The most Holy
10	538	In the Lion's den	6	8	God of Daniel
11	537	Earthly kingdom transitions and history	10–12	2	God of gods

Reasonable assumptions: Daniel was born around 628 BC, taken captive by Chaldeans in 605 (first wave of captives), and died in 536 BC.
3PSP Third person singular divine pronouns
The most common divine title referencing Jehovah in the book of Daniel is "the most High."
*The pronoun "they" in Daniel 4:25, 26 and 32 refers to angelic beings used by or sent by God. "They" are distinguished from "the most High" which refers to Jehovah.
Messianic titles or allusions in Daniel: Stone cut out without hands, Prince of princes, Messiah the prince, Messiah, One like the son of man

References

2008. *The Chronological Study Bible*. Nashville, TN: Thomas Nelson, Inc.

Whiston, William. 1987. *The Works of Josephus: New Updated Edition, Complete and Unabridged in One Volume*. Peabody, MA: Hendrickson Publishers.

The Holy Bible. 2010. *Authorized King James Version*. Nashville, TN: Holman Bible Publishers.

2009. *The Apologetics Study Bible for Students*. Nashville, TN: Holman Bible Publishers.

Wiersbe, Warren W. 2007. *The Wiersbe Bible Commentary: Old Testament*. Colorado Springs, Colorado: David C. Cook.

Marincola, John. 2003. *Herodotus: The Histories (Translated by Aubrey De Selincourt)*. New York, NY: Penguin Books.

Olmstead, AT. 1959. *History of the Persian Empire*. Chicago, Ill: The University of Chicago Press.

Horn Siegfried H. "New light on Nebuchadnezzar's madness." https://ministrymagazine.org/authors/horn–siegfried–h

Walvoord, John F. "The Nations in Prophecy." www.walvoord.com

Newton, Isaac. *Observations upon the Prophecies of Daniel.*

Encountering the God of Obadiah: The Prophet of Edom's Downfall

Archaeological and historical evidences to definitively date the writings of the prophet Obadiah have not been found, and the historical setting for this prophet's encounter with Jehovah is, at best, difficult to pin down. Some historians place the prophet Obadiah as a contemporary to Elijah, Elisha, and Joel. A date around 850 BC could be assigned to Obadiah's encounter with Jehovah based upon Judah's fall and Edom's uprising against Judah during the reign of Jehoram, the son of Jehoshaphat (2 Chronicles 21). However, some of the words spoken by Jehovah to Obadiah in the book of Obadiah more logically place the prophecy after the fall of Jerusalem to the Babylonian Empire. In support of the later date is the fact that Jehovah included Edom in the list of places that would endure His wrath when He spoke to Jeremiah around 587 BC (Jer. 25:15–28) and again when He spoke to Ezekiel during the same time period (Ezek. 25:12–17).

The timing of Obadiah's ministry is important in that this would tell us how far in advance of the downfall of Edom Jehovah foretold its demise. However, not resolving this dilemma does not diminish the fact of Jehovah's omniscience and omnipotence. Regardless of the date of Obadiah's single encounter with Jehovah, the fact remains that in this encounter, Jehovah spoke of Edom's futile efforts to prop itself up because purposes set in the mind of Jehovah cannot be resisted (Obad. 4).

It is notable that the reason offered by Jehovah for His judgment against Edom is the nation's willful neglect of and opposition to His chosen people, particularly in the time of their distress when Edom could have been their advocates. This speaks to Jehovah's commitment to His covenant relationship with Israel, a consistent personal disposition since He chose Abram and promised to bless those that blessed him and curse those that cursed him back around 2091 BC (Genesis 12:1–5).

The name of Jehovah appears seven times in this very short divine encounter, and there are five first person singular divine pronouns pointing to Jehovah's divine person. Obadiah's God is an omniscient, omnipotent, sovereign person Who is covenant relationship-driven and Who is faithful to His promises to those Who walk in covenant relationship with Him while He judges those Who defy His will. He is the God of Abraham, Isaac, and Jacob; even Esau. His relationships with these patriarchs can be studied to gain insight into His character.

References

The Holy Bible. 2010. *Authorized King James Version.* Nashville, Tennessee: Holman Bible Publishers.

Wiersbe, Warren W. 2007. *The Wiersbe Bible Commentary: Old Testament.* Colorado Springs, Colorado: David C. Cook.

Encountering the God of the Post-Captivity Prophets and Writers of Israel

In 1446 BC, the days of Moses, Israel's great lawgiver, Jehovah had foretold the nation's fall into captivity (see Lev. 26). Though He knew from the beginning that they would break the covenant relationship that He established with them, He chose them and set His affection on them. As the time of Israel's judgment for its recurrent and perpetual transgressions against Him grew near, Jehovah, knowing that His people would have to suffer the consequences of their choices, looked forward to their opportunity for restoration.

Around 700–686 BC, over a century before the Babylonian captivity began (586 BC) and many decades before Cyrus the Great was even born (approximately 600 BC), Jehovah told His prophet, Isaiah, that Cyrus would issue an edict that would begin the restoration process for His chosen people.

Sometime shortly after 539 BC, Cyrus issued this edict, known as one of the greatest humanitarian declarations of human history. The contents of this humanitarian edict have been preserved in print on the Cyrus Cylinder. Jehovah's mastery of history, before it is experienced by humanity, is further displayed in the fact that, with amazing precision, He foretold the length of Judah's captivity under Babylon. Though several dates can be selected for the beginning of Nebuchadnezzar's incursions into Judah, they all fall around 600 BC.

The edict of Cyrus was issued just after 539 BC, and this is easily reconciled with Jehovah's seventy-year forecast to Jeremiah around 588–586 BC (see Jer. 29:10–14). The 539 BC humanitarian edict of Cyrus the Great marked the beginning of the post-captivity period of Judah in particular and of Israel as a nation.

After the death of Cyrus the Great (600–529 BC), Persia continued to be the dominant world power until it fell to Alexander the Great around 330 BC. A number of kings succeeded Cyrus the Great before Persia fell. The Bible chiefly references three Persian kings besides Cyrus the Great: Darius I (522–486 BC), Xerxes I (486–465 BC), and Artaxerxes I (465–424 BC). Haggai and Zechariah prophesied and ministered during the reign of Darius I. Ezra, Nehemiah, and Esther lived and recorded events in Jewish history during the reign of Artaxerxes. And Malachi, the last of the Old Testament prophets, wrote between 430–420 BC.

All of these writings, therefore, were penned over a span of about 100 years beginning in 520 BC. Several notable non-Jewish persons and events in human history were contemporary with the persons and events recorded in these six Old Testament books.

The classical age of Greece played out during the same era as Israel's post-captivity period, extending from 500–300 BC. Democracy began in Athens around 500 BC. The Greco-Persian Wars took place between 499–449 BC. The Peloponnesian Wars (between Athens and Sparta) took place thereafter, ending around 404 BC. The Parthenon, the temple for the goddess Athena, was constructed between 447–432 BC.

A host of important historical figures emerged during the classical age of Greece. Thucydides (460–400 BC) wrote *History of the Peloponnesian War*. The writings of Herodotus (484–404 BC), considered by many to be the father of modern history, captured historical events beyond Greece and before his time. Sophocles (496–406 BC) was one of the greatest playwrights of this era, penning *Oedipus the King* and over 100 other dramas. Pericles (495–429 BC) was among the greatest politicians of the early portion of the classical age of Greece. The most famous Greek philosophers in history lived during this era, including Socrates (470–399 BC), Plato (428–347

BC), and Aristotle (384–322 BC). And of personal interest to me, Hippocrates (460–375 BC), credited by many to be the father of modern medicine, lived during this era. Without debate, Greece left an indelible imprint on human history during its golden age.

Important characters of history were not limited to Greece during the era contemporary with the writings of Israel's post-captivity prophets and historians. Siddhartha Gautama, the father of Buddhism, may have been a historical contemporary of these biblical characters. Some uncertainty plagues the dating of his life, and some believe, as I previously noted, that he lived a century earlier, during the time Judah was being overrun by Babylon. There is some evidence that he lived between 560–480 BC.

Buddha, like the philosophers of Greece, left a powerful legacy still impacting human thought to this day. Likewise, Confucius (551–479 BC), China's greatest philosopher over the course of history, had an impact on human thought that far outlived his time on earth. Many great men of history, as can be easily gathered from the aforementioned sampling, were contemporary with Haggai, Zechariah, Ezra, Nehemiah, Esther, and Malachi.

In this final chapter, the view of Jehovah as a person of history will be explored as revealed in the encounters and writings of the authors of Haggai, Zechariah, Ezra, Nehemiah, Esther, and Malachi. Though direct encounters with Jehovah are not uniformly distributed throughout these writings like they were in the writings of the prophets and kings that preceded them, a clear picture of the person of Jehovah still emerges during this era that is consistent with that which has been pervasive throughout human history.

The experiences and encounters of each of these writers with Jehovah, or the intervention of Jehovah in the lives of each of these historical characters, gives the student of history some insight into the person of his/her God. Though the historical record does not reveal that Jehovah spoke directly to all of these historical characters, a clear picture still emerges of the perception each had of Jehovah, and His interactions with them can be delineated. The divine person, Jehovah, Who initiates these interactions is unmistakably the same person Who had interacted with their forefathers over eons of time before.

Encountering the God of Haggai, the God of the Neglected Temple

The prophet Haggai may well have been an aged man when he wrote his prophecies inspiring the people who had returned to Judah, nearly two decades earlier, to finish the work of rebuilding their place of worship of Jehovah. If this is correct, then as a young man, he was contemporary with the aged prophet Daniel whose last recorded divine encounter had occurred around 537 BC.

Haggai had grown up as a captive in Babylon. As a youth, he may well have heard some of the older Hebrew captives describe the days when they worshipped Jehovah in the temple in Jerusalem. The edict issued by Cyrus during the last days of Daniel, the prophet, had given the Jews the opportunity to return to the city of David and begin rebuilding their nation. After the initial exuberance that must have permeated the Jewish communities when they returned to Jerusalem, their zeal toward rebuilding the temple where they had formerly worshipped Jehovah, the God of their fathers, had waned. Through a series of five divine encounters, Jehovah gave Haggai prophetic messages to inspire the people to attend to the important business of completing the rebuilding of His temple. All five of Haggai's encounters with Jehovah take place during the last half of the year in 520 BC.

Encounter one: Jehovah Chastises Zerubbabel and Joshua for the Complacency of the People in Not Building the Temple (Haggai 1:1–11)

The people of Judah had begun returning to their land around 538–537 BC. Though they had been back in Judah for nearly twenty years, they had failed to complete the rebuilding of the Temple of Jehovah. In August 520 BC (Haggai 1:1), Jehovah spoke to Haggai and had him deliver a message to the leaders among the people—the governor and the high priest—chastising them for the complacent attitude of the people. For Jehovah, this complacency was a statement of the value they placed on Him and on worship. They were so preoccupied with their daily lives that they had devalued their God and His house of worship had been neglected.

In His message to the leaders and the people, Jehovah reminded them that they could not prosper without His blessing and that their failure to prosper was consequent to their neglect of their covenant relationship with Him. Haggai captured Jehovah's counsel and admonishment in Haggai 1:7–11. He says, "Thus saith the LORD of hosts; Consider your ways. Go up to the mountain, and bring wood, and build the house; and I will take pleasure in it, and I will be glorified, saith the LORD. Ye looked for much, and, lo, it came to little; and when ye brought it home, I did blow upon it. Why? saith the LORD of hosts. Because of mine house that is waste, and ye run every man unto his own house. Therefore the heaven over you is stayed from dew, and the earth is stayed from her fruit. And I called for a drought upon the land, and upon the mountains, and upon the corn, and upon the new wine, and upon the oil, and upon that which the ground bringeth forth, and upon men, and upon cattle, and upon all the labour of the hands."

The God Who spoke to Haggai is omniscient, knowing the thoughts of the people (1:2). He is omnipotent, controlling the elements and the ability of the earth to produce its fruit (1:9–11). This divine person, Whom Haggai called Jehovah and the Lord of hosts, used five first person singular divine pronouns in reference to Himself in His first encounter with Haggai. Clearly, Haggai believed Him to be a single divine person.

Encounter two: Jehovah Commends the People for a Sincere Effort to Build (Haggai 1:13–15)

The response of the people to the initial message of Jehovah through Haggai was immediate and enthusiastic. About three weeks later (Haggai 1:15), Jehovah has His prophet deliver a message of approval for their response (1:13). Jehovah says simply, "I am with you" (1:13). Jehovah's response demonstrated His attitude of forgiveness and the ease with which He readily accepts their efforts to restore their covenant relationship with their covenant God.

Encounter three: The Finished Product of Building the Temple Assessed (Haggai 2:1–9)

The rebuilding of the foundation of the temple of Jehovah, completed by Zerubbabel and Joshua in October 520 BC (Haggai 2:1–3), was very modest in comparison to the temple that Solomon had built from 966–959 BC (1 Kings 6:37–38). However, Jehovah expressed His approval of their efforts and reassured His people concerning the future glory of the temple they had constructed. His covenant-minded disposition, consistent over the history of His relationship with men, is referenced in His words of reassurance at this time. Jehovah lovingly stated, "I am with you." In Haggai 2:5, Jehovah continued, "According to the word that I covenanted with you when ye came out of Egypt, so My spirit remaineth among you…" In this interaction, Jehovah used eight first person singular divine pronouns in reference to Himself.

Encounter four: Jehovah Discusses the Consecration of the Priests (Haggai 2:10–19)

Once the physical place of worship—though modest by any standard—was completed, Jehovah directed Haggai to turn his attention to the consecration of the priests who would serve in His house of worship. This showed His concern with having those with whom He was in relationship meet specific standards of conduct. In December 520 BC, Jehovah spoke with Haggai to prompt a self-examination among the priests to purge their unholy ways and enter into the blessings that accompany righteous living in covenant relationship with Him. On this occasion, He used five more first person singular divine pronouns in identifying Himself.

Encounter five: Jehovah Gives a Prophecy for Zerubbabel (Haggai 2:20–23)

In the final interaction between Haggai and Jehovah, which occurred in December 520 BC (Haggai 2:20), Jehovah instructs Haggai to give a prophetic word to the governor of the land, Zerubbabel. Using seven first person singular divine pronouns in referencing Himself, Jehovah gave a message of encouragement that proclaimed the supremacy of the future kingdom He would establish (Haggai 2:20–23). This message was quite like that delivered by Jehovah to Daniel in 603 BC and 553 BC (Dan. 2:34–35,44–45, 7:27).

As previously mentioned, the prophet Daniel may well have been a source of inspiration (indirectly or by direct contact) for Haggai during his formative years. During this encounter, Jehovah alludes to the fact that the Messiah would come through the lineage of Zerubbabel (Haggai 2:23; Matt. 1:13).

> "In that day," saith the LORD of hosts, "will I take thee, O Zerubbabel, My servant, the son of Shealtiel," saith the LORD, "and will make thee as a signet: for I have chosen thee," saith the LORD of hosts. (Hag. 2:23).

Encountering the God of Zechariah, the God Who Will Come to His Temple

Zechariah was the younger contemporary of the aged Haggai. Like Haggai, he had grown up in captivity. His prophetic ministry was inspired by Haggai and the God of Haggai. Haggai's ministry inspired the people to complete the building of the physical structure in which they were to worship the God of heaven. Zechariah's ministry inspired the people to not only build the temple of worship, but to know the person Whom they were to worship in the temple. In fact, Zechariah focuses on the fact that the God of the temple would one day come to His temple, a message intended to inspire the builders to invest their best effort into the construction of this temple. If they understood that Jehovah would one day come to the temple that they were building, surely, they would invest their best efforts into the process of restoring the temple. Through a series of nine divine encounters, one of which consisted of a series of visions, Zechariah inspires the inhabitants of Jerusalem to prepare themselves for the return of their God to live among His people.

Zechariah stands unique among the prophets as the one who makes the most concentrated effort to describe the coming of Jehovah as the prophesied Messiah. While Isaiah has the greatest number of messianic prophecies of any single prophet, he conveys them through sixty-six chapters during a ministry that spanned well over half a century. Within the confines of a mere fourteen chapters describing events that took place over a two year span of time, Zechariah gives eight incredibly precise prophesies which would apply to the coming Messiah. Jehovah was coming to His temple just over 500 years in the future!

Encounter one: Jehovah's Admonition to the People to Honor His Covenant (Zech. 1:1–6)

Shortly after Jehovah had encouraged Judah and its leaders for initiating a sincere effort to rebuild the temple, through the ministry of Haggai (Haggai 1:13–15) in October 520 BC, He sent Zechariah to admonish them to do better than their forefathers in honoring their covenant relationship with Him (Zech. 1:1–6). Through Haggai, Jehovah sent the message "I am with you" (Haggai 1:13).

Through Zechariah, Jehovah gave a supplemental message. In Zechariah 1:1–4, the prophet writes, "In the eighth month, in the second year of Darius, came the word of the LORD unto Zechariah, the son of Berechiah, the son of Iddo the prophet, saying, 'The LORD hath been sore displeased with your fathers.' Therefore say thou unto them, Thus saith the LORD of hosts; Turn ye unto Me,' saith the LORD of hosts, 'and I will turn unto you,' saith the LORD of hosts. 'Be ye not as your fathers, unto whom the former prophets have cried, saying, Thus saith the LORD of hosts; Turn ye now from your evil ways, and from your evil doings: but they did not hear, nor hearken unto Me,' saith the LORD."

Jehovah is a very present God Who pursues a covenant relationship with His people but requires a standard of conduct in order for this relationship to retain its vitality. He laments the past transgressions of Judah against Him and the consequences of these transgressions (i.e., the fractured fellowship). He desires that His presence and the desire of His people to live in His presence will prevent them from making the same mistakes after being restored to their land. In identifying His presence through the message of Zechariah in this encounter, Jehovah used seven first person singular divine pronouns. He is the same divine person Who had sought fellowship with their forefathers and now seeks a healthy relationship with them.

Encounter two: A Series of Angelic Encounters with Divine Messages (Zech. 1:7–6:8)

Zechariah is a unique book in many ways. It is sometimes mysterious. It can be quite difficult to understand all of the intricacies of the writings of this prophet. At times, His encounters resemble those of the prophet Daniel. Jehovah communicated several messages to His prophet Daniel through dreams and visions. Some of the communications from Jehovah to Zechariah are of this same nature. In fact, in February 519 BC (Zech. 1:7), Zechariah had a series of visions through which Jehovah prepared him to deliver messages to the people of Judah.

Attempting to analyze every detail of each of these visions would be a major undertaking which, if taken up, would cause the purpose of this project to be lost. Instead, I will hit the highlights of each of the seven visions experienced by Zechariah at this time, extracting at least one major message that Jehovah communicated to Zechariah through each vision. This approach will permit us to stay focused on the main historical theme that Jehovah interacted with His people with purpose and intent. It will also help to prevent digression from the theme of the consistencies of the character of the divine person encountered by Zechariah with the character of the God encountered by others throughout history.

The first of Zechariah's series of seven visions is documented in Zechariah 1:7–21. The core components of the vision are documented in Zechariah 1:8,18, and 20. The interpretation of the vision is given by an angelic being and discussed in Zech. 1:9–14,19, and 21. The overall message from this encounter, in which Zechariah sees horsemen, horns, and carpenters, is that the punishment of Judah for its violation of their covenant relationship with Jehovah has concluded and that Jehovah would like a fresh start with a people that truly desire to seek after Him. His message is one of redemption and restoration.

This is best seen when the angel communicates the words of Jehovah to Zechariah in 1:14–17. Zechariah documents, "Thus saith the LORD of hosts; 'I am jealous for Jerusalem and for Zion with a great jealousy. And I am very sore displeased with the heathen that are at ease: for I was but a little displeased, and they helped forward the affliction.' Therefore thus saith the LORD; 'I am returned to Jerusalem with mercies: My house shall be built in it,' saith the LORD of hosts, 'and a line shall be stretched forth upon Jerusalem.' Cry yet, saying, Thus saith the LORD of hosts; 'My cities through prosperity shall yet be spread abroad; and the LORD shall yet comfort Zion, and shall yet choose Jerusalem.'" (Zech. 1:14–17).

The being speaking to Zechariah is not Jehovah but an angelic ambassador. He used at least six first person singular divine pronouns when speaking of Jehovah for Whom he was delivering the message to the prophet. Jehovah is yet a relationship-seeking, merciful, and forgiving divine person.

This vision gives way to a second vision within the same encounter. In the second vision, Zechariah is shown a man with a measuring line in his hand (Zech. 2:1). This vision enlarges upon the theme of restoration introduced in the first vision. Not only is Jehovah interested in restoration for the people of Israel, He is interested in achieving restoration for lost humanity; a fractured relationship which He has not been able to mend through His chosen people because of their lack of faithfulness to Him. In this vision, The Lord, Jehovah, gives the first of eight messianic prophecies in the book of Zechariah. In Zechariah 2:10–12, Jehovah says:

> "Sing and rejoice, O daughter of Zion: for, lo, I come, and I will dwell in the midst of thee," saith the LORD. "And many nations shall be joined to the LORD in that day, and shall be My people: and I will dwell in the midst of thee," and thou shalt know that the LORD of hosts hath sent me unto thee. And the LORD shall inherit Judah his portion in the holy land, and shall choose Jerusalem again."

In this passage, Jehovah prophesies of the kingdom which He will establish through which He will dwell in the midst of His people. In this vision as a whole, six first person singular divine pronouns reference Jehovah. This vision builds on a theme established in the prophecies given to Daniel in 603 BC (Daniel 2:34–35,44–45) and 553 BC (Daniel 7:27) focusing on the idea of Jehovah's everlasting kingdom.

The angelic being who directs Zechariah through this series of visions then shows Zechariah a vision of Joshua, the high priest in 520 BC, standing in the presence of Jehovah with filthy clothes. Satan, the accuser of men, is standing beside Joshua, presumably as his accuser before Jehovah.

Joshua's sins are forgiven and he is granted a fresh start and clothed with clean clothes. In this vision, which conveys the forgiveness, cleansing, and restoration that Jehovah gives to His people despite their guilty state, Jehovah makes a proclamation which is consistent with His character throughout history. In Zechariah 3:4, Jehovah declares, "Behold, I have caused thine iniquity to pass from thee, and I will clothe thee with change of raiment."

Though Joshua symbolizes the nation of Israel in this vision, Jehovah enlarges the subject and the meaning to include those who would come into fellowship with Him through the work accomplished by the coming Messiah, when He spoke to Zechariah of "My servant the Branch" (Zech. 3:8). Twelve first person singular divine pronouns reference Jehovah during this vision.

Next, the angel shows Zechariah a golden candlestick with seven lamps, with seven pipes to the seven lamps, and with two olive trees by it (Zech. 4:2–3). It appears that these symbolize the nation of Israel and its leaders, Zerubbabel and Joshua. This vision conveys the message that Jehovah is the source of their strength to accomplish anything that they might accomplish. Jehovah says, during this vision, "Not by might, nor by power, but by My spirit," saith the Lord of hosts (Zech. 4:6). Thus, the only divine pronoun in this vision is a first person singular divine pronoun.

In Zechariah's fifth vision of this encounter, he sees a flying roll (Zech. 5:1–3) representing a standard of judgment that will be used as a standard for judgment for the whole earth. In Zechariah 5:4, Jehovah takes ownership for ultimately bringing this universal standard of judgment upon the earth. He uses two first person singular divine pronouns in His proclamation relevant to this vision.

In the immediately subsequent vision (Zech. 5:5–11), Jehovah's righteous standard is contrasted to a wicked standard, apparently adopted by His people while in Babylon. This vision depicted a people that had come out of captivity and brought with them the money-driven, wicked, ungodly approach to life of their captors in place of the standard of righteousness Jehovah always wanted for His people. An *ephah* is a unit of measurement. This vision implied that instead of measuring their progress using the righteous standard of Jehovah, God's people had adopted a different and wicked standard learned during their captivity in Babylon. This error, no doubt, had been a contributing factor to the failure of God's people to make the rebuilding of Jehovah's temple a priority over their own personal economic gains (Haggai 1:3–11) after returning to Jerusalem.

In the seventh and final vision in this series of visions seen by Zechariah, there are four chariots. Each chariot is drawn by different color horses. Each represents angels assigned to carry out the will of Jehovah in different international geographical regions. Some emphasis is placed on Babylon, the north country, and the fact that Jehovah's purposes with regards to His chosen people in the land of Babylon have been accomplished (Zech. 6:6,8).

The idea that angels play an active role in accomplishing Jehovah's agenda on the international scene was quite prevalent in the prophetic life and divine encounters of the prophet Daniel (see Dan. 4, 7, 8, 9, 10–12) a few decades before Zechariah began his prophetic ministry. This idea is supported by Zechariah's final vision in this series.

Zechariah's series of seven visions further confirms the fact that Jehovah interacts with His people through visions on occasion. There are a total of twenty-seven first person singular divine pronouns referencing Jehovah during the time Zechariah experienced this series of visions.

Encounter three: The High Priestly Prophetic Enactment (Zech. 6:9–15)

The remainder of Zechariah is filled with prophetic words and descriptions of events in his personal life that have messianic interpretations. The first of these occurs in the wake of Zechariah's series of visions in February 519 BC. Zechariah is instructed by Jehovah to take Heldai, Tobijah, and Jedaiah and go to the house of Josiah and to make crowns for Joshua, the high priest. These crowns were to be a symbol and a reminder of Jehovah's promise to have a priest and king rule upon the throne of Judah (i.e., the throne of David).

For the second time on this date (Zech. 3:8, 6:12), Jehovah prophesies to Zechariah of the coming Messiah, whom He refers to as "The BRANCH." Jehovah instructs Zechariah, "And speak unto him [Joshua, the high priest], saying, 'Thus speaketh the LORD of hosts, saying, Behold the man whose name is The BRANCH; and he shall grow up out of his place, and he shall build the temple of the LORD: Even he shall build the temple of the LORD; and he shall bear the glory, and shall sit and rule upon his throne; and he shall be a priest upon his throne: and the counsel of peace shall be between them both'" (Zech. 6:12–13).

Jehovah informs Zechariah that there would be a counsel of peace between Himself—Jehovah—and this prophesied future man, the coming Messiah, "The BRANCH" whom He would bring forth (Zech. 3:8). It is this man, "The BRANCH," that will build the temple of Jehovah. This message was to be a source of motivation in Zechariah's day for the people to make the rebuilding of Jehovah's temple a priority. However, more importantly, it made reference to the work of the Messiah in the kingdom of which Daniel had spoken during his ministry (Daniel 2:44–45, 7:13–14, 7:27). While there are no divine pronouns in this encounter, the covenant name of Jehovah appears eight times, thus identifying His divine personhood in the mind and experience of Zechariah.

Encounter four: Jehovah Calls the People to Sincere Service and Worship (Zech. 7)

Nearly two full years pass (Zech. 7:1), and the people that have returned from captivity are making progress in the reconstruction of the temple. They are, however, wearied by worship traditions not instituted by God that do nothing to enhance their relationship with Jehovah; they are experienced as mere empty traditions. Thus, they inquired whether they should continue these traditions (Zech. 7:3).

Jehovah spoke to Zechariah in His fourth encounter with the prophet and gave the response that these were the traditions of men. These were not worship ceremonies that He had instituted. They commemorated events that could have been avoided had the people simply lived in covenant relationship with Jehovah and obeyed His words sent by His prophets (Zech. 7:4–7,13–14). The disregard of Jehovah's people for His covenant had caused the events that they were remembering with burdensome rituals. Such ritualistic worship was unnecessary and unfruitful. Jehovah was really drawing them away from ritualistic worship and emphasizing instead a lifestyle of covenant relationship with Him (Zech. 7:8–10).

In connecting their past national conduct with their past national judgment and drawing them into a heartfelt covenant relationship with Him, Jehovah used four first person singular divine pronouns (Zech. 7:5,13,14). The covenant name of God appears ten times in the record of Zechariah's fourth encounter with Jehovah.

Encounter five: Jehovah's Return to Jerusalem (Zech. 8)

Linked to the inquiry concerning ritualistic worship, but in a separate encounter with Zechariah, Jehovah gave an additional message to His people through His prophet. This message focused on the fact that after their judgment was complete in the land of Babylon and that He was determined to return to Jerusalem to restore covenant relationship with His people. Since His people had begun in earnest to honor Him by committing to complete the rebuilding of the temple, He has been among them (Haggai 1:13–15).

In the fifth encounter of Zechariah with Jehovah, Jehovah used seventeen first person singular divine pronouns in reference to Himself. The conciliatory tone of Jehovah and His genuine pursuit of and value of covenant relationship with His people is pervasive throughout this encounter.

Encounter six: Jehovah Shares with Zechariah a Contrast of Coming Kings (Zech. 9)

What Zechariah presents here as a prophetic message—including the memorable "Palm Sunday Messianic Prophecy" in which the Messiah would enter Jerusalem riding on a donkey—is a poignant contrast of future conquerors and kings. This prophecy was written in 518 BC.

Alexander the Great rode into Jerusalem as a mighty conqueror on a great war stallion with the intent to subdue God's people in 332 BC, nearly 200 years later. God intervened to save His people from destruction on this occasion. At some point, somehow Alexander was made aware of the prophecy of Daniel concerning his success in conquering the Persian Empire. Daniel had this initial vision in 553 BC. In 518 BC, Zechariah was given a vision consistent with Daniel's and supplemental to it (Zech. 9:1-8).

Josephus, the great Jewish historian in the days of the Roman Empire, gave a detailed account of Alexander's encounter in Jerusalem as these prophecies were fulfilled hundreds of years after Jehovah revealed them to His prophets. In the encounter between Zechariah and Jehovah, recorded in Zechariah 9, Zechariah is allowed to see into the future and witness the breathtaking fear and dread of the people of Jerusalem as the great and mighty Alexander rode through their city as a coming conqueror.

In direct contrast to the prophesied coming of the king of Greece (Zech. 9:13), Zechariah is given a glimpse of the coming of the prophesied Messiah. Zechariah records the following observation concerning Israel's coming Messiah:

> "Rejoice greatly, O daughter of Zion; shout, O daughter of Jerusalem: behold, thy King cometh unto thee: he is just, and having salvation; lowly, and riding upon an ass, and upon a colt the foal of an ass." (Zech. 9:9).

All four of the gospel writers record the fulfillment of the messianic portion of Zechariah's prophetic revelation. Each wrote of the day that Jesus rode into Jerusalem sitting upon a donkey on the Sunday before Passover over 500 years after Zechariah's prophecy and over 300 years after Alexander the Great had come through Jerusalem, riding on a war stallion (Matt. 21:1–11; Mark 11:1–11; Luke 19:29–44; John 12:12–19).

During this, His sixth encounter with Zechariah, Jehovah used ten first person singular divine pronouns in reference to Himself. Several third person singular divine pronouns are also used referencing the divine person Who is interacting with Zechariah in this encounter.

Encounters seven and eight: Jehovah Shares with Zechariah a Contrast of Earthly Shepherds and Israel's True Divine Shepherd (Zech. 10–11)

In an encounter with Zechariah, presumably also in 518 BC, Jehovah encouraged the prophet that He would enlarge the number of people returning to Jerusalem. As a shepherd gathers his sheep, Jehovah would gather back to Judah His people scattered across the nations (Zech. 10:3,6–12). This is contrasted to the unprotected state of the people that are not the sheep of His flock, the people that do not have Jehovah as their divine shepherd (Zech. 11:1–7). Though the non-Jew is an obvious member of this unprotected flock (Zech. 11:1–3), there are some among the Jews who refuse to follow Jehovah as their divine shepherd (Zech. 11:4–7).

In an apparent object lesson that follows his seventh encounter with Jehovah, Zechariah becomes chief shepherd over a flock and hires some under shepherds. He even acquires the tools of the trade—a rod and a staff (Zech. 11:7–8). When the message of his object lesson becomes apparent to the unrighteous people of influence, and their unrighteousness is exposed, they offer the prophet a fee to end this public display (Zech. 11:7–12). The fee they offer is the price at which a slave had been valued since Jehovah gave the law in 1446 BC (Exodus 21:32).

In His eighth encounter with the prophet Zechariah, Jehovah instructed the prophet to take the price and cast it unto the potter in the temple (Zech. 11:13). This exchange between Zechariah and the people of influence in Jerusalem in 518 BC, unknown to the prophet, was laden with messianic inklings. Zechariah documents, "And the LORD said unto me, 'Cast it unto the potter: a goodly price that I was prised at of them.' And I took the thirty pieces of silver, and cast them to the potter in the house of the LORD" (Zech. 11:13).

The phrase "a goodly price that I was priced at of them" is critical. Some Bible teachers believe that this phrase reflected the prophet's sarcasm regarding the value the people offered him to suspend his rather pricey object lesson, a pittance compared to the personal cost of acting out the lesson. While this is a reasonable contention, another reasonable contention is that this was a part of Jehovah's response to the price the Jewish leaders offered to suspend a lesson that He wanted them to hear, and thus, Jehovah was saying, "Cast it unto the potter: a goodly price that I was priced at of them."

So the *I* in this phrase is a first person singular divine pronoun. This being the case, this phrase linked the personal value placed on Jehovah by the Jewish leaders in Zechariah's days with the value placed on the person of the Messiah over 500 years later when Jesus was betrayed by Judas Iscariot for thirty pieces of silver (Matt. 26:14–15, 27:1–10). Jehovah was foretelling the price that would be placed on His head when He came in human form as the shepherd of Israel; it was the price of a slave.

The two chapters that record these two encounters between Zechariah and Jehovah contain twenty-one first person singular divine pronouns, including the one in this messianic prophecy. Zechariah is clear that the object lesson was prompted by Jehovah and was a reflection of His character as a divine person with the heart of a pure and righteous shepherd toward His people. The Jehovah known by Moses as he led Israel between 1446–1406 BC and the one known by King David throughout his life (1040–970 BC) had the heart of a shepherd. The Jehovah known by Zechariah in 518 BC had the same heart. The God known by the disciples during the earthly ministry of Jesus also had the heart of a shepherd (John 10:1–18).

Encounter nine: Jehovah's Final Encounter with Zechariah (Zech. 12–14)

Zechariah's final encounter with Jehovah is a lengthy prophecy addressing issues pertaining to the first and second appearance of Israel's Messiah. It is a complex interaction in which Jehovah dispenses a great deal of information to His prophet concerning future events. It is significant that this encounter begins with a description of Jehovah's credentials.

> "The burden of the word of the LORD for Israel," saith the LORD, "which stretcheth forth

> the heavens, and layeth the foundation of the earth, and formeth the spirit of man within him." (Zech. 12:1)

Zechariah was already fully aware of these credentials. Over the course of two years and eight prior encounters with Jehovah, the divine personhood of Jehovah was now no mystery to the priest and prophet. It is rational, therefore, to conclude that these introductory remarks were made because of the gravity of the material about which Jehovah wished to have a conversation with Zechariah. The time frame over which the prophecies discussed in this encounter would unfold ranged from hundreds of years to some, as yet, undefined duration.

Zechariah had to be sure that the messenger had infallible credentials. The messenger is thus identified by the covenant name of God—"the Lord" or Jehovah. This makes Him the person Who had interacted with the fathers of the nation in years gone by. Moreover, He is the creator of the heavens and the earth and therefore lord of these created things as well. Finally, He is the giver of life, and thus, the God of life and death. His omniscience, omnipotence, omnipresence, and sovereignty are unquestionable after these introductory remarks, and His authority to make the proclamations that follow, uncontestable.

What follows in chapters 12–14 is a divine proclamation concerning future events pertaining to the Messiah, the nation of Israel, and the global impact of the events discussed. It will suffice for the purpose of this work to examine the messianic comments made by Jehovah during this final encounter with Zechariah.

The first messianic prophecy is found in Zechariah 12:10. Jehovah proclaims, "And I will pour upon the house of David, and upon the inhabitants of Jerusalem, the spirit of grace and of supplications: and they shall look upon Me whom they have pierced, and they shall mourn for him, as one mourneth for his only son, and shall be in bitterness for him, as one that is in bitterness for his firstborn" (Zech. 12:10).

In the gospel penned by the Apostle John, the messianic application of the words spoken by Jehovah to His prophet, Zechariah, is confirmed. When discussing the closing scene at Calvary, John records, "But when they came to Jesus, and saw that he was dead already, they brake not his legs: But one of the soldiers with a spear pierced his side, and forthwith came there out blood and water. And he that saw it bare record, and his record is true: and he knoweth that he saith true, that ye might believe. For these things were done, that the scripture should be fulfilled, A bone of him shall not be broken. And again another scripture saith, They shall look on him whom they pierced" (Jn. 19:33–37).

John thus believed that the words spoken by Jehovah to Moses in 1446 BC (Exod. 12:46) and those spoken to Zechariah in 518 BC (Zech. 12:10) were prophetically spoken of Jesus Christ. Paul tied the Messiah to the prophecy of Moses when he wrote to the Corinthian church in 55 AD (1 Cor. 5:7). John tied the sacrifice of the Messiah on Calvary to the prophecy penned by Zechariah because of the piercing of Jesus in his side. What makes this most revealing, concerning the nature of Jehovah and the Messiah, is that when Jehovah spoke to Zechariah, He said, "And they shall look upon Me whom they have pierced, and they shall mourn for him."

John, led by the spirit of God, said, "They shall look on him whom they pierced." It appears that Jehovah equates Himself with the one who is pierced, and John equates Jesus with Jehovah. When speaking to Zechariah and proclaiming this messianic prophecy, Jehovah used nine first person singular divine pronouns to identify Himself.

Jehovah goes on to describe what would be accomplished by the piercing of Messiah. Jehovah reveals, "In that day there shall be a fountain opened to the house of David and to the inhabitants of Jerusalem for sin and for uncleanness" (Zech. 13:1). The piercing of the hands of the Messiah is also foretold (Zech. 13:6).

Jehovah then further illuminates the mind of Zechariah concerning the nature of the coming Messiah. Zechariah captures this revelation in Zechariah 13:6–7 by writing, "And one shall say unto him, What are these wounds in thine hands? Then he shall answer, Those with which I was wounded in the house of my friends. 'Awake, O sword, against My shepherd, and against the man that is My fellow,' saith the LORD of hosts: 'smite the shepherd, and the sheep shall be scattered: and I will turn Mine hand upon the little ones.'"

It is theologically scintillating that Jehovah described the coming Messiah as "My shepherd" and "the man that is My fellow" (Zech. 13:7). Zechariah understands that Jehovah is the divine person speaking to him, that Jehovah is speaking of a man who will one day come and will suffer physical wounds for sin and for uncleanness, the Messiah will be a shepherd chosen by Jehovah, and finally, that the Messiah will be working with or for Jehovah.

Based upon the earlier comment of Jehovah in Zechariah 12:10, however, it is consistent to conclude that Jehovah would reside within the body of the Messiah since Jehovah claimed the piercing of the Messiah as His own piercing. Paul's letters confirm this interpretation in Colossians 2:9 and 2 Corinthians 5:19. The writers of the gospel according to Matthew and Mark confirm that Jesus applied Zechariah 13:6–7 to his experiences during the Passion Week (Matt. 26:31; Mark 14:27). Jehovah used eleven first person singular divine pronouns during the portion of His final conversation with Zechariah pertaining to the Messiah as the suffering shepherd (Zech. 13).

Finally, in Zechariah 14:9, we find the following statement: "And the LORD shall be king over all the earth: in that day shall there be one LORD, and his name one."

Zechariah 14 is held by many scholars to be apocalyptic in its time focus. Jehovah declares that a final battle involving Jerusalem and its interests will take place. Jehovah will defend Jerusalem at this time. The ultimate outcome will be an overwhelming victory by Jehovah and He will be king over all the earth. Zechariah described this king over the earth and says there shall be "One Lord, and His name One."

No doubt, Zechariah understood that Jehovah was this divine person Who would rule the earth. Of this worldwide rule, Jehovah declared to the prophet Isaiah that every knee would bow unto Him and every tongue would swear submission to Him (Is. 45:23). Paul saw the prophecies of Jehovah to Isaiah around 700 BC and to Zechariah around 518 BC as being fulfilled by the world's eventual submission to Jesus Christ, thus making Jesus, the Messiah, the human manifestation of Jehovah.

Summary and Conclusions: The God of Haggai and Zechariah

Haggai was born during the Babylonian captivity. He had grown up as a Babylonian Jew and did not experientially know about life in Jerusalem or about worship in the temple of Jehovah. He likely heard of these things from his elders and may well have heard much about the elderly prophet Daniel and the great things Jehovah had accomplished for His people through the ministry of Daniel. Toward the end of Daniel's life, Cyrus the Great gave a proclamation allowing the Jews to return to their land (around 539 BC).

Haggai was among those that returned to Jerusalem. After the initial excitement waned and the reality of the hard work of restoration hit them, the Jews were not zealous about rebuilding the temple of Jehovah. They also lacked the zeal to recover the purity of fellowship, worship, and covenant living that Jehovah desired for His people.

The ministry of the aging prophet, Haggai, according to the historical record he left, covers the last five months of 520 BC. Haggai records five encounters with Jehovah in which Jehovah gives him words to share with His people concerning their need to complete the rebuilding of the temple and their need to live up to an expected standard as His covenant people. Twenty-six first person singular divine pronouns are spoken by Jehovah during these five encounters, confirming His divine person.

Based upon the encounters Haggai has with Jehovah, he sees Jehovah as a covenant relationship-oriented person Who intensely desires a relationship with His people but has expectations that His people must meet in order for this desired relationship to be healthy.

Zechariah is a younger man, a priest, and a prophet when the people of Judah return from the Babylonian captivity. His first encounter with Jehovah occurs within a month of Haggai's third encounter.

Zechariah goes on to have nine encounters with Jehovah over a period of two years as documented in his record. While Jehovah's encounters with Haggai were primarily for the purpose of preparing Haggai to motivate the people to be vigilant in their work of rebuilding the temple, His encounters with Zechariah focused more on the person Who was the Lord of the temple, the work Jehovah had already done for the purpose of preserving His relationship with them, the fact that He desired to live among them, and the work He was yet to do to sustain a covenant relationship with His people.

It is this line of reasoning that is pervasive throughout the encounters of Jehovah with Zechariah and that ultimately caused the written record of Zechariah's prophetic ministry to have the densest accumulation of messianic prophecies in the Old Testament. While Isaiah's writings have the highest volume of messianic prophecies by far, he takes sixty-six chapters to accomplish this feat. Within the space of fourteen chapters, Zechariah records at least eight messianic prophecies.

Jesus and his disciples reference the messianic prophecies that Jehovah spoke to Zechariah on several occasions. Just as a study of the many messianic prophecies in the book of Isaiah—when they are taken as a whole and within the context of the divine person with Whom Isaiah was speaking— reveals how strongly Jehovah identified with the Messiah; so a study of Zechariah's messianic prophecies, taken in the context of the Jehovah known to Zechariah, reveals that Jehovah is one divine person but that He sees the coming Messiah as the human manifestation of Himself.

There are over 100 first person singular divine pronouns spoken by Jehovah in reference to Himself during His nine encounters with Zechariah. No doubt, Zechariah understood and taught that Jehovah desired to dwell among His people and had expended great efforts to accomplish this feat. The rebuilding of the temple was a way that the people could facilitate this process. However, Jehovah looked toward an even more intimate means of coming to live with His people. Over 500 years would go by before this intimate relationship between Jehovah and His people would become a reality, when Jesus, the Messiah, would come and fulfill the messianic prophecies spoken by Jehovah to Zechariah and many others before him.

Divine Interactions with Jehovah in the Days of Artaxerxes, King of Persia

Herodotus captured a cross-cultural account of history during the early portion of the classical era of Greece. His attention to detail and his attempt to respect the facts of history in large part contributed to him being called, by many, the father of modern history. Thucydides wrote a more focused history. He captured the details of the wars fought between Sparta and Athens, the two major centers of Greek cultural and political life during this era.

Ezra, a priest and a scribe of the law of Moses, was a historian of equal veracity. He was contemporary with Herodotus and Thucydides. His writings captured the history of his people, the Jews, during the reigns of Cyrus the Great, Darius I, Xerxes, and Artaxerxes.

Cyrus the Great was the first and most famous ruler of the Persian Empire. He is most remembered for his humanitarian edict allowing all the captured and oppressed people of the Babylonian Empire to return to their home countries after he conquered the Babylonian Empire in 539 BC. He ruled the Persian Empire from 560–529 BC. Darius I was born in 550 BC. He ruled the Persian Empire from 522–486 BC. Ezra makes note of his status as a contemporary with Haggai and Zechariah (Ezra 6:14–15). Xerxes ruled the Persian Empire from 486–465 BC and is thought by many scholars to be the Ahasuerus of the Bible. Artaxerxes ruled the Persian Empire from 465–424 BC and is also thought by many scholars to be the Ahasuerus of the Bible.

Ezra and Nehemiah are contemporary with Artaxerxes (Ezra 7:1–6; Nehemiah 2:1). Esther is contemporary with Ahasuerus (Esther 2:16). If Ahasuerus is Artaxerxes, Esther is contemporary with Ezra and Nehemiah. If Ahasuerus is Xerxes, Esther predated Ezra and Nehemiah slightly but can still be considered their contemporary in relative timeframe.

I believe that sufficient evidence substantiates the scholarly perspective that Ahasuerus was Artaxerxes, and thus, the events in the book of Esther are contemporary to the events of Ezra and

Nehemiah. First, Josephus, the great Jewish historian of the Roman Empire, contends that Artaxerxes is Ahasuerus. Secondly, the Greek translation of the Septuagint makes Artaxerxes the same person as Ahasuerus of the book of Esther. Finally, Nehemiah makes special note of the presence of the queen when he petitioned the king for a leave of absence to rebuild the walls of Jerusalem (Neh. 2:6). Since the authority rested with the king and the request was addressed only to the king, and since the queen's presence would have served no other special political or historical purpose, I contend that Nehemiah made note of the presence of the queen because she was Esther, the Jewish queen of the Persian Empire. Moreover, her presence may well have helped to embolden Nehemiah in his request; after all, Jerusalem was also "the city, the place of her fathers' sepulchres" (Neh. 2:1–3). We will assume that Artaxerxes is the Persian king who married Esther and in whose court both Ezra and Nehemiah served.

Thus, Ezra, Nehemiah, and Esther are all contemporaries within a couple of decades of each other, and the similarities in the God they each experienced should be informative. History does yield evidence of Jehovah's interventions in each of their lives. From the accounts of history documented in the books that bear their names, one can gain a view of Jehovah that is consistent with that which had been demonstrated by His interactions with others that preceded them.

Encountering the God of Ezra

Ezra documents three distinct interventions by Jehovah in his life. He discusses these interventions in chapters 7–10 of his record. All three encounters take place in the year 458 BC. In the first six chapters of his book, Ezra gives the historical preface to the personal interventions of Jehovah in his life. Before discussing the personal encounters between Ezra and Jehovah, the historical preface Ezra lays out should be examined because it is foundational to understanding the mindset Ezra brings to these encounters. Understanding this preface is also foundational to knowing Ezra's preconceptions regarding the person of Jehovah.

First, as a historian, Ezra documented that Cyrus the Great had issued an edict charging the people of Judah to go up to Jerusalem and build the house of God there (see Ezra 1:1–4). It is commonly taught that Cyrus was shown the prophecy of Isaiah which foretold this magnanimous act. Isaiah recorded this prophecy over 150 years before Cyrus performed it. Cyrus may well have formulated his understanding of the deity he called "The Lord God of heaven" (Ezra 1:2) and "The Lord God of Israel" (Ezra 1:3) by interacting with Daniel who was still active in political spheres at that time. It is notable that four third person singular divine pronouns are used in reference to Jehovah in Ezra's documentation of Cyrus' letter (Ezra 1:1–4).

As a historian, Ezra also gives attention to the order from King Darius that allowed the rebuilding of the temple in the time of Haggai and Zechariah. The content of the letter from King Darius is recorded in Ezra 6:6–12. In this letter, Darius gives detailed instructions regarding the provisions to be made for the Israelites to rebuild the temple. Darius refers to Jehovah as "the God of heaven" and uses a third person singular divine pronoun in reference to Him.

Finally, when Ezra made his journey to Jerusalem, he carried with him a letter from King Artaxerxes which authorized the work he set out to do in the city of his fathers. The content of this letter is recorded in Ezra 7:11–26 and calls Ezra's God "Jehovah," "the God of heaven," "the God of Israel," and "the God of Jerusalem," and uses a third person singular divine pronoun (Ezra 7:11) in reference to Him.

Each of these three letters—the letter from Cyrus, the letter from Darius, and the letter from Artaxerxes—are consistent with the idea that Jehovah is a divine person Who intervenes in the affairs of men with purpose and intent. He worked through each of these Persian kings to accomplish the restoration of His chosen people and to progressively rebuild the city and the temple where His worship was centered.

CHAPTER EIGHT

Jehovah's Interventions in the Book of Ezra

Ezra's personal encounters with Jehovah begin in March 458 BC (Ezra 7:7). Compared with the first six chapters of the book of Ezra, the writing style changes noticeably at the beginning of chapter 7. The actions and events become present tense and involve the author. Ezra is, therefore, personally experiencing the mercy extended to him by the Persian king, Artaxerxes, and crediting this favor to "the hand of Jehovah upon him" (Ezra 7:6).

This is consistent with the idea that Ezra believed that Jehovah was a personal God Who moved with purpose and intent in the lives of His chosen people. Furthermore, Ezra believed that Jehovah had the ability to impact the decisions of others, even those in authority over him, like the king of Persia. Ezra 7:27–28 confirms that this was Ezra's line of thought. The heart of the king, his counsellors, and his mighty princes were all influenced by Jehovah, and thus, it was the mercy of Jehovah that resulted in Ezra's ability to return to Jerusalem. This understanding of the person of Jehovah gave Ezra courage and strength.

Ezra also credited Jehovah's "good hand upon him" for his safe journey from Persia to Palestine (Ezra 7:9, 8:18, 8:21-23, 8:31). When Ezra and his co-travelers encountered difficulties, they sought the intervention of their God because they believed that He would personally intervene on their behalf. Ezra credited the person he knew as Jehovah for their successes along the way (see Ezra 8:18, 23, 31). For example, in Ezra 8:21-23, Ezra reveals,

> "Then I proclaimed a fast there, at the river of Ahava, that we might afflict ourselves before our God, to seek of Him a right way for us, and for our little ones, and for all our substance. For I was ashamed to require of the king a band of soldiers and horsemen to help us against the enemy in the way: because we had spoken unto the king, saying, The hand of our God is upon all them for good that seek Him; but His power and His

> wrath is against all them that forsake Him. So we fasted and besought our God for this: and He was intreated of us."

While the record does not reflect that Jehovah spoke directly to Ezra, Ezra's perception of the person of Jehovah is evidenced by his repeated use of third person singular divine pronouns in reference to his God. There are seven third person singular divine pronouns in the scriptures describing God's presence and provision for Ezra during his journey from Babylon to Jerusalem (Ezra 7:9, 8:18,21–23,31).

The encounters of Ezra with Jehovah after he arrived in Jerusalem are consolidated into a single documentable historical occurrence. These encounters may well have been numerous, but one shall suffice to demonstrate that Ezra encountered Jehovah after he arrived in Jerusalem.

Ezra 9 documents the fervent heart and intercessory prayer of Ezra to God on behalf of a people that had violated their covenant agreement with Jehovah. A similar attitude of prayer had been demonstrated by Daniel in 539 BC when he realized that the seventy-year period of captivity prophesied by Jeremiah was drawing to a close (Dan. 9:4–19). Daniel prayed to a God of mercy to forgive His people as they transitioned out of the period of captivity.

In July or August of 458 BC, Ezra discovered that the Jews living in Jerusalem had been transgressing the laws given in 1446 BC by Jehovah, prohibiting marriage to people who were not worshippers of Jehovah (Exod. 34:11–16). He prays fervently for Jehovah's forgiveness of this transgression (Ezra 9:5–15). Like Daniel, Ezra perceived that the person he knew as Jehovah was a powerful and present relationship-oriented God. He had been the same person Who had given the laws to Moses in 1446 BC and had seen generation after generation violate His covenant with them. He had longed for a sustained covenant relationship with His chosen people but maintained the necessity of obedience to a set standard of life in order for this covenant relationship to remain intact. He had allowed the consequences of their transgression of this covenant relationship to come upon them beginning in 609 BC and culminating in the fall of Jerusalem in 586 BC. And thus, Jehovah was a God of judgment. However, He was also a God of mercy and forgiveness as demonstrated repeatedly throughout this same expanse of time.

Finally, Ezra understands that Jehovah is a God of action and not just words. Ezra acts to correct this transgression among the people and institutes a process of purification among the people (Ezra 10:9–11,16–17). Two additional third person singular divine pronouns occur in the last two chapters of Ezra. In all, there are sixteen third person singular divine pronouns in the book of Ezra with nine of them occurring in portions that pertain to the personal life of Ezra as a scribe and leader among the people (Ezra 7–10). The covenant name of Jehovah appears over three dozen times in the book of Ezra.

As previously argued in this work, I believe that Artaxerxes of the book of Ezra is the same person as Ahasuerus of the book of Esther. In Ezra 3–6, the author speaks extensively of the challenges faced by the Jews from people that did not want to see Jerusalem, its walls, or its temple rebuilt. Most of chapter 3, the beginning and end of chapter 4 (Ezra 4:1–5, 23b), and chapters 5–6 are devoted to the opposition the Jews faced during the reign of Cyrus and Darius. This opposition was eventually overcome, ending with the completion of the temple rebuild in the sixth year of Darius (516 BC).

A significant portion of chapter 4, however, is devoted to recording the situation faced in the days of Ezra. Ezra notes that in the early days of Ahasuerus, who is Artaxerxes, a letter was written to Artaxerxes that resulted in the total cessation of efforts to rebuild the walls of Jerusalem (Ezra 4:6–7,23). Because extensive detail is given to the discussion of opposition under Cyrus and Darius and separately to opposition under Artaxerxes, and there is no separate discussion of opposition under Ahasuerus, I believe that Ezra 4:5 and Ezra 4:6 both refer to the early days of Artaxerxes and that both names identify the same person. It would be inconsistent with the pattern of Ezra, as a historian, to mention opposition under Xerxes (if as some have asserted Xerxes is Ahasuerus) and give no details in the rest of his book regarding this as a separate period of opposition. It is more consistent with the writing style of Ezra, as a historian, to contend that he used the two names synonymously.

Jehovah's Interventions for Esther

Artaxerxes began to reign in 465 BC. In 462 BC, three years after Artaxerxes became king, Vashti was deposed (Esther 1:3, 19). Though the record reports that Vashti's removal was consequent to her own choices, an argument can be made that the condition of Vashti's heart was due to a direct intervention by Jehovah. If so, Jehovah hardened the heart of Vashti in order to make room for Esther to become queen in her stead.

The hardening of the heart of Pharaoh in 1446 BC (Exod. 7:1–5) set a precedent for the principle that Jehovah can influence the heart of an individual to their own demise in order to bring about a good purpose in the life of His chosen people. The sequence of events leading to the deposing of Queen Vashti constituted the first direct divine intervention of Jehovah in the life of Esther.

Jehovah's second intervention in the life of Esther is seen when Jehovah turned the heart of Artaxerxes toward Esther between December 458 and January 457 BC. Artaxerxes made Esther the new queen of Persia (Esther 2:16–20). This was in the seventh year of the reign of Artaxerxes. It was approximately six months after Artaxerxes had granted Ezra, a member of his court, leave to return to Jerusalem to rebuild the walls of the city (Ezra 7:6–9).

The third intervention of Jehovah in the life of Esther is one of the most memorable portions of this historical account. In her fifth year as queen, 453 BC, Esther's character is challenged. Haman had succeeded in getting the king's authorization to permit the slaughter of the Jews, partly due to the lifestyle and standards they adhered to as required by their covenant relationship with Jehovah (Esther 3:7–8). The royal policies and actions of Ahasuerus in Esther at this time are consistent with the policies and actions of Artaxerxes (and Ahasuerus) in Ezra 4:6–23.

When the letters were sent out authorizing the planned slaughter of the Jews, Mordecai petitioned the young queen to use her influence to disannul this evil (Esther 4:8). The young queen was daunted and made excuses (Esther 4:10–11). Mordecai gave her some wise counsel (Esther 4:13–14) which she accepted. Though uncertain of the personal ramifications of this decision, Esther put the counsel of Mordecai into action (Esther 4:15–17).

The divine encounter occurs after Esther, Mordecai, and other concerned parties had fasted and prayed three days, seeking the intervention of a God they believed to be approachable and powerful. Jehovah intervened in the life of Esther in that He gave her favor in the sight of the king. The intervention of Jehovah in Esther's life prevented her execution for daring to come before the king without a personal invitation from him. Esther 5:1–8 documents the details of Jehovah's intervention on behalf of Esther in this encounter.

Jehovah's Interventions for Mordecai

Jehovah also intervenes in the life of Esther's uncle, Mordecai, at least three times during the reign of Esther. It was because of Jehovah's first intervention in Mordecai's life that Mordecai found himself in the right place at the right time to overhear the assassination attempt against Ahasuerus, or Artaxerxes (Esther 2:21–23) after Esther had been elevated to the throne as queen.

Esther's third encounter with Jehovah was intricately linked with Mordecai's second divine encounter. These encounters occurred in 453 BC. Mordecai's concept of Jehovah is evident from the beginning of his second encounter with Jehovah. Based upon his understanding of the character of Jehovah, Mordecai counseled Esther, "Think not with thyself that thou shalt escape in the king's house, more than all the Jews. For if thou altogether holdest thy peace at this time, then shall there enlargement and deliverance arise to the Jews from another place...and who knoweth whether thou art come to the kingdom for such a time as this?" (Esther 4:13–14).

This counsel reveals that Mordecai believed that Jehovah was omnipotent. Mordecai's God, Who inspired and counseled the heart and mind of Mordecai during this crisis, was fully aware of their situation and would bring deliverance by some means. Jehovah was not limited to using Esther and her position to achieve His objectives. He was able to influence other people and other situations to accomplish whatever was His will.

The encouragement and inspiration that guided Mordecai at this time was an intervention by Jehovah in his life. Mordecai gladly embraced Esther's plan of fasting and seeking Jehovah's intervention. Jehovah's protection of Esther and His protection of the Jewish people was the final product of their combined faith in Him.

The third intervention of Jehovah in the life of Mordecai came on what could well have been the eve of Mordecai's death. Haman, who harbored a great disdain for Mordecai and had plotted his death, would have spoken to the king to request Mordecai's execution the next morning (Esther 5:11–14). Instead, Jehovah intervened on the night before Haman's plan was implemented and influenced the mind of the king (Esther 6:1–10). This intervention by Jehovah ultimately leads to Haman's demise and Mordecai's promotion to a position of great influence in Persian political decision–making (Esther 7:9–8:2, 10:1–3).

Jehovah's General Interventions in the Book of Esther

In the final group of interventions by Jehovah documented in the book of Esther, Jehovah used the positions of influence that He had given to Esther and Mordecai to achieve the ultimate preservation of the entire nation of Israel. In doing this, Jehovah accomplished the preservation of the lineage of the coming Messiah. First, in June 453 BC, Esther and Mordecai were given the ability to influence the heart of Ahasuerus and to reverse the plan of Haman to destroy the Israelites (Esther 8:3–9,12). Then, in March 452 BC, the redemptive plan that was authorized nine months earlier because of the intervention of Jehovah was actually implemented (Esther 9:1,15,17,19,21).

Though no words spoken by Jehovah are recorded in the entire book of Esther, and the covenant name of Jehovah does not occur in this book, the interventions of Jehovah on the behalf of Esther and Mordecai and toward the ultimate preservation of the whole nation and the lineage of the coming Messiah are undeniable. There are no less than three divine interventions for Esther, three for Mordecai, and an additional two directly resulting in the preservation of the entire nation and the seed of the Messiah.

These events speak of Jehovah as a personal God Who directly intervenes in the lives of those who are in relationship with Him in order to bring about good in their lives and to preserve them from evil. Furthermore, His omnipotence, omniscience, and omnipresence are demonstrated by His ability to hear even secret conversations and to influence the hearts of people in positions of influence, even when they are not in relationship with Him. The sovereignty of Jehovah is unmistakable in the historical accounts documented in the book of Esther.

Jehovah's Interventions in the Book of Nehemiah

The book of Nehemiah continues the theme of the direct intervention of Jehovah in the lives of His people and the personal attributes of His divine person as presented in the books of Ezra and Esther. While Ezra's personal encounters with Jehovah occur during the seventh year of Artaxerxes (Ezra 7:6–8), Esther becomes queen during the seventh year of Artaxerxes (Esther 2:16–17), and Mordecai is promoted within the kingdom of Persia during the twelve-year of Artaxerxes (Esther 3:7, 8:1,2,9), Nehemiah uttered his first two documented prayers to Jehovah during the twentieth year of the reign of Artaxerxes (Nehemiah 1:4–11, 2:1–4). Nehemiah documents no less than twelve interactions with Jehovah in his short book.

A prayer to Jehovah from Nehemiah and other national leaders of the day is among the documented exchanges with Jehovah in the book of Nehemiah (Nehemiah 9). In fact, the majority of the divine interactions in the book of Nehemiah are prayers to Jehovah and provide good insight into the perception of the character of Jehovah during Nehemiah's lifetime.

The Setting for Nehemiah's Encounters with Jehovah: First Three Interactions (Nehemiah 1–2)

The historical setting for Nehemiah's relationship with Jehovah is established in the first two chapters of his book; the first three interactions between Nehemiah and Jehovah are documented in these two chapters. Though many of the Jews had returned to Judah and Jerusalem, the nation and the city had failed to regain any socio-political footing, and even its important physical structures had not been restored and maintained.

Cyrus the Great had issued the verdict that allowed the first Jews to return to Jerusalem around 539 BC. Zerubbabel, Haggai, and Zechariah had been instrumental in restoring the foundation of the temple in Jerusalem between 520–516 BC during the reign of Darius I. With the permission of King Artaxerxes, Ezra had been the driving force behind a spiritual awakening and rededication of the people of Judah to the principles and person of Jehovah in 458 BC. But the walls of Jerusalem continued to be a ruinous heap and a disgrace in comparison to what the people knew of from the history of this great city.

After he received a negative status report concerning Jerusalem in November 445 BC (Nehemiah 1:1–3), Nehemiah directed a prayer to Jehovah Whom he believed to be a divine advocate. Two interesting historical notes attend Nehemiah's initial prayer. First, Nehemiah clearly believed that Moses was a real historical figure who had encountered Jehovah between 1446–1406 BC and to whom Jehovah had prophesied the series of events that had befallen the nation of Israel (Nehemiah 1:8–9; Leviticus 26; Deut. 28:15–68). Second, the pattern of Nehemiah's prayer (Nehemiah 1:5–11) was quite similar to the prayer offered to Jehovah by Daniel in 539 BC (Daniel 9:4–19). Both prayers characterize the person of Jehovah as a righteous and merciful judge and advocate. Both prayers acknowledge that the nation had violated its covenant relationship with Jehovah and experienced the negative consequences of its wrongdoing and the broken fellowship. Both prayers seek the favor of an omnipotent, omniscient, sovereign, merciful, and approachable

God in the very practical form of an intervention on the behalf of His chosen people.

Nehemiah's perception of the person of Jehovah, "the God of heaven," is best summed up at the very beginning of his prayer. He begins his first documented prayer to Jehovah saying, "I beseech thee, O LORD God of heaven, the great and terrible God, that keepeth covenant and mercy for them that love Him and observe His commandments" (Neh. 1:5).

Nehemiah's grand view of the person of Jehovah is evident by the titles he attributes to Him. Importantly, this great God is relationship-oriented and full of mercy, attributes that have been recognized consistently by Nehemiah's predecessors. It should not go unnoticed that Nehemiah used two third person singular divine pronouns in reference to Jehovah. These two third person singular divine pronouns support the idea that Nehemiah understands that Jehovah is the same person Who gave the commandments and prophecy to Moses almost a full millennium earlier.

In his reference to Jehovah's interactions with Moses, Nehemiah recalled six first person singular divine pronouns spoken by Jehovah in reference to Himself (Nehemiah 1:8–9). The use of the pronouns *Thine*, *Thou*, *Thee*, and *Thy* in the rest of Nehemiah's prayer can justly be assumed to refer to the same divine person referenced in verses 5, 8, and 9. There are twenty-five such pronouns in this prayer. In total, then, Nehemiah's prayer has thirty-three singular divine pronouns referencing Jehovah. As he contemplates how to use his God-given political position to the advantage of his people, Nehemiah prays and fasts, seeking Jehovah's intervention.

The evidence of Jehovah's intervention is seen four to five months later (Nehemiah 2:1) in an exchange that takes place between Nehemiah and King Artaxerxes (Nehemiah 2:1–8). As Nehemiah is performing his service to the king, the king takes note of the emotional burden of Nehemiah. Consistent with His interventions for Ezra, Mordecai, and Esther, Jehovah influenced the heart of the king in favor of Nehemiah. Nehemiah is fully cognizant of the recent history of each of these individuals with King Artaxerxes.

In 458 BC, Ezra had received a letter from the king allowing him to return to Jerusalem to teach the people the laws and principles of Jehovah (Ezra 7:6–10,11–26) because of Jehovah's hand upon him (Ezra 7:6). In 453 BC, Mordecai had been elevated to a high position in the Persian Empire because of Jehovah's interventions (Esther 3:7, 6:1–10, 8:1–2, 10:1–3). In 458–7 BC, Esther had been given the position of queen (Esther 2:16–20), a position given by Jehovah to accomplish His purposes (Esther 4:12–14). Nehemiah's knowledge of these recent events, and the visible testimony of Jehovah's power to influence the hearts of men—the presence of Queen Esther—emboldened Nehemiah to explain his perceptible emotional burden and make his request to King Artaxerxes after an "on the spot" prayer to "the God of heaven." Consistent with His behavior pattern, Jehovah influenced the king's heart favorably for His people, and Nehemiah's request was granted in April 444 BC. Nehemiah attributed this to "the good hand of my God upon me."

Nehemiah 2:6 deserves a brief examination. Nehemiah says, "And the king said unto me (the queen also sitting by him) For how long shall thy journey be? and when wilt thou return? So it pleased the king to send me; and I set him a time" (Neh. 2:6).

Jamieson, Fausset, and Brown conclude that the evidence points to Esther being the queen on this occasion. The very fact that this footnote is included in the scripture is likely because the queen's story was significant to Nehemiah's account. Nehemiah was encouraged by his knowledge of Jehovah's hand in elevating Esther to the throne as queen. He was also encouraged by the influence Esther had exhibited in the process of Mordecai's promotion. Finally, it was likely partly due to Esther's influence that Artaxerxes overall seemed to be a pro-Jewish Persian ruler from a historical perspective.

Having obtained favor of King Artaxerxes, Nehemiah set out to Jerusalem with promise and purpose. His purpose was driven by his ongoing relationship with Jehovah. Nehemiah's third interaction with Jehovah acknowledges the fact that Jehovah continued to influence the mind and purpose of Nehemiah, even after he arrived in Jerusalem (Nehemiah 2:11–20). Nehemiah refers back to his awareness of Jehovah and Jehovah's involvement when he is confronted by oppositional forces in Jerusalem (Nehemiah 2:18–20). He used two third person singular divine pronouns in reference to Jehovah when he verbally reprimanded Sanballat, Tobiah, and Geshem.

Nehemiah's Constant Companion: Jehovah's Interventions as Nehemiah Worked

The next three interactions between Nehemiah and Jehovah take place during the rebuilding project. When the enemies of the Jews tried to thwart their rebuilding project under the leadership of Nehemiah, the righteous indignation of Nehemiah was aroused. Nehemiah prayed to his God for protection and for the failure of the harmful schemes of the enemies outside of the nation of Israel. The principles of this prayer are found in Nehemiah 4:4,5,9. Nehemiah communicated his confidence in Jehovah, and thus, his perception of the character of Jehovah in Nehemiah 4:14. Nehemiah had no doubt that Jehovah would accomplish that which He had placed as a purpose into the heart of His servant (Nehemiah).

Next, Nehemiah had to confront the forces within the nation of Israel that were working against his God-given purposes. Jehovah had given Moses instructions concerning social interactions between different socio-economic groups within the nation of Israel (Lev. 25:35–42). The principles embodied in Jehovah's instructions prevented the abuse of the poor and encouraged equality and upward mobility throughout the nation.

The Jews that were living in Judah in 444 BC were not living by these principles and were oppressing the poor among the nation. The economic inequalities and the social hardships that resulted were undermining the unity of the nation and they undermined Nehemiah's ability to accomplish what Jehovah had purposed in his heart to do. Nehemiah addressed this issue in Nehemiah 5. His consciousness toward his God is evident in his prayer to Jehovah after addressing this matter (Nehemiah 5:18–19). Nehemiah's actions are driven by his mindfulness of his relationship with Jehovah as well as his service to Jehovah and the people of His covenant relationship.

Even among those in leadership and who were closer confidants for Nehemiah, there were enemies to the purpose God had given Nehemiah. In Nehemiah 6, Nehemiah details the underhanded attempts of Sanballat, Tobiah, and Geshem to undermine God's purpose in him. People like Shemaiah (Nehemiah 6:10) and Noadiah (Nehemiah 6:14) who could influence the thinking and actions of Nehemiah were not immune to the scheming of Nehemiah's enemies and used their influence to undermine Nehemiah's God-given purposes.

Nehemiah's relationship with Jehovah and Jehovah's involvement with Nehemiah helped him overcome even these challenges. Nehemiah's dependence upon Jehovah and his God consciousness are clearly depicted in Nehemiah 6:12–16. Nehemiah believed that Jehovah was intricately involved in his life in order to allow him to successfully accomplish the purpose He had placed in his heart. The rebuilding of the wall around Jerusalem was completed in August 444 BC.

Nehemiah did not see his purpose as limited to the physical task of rebuilding the walls of Jerusalem. The welfare of the nation and the restoration of a right relationship between the people of Judah and Jerusalem and their God was the larger God-given purpose of Nehemiah. The rest of Nehemiah touches on the accomplishment of this larger purpose. The organization of the people was an important part of restoring the community. Nehemiah attributed the idea of organizing the community to the intervention of Jehovah (Nehemiah 7:5). This project was completed within a month of the completion of the wall (Nehemiah 7:73).

Ezra's teaching was instrumental in this phase of Nehemiah's work. As a scribe and priest, Ezra helped provide education and restoration of the people to their rightful relationship with Jehovah. Ezra's teaching was rooted in the written laws Jehovah had given His chosen people many years ago. Over a millennium after these laws were first given (1446–1406 BC), they still remained practical guidelines for a healthy covenant relationship with Jehovah (Nehemiah 8).

Nehemiah, Ezra, and the leaders of the nation at that time lead the people in a prayer for the nation as they rededicate themselves to Jehovah worship and to the pursuit of a right relationship with Him (Nehemiah 9). This ceremonial process ends with a personal commitment by the leaders and the people to apply the principles of the laws of Jehovah, issued to Moses 1,000 years ago, to their daily lives in 444 BC (Nehemiah 10:29). The prayer of Nehemiah, Ezra, and the leaders in Nehemiah 9 and the oath of the people in Nehemiah 10 give great insight into the understanding of the people and the leaders about the character of Jehovah. In Nehemiah 9:6, they acknowledge the singleness and sovereignty of Jehovah.

> Thou, *even* Thou, *art* LORD alone; Thou hast made heaven, the heaven of heavens, with all their host, the earth, and all *things* that *are* therein, the seas, and all that *is* therein, and Thou preservest them all; and the host of heaven worshippeth Thee. (Neh. 9:6)

They understood that this Jehovah was the same person Who had called Abraham, the father of their nation, around 2091 BC—almost 1,650 years earlier—according to Genesis 12 (Nehemiah 9:7–8). They believed that Jehovah was the same person Who had been with Moses and their fathers through the saga of Egypt, the Great Exodus, Sinai, and the wilderness between 1446–1406 BC (Nehemiah 9:9–24). In their minds, Jehovah had been with Joshua and had led the judges who rescued the people from oppression by the nations that occupied the land He had given them in the years after the death of Moses (Nehemiah 9:25–29). He had also sent His word, through His spirit, using the mouths of various prophets to correct them over hundreds of years (Nehemiah 9:30–31) because of His inherent personal attributes of mercy and grace.

Finally, they recognized and acknowledged that the great, the mighty, the fearful—to be revered or awed—merciful, relationship-oriented God to Whom they were praying had been righteous in allowing them to suffer the bondage, oppressions, and hardships they had experienced beginning in 722 BC and extending to their present day (Nehemiah 9:32–37). Understanding their national history with Jehovah over more than a millennium of time, they were seeking a right relationship with Jehovah based on His mercy and His other personal attributes coupled with their commitment to value and practice a healthy spiritual lifestyle consistent with the standards of conduct He required (Nehemiah 10:28–29).

In the covenant that they were now professing, the leaders and the people again acknowledged the personhood of Jehovah using two third person singular divine pronouns in reference to Him (Nehemiah 10:29). Pronouns like *Thy*, *Thou*, and *Thee* are used nearly seventy-five times in the lengthy prayer and dedication service documented in Nehemiah 9–10. They all refer to the same divine person acknowledged by the covenant name Jehovah, beginning in Nehemiah 9:3, and identified by the pronouns *Who* (Nehemiah 9:7, 32) and *His* (Nehemiah 10:29). The omnipresence, omnipotence, omniscience, and sovereignty of Jehovah is unquestionable in the minds of the people gathered for this dedication service in 444 BC. This service constitutes Nehemiah's eighth interaction with Jehovah.

The last four documented encounters between Nehemiah and Jehovah are all found in chapter 13. Each is a simple prayer uttered by Nehemiah toward Jehovah, giving testimony to his constant awareness of the person and presence of Jehovah and his mindfulness to seek out Jehovah's mind and to strive to please Him.

Nehemiah 13:14 documents Nehemiah's prayer to Jehovah after addressing some process and procedure inadequacies with the keepers of the money for the ministers of Jehovah. In Nehemiah 13:22, Nehemiah sought the approval of Jehovah after he had made a diligent effort to cleanse the Levites, the ministers of Jehovah. In Nehemiah 13:23–29, Nehemiah extended this purging of the priesthood to include the families of the priests and sought the approval of Jehovah for this effort. He offered his final prayer, seeking the approval of Jehovah in Nehemiah 13:31.

Nehemiah's encounters with Jehovah may have been spread out over as many as twelve years (Nehemiah 5:14) and thus may have taken place between 445–432 BC. The twelve encounters with Jehovah recorded in Nehemiah emphasize his constant awareness of the person and presence of Jehovah and his attitude of seeking

Jehovah's approval and a right relationship with Him at all times and in all areas of his life. Nehemiah sees Jehovah as the God of heaven and the God of history. Nehemiah's God is aware of all things and is master over them all. He is a righteous judge and a God of mercy. It is Nehemiah's goal to seek the approval of this omnipotent, omniscient, omnipresent, sovereign person and to have His good hand on him in everything that he endeavors to do.

Summary and Conclusions: Encounter Jehovah in the Days of Artaxerxes

Identifying the encounters of Jehovah with His people during the reign of Artaxerxes is more challenging than during any other era in the Old Testament period. This is because the three books of the Bible that document the encounters of the people of history with the God of history during this era never record any of the words directly spoken by Jehovah to the people with whom He interacted. Though there is no documentation of any words directly spoken by Jehovah during this era, His presence and His activities in the lives of His chosen people remain discernable.

The person of Jehovah is documented by the appearance of His covenant name, Jehovah, almost seventy times in the writings of Ezra, Nehemiah, and Esther. Since the only words spoken directly by Jehovah, as recorded in these books, were the words that Ezra said He had spoken through His prophets (Ezra 9:11–12) and the words that Nehemiah recalled Jehovah had spoken to Moses (Nehemiah 1:8–9), there are only six first person singular divine pronouns referencing Jehovah in these books. Even third person singular divine pronouns are used sparingly in Ezra, Nehemiah, and Esther.

In sum, fewer than twenty singular divine pronouns reference Jehovah in Ezra. Only about one half of those occur in the portion of his book that discussed Ezra's personal encounters with Jehovah. Only a half dozen third person singular divine pronouns reference Jehovah in Nehemiah's record, and they are limited to three references (Nehemiah 1:5, 2:20, 10:29). However, because their use occurs during exchanges in which Nehemiah used the third person singular pronouns previously noted, nearly 100 pronouns like *Thee, Thine, Thou,* and *Thy*, it can be argued, also reference the person of Jehovah in Nehemiah's book. No divine pronouns are recorded in the book of Esther. The less personal divine name or title "God" is used ninety-four times by Ezra and seventy-four times by Nehemiah in their writings. Not even this name or title can be found in Esther.

The presence of Jehovah and His interventions on the behalf of the historical figures that are prominent in these three books is evident, despite a dearth of divine pronouns. Three interventions by Jehovah on behalf of Ezra, the scribe and priest, can be seen in the book of Ezra. The book of Esther documents at least three interventions by Jehovah in the life of Esther, three in the life of Mordecai, and two additional interactions that can be argued to be common to the life of Esther, Mordecai, and the Jewish nation. A dozen interactions in the book of Nehemiah involve Nehemiah and Jehovah. The majority of these are prayers offered or answered in the form of interventions by Jehovah on the behalf of Nehemiah.

Thus, the consistent theme concerning the person of Jehovah during the reign of Artaxerxes is that Jehovah intervenes in the lives of His chosen people in order to bring them to a positive expected end or in order to accomplish His purposes for their lives. He is a covenant relationship-oriented, omnipotent, omniscient, omnipresent, sovereign divine person Who takes a personal interest in the well-being of His chosen people.

Table 8.1 Encountering God with Haggai

	Date BC	Description	Reference	FPSP
1	Aug 520	Chastening for not completing building of the temple	1:1–11	5
2	Sept 520	Approval for beginning a sincere effort to build temple	1:13–15	1
3	Oct 520	Work of temple assessed	2:1–9	8
4	Dec 520	Consecration of priests addressed	2:10–19	5
5	Dec 520	Prophecy to Zerubbabel	2:20–23	7

FPSP First person singular divine pronouns
3PSP Third person singular divine pronouns

Table 8.2 Encountering God with Zechariah

	Date BC	Description	Reference	FPSP	3PSP
1	Oct/Nov 520	Admonition to do better than forefathers in covenant with Jehovah	1:1–6	7	1
2	Feb 519	**Series of vision/angelic encounters**			
2.1		Redemption of the nation: Angelic horsemen, horns and carpenters	1:7–21	6	
2.2		Restoration: Measuring line	2	6	5
2.3		Cleansing: Joshua and Satan	3	12	2
2.4		Prevailing by the spirit of God: Candlestick and olive trees	4	1	
2.5		Standard for judgment: Flying roll	5:1–4	2	
2.6		Wickedness in the land: Ephah	5:5–11		
2.7		Spirits throughout the earth: Horses	6:1–8		
3	Feb 519	High priestly prophetic enactment	6:9–15		
4	Dec 518	Call to sincere service and worship	7	4	1
5		Jehovah's return to Jerusalem	8	17	
6		Prophetic contrast of conquerors	9	10	9
7-8		Prophetic contrast of shepherds	10–11	21	3
9		Final encounter	12–14	21	3

FPSP First person singular divine pronouns
3PSP Third person singular divine pronouns

Table 8.3 Messianic prophecies in Haggai and Zechariah

	Messianic prophecy	Reference
1	"I will fill this house with glory"	Hag. 2:6-9
2	Zerubbabel in messianic lineage	Hag. 2:23
3	"I will dwell in the midst of thee"	Zech. 2:10-12
4	"I will bring forth my servant the Branch"	Zech. 3:8
5	The man, the Branch will grow up, rule and be priest	Zech. 6:12-13
6	The king will come riding upon a donkey	Zech. 9:9, 16
7	Thirty pieces of silver paid and cast away as his price	Zech. 11:12-13
8	Pierced	Zech. 12:10
9	Wounds in the hands of the man who is Jehovah's fellow	Zech. 13:6-7
10	Jehovah will be king and One Lord, with One name	Zech. 14:9

Table 8.4 Divine interactions with Jehovah in the days of Artaxerxes, King of Persia

Encounter	Date BC	Description	Reference	3PSP
		Ezra's report		
Note #1	539 BC	Order from King Cyrus	Ezr. 1:1–4	4
Note #2	538-520	Early post-captivity worship	Ezr. 3:1–11 Hag. 2, Ps. 136	2
Note #3	520	Order from King Darius	Ezr. 6:1, 6–12	1
Note #4	Mar 458	Order from King Artaxerxes	Ezr. 7:11–26	1
Ezra1	Mar 458	Divine favor with Artaxerxes (Ezra)	Ezr. 7:6–7, 27–28	
Ezra2	Mar 458	Divine favor for the journey	Ezr. 7:9 Ezr. 8:18, 21–23, 31	7

Ezra3	July/ Aug 458	Divine favor in Jerusalem	Ezr. 9:8, 10:9–11, 16–17	2
Esther1	462	Influencing the heart of Vashti	Esth. 1:10–19	
Esther2	Dec-Jan 458-7	Influencing the heart of Artaxerxes	Esth. 2:16–20	
Esther3	Mar 453	Jehovah influences Esther's heart and preserves her life	Esth. 4–5	
Mordecai1	Mar 453	Assassination plot revealed to Mordecai	Esth. 2:21–23	
Mordecai2	453	Counseling Mordecai in crisis	Esth. 3–4	
Mordecai3	453	The restless king/Haman's defeat	Esth. 6	
Nation1	June 453	Redemptive plan instituted	Esth. 7–8	
Nation1	Mar 452	Redemptive plan implemented	Esth. 9	

Note — Historical note documented by Ezra. Date of past event noted in table.
Ezra# — Divine encounter or intervention involving Ezra
Esther# — Divine encounter or intervention involving Esther
Mordecai# — Divine encounter or intervention involving Mordecai
Nation# — Divine intervention involving or benefitting the nation of Israel
"the Lord" — (ie. Jehovah) occurs thirty-seven times in Ezra
FPSP — First person singular divine pronouns
3PSP — Third person singular divine pronouns

Table 8.5 Nehemiah's report and his ten prayers

	Description	Reference	FPSP	3PSP
1	Prayer of despair	1:1, 5–11	6	2
2	Prayer for favor with the king	2:1–8		

3	Early divine counsel in Jerusalem	2:11–20		
4	Prayer of righteous indignation	4:4, 5, 9, 14		2
5	Prayer for blessing after abolishing abuses of poor Jews by rich	5:18–19		
6	Prayer for strength in adversity	6:12–16		
7	The reorganization of the people	7:5		
8	Prayer for the covenant people	9		
	The people enter covenant	10:29		2
9	Prayer for Jehovah's approval after installing treasury officers	13:14		
10	Prayer for Jehovah's approval after ordering cleansing of Levites	13:22		
11	Prayer for Jehovah's approval after purging the priesthood	13:23–29		
12	Prayer for Jehovah's approval at the conclusion of his work	13:30–31		

"the Lord" (i.e. Jehovah) occurs twenty-two times in Nehemiah
FPSP First person singular divine pronouns
3PSP Third person singular divine pronouns
Nehemiah's first prayer was offered in 445 BC.
Nehemiah's subsequent prayers were offered in 444 BC.

References

Marincola, John. 2003. *Herodotus: The Histories (Translated by Aubrey De Selincourt)*. New York, NY: Penguin Books, 2003.

Olmstead, AT. 1959. *History of the Persian Empire*. Chicago, Ill: The University of Chicago Press, 1959.

Jamieson, R., Fausset, A. R. & Brown, D. 1997. *Commentary Critical and Explanatory on the Whole Bible*. Oak Harbor, WA: Logos Research Systems, Inc.

Whiston, William. 1987. *The Works of Josephus: New Updated Edition, Complete and Unabridged in One Volume*. Peabody, MA: Hendrickson Publishers.

The Holy Bible. 2010. *Authorized King James Version*. Nashville, Tennessee: Holman Bible Publishers.

Wiersbe, Warren W. 2007. *The Wiersbe Bible Commentary: Old Testament*. Colorado Springs, Colorado: David C. Cook.

The Apologetics Study Bible for Students. Nashville, TN: Holman Bible Publishers, 2009.

The Chronological Study Bible. Nashville, TN: Thomas Nelson, Inc., 2008.

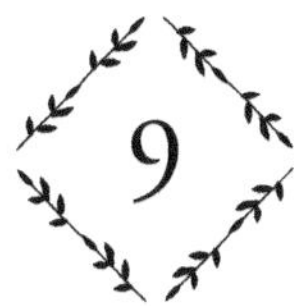

Encountering the God of Malachi, the Last Old Testament Prophet

Malachi was the final historically documented authoritative prophetic voice of the Old Testament. His prophetic ministry was probably influenced by the leadership and the social and spiritual renewal that Nehemiah's ministry had brought to Judah and Jerusalem between 445–432 BC. Malachi may well have been a young man during this time of spiritual renewal. When the renewed commitment of Jehovah's chosen people to their covenant relationship with Him began to wane again, He sanctioned the ministry of Malachi to promote their awareness of their faults and their recommitment to their covenant relationship with Him. The record of Malachi's encounters with Jehovah were probably penned between 430–420 BC. Outside of the land of Judah, Malachi was contemporary with Socrates, Hippocrates, and Plato of the classical Greek era.

It was noted above that during the reign of the Persian king Artaxerxes, there were no words recorded that were directly spoken by Jehovah to the leaders within the Jewish nation. The final prophet ordained by Jehovah before the long awaited earthly ministry of Messiah began had three historically documented encounters with Jehovah. Jehovah, the divine person Who had been pursuing a covenant relationship with the Jews and with humanity for millennia before Malachi encountered Him, spoke with Malachi—and through

Malachi, His chosen people—about the disregard and disrespect that the people continued to show for Him and for their covenant relationship with Him. Jehovah uttered the two messianic prophecies most proximate to the coming of Messiah into the ears of Malachi during His final encounter with His last sanctioned pre-messianic prophet.

Encounter one: Jehovah's Case to Malachi Against the People of Judah (Mal. 1)

Malachi's first documented encounter with Jehovah begins with a very powerful proclamation by Jehovah. In Malachi 1:2, Jehovah declares to His chosen people, "I have loved you." After proclaiming His love and giving Malachi the information needed to defend His proclamation as fact, Jehovah proceeded to decry the failure of His people to understand and embrace His affection. Their choices and actions dishonored Him and dishonored His love relationship with them.

The actions of one person toward another demonstrates the value that they place on that person and on their relationship with that person. The actions of the people of Israel indicated how little they valued Jehovah and their relationship with Him. Furthermore, Jehovah argued that He was so much more valuable than might be concluded by observing the actions of His chosen people toward Him. In fact, the actions of the Jews actually communicated contempt for Jehovah instead of love for Him. Jehovah's message to His people was that such behavior was beneath Him and would not be accepted if they wanted to have a healthy covenant relationship with Him.

In this first encounter of Jehovah with Malachi, Jehovah focused on His personal worth and Israel's failure to understand and appreciate His worth. He used nineteen first person singular divine pronouns in identifying Himself in this interaction with Malachi. No doubt, Malachi was equipped to passionately communicate Jehovah's message to His people after this encounter.

Encounter two: Jehovah's Case to Malachi Against the Priests of Judah (Mal. 2:1–9)

Jehovah then presented to Malachi accusations against those in the priesthood with the foretelling of many blessings lost and hardships to come if they continued their collective mishandling of spiritual responsibility and personal relationship with Him. During this encounter, Jehovah reminisced about His relationship with the priests when the priesthood was first established. He waxed nostalgic about the pervasive attitude of reverence for Him among the early Levites and their pursuit to please Him by living out His commandments and leading others in proper worship before Him. He lamented the contrast between these former days and the attitudes the priests in Malachi's day exhibited. It saddened Jehovah that the priests could no longer be regarded with respect by Him or by the people because they no longer embodied the pursuit of a right relationship between the people and Jehovah.

Malachi 2:10–17 gives the prophet's record of when he delivered his message from Jehovah to the people of Judah. Remembering the greatness of Jehovah as Jehovah had communicated it during his first encounter with Him (Mal. 1:11,14), Malachi pleaded with his listeners to reverence the One God Who had created them. He implored them not to disrespect Jehovah and the privilege He had extended to them of having a covenant relationship with Him (Mal. 2:10–11). Malachi also addressed the emptiness of the acts of worship of the people, in the eyes of Jehovah, because their heart was not devoted to Him (Mal. 2:12–13). Malachi went on to tell his countrymen that their refusal to embrace a lifestyle of pursuing covenant relationship with Jehovah had negatively impacted how they lived out their human relationships.

Just as they had no reverence for their relationship with Jehovah, they also had no reverence for the most sacred of human relationships—the marriage covenant relationship. Jehovah considered their lack of regard for these special relationships—the covenant relationship with Jehovah and the covenant relationship between man and woman in marriage—an act of violence. He did not look favorably upon divorce or upon any dismissal of sacred covenant relationship

(Mal. 2:13–16). Excusing these acts of misconduct against Jehovah and against each other and attempting to justify themselves in the eyes of Jehovah was intolerable, taught Malachi (Mal. 2:17).

Malachi believed that he had received his message directly from the mouth of Jehovah. In His message to the general populous of Judah (Mal. 1), Jehovah identified Himself by the use of nineteen first person singular divine pronouns. His personal investment in His message and His relationship with His people was communicated through expressions like "My honor," "My fear," "My name," and "Mine altar." He also calls Himself a Father (Mal. 1:6) and a great King (Mal. 1:14) during this first encounter with Malachi.

Fourteen additional first person singular divine pronouns were used by Jehovah in reference to Himself during His second encounter with Malachi. In this encounter, He prepared the prophet to address the ineptitude of the priests separately from the people in general. Understanding that he had received his ministerial preparation and instruction from the person of Jehovah, Malachi delivered his message with passion, fearlessness, and conviction using seven third person singular divine pronouns to reference the One Who had commissioned him. Malachi spoke to them of the "One God" that created them and used the covenant name, Jehovah, and the familiar titles, "the Lord of hosts" and "the God of Israel," in reference to Jehovah.

Encounter three: Jehovah's Promised Remedy, Relationship Through Messiah (Mal. 3–4)

Thousands of years earlier, when Adam and Eve had shown disdain for their covenant relationship with Jehovah and He had issued judgment upon them for their act of contempt, He cushioned the impact of their great loss with the first messianic prophecy in history (Gen. 3:15). As the pre-messianic era closed and Jehovah proclaimed pending judgment upon His covenant people for their perpetual contempt of Him and of their covenant relationship with Him, He closed the post-captivity, pre-messianic period with two final messianic prophecies.

In His third and final encounter with Malachi, Jehovah gave the hope of the coming Messiah who would purify the people of God and enable them to offer acceptable offerings to Jehovah by reestablishing a right relationship between them and Him. Later, history revealed that John the Baptist was the messenger who prepared the way of Jehovah (Mal. 3:1 and John 1:23). Nearly 300 years earlier, Isaiah had also prophesied the preceding of the earthly ministry of Messiah by a chosen messenger (Isaiah 40:3). A century earlier, when Jehovah used the ministry of Haggai and Zechariah to motivate His people to complete the reconstruction of the temple, He had pronounced several messianic prophecies to Zechariah. Now, in His third encounter with Malachi, the Lord said, "The Lord, Whom ye seek, shall suddenly come to His temple" (Mal. 3:1).

To the student of history and the discerner of Jehovah's words, Jehovah unmistakably identified Himself with the coming Messiah and as the coming Messiah who would purify His chosen people. In Mal. 3:5, Jehovah said, "I will come near to you to judgment," declaring that He would not overlook their continued lifestyle of reproach, but that He Himself would deliver them from this hopelessness through the earthly ministry of the Messiah.

In an oft referenced passage from the third encounter between Jehovah and Malachi, Jehovah addressed another example of Israel's irreverence for Him, the blessings that would follow if they walked in His covenant, and the negative consequences of their failure to walk in covenant relationship with Him (Mal. 3:6–14). While He used the example of their disregard for the principle of tithing within His covenant, His larger message to them concerned the condition of their hearts and minds. They failed to value Jehovah and their covenant relationship with Him. Malachi expressed his understanding of Jehovah's larger message in his response in Malachi 3:15–16. Jehovah spoke back to Malachi in 3:17, and Malachi summarized the tone of his actual message to the nation on this matter in Malachi 3:18.

Enlarging upon the statement He made in Malachi 3:17, in Malachi 4, Jehovah contrasted the unfortunate end of those who continued to disrespect His covenant with the blissful end that awaited those who revered Him and pursued a lifestyle that honored the principles and practices He had taught through Moses at Sinai over 1,000 years earlier. Those who lived their lives without regard for their covenant relationship with Jehovah would face the wrath of His judgment. Those who chose to walk in His covenant would prosper (Mal. 4:1–4).

It is noteworthy that the last statement made by Jehovah in His third and final encounter with Malachi, indeed the last statement that history recorded as spoken by Jehovah during the period of the old covenant, constituted a messianic prophecy. In Malachi 4:5–6, Jehovah says, "Behold, I will send you Elijah the prophet before the coming of the great and dreadful day of the LORD: And he shall turn the heart of the fathers to the children, and the heart of the children to their fathers, lest I come and smite the earth with a curse."

This prophecy is a part of the same encounter between Jehovah and Malachi that began with the words, "Behold, I will send My messenger, and he shall prepare the way before Me" (Mal. 3:1). Jesus himself and the writers of the gospels understood that these two messianic prophecies were intricately linked.

In Matthew 11:10, while speaking about John the Baptist, Jesus quoted Malachi 3:1 and then linked John the Baptist to Mal. 4:5 as the "Elias, which was to come" in Matthew 11:14. At the mount of Transfiguration (Matt. 17:9–13), Jesus reconfirmed that he intended to imply that John the Baptist was the "Elijah to come" prophesied by Jehovah in Mal. 3:1 and 4:5. And Luke, the physician and historian, recorded that an angel linked John the Baptist to the prophecy uttered by Jehovah to Malachi in Mal. 4:5–6, saying of the unborn prophet, "He shall go before Him in the spirit and power of Elias…"

Jehovah used twenty-seven first person singular divine pronouns in reference to Himself in His final encounter with Malachi (Mal. 3–4). He made His love for His chosen people, His expectation of the pursuit of righteousness in those who desire to walk in covenant relationship with Him, and His promise to be the One Who would make this righteousness possible through His personal work as the coming Messiah all clear in this final encounter of the old covenant. Jehovah's identification with the person of the Messiah is abundantly clear from an examination of the words He spoke to His prophets. Any doubts are erased when the life and words of Messiah and the men he commissioned to spread his teachings are honestly examined in the light of the encounters of Jehovah with the men of the Old Testament.

Summary and Conclusions: The God of Malachi

The biblically recorded history of the encounters of Jehovah with the men of the Old Testament closes with the three encounters of Malachi. Malachi, it appears, was commissioned by Jehovah to give a final word of reproof and prophecy to His people when the renewed fervor that was ignited and sustained under the ministry of Nehemiah began to wane. The three historically documented encounters of Malachi with Jehovah include two words of reproof and two words of prophecy.

The words of reproof center around Jehovah's love for His chosen people and the irreverence of Jehovah's people for Him demonstrated by their lack of commitment to living out a covenant relationship with Him. In His final encounter with Malachi, Jehovah focused on His highly anticipated coming remedy to the perpetually broken relationship—the prophesied Messiah. The final encounter contains two messianic prophecies.

Within the three historically documented encounters of Jehovah with His final prophet of the Old Testament, there are sixty first person singular divine pronouns spoken by God. Fourteen third person singular divine pronouns are also contained within Malachi's historical documentation. Just as Jehovah had begun His history with mankind with the pursuit of relationship when He created Adam and Eve thousands of years earlier, so the Old Testament concludes with a proclamation of Jehovah's love relationship with His chosen people. Just as He had pronounced judgment for humanity's rejection of Him and promised a coming remedy in the Garden of Eden, so in Malachi He pronounced judgment for the irreverence and lack of commitment of Israel and promised the coming remedy of the coming Messiah.

Table 9.1 Malachi's Divine Encounters

	Description	Reference	FPSP	3PSP
	Jehovah's case against Judah and His solution			

1	Chastisement of the people: Their contempt of their God demonstrated by their actions	Malachi 1	19	3
2	Chastisement of the priests: Failure to revere the standards of their covenant relationship with God	Malachi 2	14	7
3	Prophesy of the coming remedy/ Messiah: Relationship through the coming Messiah	Malachi 3	27	4

FPSP First person singular divine pronouns
3PSP Third person singular divine pronouns
Malachi's ministry takes place around 430 BC

Table 9.2 Messianic prophecies in Malachi

	Messianic prophecy	**Reference**
1	Messenger to precede the coming of Jehovah	Malachi 3:1–3
2	Messenger likened to Elijah	Malachi 4:5–6

References

The Holy Bible. 2010. *Authorized King James Version.* Nashville, Tennessee: Holman Bible Publishers.

Wiersbe, Warren W. 2007. *The Wiersbe Bible Commentary: Old Testament.* Colorado Springs, Colorado: David C. Cook.

The Apologetics Study Bible for Students. Nashville, TN: Holman Bible Publishers, 2009.

The Chronological Study Bible. Nashville, TN: Thomas Nelson, Inc., 2008.

Bibliography

Barton, Ruth (September 1998), "Huxley, Lubbock, and Half a Dozen Others": *Professionals and Gentlemen in the Formation of the X Club, 1851–1864*, Isis, Chicago: University of Chicago Press, 89 (3): 410–444, JSTOR 237141, OCLC 83940246, doi:10.1086/384072

Barton, Ruth (March 1990), "'An Influential Set of Chaps." *The X–Club and Royal Society Politics 1864–85, The British Journal for the History of Science*, Cambridge: Cambridge University, 23 (1): 53–81, JSTOR 4026802, doi:10.1017/S0007087400044459.

http://www.pewforum.org/2016/12/13/religion-and-education-around-the-world.

http://www.pewforum.org/2017/04/26/in-america-does-more-education-equal-less-religion.

Shapiro, Robert. *Origins: A Skeptic's Guide to the Creation of Life on Earth*. New York, NY: Bantam Books, 1986.

Johnson, Phillip E. *Darwin on Trial*. Downers Grove, Ill: InterVarsity Press, 1993.

Lubenow, Marvin L. *Bones of Contention*. Grand Rapids, MI: Baker Books, 2004.

Behe, Michael J. *Darwin's Black Box*. New York, NY: Free Press, 2006.

Denton, Michael. *Evolution: A Theory in Crisis*. Chevy Chase, MD: Adler & Adler, 1986.

Morris, Henry. *Men of Science—Men of God.* Green Forest, AR: Master Books, 1988.

The Holy Bible. *Authorized King James Version.* Nashville, TN: Holman Bible Publishers, 2010.

Wiersbe, Warren W. *The Wiersbe Bible Commentary: Old Testament.* Colorado Springs, Colorado: David C. Cook, 2007.

The Apologetics Study Bible for Students. Nashville, TN: Holman Bible Publishers, 2009.

The Chronological Study Bible. Nashville, TN: Thomas Nelson, Inc., 2008.

Ann Spangler. *The Names of God Bible.* Grand Rapids, MI: Baker Publishing Group, 2014.

The Jewish Study Bible (Second edition). New York, New York: Oxford University Press, 2014.

Spurgeon, Charles H. *Treasury of David: Classic Reflections on the Wisdom of the Psalms.* Peabody, MA: Hendrickson Publishers, 1876.

Danziger, Hillel and Scherman, Nossom. *Tehillim.* Brooklyn, NY: Mesorah Publications, 2012.

Keller, Werner. *The Bible as History (2nd Edition).* New York, NY: Bantam Books, 1988.

Marincola, John. *Herodotus: The Histories (Translated by Aubrey De Selincourt).* New York, NY: Penguin Books, 2003.

Olmstead, AT. *History of the Persian Empire.* Chicago, Ill: The University of Chicago Press, 1959.

Jamieson, R., Fausset, A. R. & Brown, D. *Commentary Critical and Explanatory on the Whole Bible*. Oak Harbor, WA: Logos Research Systems, Inc., 1997.

Whiston, William. *The Works of Josephus: New Updated Edition, Complete and Unabridged in One Volume*. Peabody, MA: Hendrickson Publishers, 1987.

Newton, Isaac. *Observations upon the Prophecies of Daniel.*

Horn Siegfried H. "New Light on Nebuchadnezzar's Madness." https://ministrymagazine.org/authors/horn-siegfried-h

Walvoord, John F. "The Nations in Prophecy." www.walvoord.com

Lockyer, Herbert. *All the Divine Names and Titles in the Bible*. Grand Rapids, MI: Zondervan Publishing House, 1975.

Lockyer, Herbert. *All the Messianic Prophecies of the Bible*. Grand Rapids, MI: Zondervan Publishing House, 1973.

Leston, Stephen. *The Bible in World History*. Urichsville, OH: Barbour Publishing Inc., 2011.

Baxter, J. Sidlow. *Explore the Book, Complete in One Volume*. Grand Rapids, MI: Zondervan Publishing House, 1966.

Robinson, Jeffrey S. *Satan as He Wants to be Seen*. North Charleston, SC: CreateSpace Independent Publishing, 2014.

Mears, Henrietta C. *What the Bible is All About*. Ventura, CA: Regal Books, 1999.

McKinney, Kevin. *The Bible as History. Second Edition*. Tom Raley, 2013.

Price, Randall. *The Stones Cry Out: What Archaeology Reveals About the Truth of the Bible*. Eugene, OR: Harvest House Publishing, 1997.

http://www.bible-history.com

Pyles, David. "A Double Portion of Thy Spirit. Miracle of Elijah and Elisha" *http://www.bcbsr.com/survey/eli.html*

Mykytiuk, Lawrence. "50 People in the Bible Confirmed Archaeo logically." http://biblicalarchaeology.org

http://calligraphyforgod.com/biblestudy/elishacharacterstudy.html

http://quatr.us/timelines/1000bc.htm

http://crystalinks.com/indiahistory.html

http://formerthings.com/necho.htm

http://www.livius.org/articles/person/necho-ii/

http://nabataea.net/solhez2.html

http://www.ancient_eu/babylon/

http://www.britannica.com/biography/Sennacherib

http://www.ancient.eu/timeline/babylon/

http://www.ancient.eu/timeliine/assyria/

https://www.britannica.com/biography/Merodach-Baladan

http://www.jewishencyclopedia.com/articles//2871-ben-hadad

Mark, Joshua J. "Jezebel: Princess of Sidon, Queen of Israel." Ancient History Encyclopedia. http://www.ancient.eu/article/92/

http://www.livius.org/articles/place/tyre/

http://www.apologeticspress.org/apcontent.aspx?category=13&article=1790

https://teldan.wordpress.com/house-of-david-inscription/

http://www.lwbc.co.uk/davids_psalms.htm

http://www.blueletterbible.org/study/parallel/paral18.cfm

Hoffmeier, James. *The Arm of God Versus the Arm of Pharaoh in the Exodus Narratives.* Biblica:67(3); p. 378–386, 1986.

Livingston, David. "The Plagues and The Exodus." http://www.dvidlivingston.com/plagues.htm

Yeager, Brian. "Numbers Outlined." www.wordsoftruth.net/sermons.htm

Copeland, Mark A. "The Book of Job." https://www.executableoutlines.com/job.htm

Chisolm, RB. *The Chronology of the Book of Judges: A Linguistic Clue to Solving a Pesky Problem.* Journal of The Evangelical Theological Society:52(2); p. 247–255, 2009.

About the Author

Napoleon Burt is a lifelong learner and passionate educator. He received portions of his formal education from Berean Bible Institute, Southern Bible Institute, Kent State University, the Northeastern Ohio Universities College of Medicine (now called the Northeast Ohio Medical University), the Cleveland Clinic Foundation, the University of Cincinnati Medical Center, and Cincinnati Children's Hospital Medical Center. He has published a dozen articles in the medical literature over his career.

Dr. Burt has always been passionate about teaching. He taught in medical residency programs at the Medical University of South Carolina and Children's Medical Center Dallas. He was the director of the pediatric anesthesiology fellowship program at the University of Texas Southwestern Medical Center in Dallas, Texas, and won several awards as a clinician educator during his career in academic medicine.

As a student of the Bible, Dr. Burt began systematically studying and memorizing the Bible as a teenager. He served for several years as Director of Christian Education in the Carolina District Council of the International Pentecostal Young People's Union of the PAW. He has been active in ministry in differing capacities since 1989. He has taught several classes on the compatibility of science and the Bible and continues to serve as a Bible teacher in his local church.

Dr. Burt has spent years immersed in medical science and devoted to educating himself and others. Simultaneously, he has spent the majority of his adult life systematically studying and teaching others how to study the Bible. This background has qualified him to help students of the Bible and students of science correctly apply principles that undergird life and learning in both disciplines (science and medicine) and draw clear and practical conclusions from all the relevant information available to them.

CPSIA information can be obtained
at www.ICGtesting.com
Printed in the USA
FSHW022116230320

9 781645 159827